THE HEROIC LEGEND OF
ARSLAN

STORY BY
YOSHIKI TANAKA

MANGA BY
HIROMU ARAKAWA

4

THE HEROIC LEGEND OF
ARSLAN

TABLE OF CONTENTS

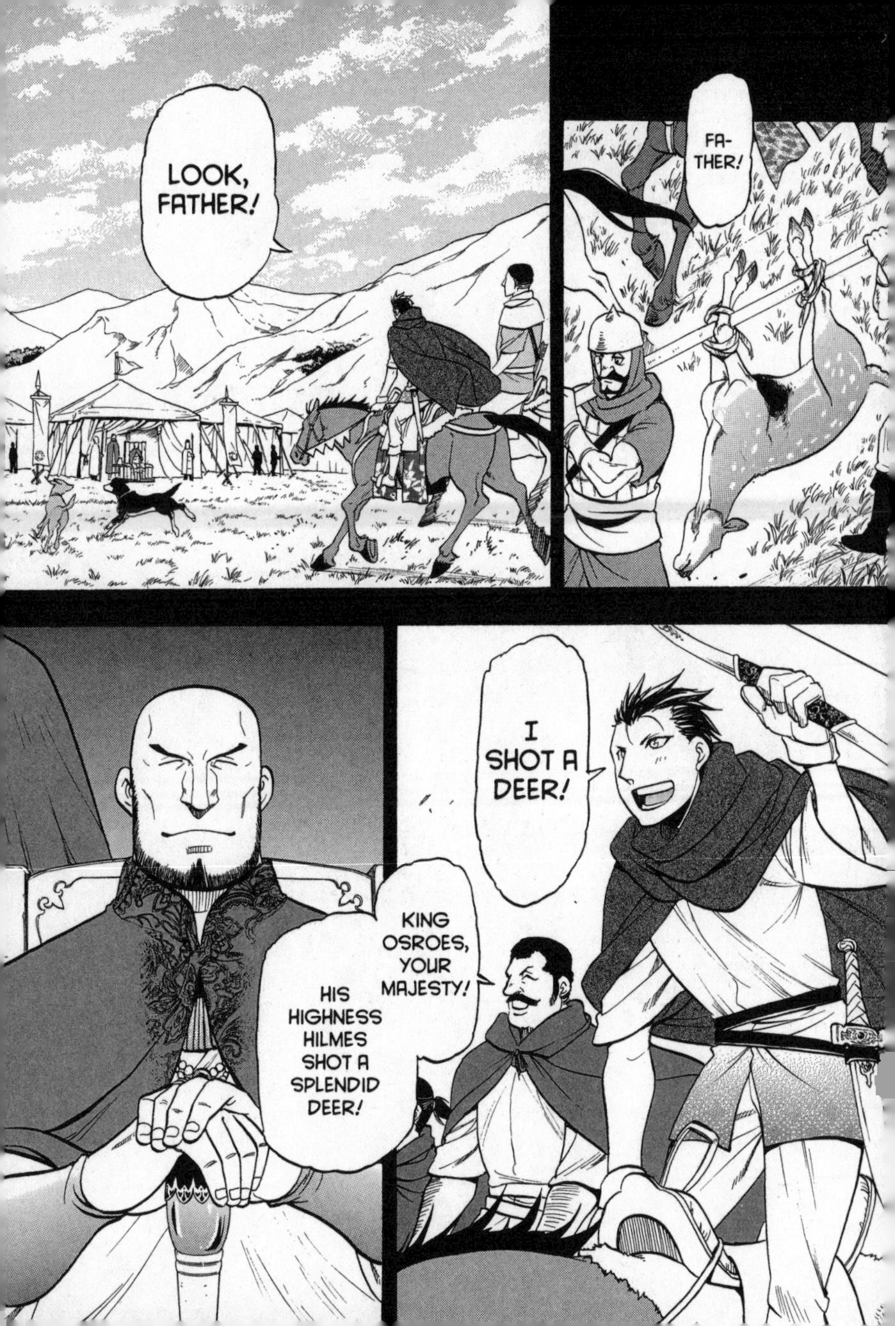
FA-
THER!
LOOK, FATHER!
I SHOT A DEER!
KING OSROES, YOUR MAJESTY!
HIS HIGHNESS HILMES SHOT A SPLENDID DEER!

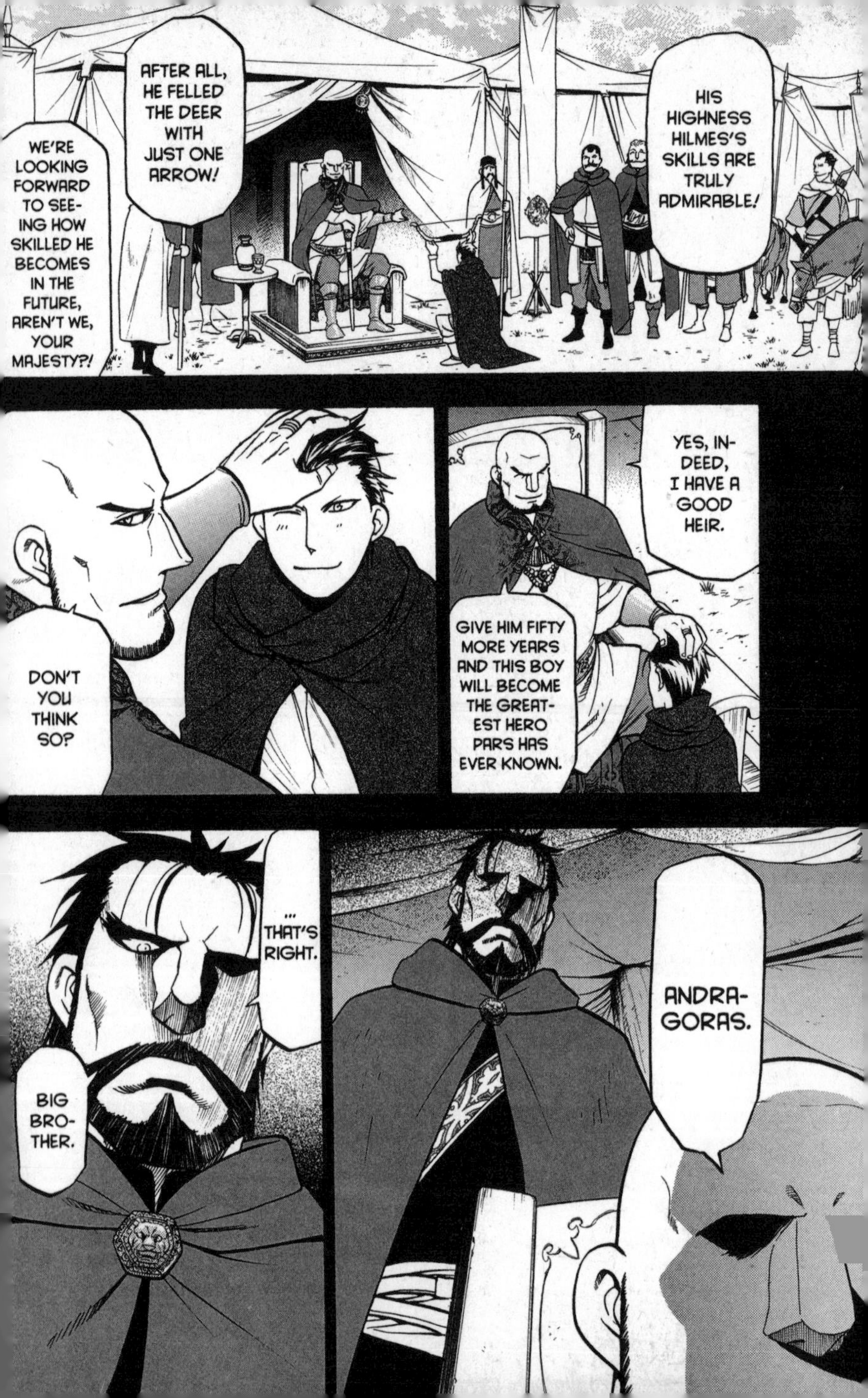
HIS HIGHNESS HILMES'S SKILLS ARE TRULY ADMIRABLE!
AFTER ALL, HE FELLED THE DEER WITH JUST ONE ARROW!
WE'RE LOOKING FORWARD TO SEE-ING HOW SKILLED HE BECOMES IN THE FUTURE, AREN'T WE, YOUR MAJESTY?!
YES, IN-DEED, I HAVE A GOOD HEIR.
GIVE HIM FIFTY MORE YEARS AND THIS BOY WILL BECOME THE GREAT-EST HERO PARS HAS EVER KNOWN.
DON'T YOU THINK SO?
ANDRA-GORAS.
... THAT'S RIGHT.
BIG BROTHER.

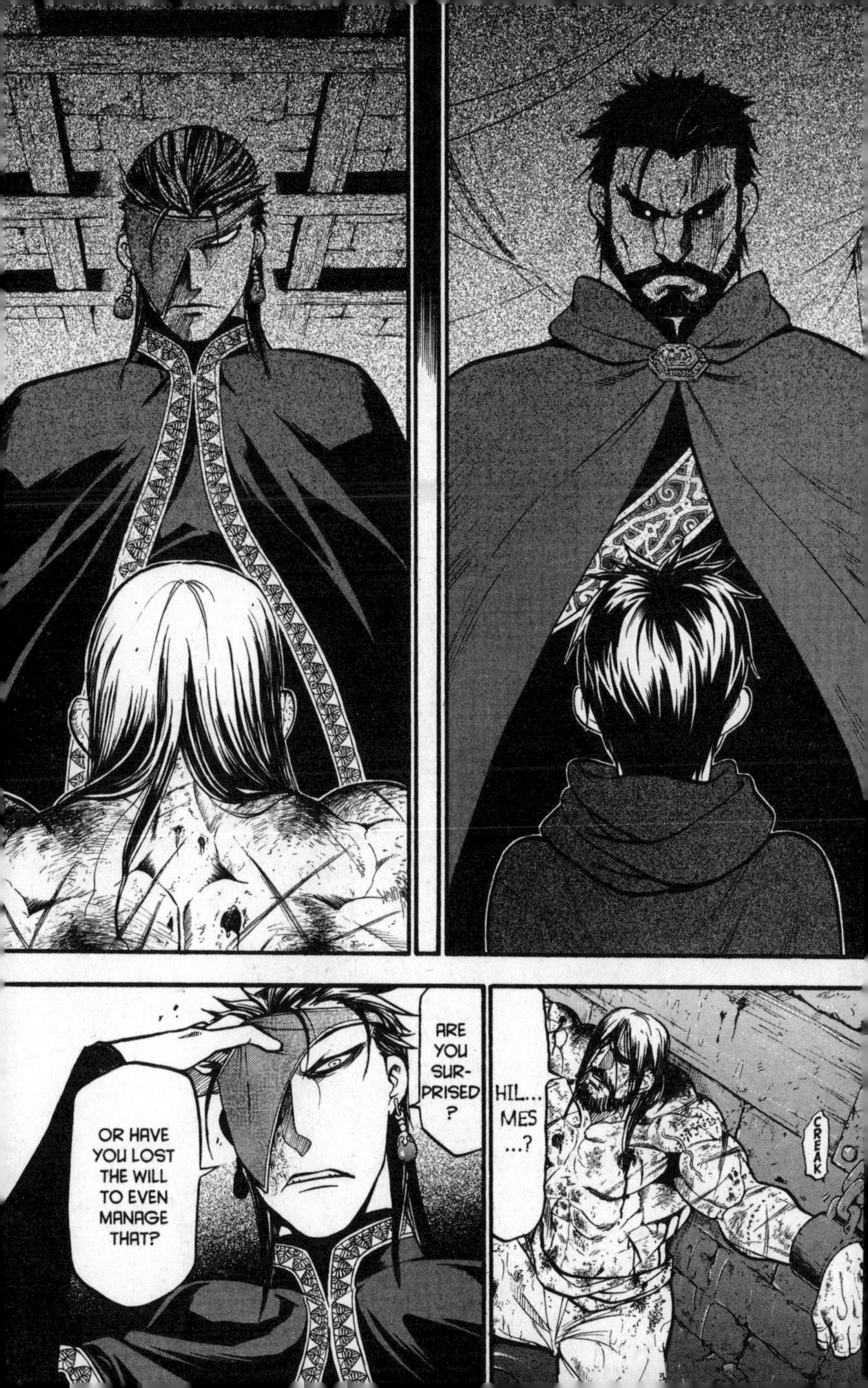
HIL... MES ...?
CREAK
ARE YOU SURPRISED?
OR HAVE YOU LOST THE WILL TO EVEN MANAGE THAT?

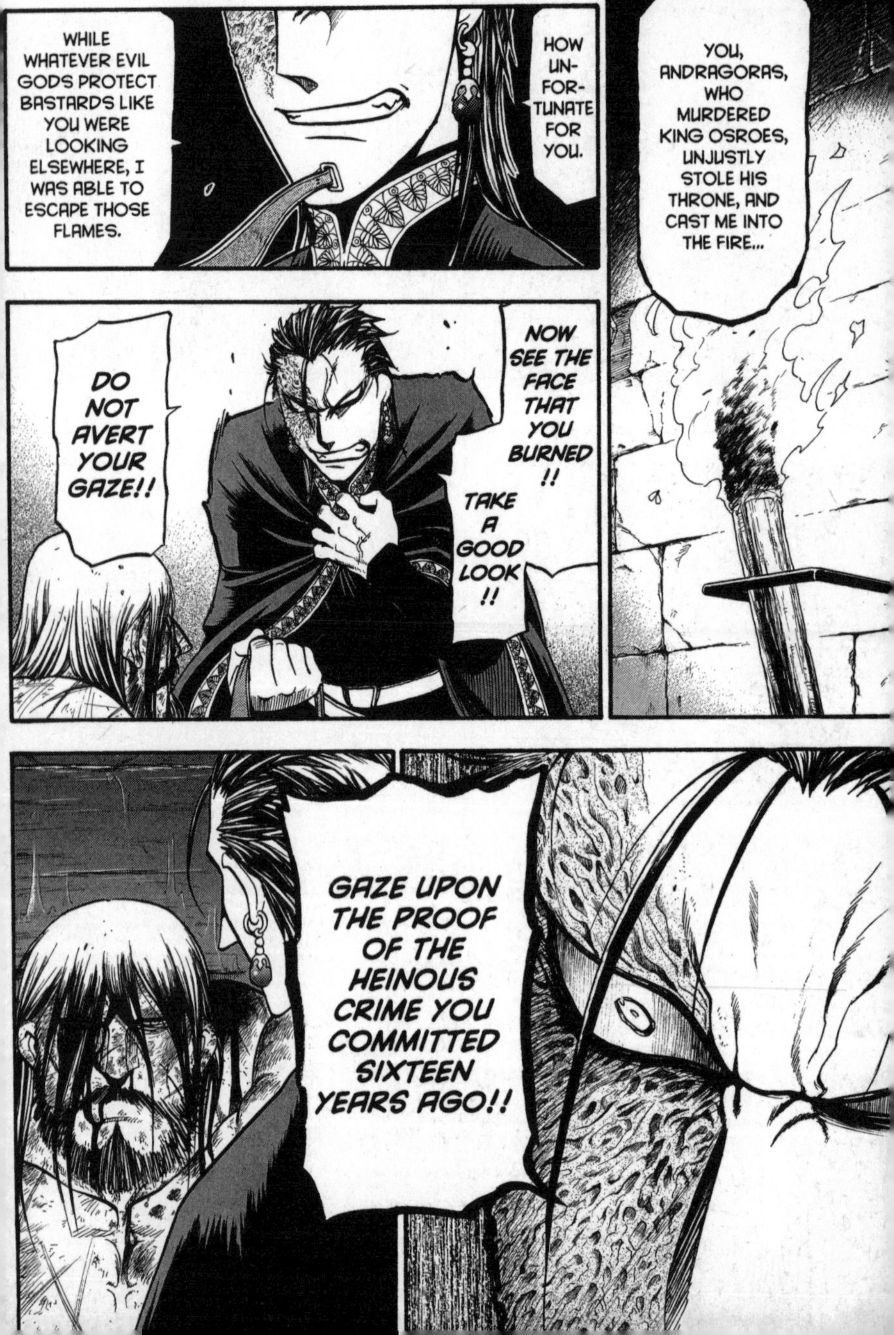
YOU, ANDRAGORAS, WHO MURDERED KING OSROES, UNJUSTLY STOLE HIS THRONE, AND CAST ME INTO THE FIRE...
HOW UN-FOR-TUNATE FOR YOU.
WHILE WHATEVER EVIL GODS PROTECT BASTARDS LIKE YOU WERE LOOKING ELSEWHERE, I WAS ABLE TO ESCAPE THOSE FLAMES.
NOW SEE THE FACE THAT YOU BURNED!!
TAKE A GOOD LOOK!!
DO NOT AVERT YOUR GAZE!!
GAZE UPON THE PROOF OF THE HEINOUS CRIME YOU COMMITTED SIXTEEN YEARS AGO!!

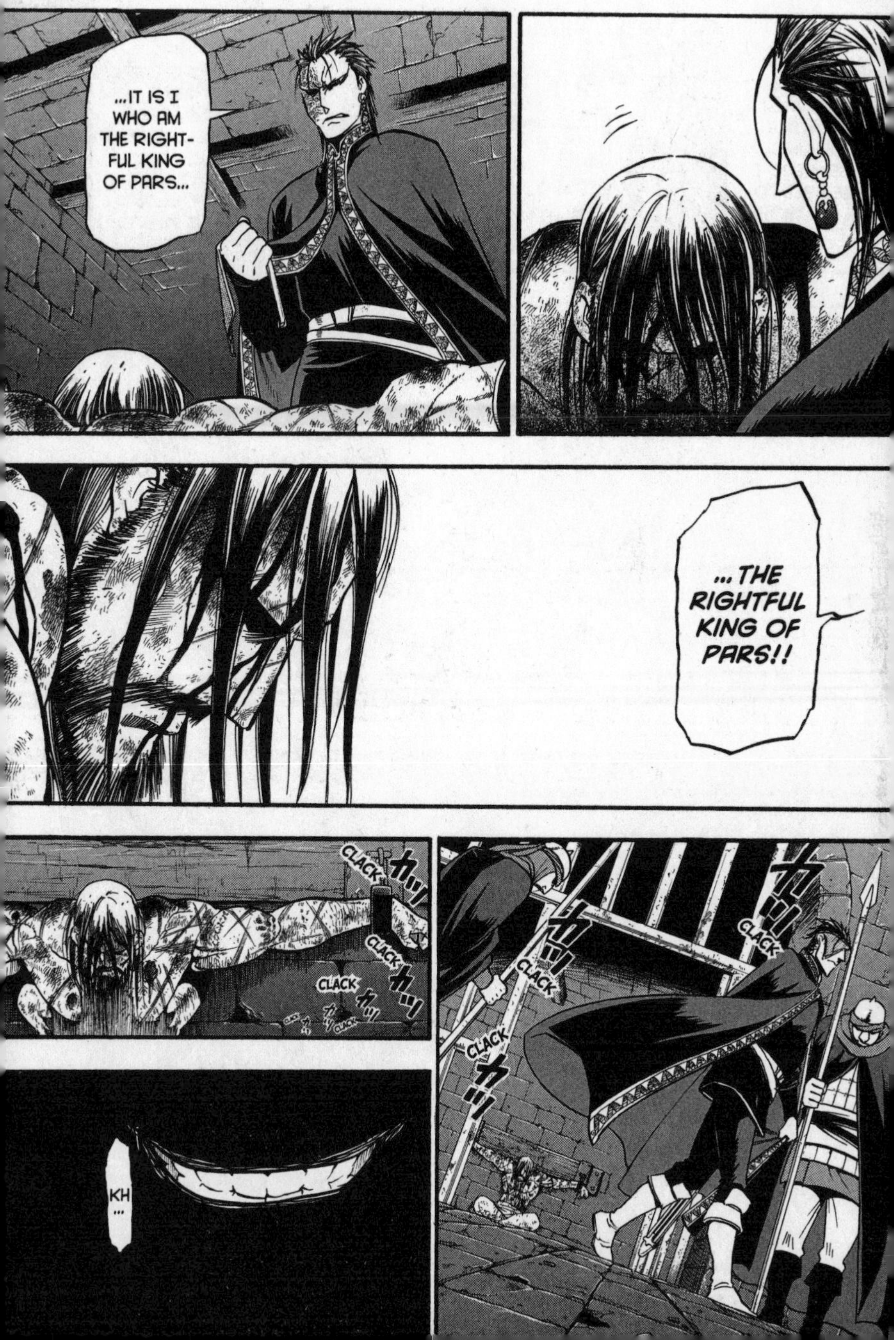
...IT IS I WHO AM THE RIGHT-FUL KING OF PARS...
...THE RIGHTFUL KING OF PARS!!
CLACK
CLACK
CLACK
CLACK
CLACK
CLACK
CLACK
CLACK
KH ...

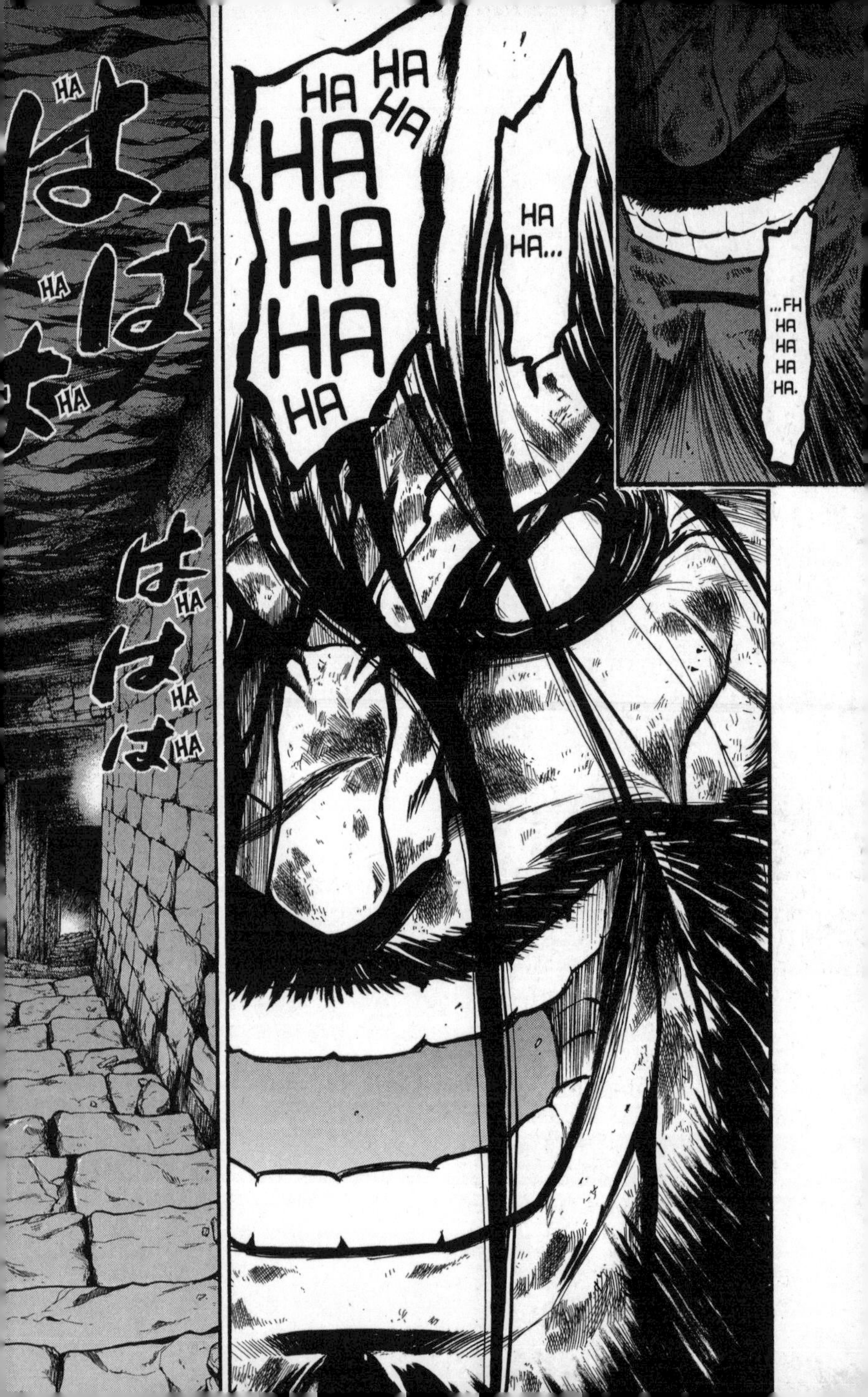

...FH HA HA HA HA.
HA HA...
HA HA HA HA HA HA HA HA
ははは
HA HA HA
ははは
HA HA HA

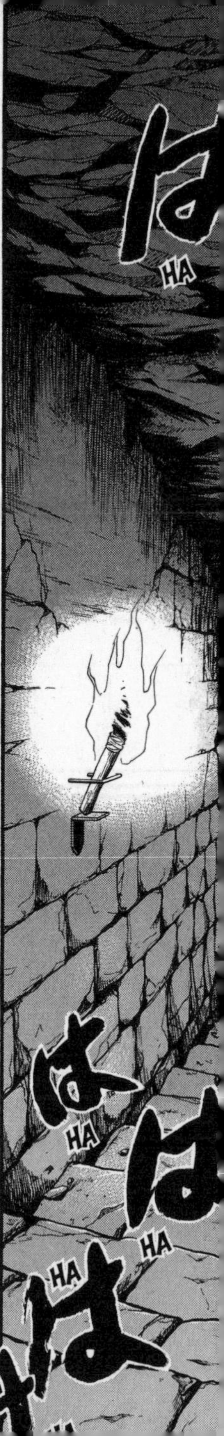
は
HA
は
HA
は
HA
は
HA

Chapter 20: The Lord of the Fortress at Kashan

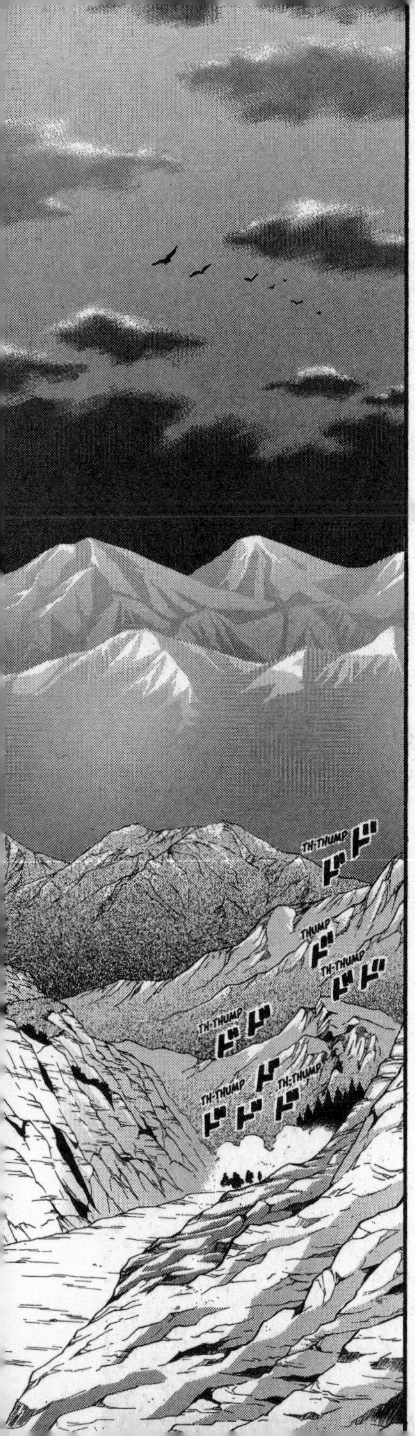
TH-THUMP
ドド
THUMP
ド
TH-THUMP
ドド
TH-THUMP
ドド
TH-THUMP
ドドド
TH-THUMP

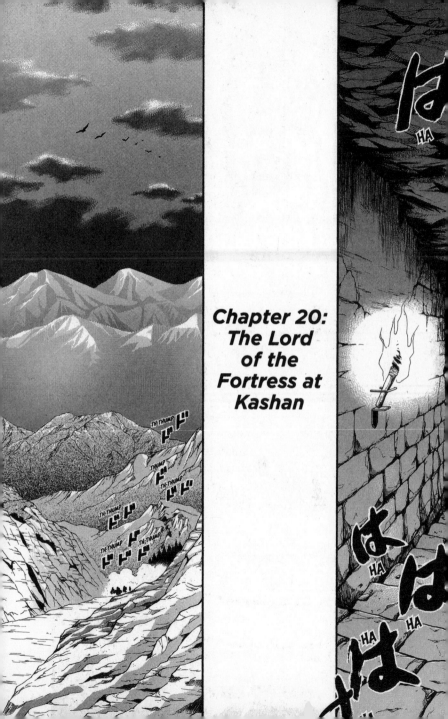

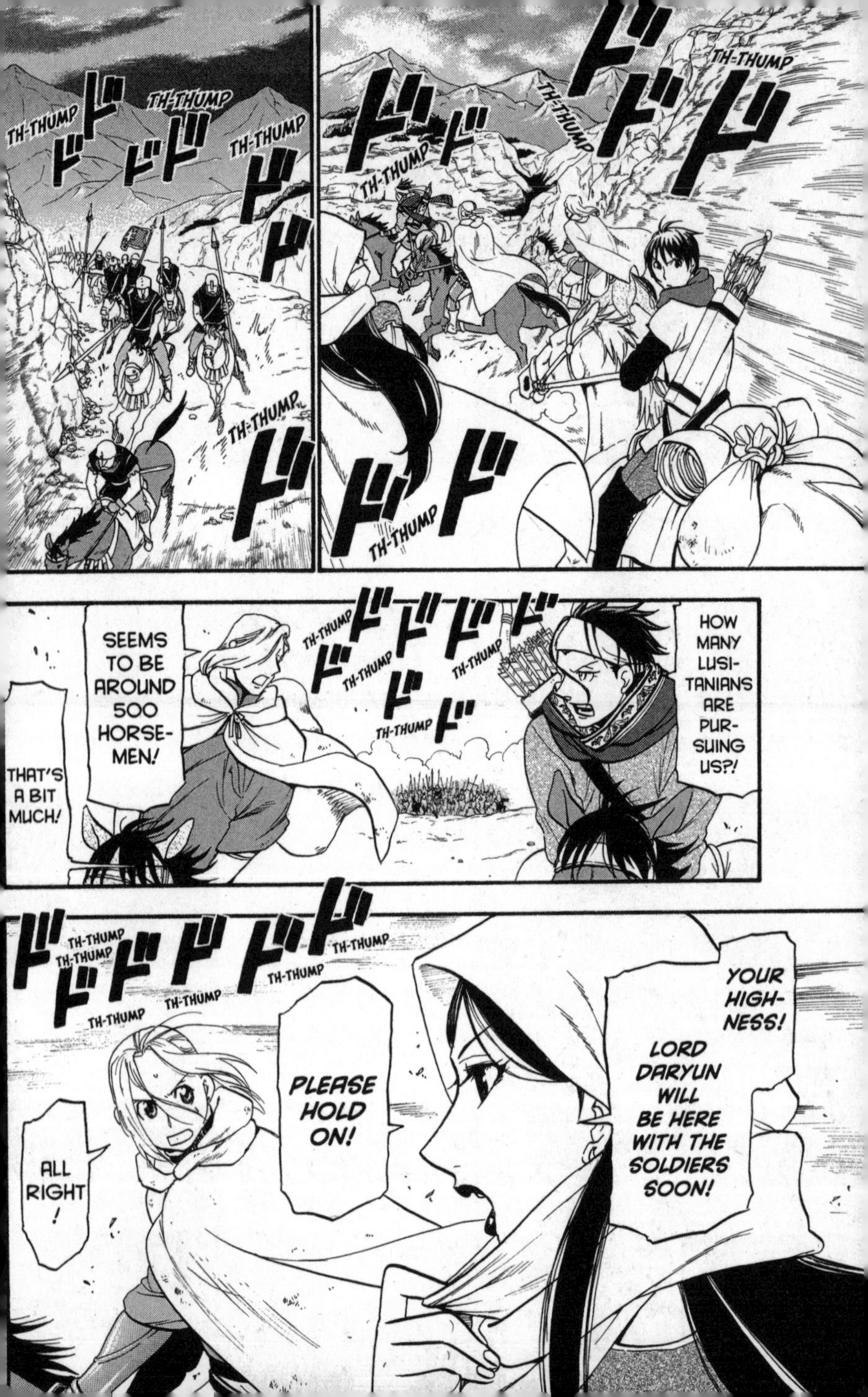
TH-THUMP
TH-THUMP
TH-THUMP
TH-THUMP
TH-THUMP
TH-THUMP
TH-THUMP
TH-THUMP
TH-THUMP
TH-THUMP
TH-THUMP
TH-THUMP
HOW MANY LUSITANIANS ARE PURSUING US?!
SEEMS TO BE AROUND 500 HORSEMEN!
THAT'S A BIT MUCH!
TH-THUMP
TH-THUMP
TH-THUMP
TH-THUMP
TH-THUMP
TH-THUMP
YOUR HIGHNESS! LORD DARYUN WILL BE HERE WITH THE SOLDIERS SOON!
PLEASE HOLD ON!
ALL RIGHT!

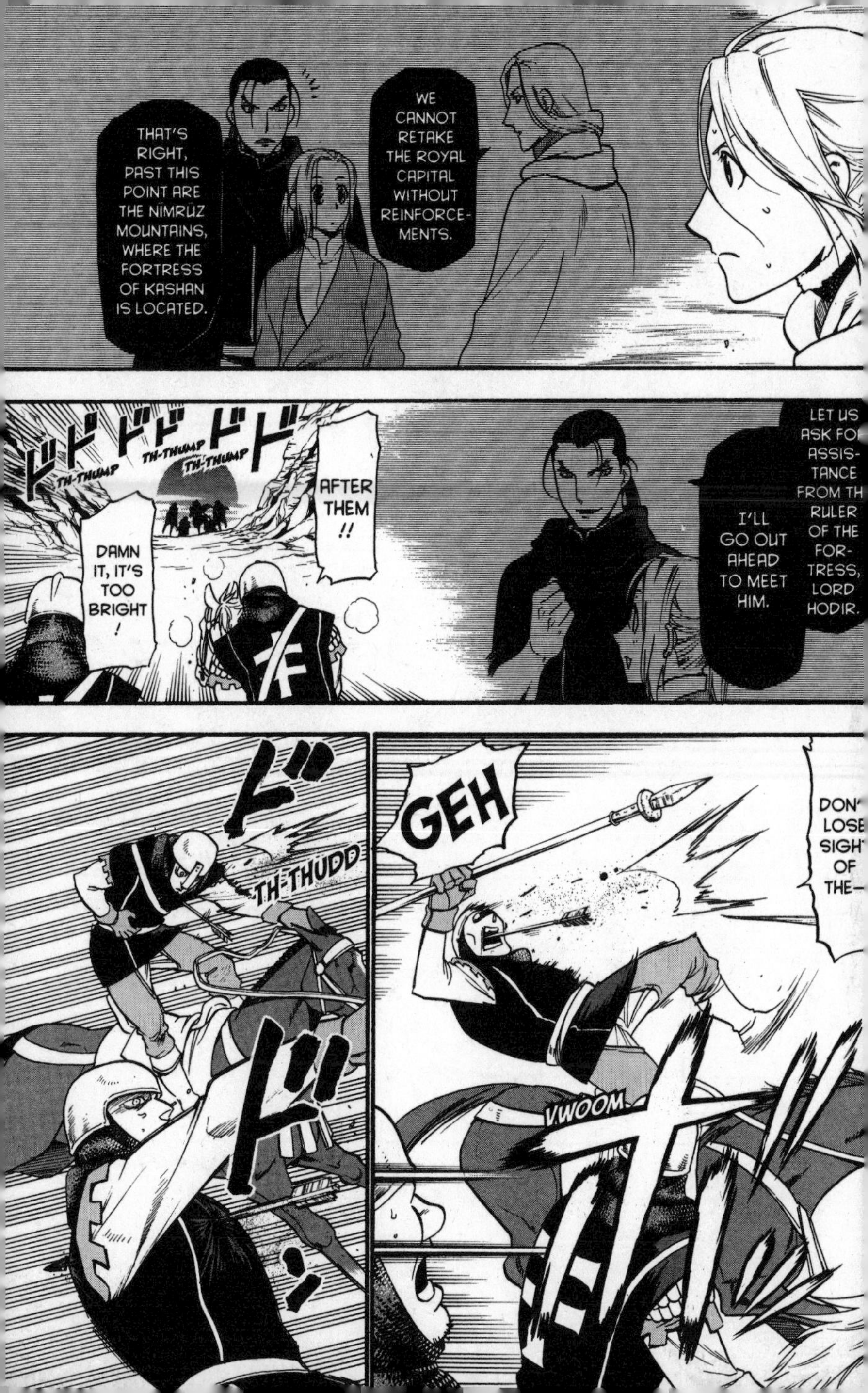
WE CANNOT RETAKE THE ROYAL CAPITAL WITHOUT REINFORCE-MENTS.
THAT'S RIGHT, PAST THIS POINT ARE THE NIMRUZ MOUNTAINS, WHERE THE FORTRESS OF KASHAN IS LOCATED.
LET US ASK FO ASSIS-TANCE FROM TH RULER OF THE FOR-TRESS, LORD HODIR.
I'LL GO OUT AHEAD TO MEET HIM.
TH-THUMP TH-THUMP TH-THUMP
AFTER THEM!!
DAMN IT, IT'S TOO BRIGHT!
DON' LOSE SIGH OF THE—
GEH
VWOOM
TH-THUDD

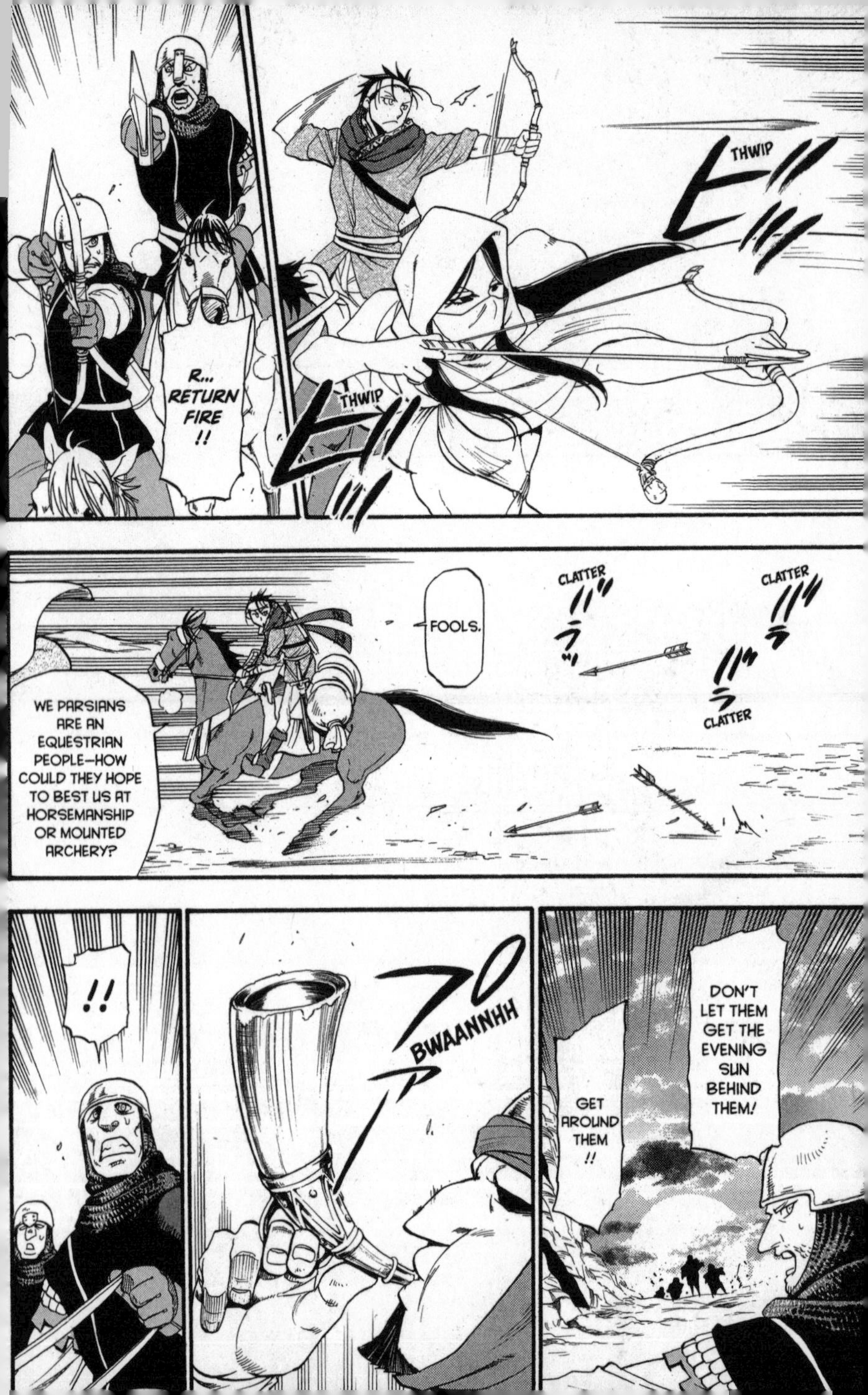
THWIP
THWIP
R... RETURN FIRE !!
CLATTER
CLATTER
CLATTER
FOOLS.
WE PARSIANS ARE AN EQUESTRIAN PEOPLE—HOW COULD THEY HOPE TO BEST US AT HORSEMANSHIP OR MOUNTED ARCHERY?
DON'T LET THEM GET THE EVENING SUN BEHIND THEM!
GET AROUND THEM !!
BWAANNHH
!!

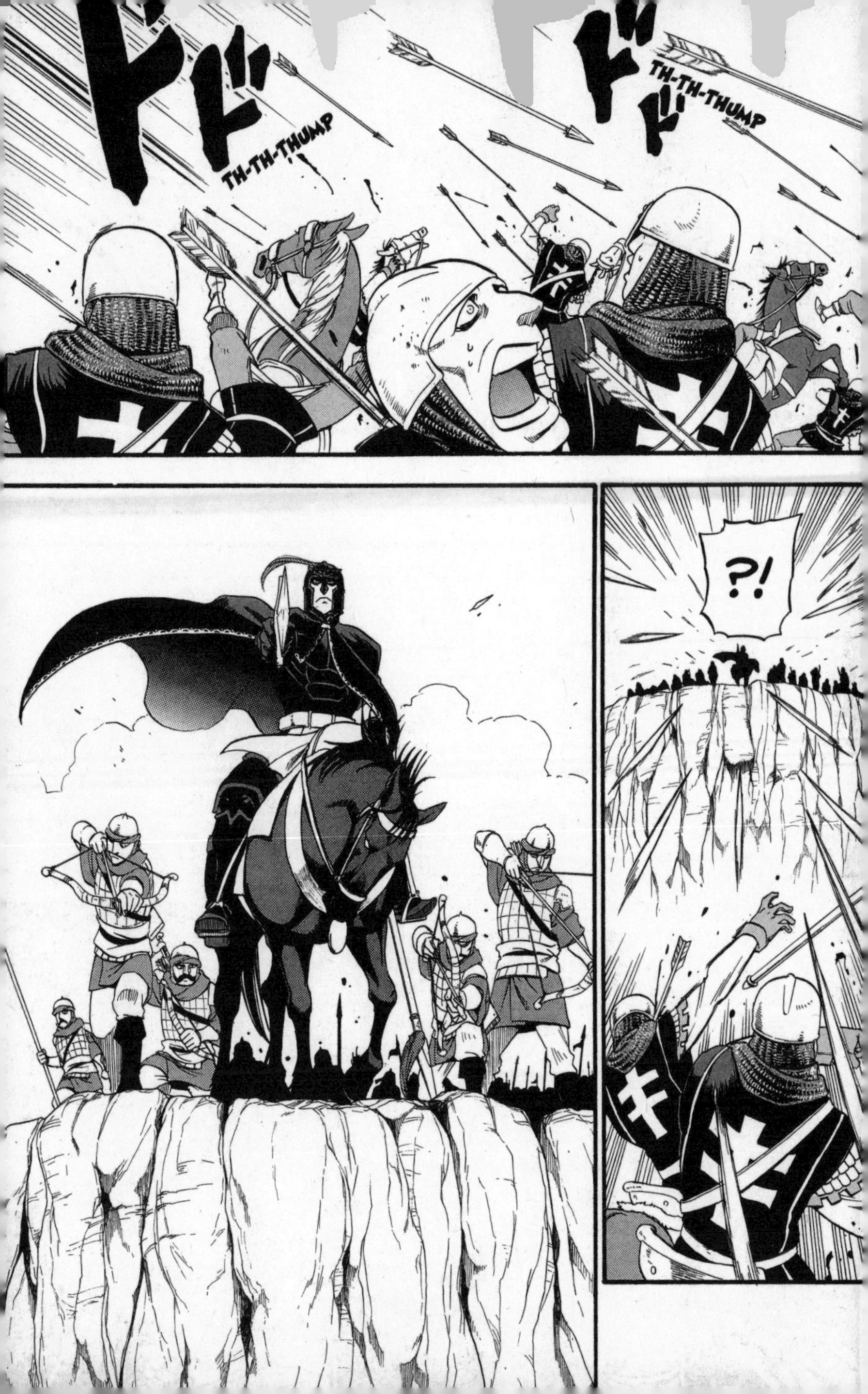
ドド
TH-TH-THUMP
ドド
TH-TH-THUMP
?!

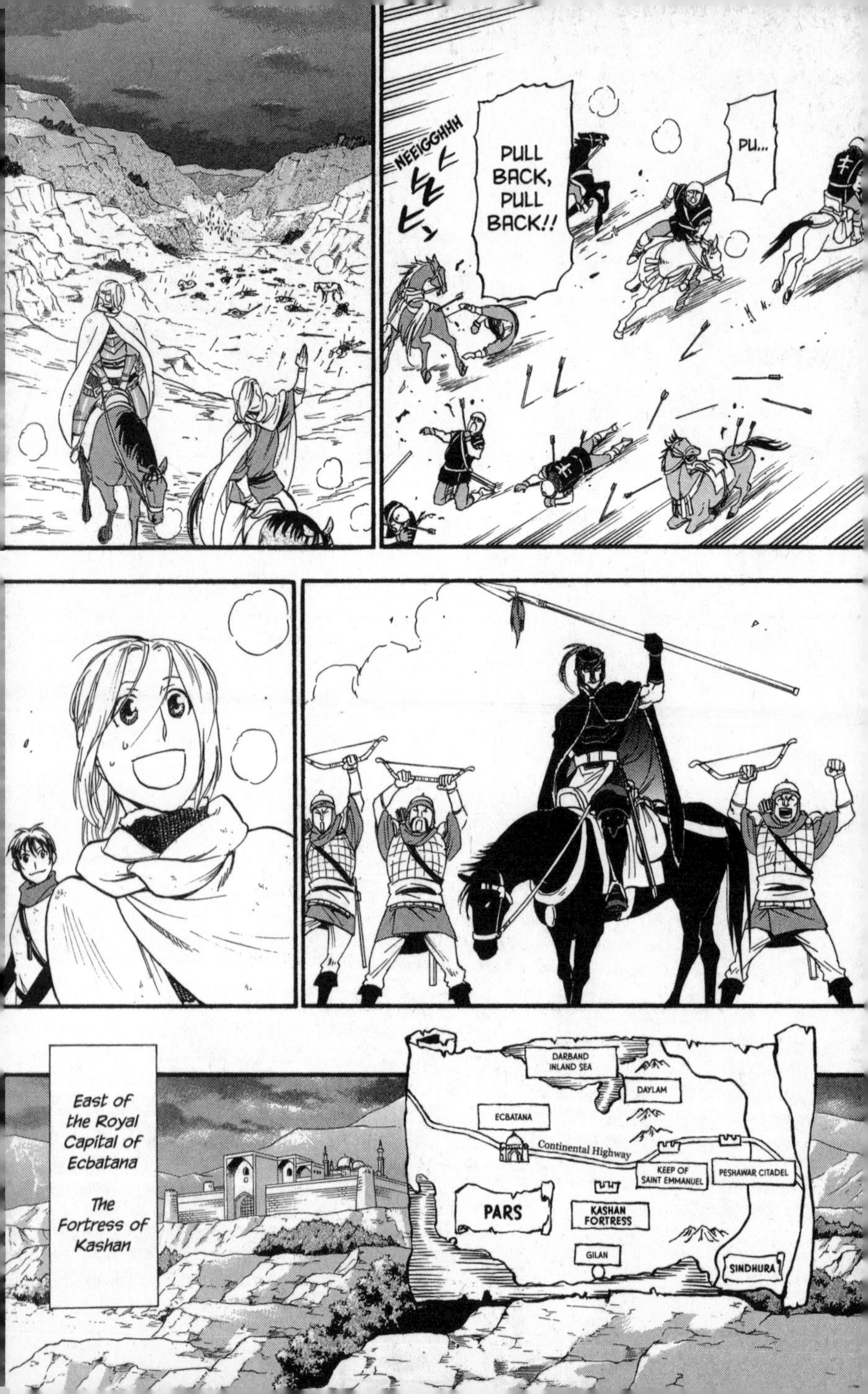
PU...
PULL BACK, PULL BACK!!
NEEIGGHHH
DARBAND INLAND SEA
DAYLAM
ECBATANA
Continental Highway
KEEP OF SAINT EMMANUEL
PESHAWAR CITADEL
PARS
KASHAN FORTRESS
GILAN
SINDHURA
East of the Royal Capital of Ecbatana
The Fortress of Kashan

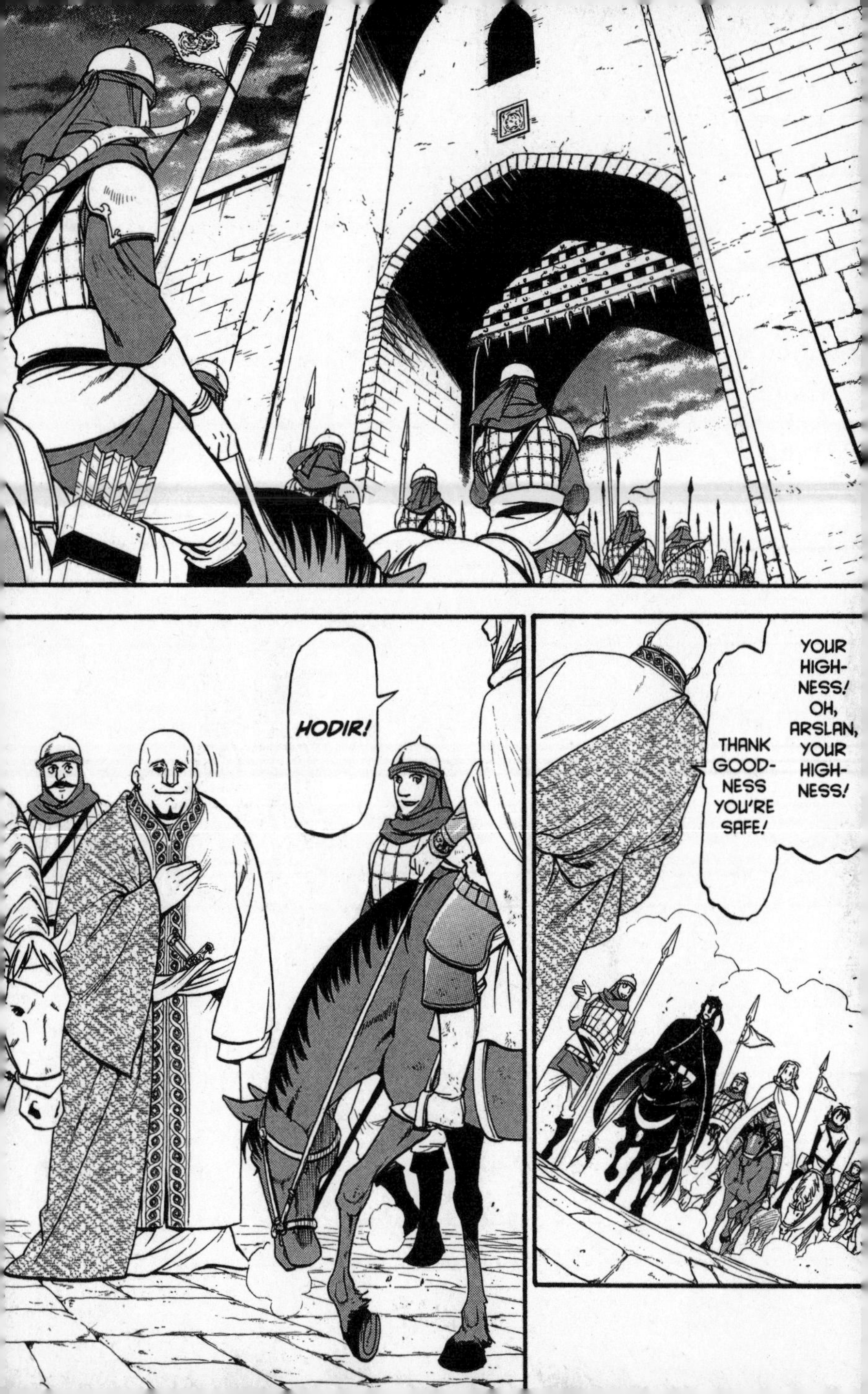
YOUR HIGHNESS! OH, ARSLAN, YOUR HIGHNESS!
THANK GOODNESS YOU'RE SAFE!
HODIR!

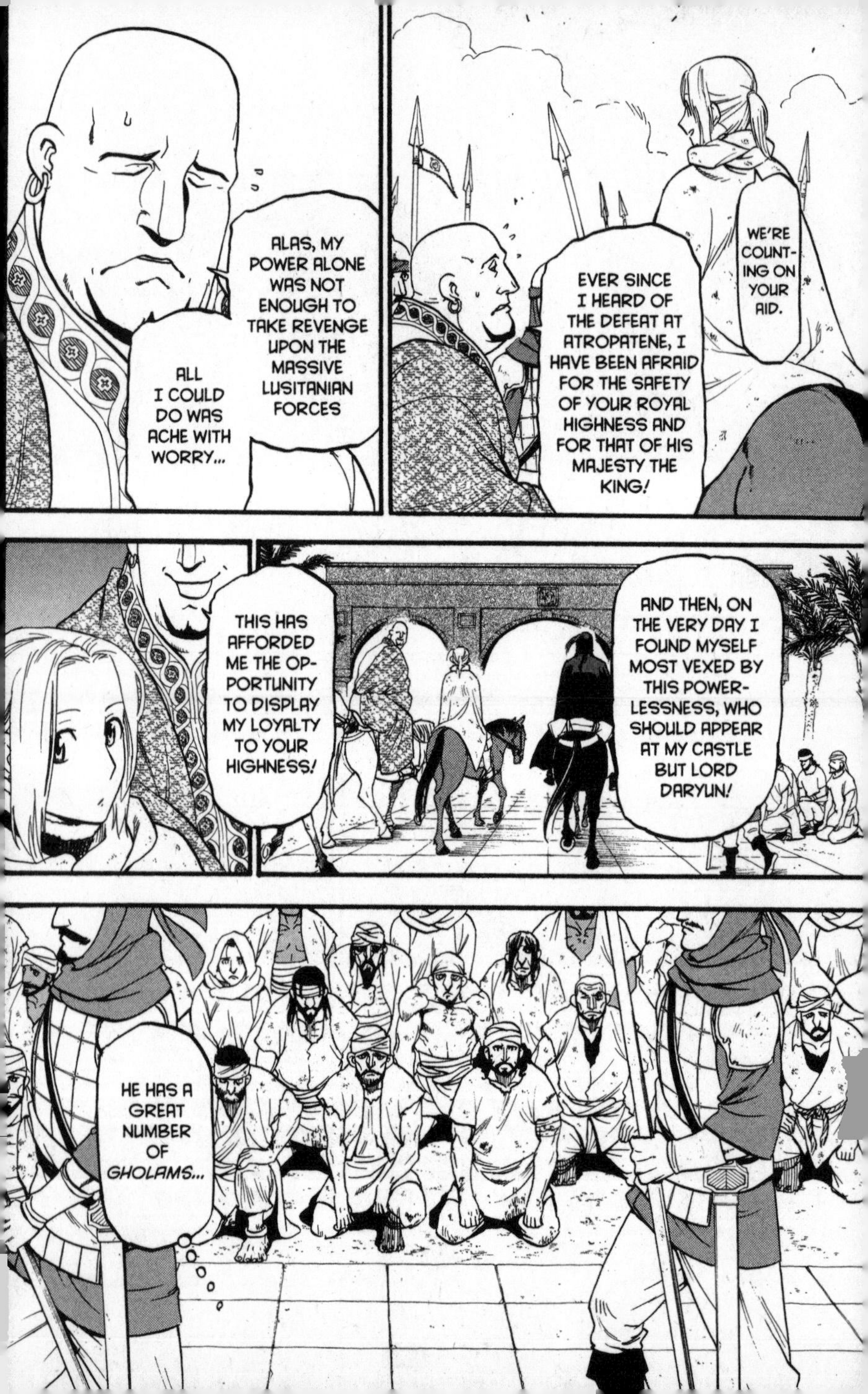
WE'RE COUNTING ON YOUR AID.
EVER SINCE I HEARD OF THE DEFEAT AT ATROPATENE, I HAVE BEEN AFRAID FOR THE SAFETY OF YOUR ROYAL HIGHNESS AND FOR THAT OF HIS MAJESTY THE KING!
ALAS, MY POWER ALONE WAS NOT ENOUGH TO TAKE REVENGE UPON THE MASSIVE LUSITANIAN FORCES
ALL I COULD DO WAS ACHE WITH WORRY...
AND THEN, ON THE VERY DAY I FOUND MYSELF MOST VEXED BY THIS POWERLESSNESS, WHO SHOULD APPEAR AT MY CASTLE BUT LORD DARYUN!
THIS HAS AFFORDED ME THE OPPORTUNITY TO DISPLAY MY LOYALTY TO YOUR HIGHNESS!
HE HAS A GREAT NUMBER OF *GHOLAMS*...

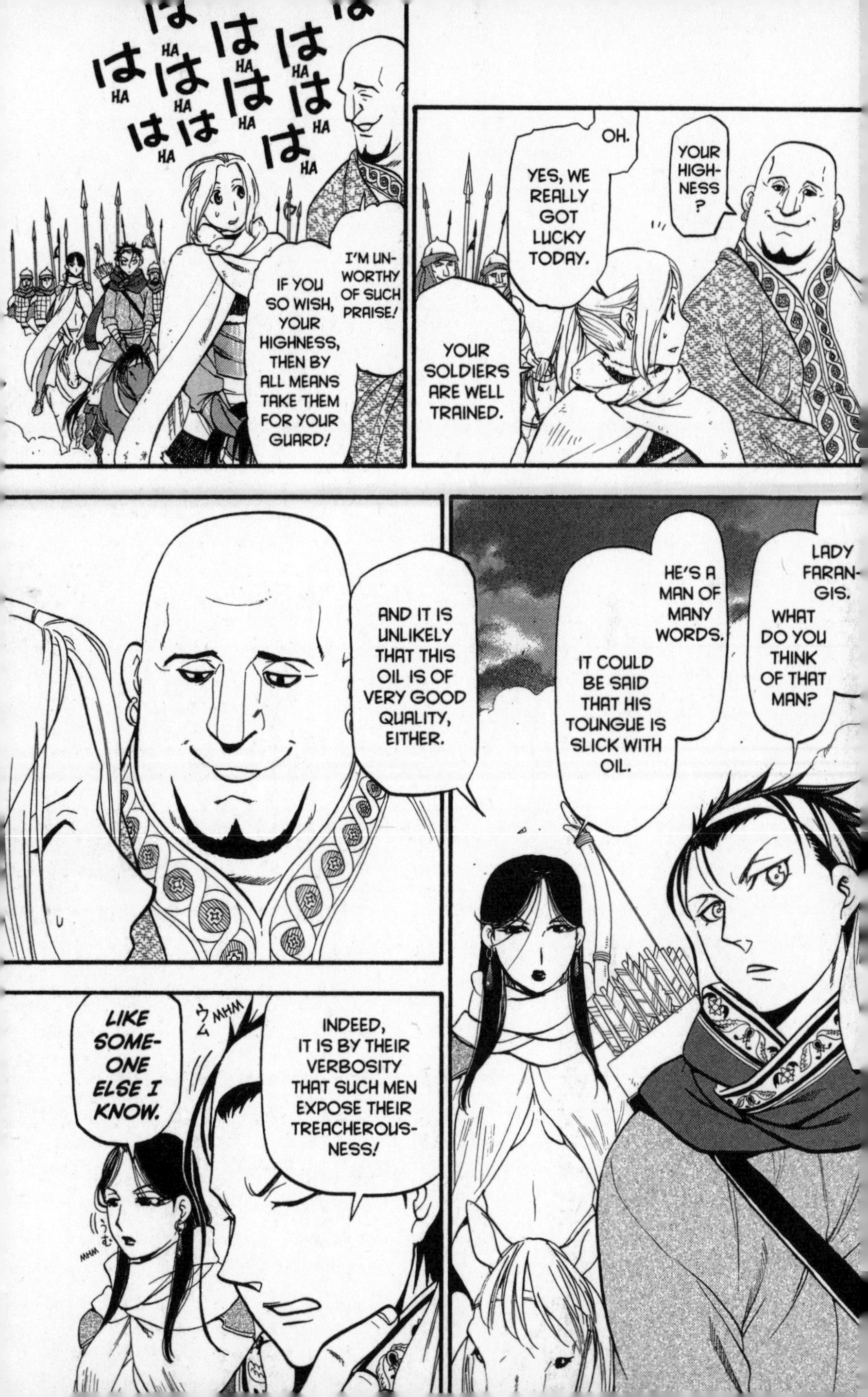
YOUR HIGHNESS?
OH.
YES, WE REALLY GOT LUCKY TODAY.
YOUR SOLDIERS ARE WELL TRAINED.
ははははははははは
HA HA HA HA HA HA HA HA HA
I'M UNWORTHY OF SUCH PRAISE!
IF YOU SO WISH, YOUR HIGHNESS, THEN BY ALL MEANS TAKE THEM FOR YOUR GUARD!
LADY FARANGIS.
WHAT DO YOU THINK OF THAT MAN?
HE'S A MAN OF MANY WORDS.
IT COULD BE SAID THAT HIS TOUNGUE IS SLICK WITH OIL.
AND IT IS UNLIKELY THAT THIS OIL IS OF VERY GOOD QUALITY, EITHER.
ウム MHM
INDEED, IT IS BY THEIR VERBOSITY THAT SUCH MEN EXPOSE THEIR TREACHEROUSNESS!
LIKE SOMEONE ELSE I KNOW.
うむ MHM

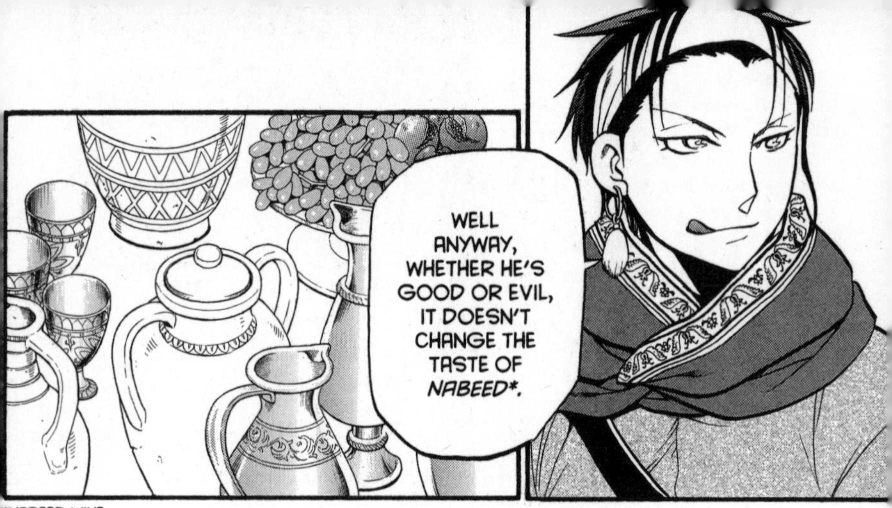
WELL ANYWAY, WHETHER HE'S GOOD OR EVIL, IT DOESN'T CHANGE THE TASTE OF *NABEED**.

*NABEED=WINE

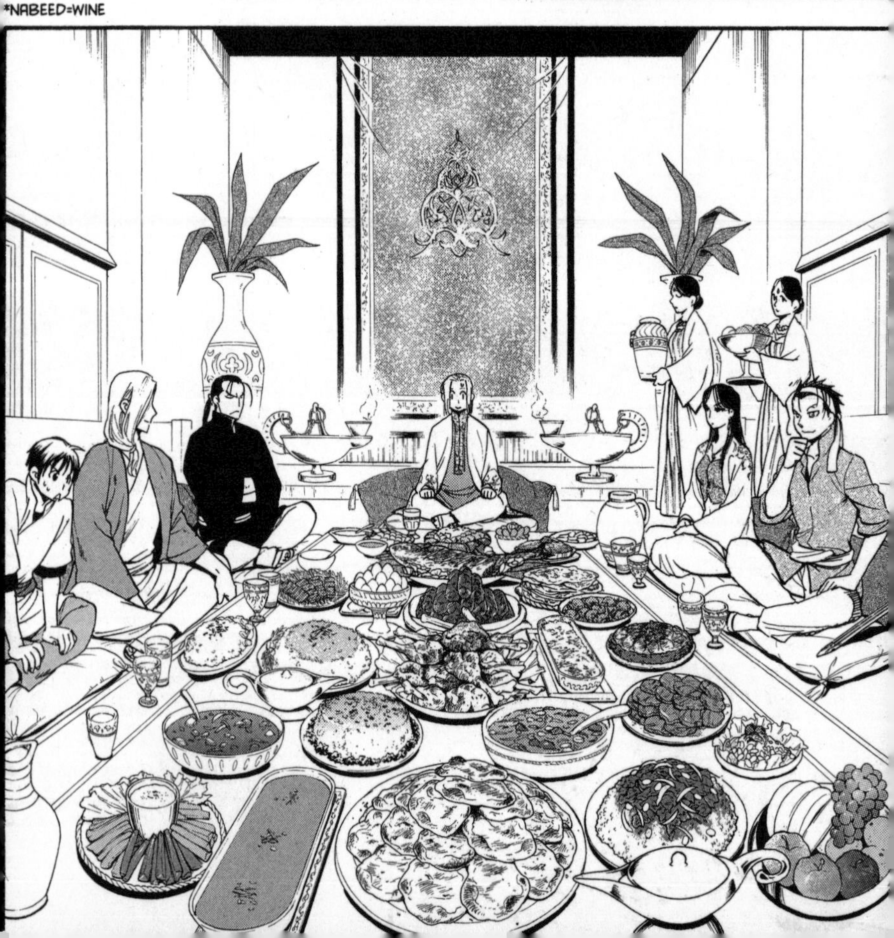

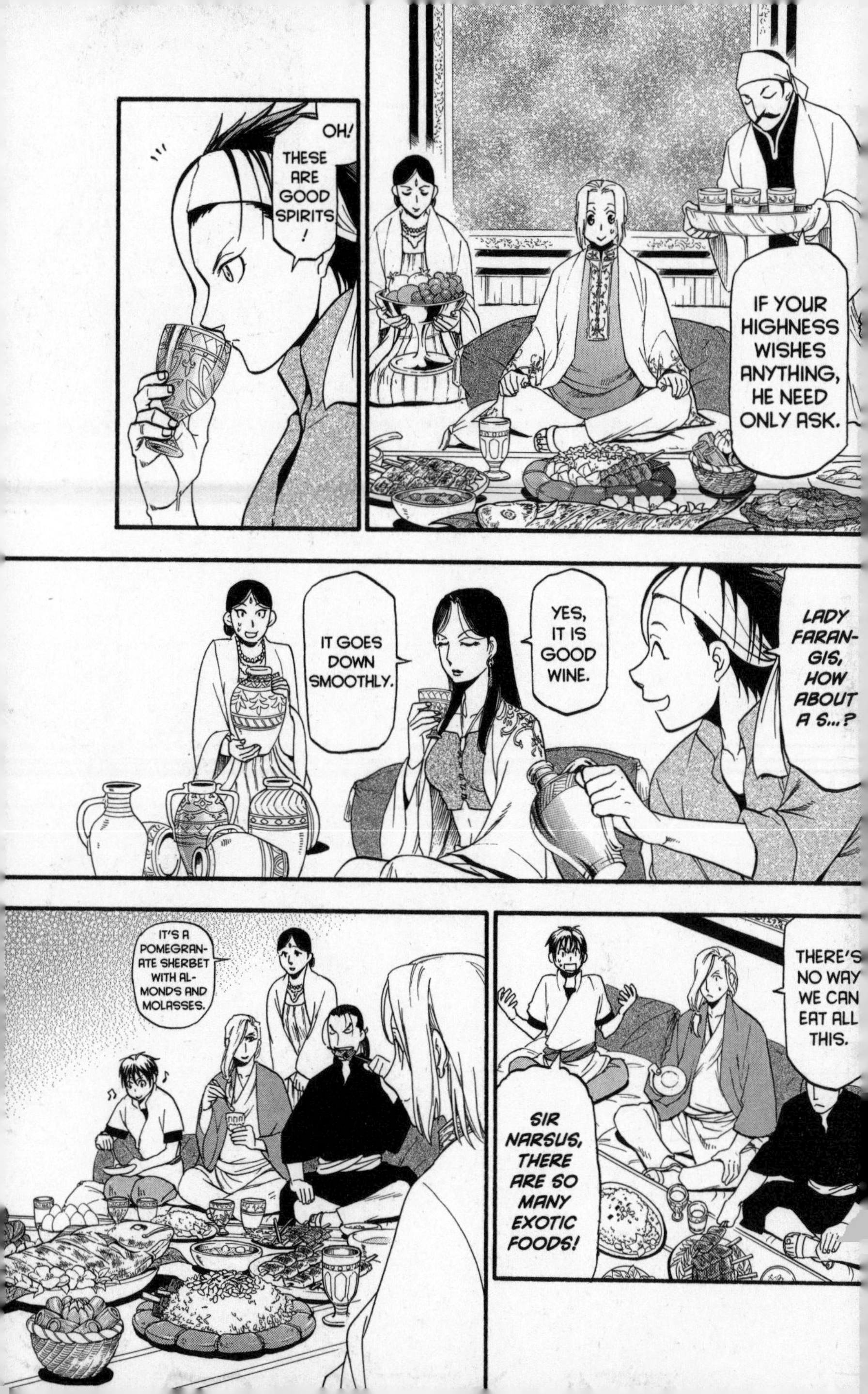
IF YOUR HIGHNESS WISHES ANYTHING, HE NEED ONLY ASK.
OH! THESE ARE GOOD SPIRITS!
LADY FARANGIS, HOW ABOUT A S...?
YES, IT IS GOOD WINE.
IT GOES DOWN SMOOTHLY.
THERE'S NO WAY WE CAN EAT ALL THIS.
SIR NARSUS, THERE ARE SO MANY EXOTIC FOODS!
IT'S A POMEGRANATE SHERBET WITH ALMONDS AND MOLASSES.

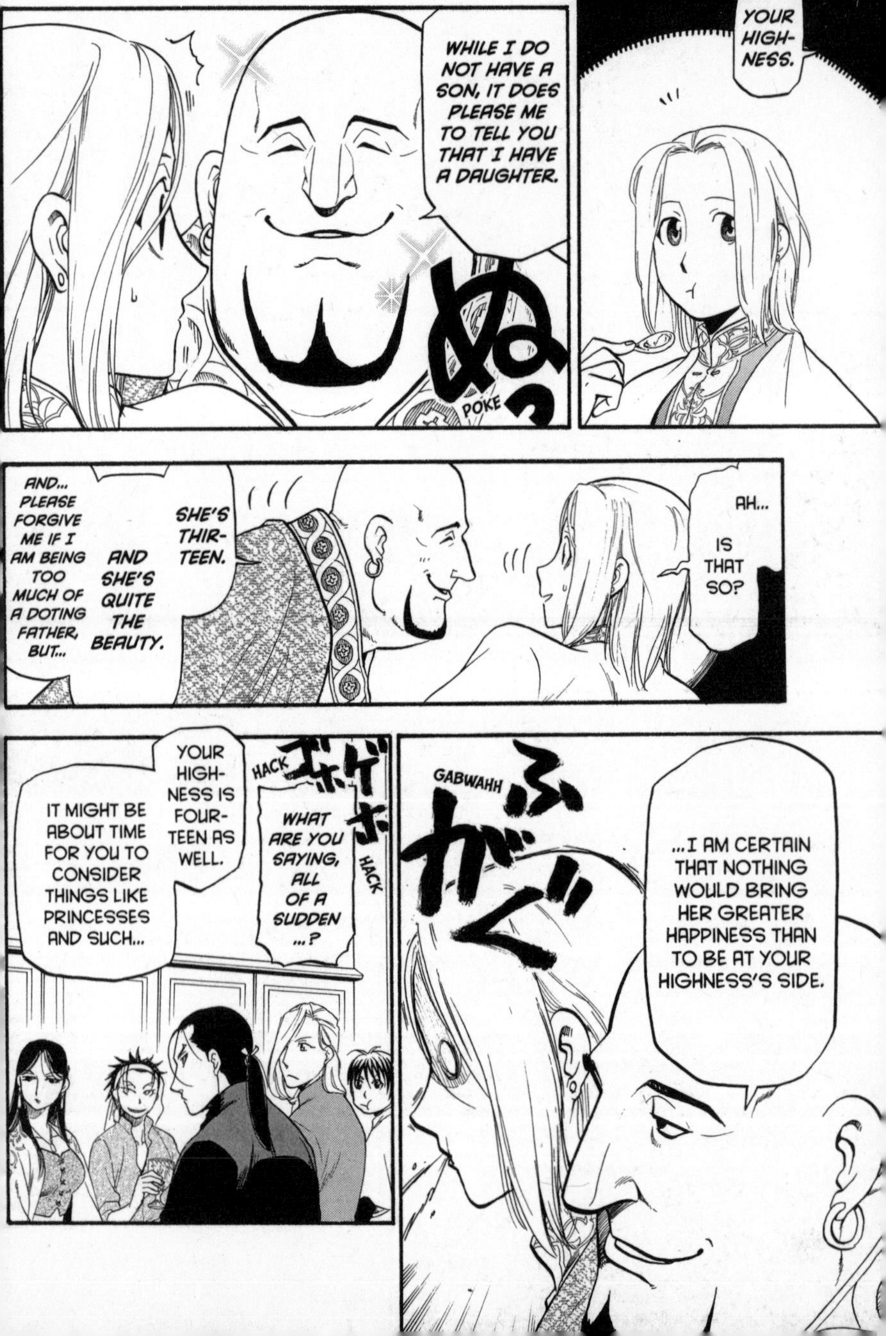
YOUR HIGHNESS.
WHILE I DO NOT HAVE A SON, IT DOES PLEASE ME TO TELL YOU THAT I HAVE A DAUGHTER.
POKE
AH... IS THAT SO?
SHE'S THIRTEEN.
AND SHE'S QUITE THE BEAUTY.
AND... PLEASE FORGIVE ME IF I AM BEING TOO MUCH OF A DOTING FATHER, BUT...
GABWAHH
...I AM CERTAIN THAT NOTHING WOULD BRING HER GREATER HAPPINESS THAN TO BE AT YOUR HIGHNESS'S SIDE.
HACK
HACK
WHAT ARE YOU SAYING, ALL OF A SUDDEN ...?
YOUR HIGHNESS IS FOURTEEN AS WELL.
IT MIGHT BE ABOUT TIME FOR YOU TO CONSIDER THINGS LIKE PRINCESSES AND SUCH...

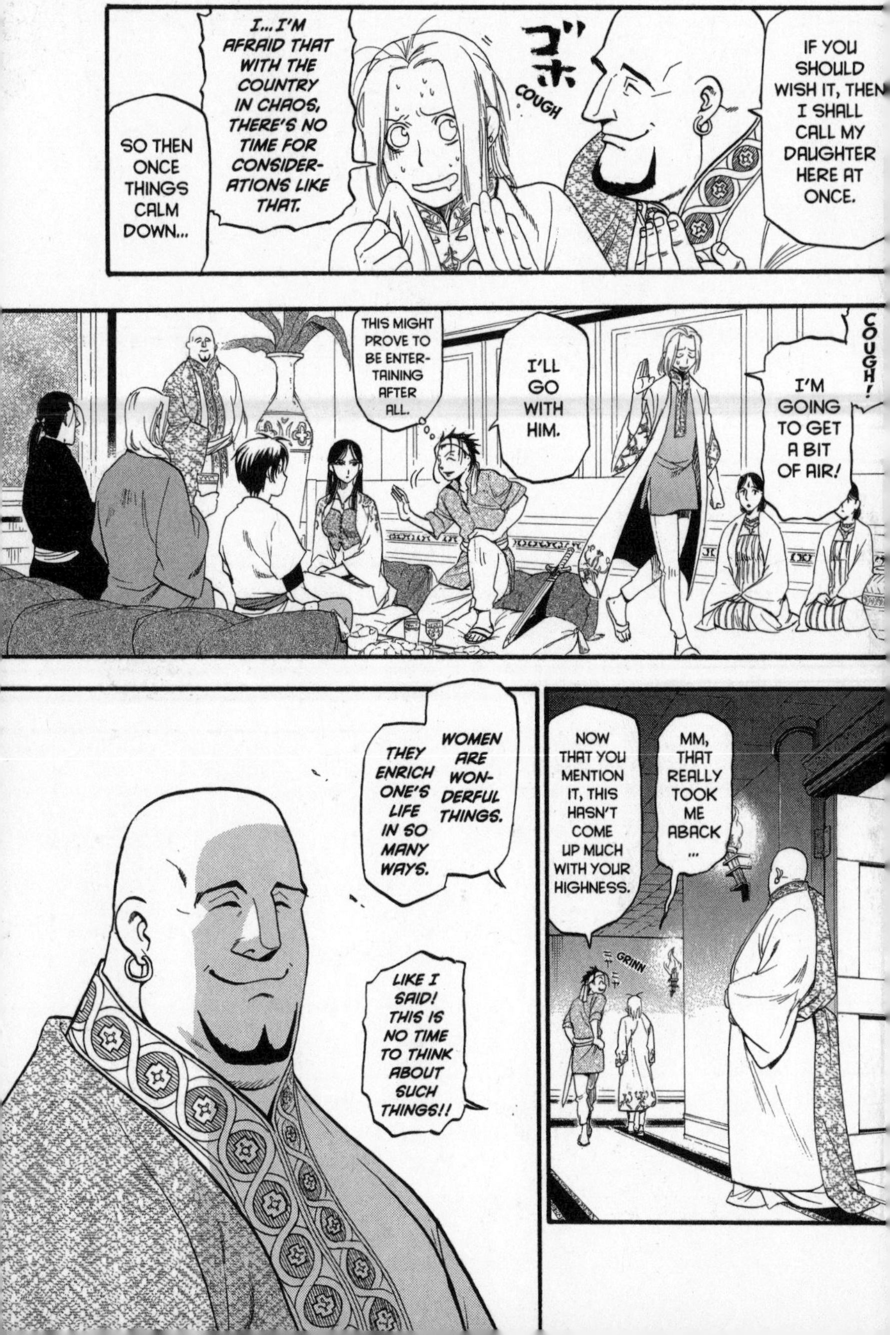
IF YOU SHOULD WISH IT, THEN I SHALL CALL MY DAUGHTER HERE AT ONCE.
ゴホ
COUGH
I... I'M AFRAID THAT WITH THE COUNTRY IN CHAOS, THERE'S NO TIME FOR CONSIDER-ATIONS LIKE THAT.
SO THEN ONCE THINGS CALM DOWN...
COUGH!
I'M GOING TO GET A BIT OF AIR!
I'LL GO WITH HIM.
THIS MIGHT PROVE TO BE ENTER-TAINING AFTER ALL.
MM, THAT REALLY TOOK ME ABACK ...
NOW THAT YOU MENTION IT, THIS HASN'T COME UP MUCH WITH YOUR HIGHNESS.
GRINN
WOMEN ARE WON-DERFUL THINGS.
THEY ENRICH ONE'S LIFE IN SO MANY WAYS.
LIKE I SAID! THIS IS NO TIME TO THINK ABOUT SUCH THINGS!!

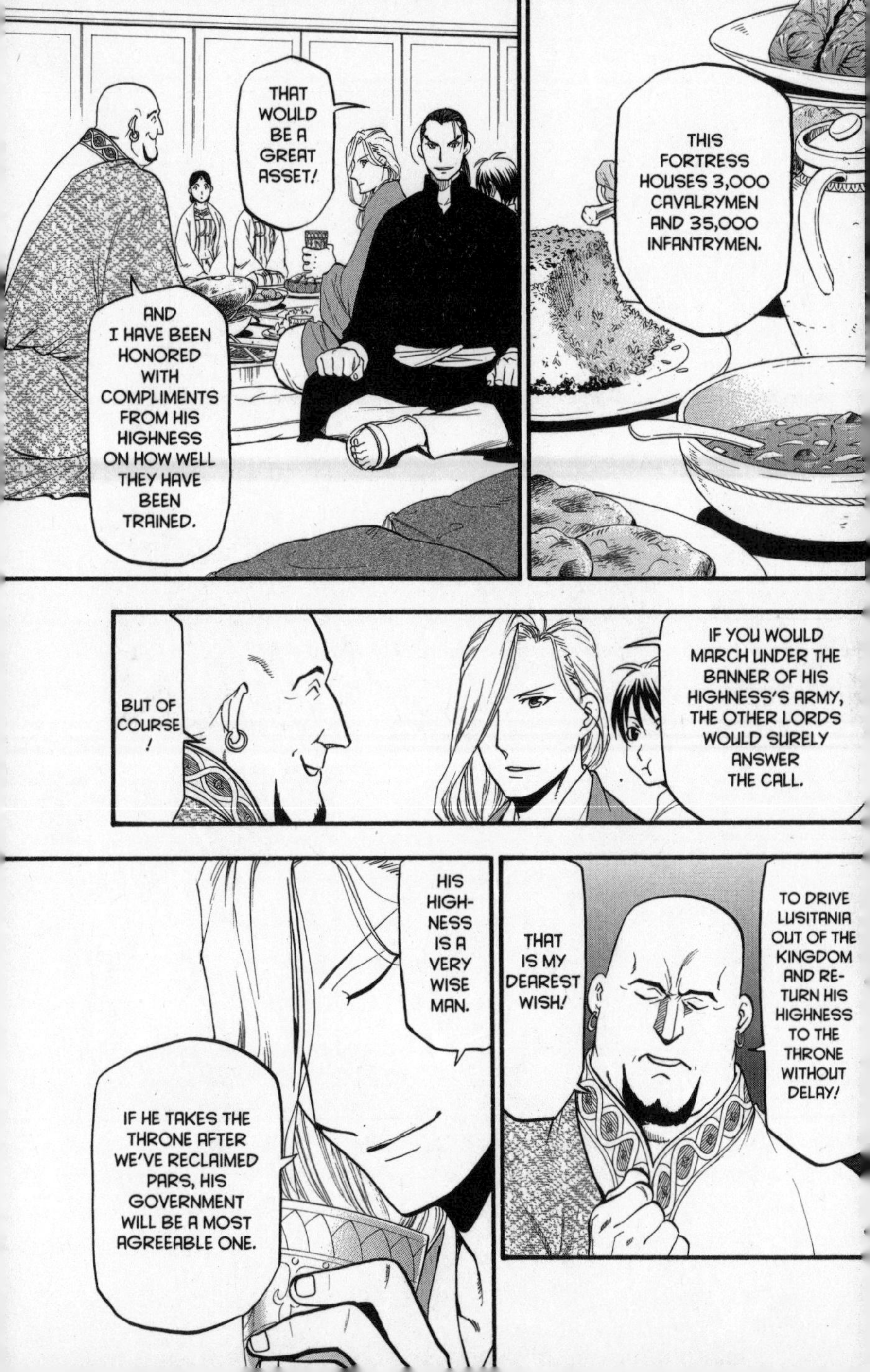
THIS FORTRESS HOUSES 3,000 CAVALRYMEN AND 35,000 INFANTRYMEN.
THAT WOULD BE A GREAT ASSET!
AND I HAVE BEEN HONORED WITH COMPLIMENTS FROM HIS HIGHNESS ON HOW WELL THEY HAVE BEEN TRAINED.
IF YOU WOULD MARCH UNDER THE BANNER OF HIS HIGHNESS'S ARMY, THE OTHER LORDS WOULD SURELY ANSWER THE CALL.
BUT OF COURSE!
TO DRIVE LUSITANIA OUT OF THE KINGDOM AND RETURN HIS HIGHNESS TO THE THRONE WITHOUT DELAY!
THAT IS MY DEAREST WISH!
HIS HIGHNESS IS A VERY WISE MAN.
IF HE TAKES THE THRONE AFTER WE'VE RECLAIMED PARS, HIS GOVERNMENT WILL BE A MOST AGREEABLE ONE.

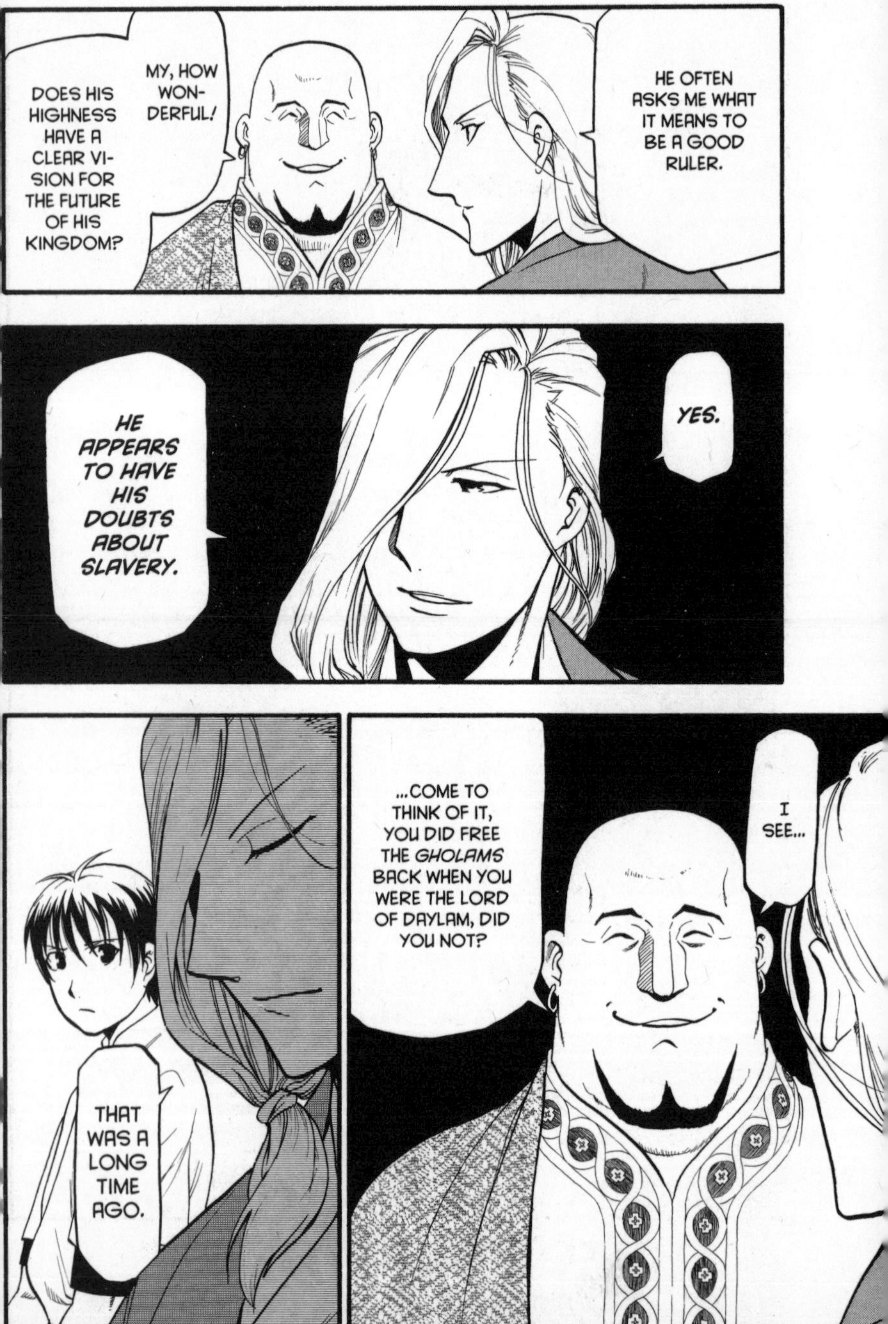
HE OFTEN ASKS ME WHAT IT MEANS TO BE A GOOD RULER.
MY, HOW WON-DERFUL!
DOES HIS HIGHNESS HAVE A CLEAR VI-SION FOR THE FUTURE OF HIS KINGDOM?
YES.
HE APPEARS TO HAVE HIS DOUBTS ABOUT SLAVERY.
I SEE...
...COME TO THINK OF IT, YOU DID FREE THE GHOLAMS BACK WHEN YOU WERE THE LORD OF DAYLAM, DID YOU NOT?
THAT WAS A LONG TIME AGO.

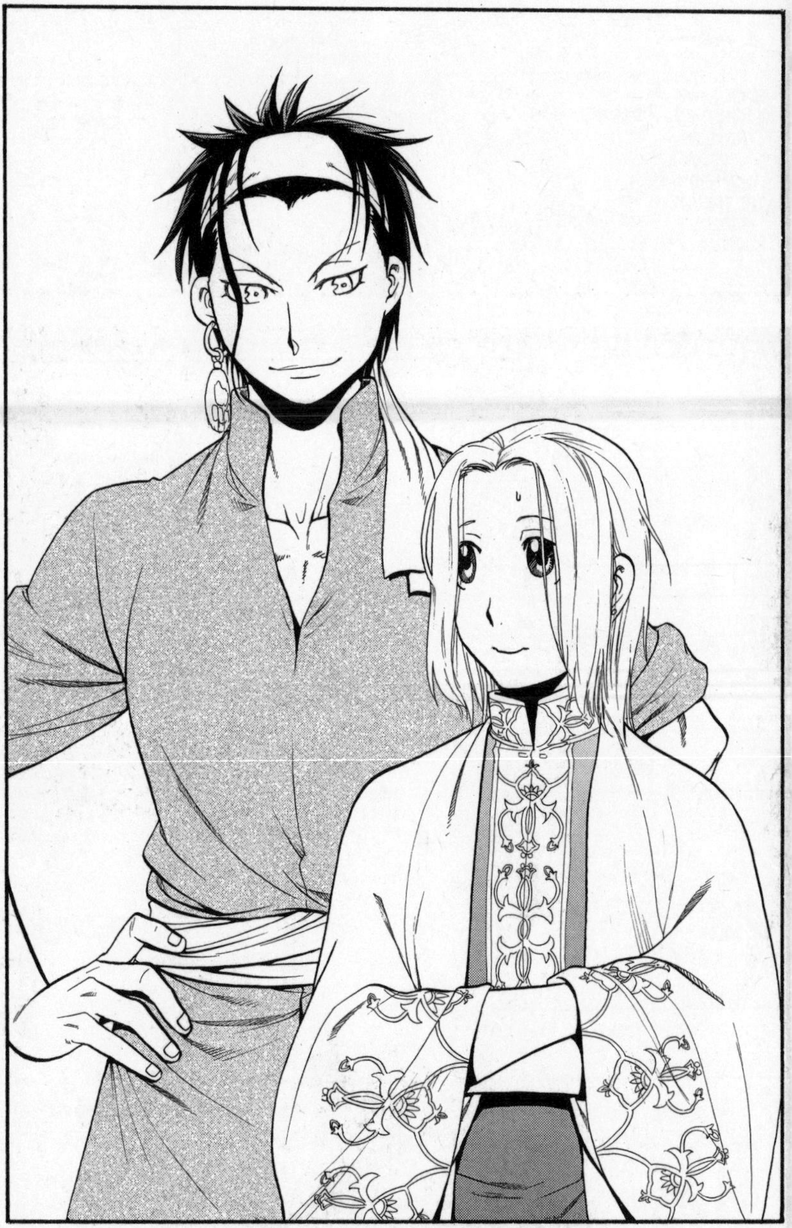

Chapter 22: Hodir's Plot

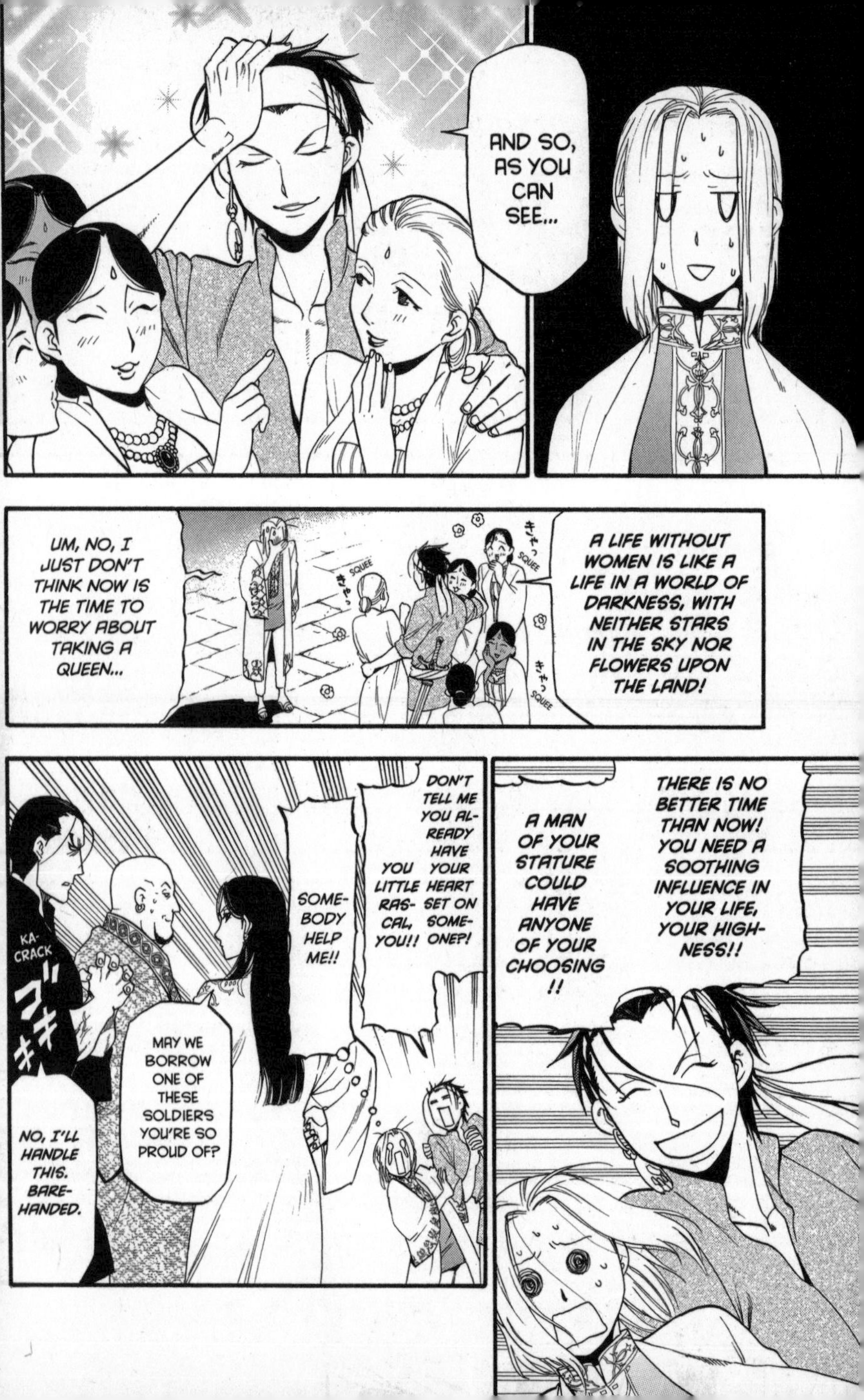
AND SO, AS YOU CAN SEE...
A LIFE WITHOUT WOMEN IS LIKE A LIFE IN A WORLD OF DARKNESS, WITH NEITHER STARS IN THE SKY NOR FLOWERS UPON THE LAND!
きゃっ SQUEE
きゃっ SQUEE
きゃっ SQUEE
UM, NO, I JUST DON'T THINK NOW IS THE TIME TO WORRY ABOUT TAKING A QUEEN...
THERE IS NO BETTER TIME THAN NOW! YOU NEED A SOOTHING INFLUENCE IN YOUR LIFE, YOUR HIGHNESS!!
A MAN OF YOUR STATURE COULD HAVE ANYONE OF YOUR CHOOSING!!
DON'T TELL ME YOU ALREADY HAVE YOUR HEART SET ON SOMEONE?!
YOU LITTLE RASCAL, YOU!!
SOMEBODY HELP ME!!
MAY WE BORROW ONE OF THESE SOLDIERS YOU'RE SO PROUD OF?
KA-CRACK
NO, I'LL HANDLE THIS. BAREHANDED.

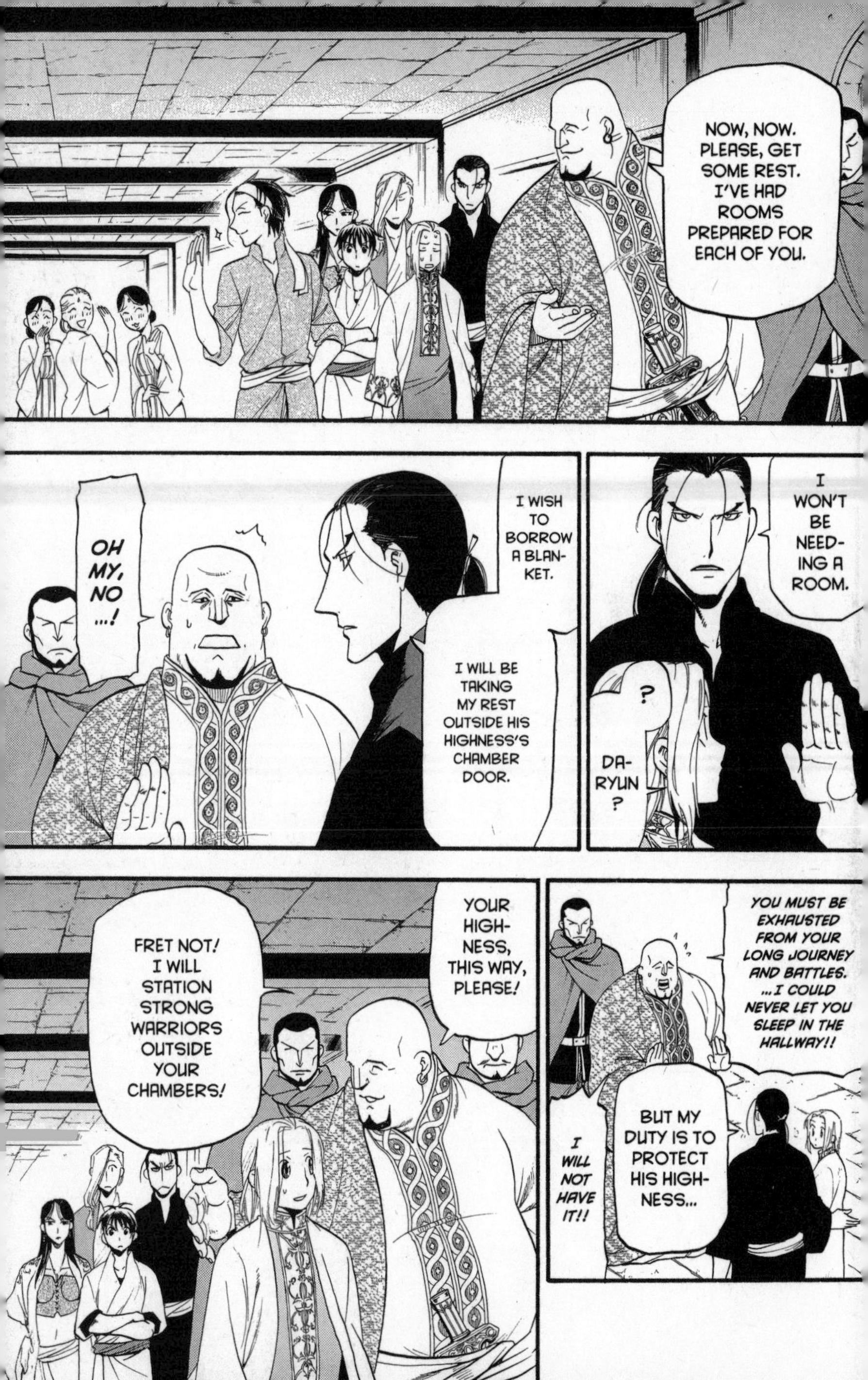
NOW, NOW. PLEASE, GET SOME REST. I'VE HAD ROOMS PREPARED FOR EACH OF YOU.
I WON'T BE NEEDING A ROOM.
?
DARYUN?
I WISH TO BORROW A BLANKET.
I WILL BE TAKING MY REST OUTSIDE HIS HIGHNESS'S CHAMBER DOOR.
OH MY, NO...!
YOU MUST BE EXHAUSTED FROM YOUR LONG JOURNEY AND BATTLES. ...I COULD NEVER LET YOU SLEEP IN THE HALLWAY!!
BUT MY DUTY IS TO PROTECT HIS HIGHNESS...
I WILL NOT HAVE IT!!
YOUR HIGHNESS, THIS WAY, PLEASE!
FRET NOT! I WILL STATION STRONG WARRIORS OUTSIDE YOUR CHAMBERS!

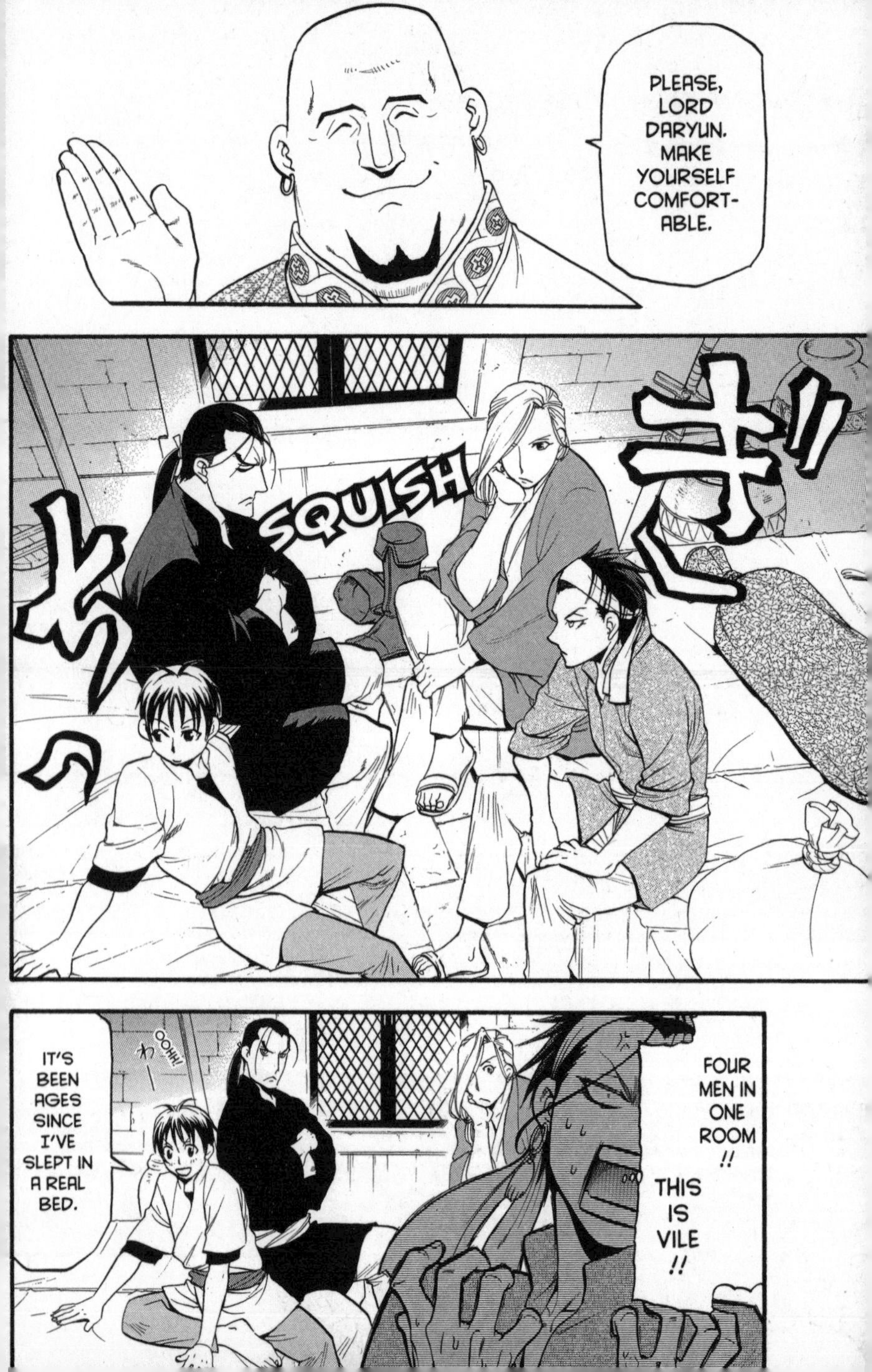
PLEASE, LORD DARYUN. MAKE YOURSELF COMFORT-ABLE.
SQUISH
FOUR MEN IN ONE ROOM!!
THIS IS VILE!!
OOHH!
IT'S BEEN AGES SINCE I'VE SLEPT IN A REAL BED.

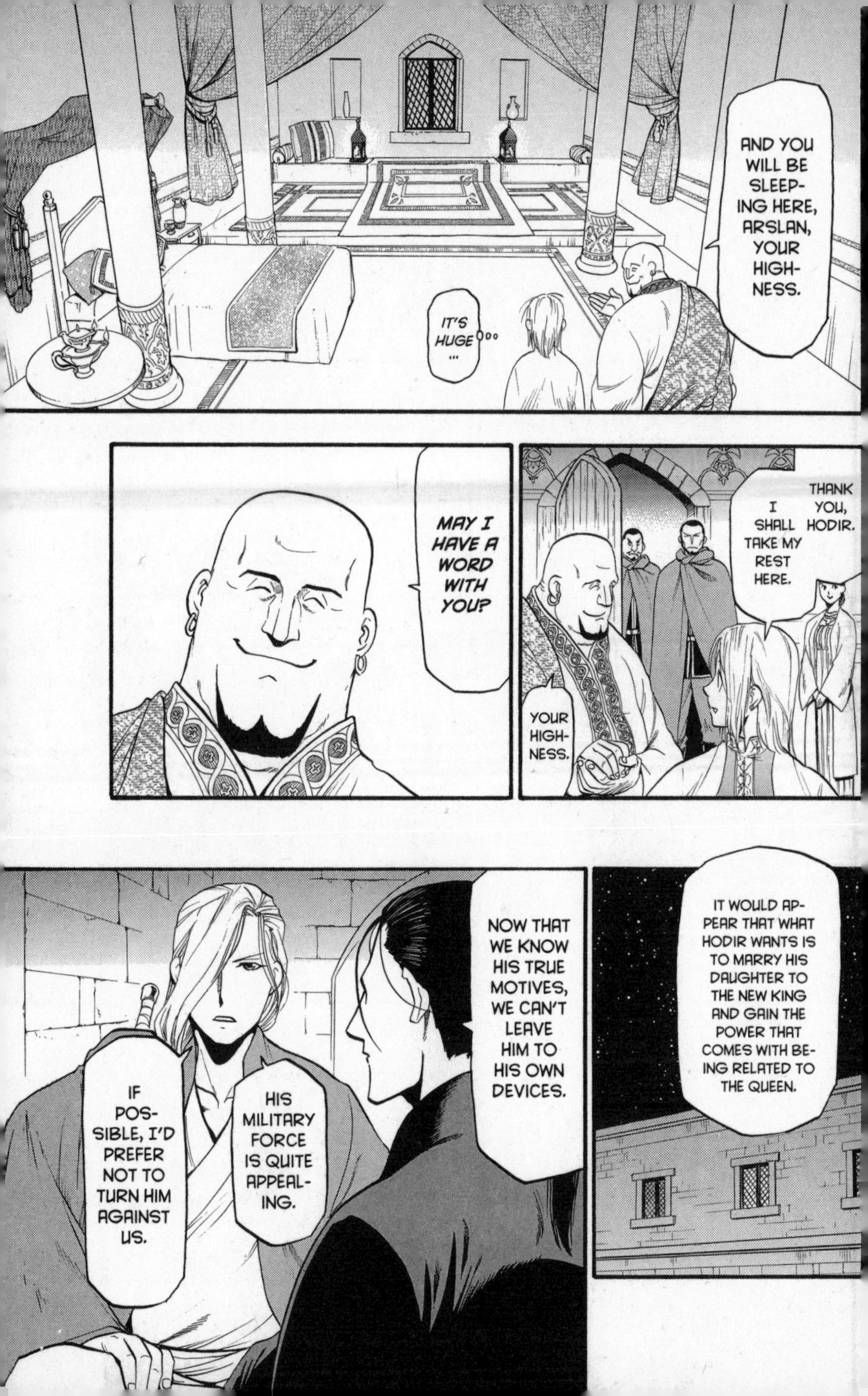
AND YOU WILL BE SLEEPING HERE, ARSLAN, YOUR HIGHNESS.
IT'S HUGE...
THANK YOU, HODIR.
I SHALL TAKE MY REST HERE.
YOUR HIGHNESS.
MAY I HAVE A WORD WITH YOU?
IT WOULD APPEAR THAT WHAT HODIR WANTS IS TO MARRY HIS DAUGHTER TO THE NEW KING AND GAIN THE POWER THAT COMES WITH BEING RELATED TO THE QUEEN.
NOW THAT WE KNOW HIS TRUE MOTIVES, WE CAN'T LEAVE HIM TO HIS OWN DEVICES.
HIS MILITARY FORCE IS QUITE APPEALING.
IF POSSIBLE, I'D PREFER NOT TO TURN HIM AGAINST US.

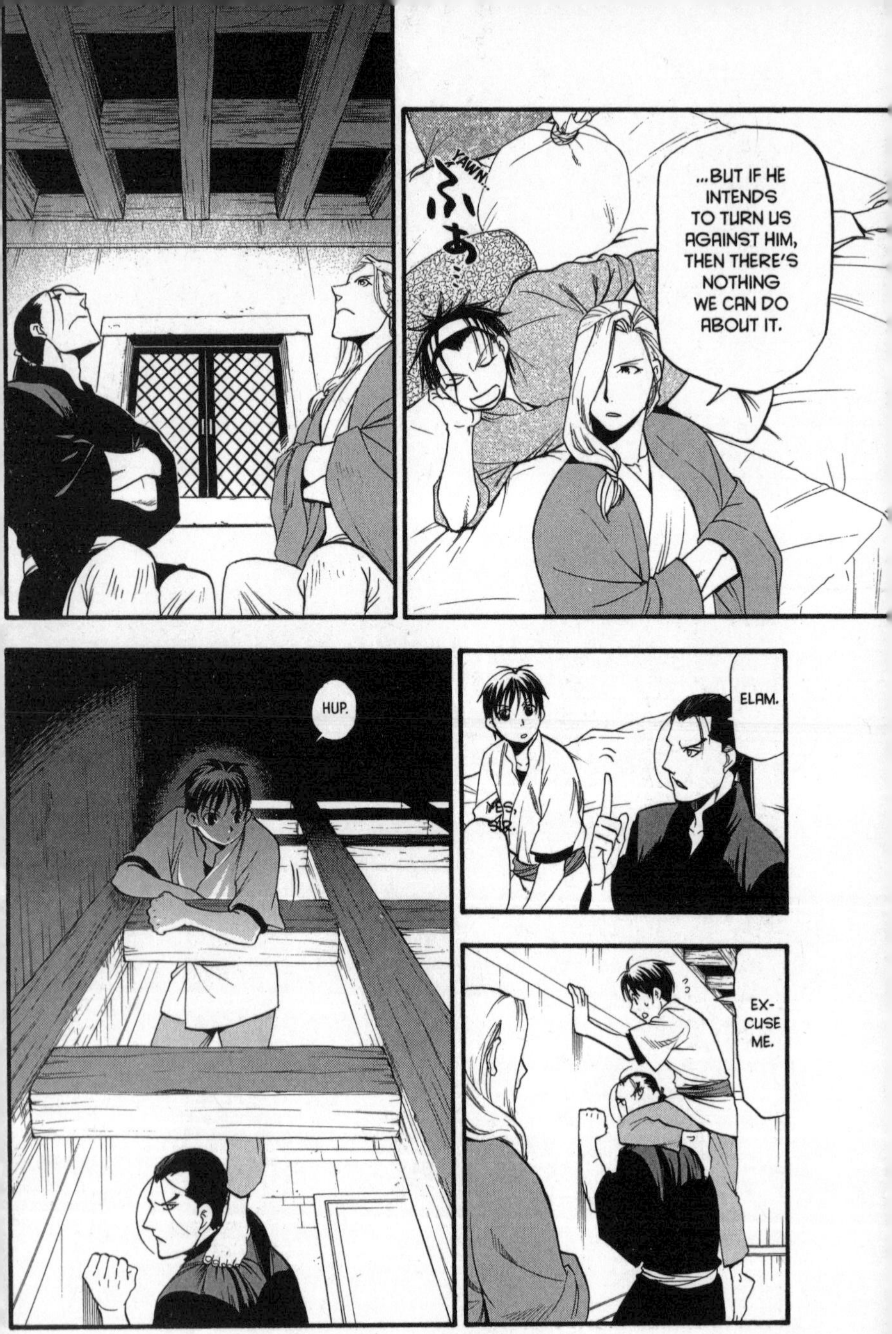
...BUT IF HE INTENDS TO TURN US AGAINST HIM, THEN THERE'S NOTHING WE CAN DO ABOUT IT.
YAWN...
ふあ…
ELAM.
YES, SIR.
EX-CUSE ME.
HUP.

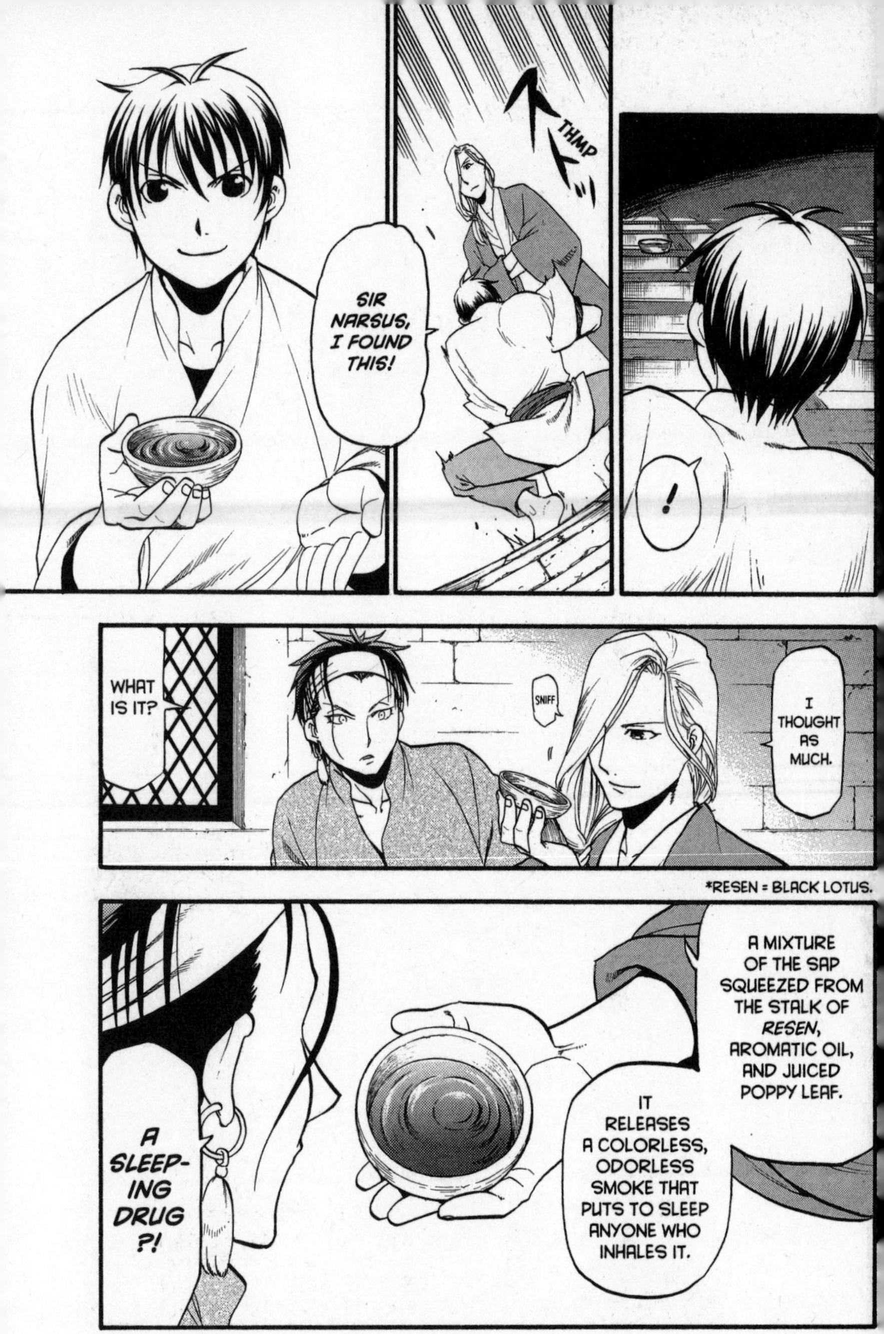
!
THMP
SIR NARSUS, I FOUND THIS!
I THOUGHT AS MUCH.
SNIFF
WHAT IS IT?
A MIXTURE OF THE SAP SQUEEZED FROM THE STALK OF *RESEN*, AROMATIC OIL, AND JUICED POPPY LEAF.
IT RELEASES A COLORLESS, ODORLESS SMOKE THAT PUTS TO SLEEP ANYONE WHO INHALES IT.
A SLEEPING-DRUG?!

*RESEN = BLACK LOTUS.

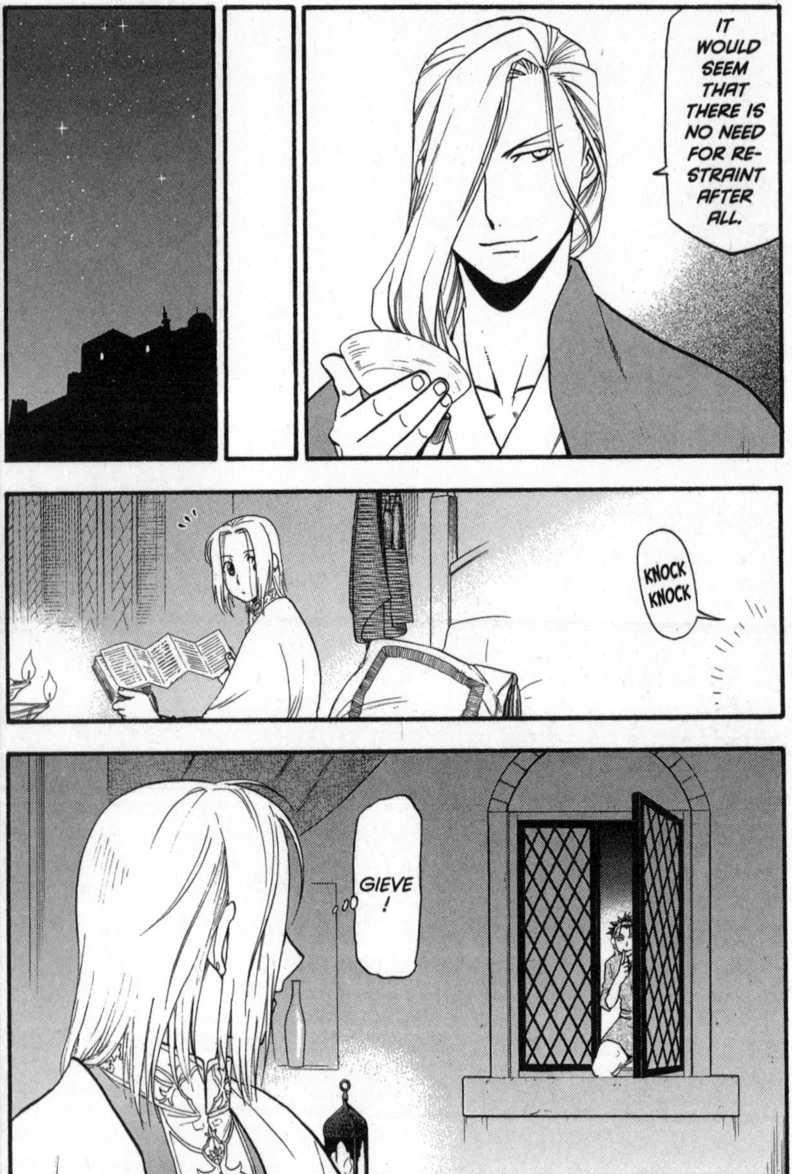
IT WOULD SEEM THAT THERE IS NO NEED FOR RE-STRAINT AFTER ALL.
KNOCK KNOCK
GIEVE !

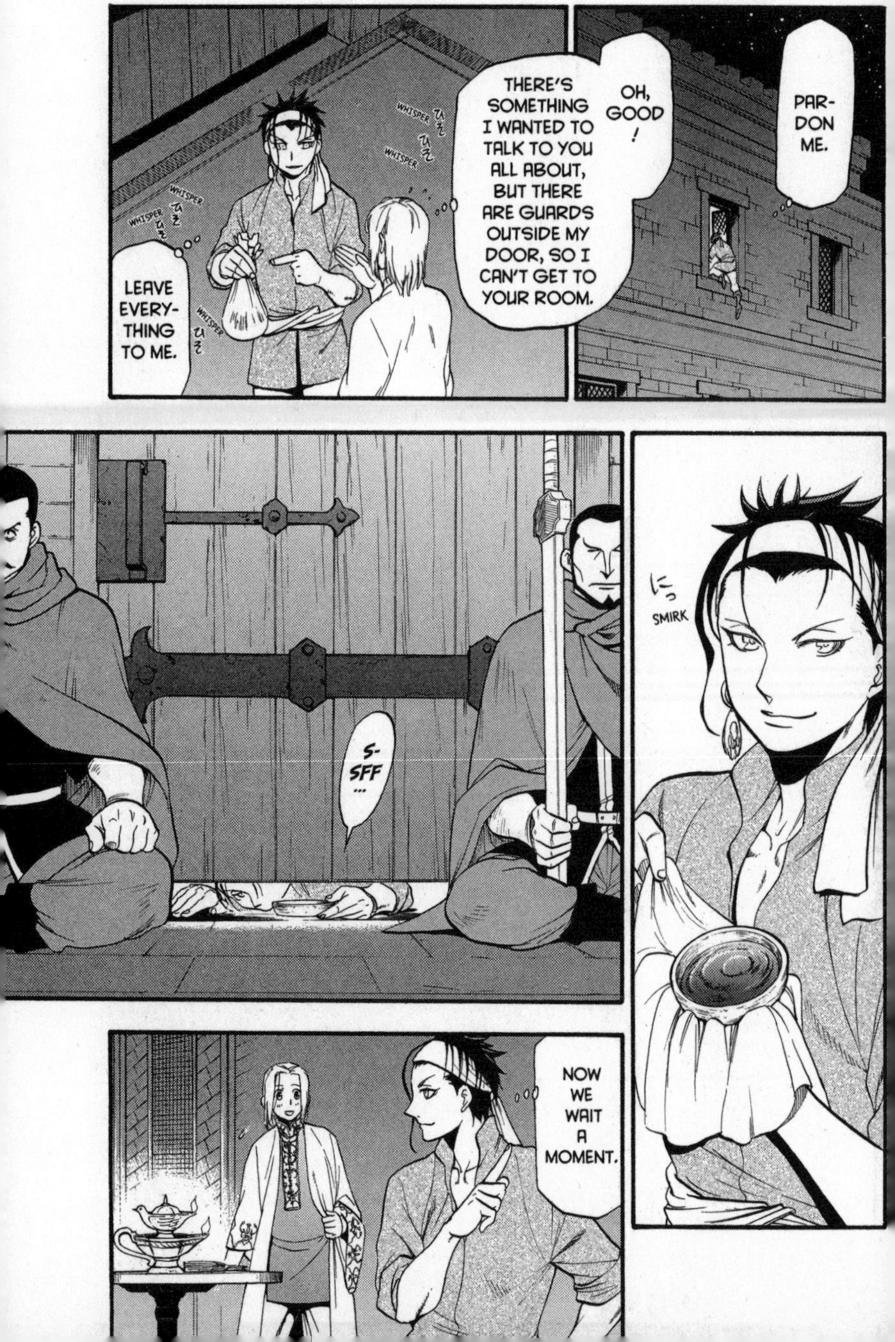
PAR-DON ME.
OH, GOOD!
THERE'S SOMETHING I WANTED TO TALK TO YOU ALL ABOUT, BUT THERE ARE GUARDS OUTSIDE MY DOOR, SO I CAN'T GET TO YOUR ROOM.
WHISPER
WHISPER
WHISPER
WHISPER
WHISPER
LEAVE EVERY-THING TO ME.
にっ
SMIRK
S-SFF...
NOW WE WAIT A MOMENT.

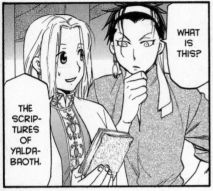

WHAT IS THIS?
THE SCRIPTURES OF YALDABAOTH.
IT WAS GIVEN TO ME BY A LUSITANIAN I KNOW, BUT I CAN'T READ LUSITANIAN SCRIPT.
DISPOSE OF THAT THING!
HA HA... THAT'S WHAT ELAM TOLD ME.
"...OTHER PEOPLE HAVE THINGS THAT ARE PRECIOUS."

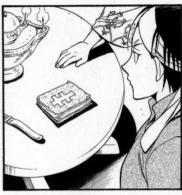

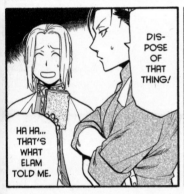

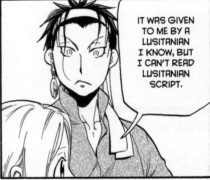

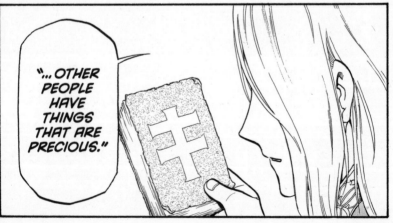

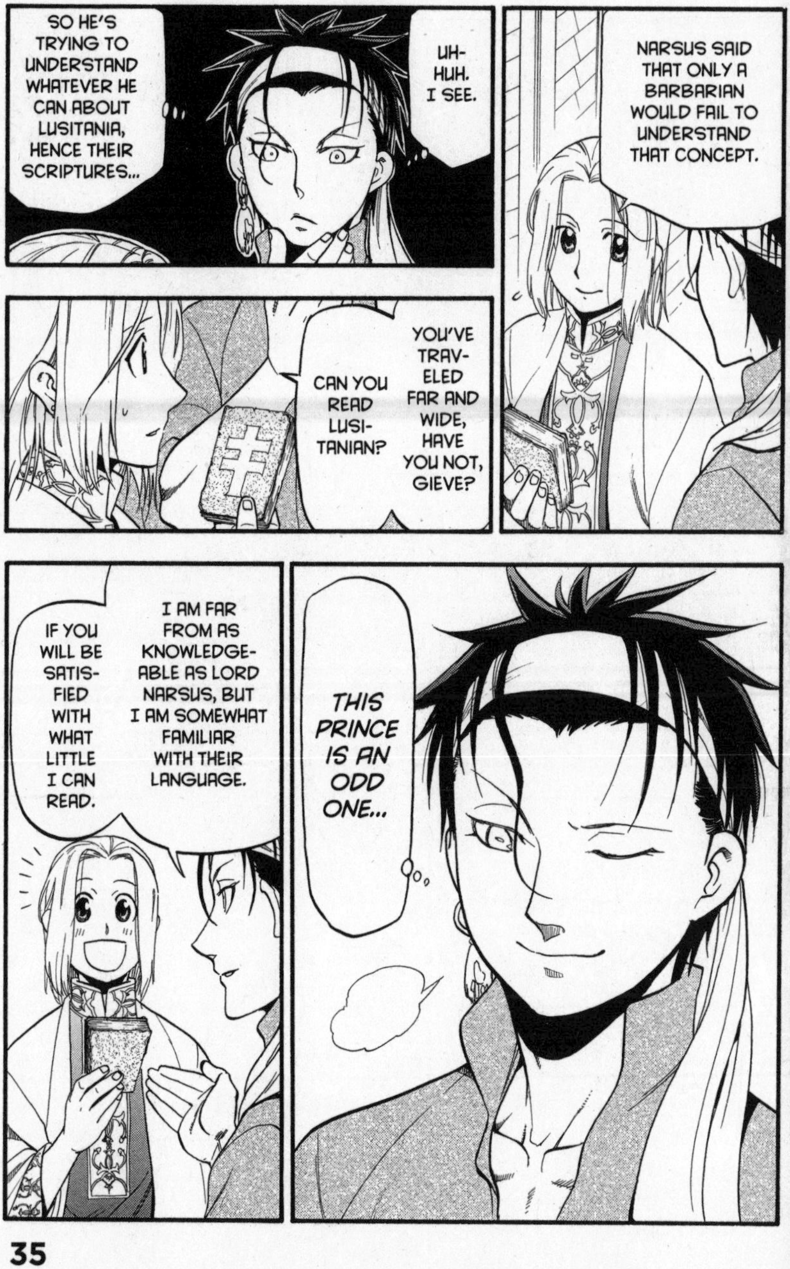
NARSUS SAID THAT ONLY A BARBARIAN WOULD FAIL TO UNDERSTAND THAT CONCEPT.
UH-HUH. I SEE.
SO HE'S TRYING TO UNDERSTAND WHATEVER HE CAN ABOUT LUSITANIA, HENCE THEIR SCRIPTURES...
YOU'VE TRAVELED FAR AND WIDE, HAVE YOU NOT, GIEVE?
CAN YOU READ LUSITANIAN?
THIS PRINCE IS AN ODD ONE...
I AM FAR FROM AS KNOWLEDGEABLE AS LORD NARSUS, BUT I AM SOMEWHAT FAMILIAR WITH THEIR LANGUAGE.
IF YOU WILL BE SATISFIED WITH WHAT LITTLE I CAN READ.

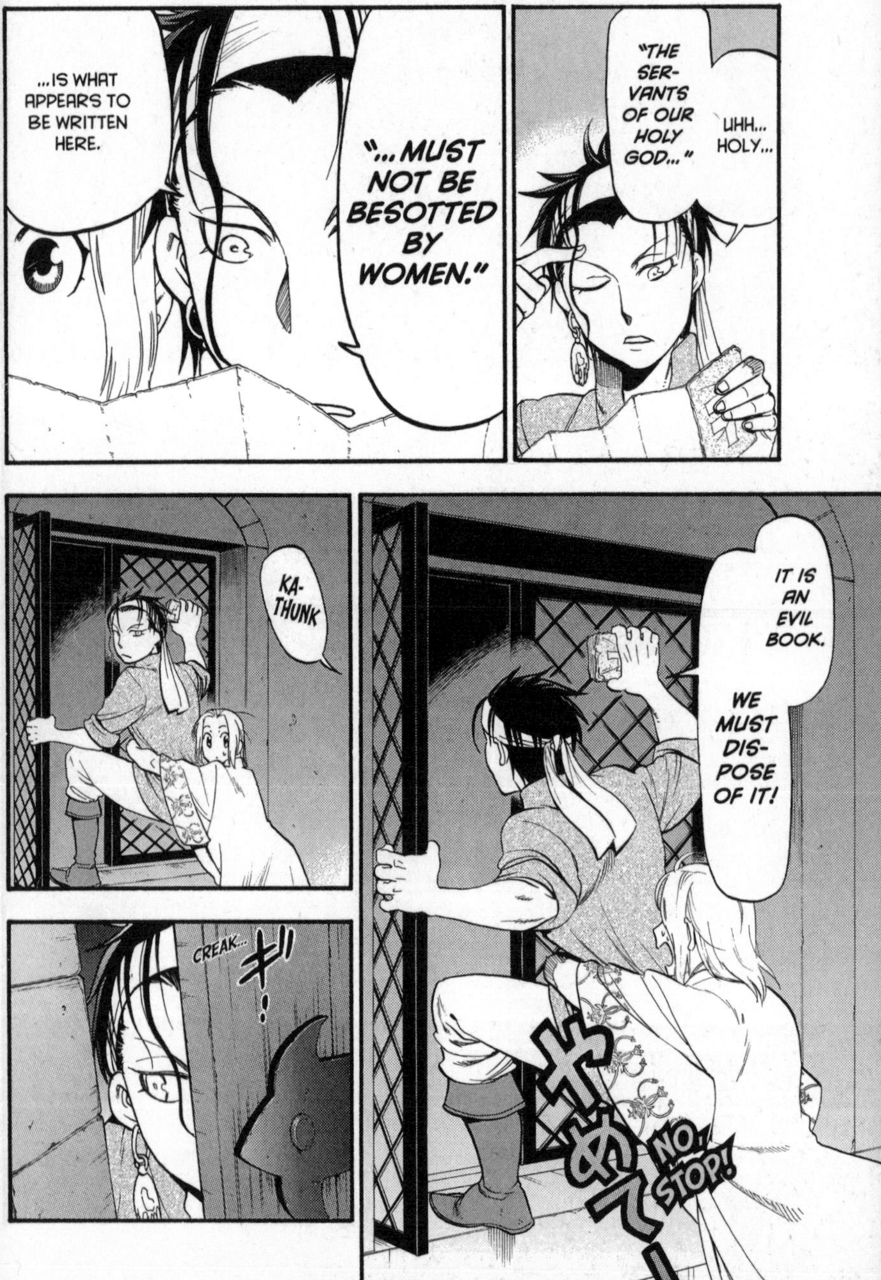
UHH... HOLY...
"THE SERVANTS OF OUR HOLY GOD..."
"...MUST NOT BE BESOTTED BY WOMEN."
...IS WHAT APPEARS TO BE WRITTEN HERE.
IT IS AN EVIL BOOK.
WE MUST DISPOSE OF IT!
NO, STOP!
KA-THUNK
CREAK...

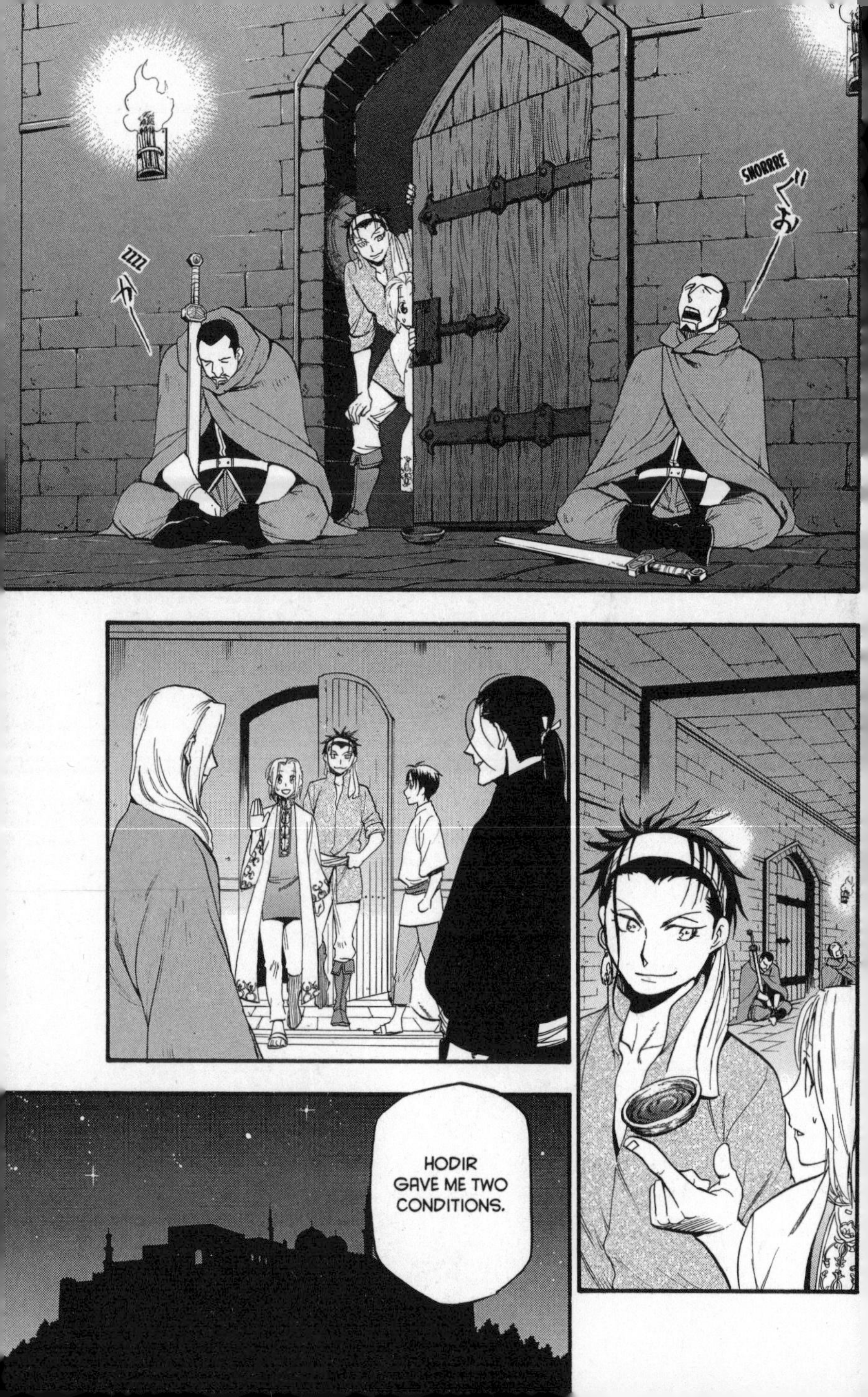
SNORRRE
ZZZZ
HODIR GAVE ME TWO CONDITIONS.

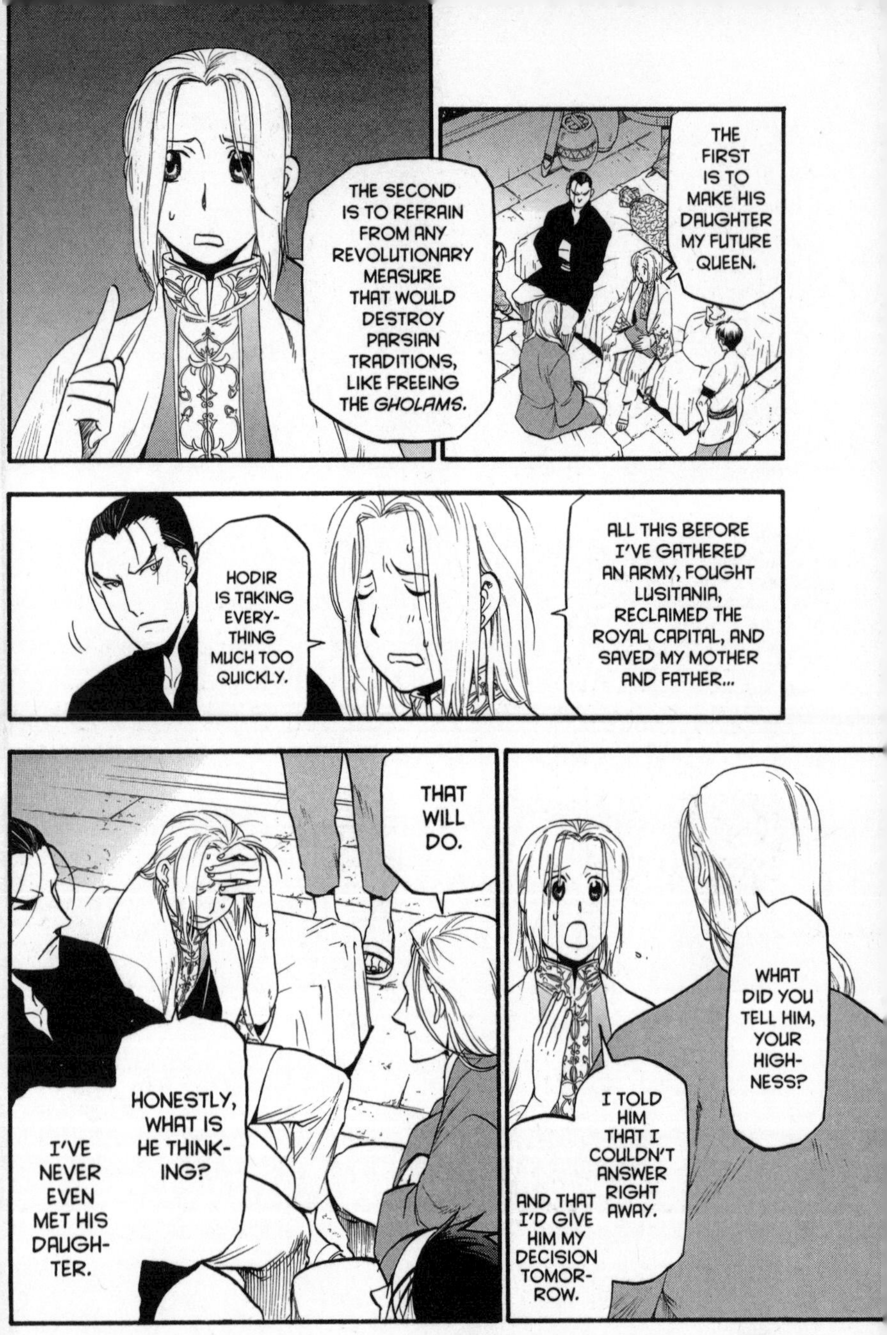
THE FIRST IS TO MAKE HIS DAUGHTER MY FUTURE QUEEN.
THE SECOND IS TO REFRAIN FROM ANY REVOLUTIONARY MEASURE THAT WOULD DESTROY PARSIAN TRADITIONS, LIKE FREEING THE *GHOLAMS*.
ALL THIS BEFORE I'VE GATHERED AN ARMY, FOUGHT LUSITANIA, RECLAIMED THE ROYAL CAPITAL, AND SAVED MY MOTHER AND FATHER...
HODIR IS TAKING EVERYTHING MUCH TOO QUICKLY.
WHAT DID YOU TELL HIM, YOUR HIGHNESS?
I TOLD HIM THAT I COULDN'T ANSWER RIGHT AWAY.
AND THAT I'D GIVE HIM MY DECISION TOMORROW.
THAT WILL DO.
HONESTLY, WHAT IS HE THINKING?
I'VE NEVER EVEN MET HIS DAUGHTER.

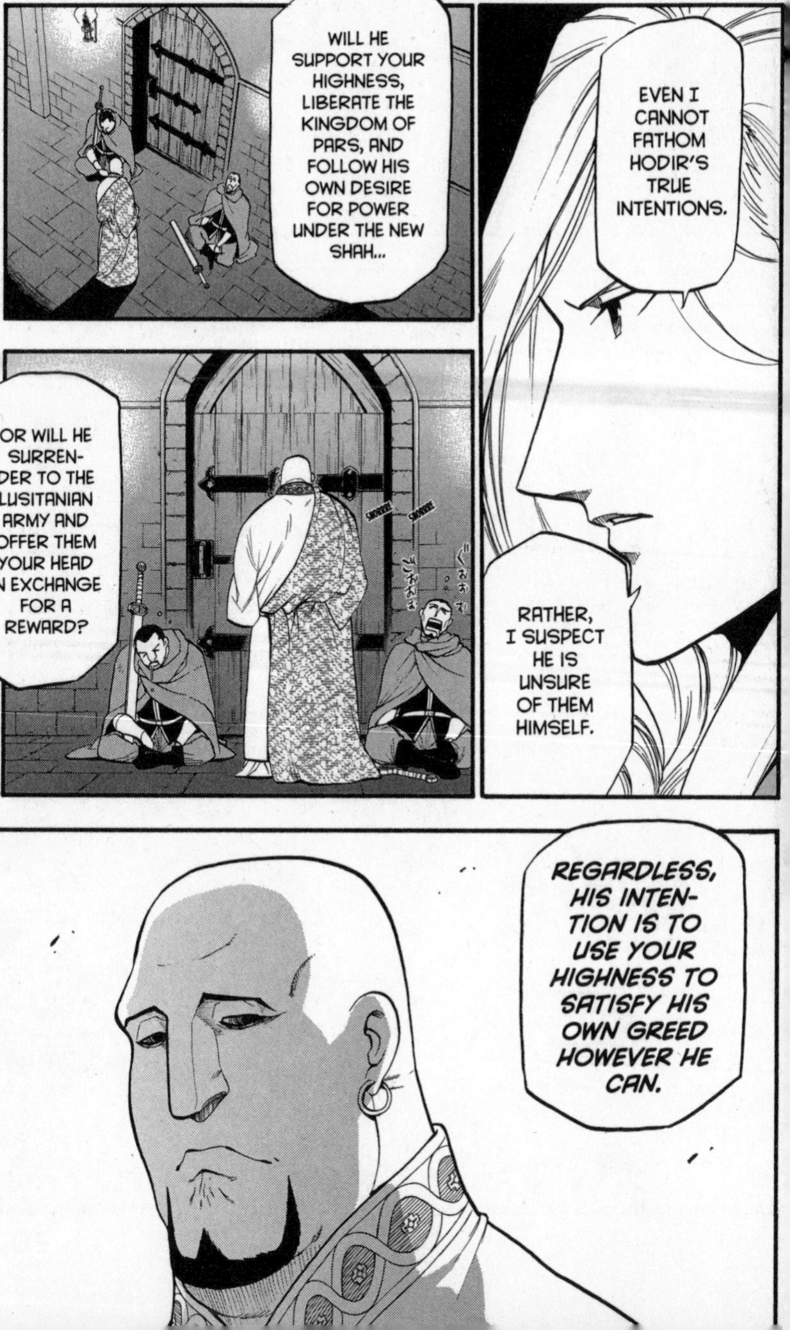
EVEN I CANNOT FATHOM HODIR'S TRUE INTENTIONS.
RATHER, I SUSPECT HE IS UNSURE OF THEM HIMSELF.
WILL HE SUPPORT YOUR HIGHNESS, LIBERATE THE KINGDOM OF PARS, AND FOLLOW HIS OWN DESIRE FOR POWER UNDER THE NEW SHAH...
OR WILL HE SURRENDER TO THE LUSITANIAN ARMY AND OFFER THEM YOUR HEAD IN EXCHANGE FOR A REWARD?
REGARDLESS, HIS INTENTION IS TO USE YOUR HIGHNESS TO SATISFY HIS OWN GREED HOWEVER HE CAN.

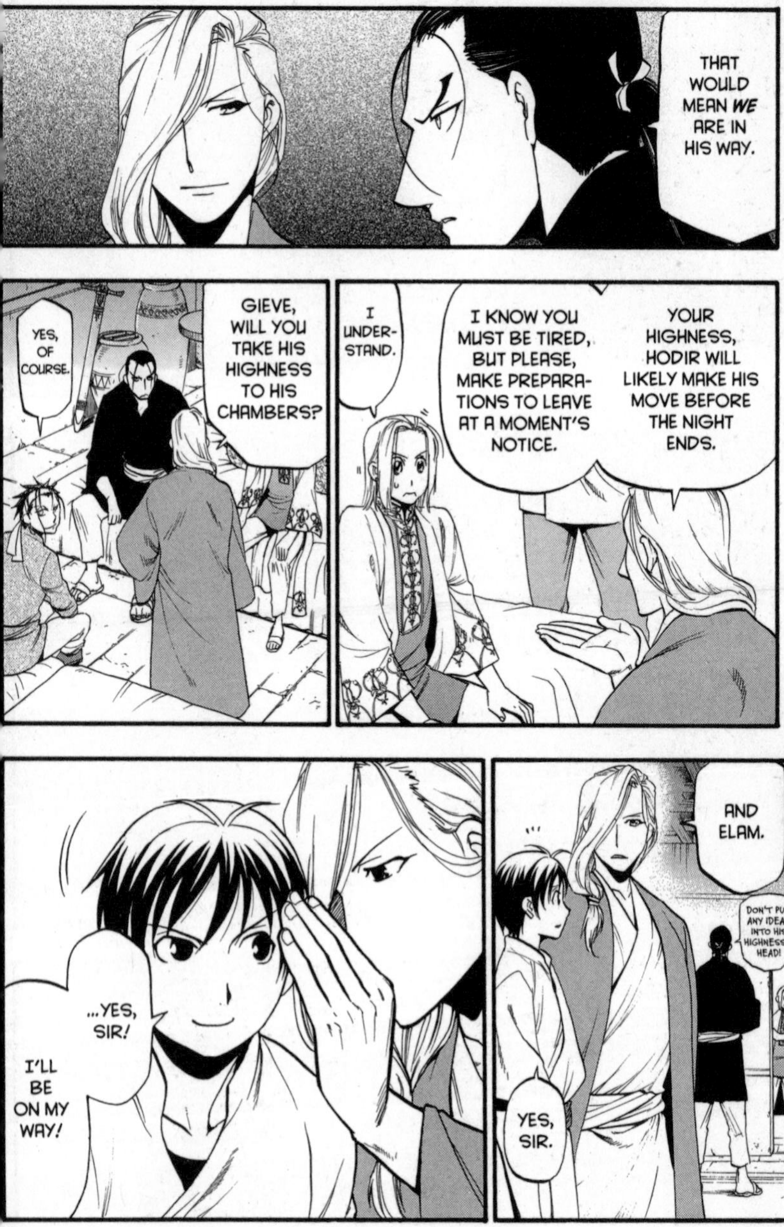
THAT WOULD MEAN *WE* ARE IN HIS WAY.
YOUR HIGHNESS, HODIR WILL LIKELY MAKE HIS MOVE BEFORE THE NIGHT ENDS.
I KNOW YOU MUST BE TIRED, BUT PLEASE, MAKE PREPARATIONS TO LEAVE AT A MOMENT'S NOTICE.
I UNDERSTAND.
GIEVE, WILL YOU TAKE HIS HIGHNESS TO HIS CHAMBERS?
YES, OF COURSE.
AND ELAM.
DON'T PUT ANY IDEAS INTO HIS HIGHNESS'S HEAD!
YES, SIR.
...YES, SIR!
I'LL BE ON MY WAY!

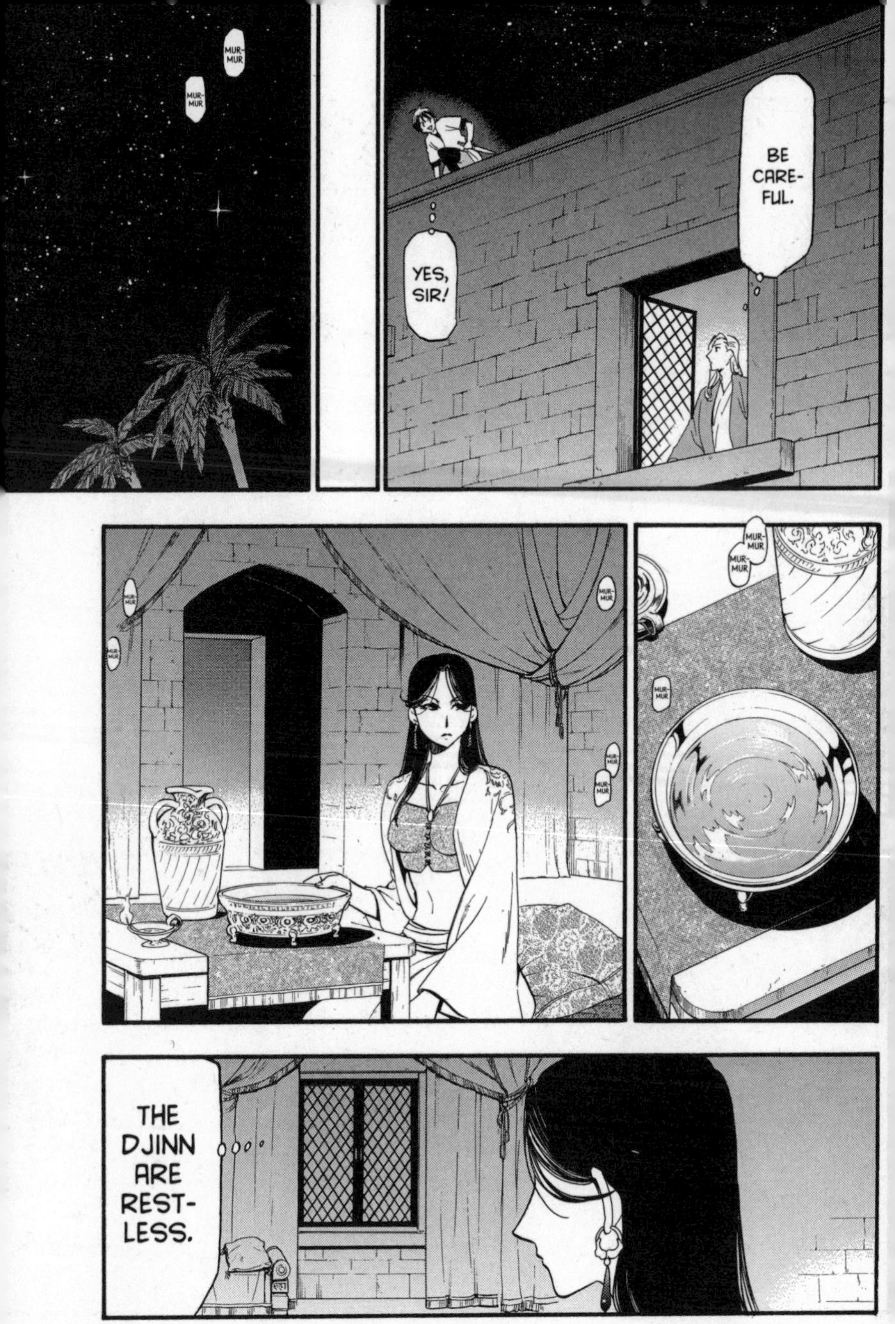
BE CARE-FUL.
YES, SIR!
MUR-MUR
MUR-MUR
MUR-MUR
MUR-MUR
MUR-MUR
MUR-MUR
MUR-MUR
MUR-MUR
MUR-MUR
MUR-MUR
THE DJINN ARE REST-LESS.

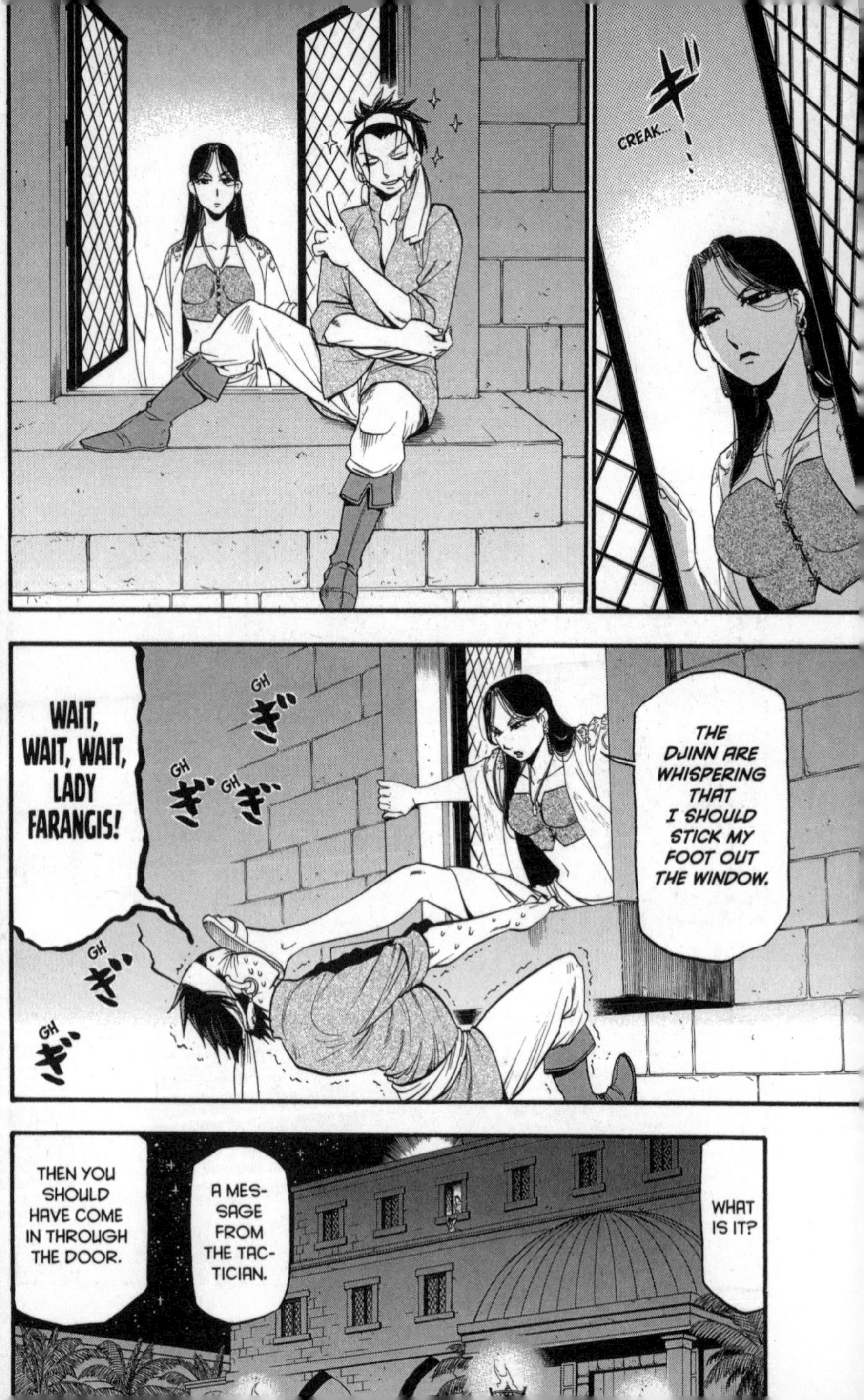
ギ
CREAK...
THE DJINN ARE WHISPERING THAT I SHOULD STICK MY FOOT OUT THE WINDOW.
GH ぎ
GH ぎ
GH ぎ
WAIT, WAIT, WAIT, LADY FARANGIS!
GH ぎ
GH ぎ
WHAT IS IT?
A MES-SAGE FROM THE TAC-TICIAN.
THEN YOU SHOULD HAVE COME IN THROUGH THE DOOR.

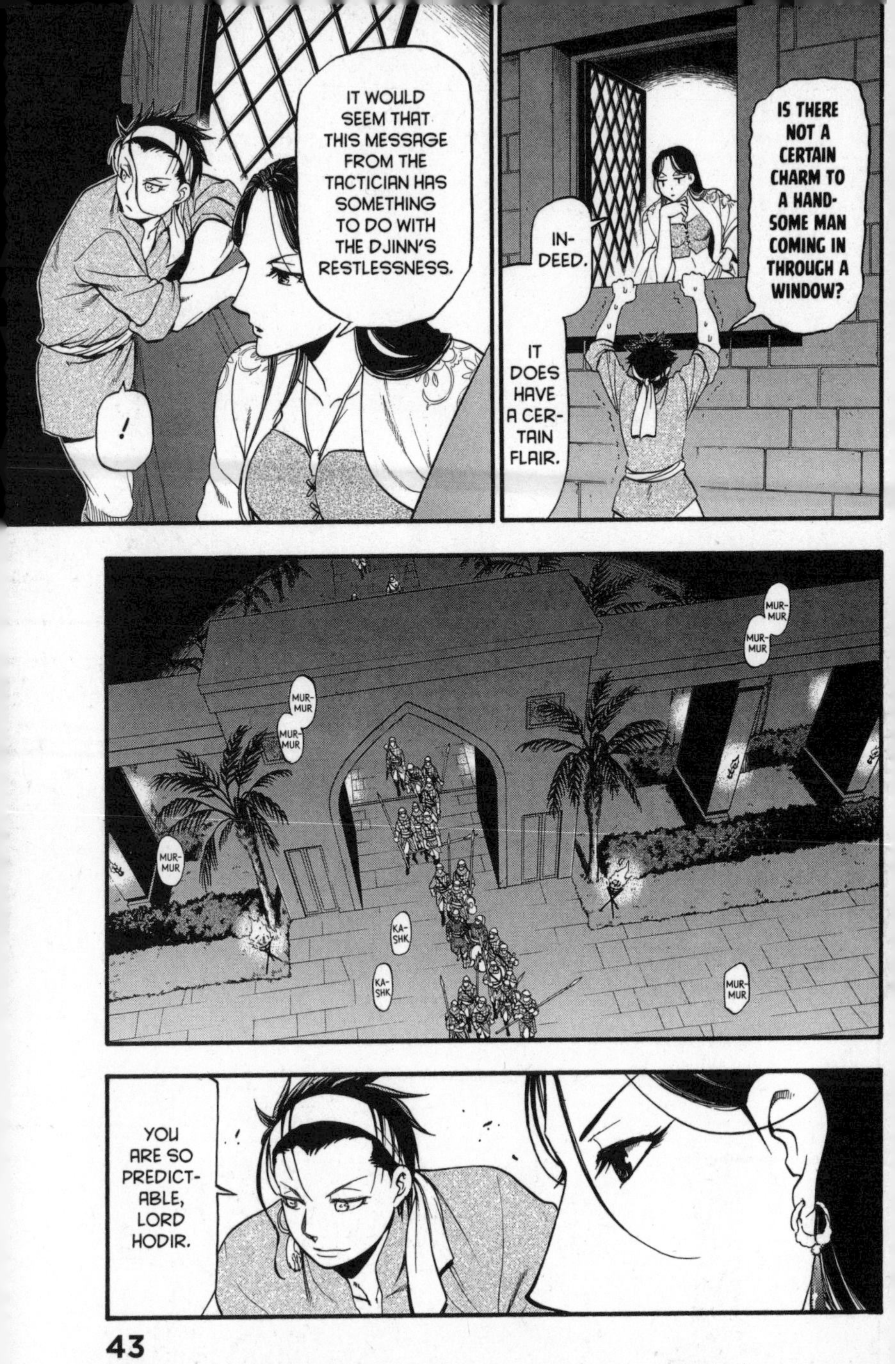
IS THERE NOT A CERTAIN CHARM TO A HANDSOME MAN COMING IN THROUGH A WINDOW?
IN-DEED.
IT DOES HAVE A CER-TAIN FLAIR.
IT WOULD SEEM THAT THIS MESSAGE FROM THE TACTICIAN HAS SOMETHING TO DO WITH THE DJINN'S RESTLESSNESS.
!
MUR-MUR
MUR-MUR
MUR-MUR
MUR-MUR
MUR-MUR
MUR-MUR
KA-SHK
KA-SHK
YOU ARE SO PREDICT-ABLE, LORD HODIR.

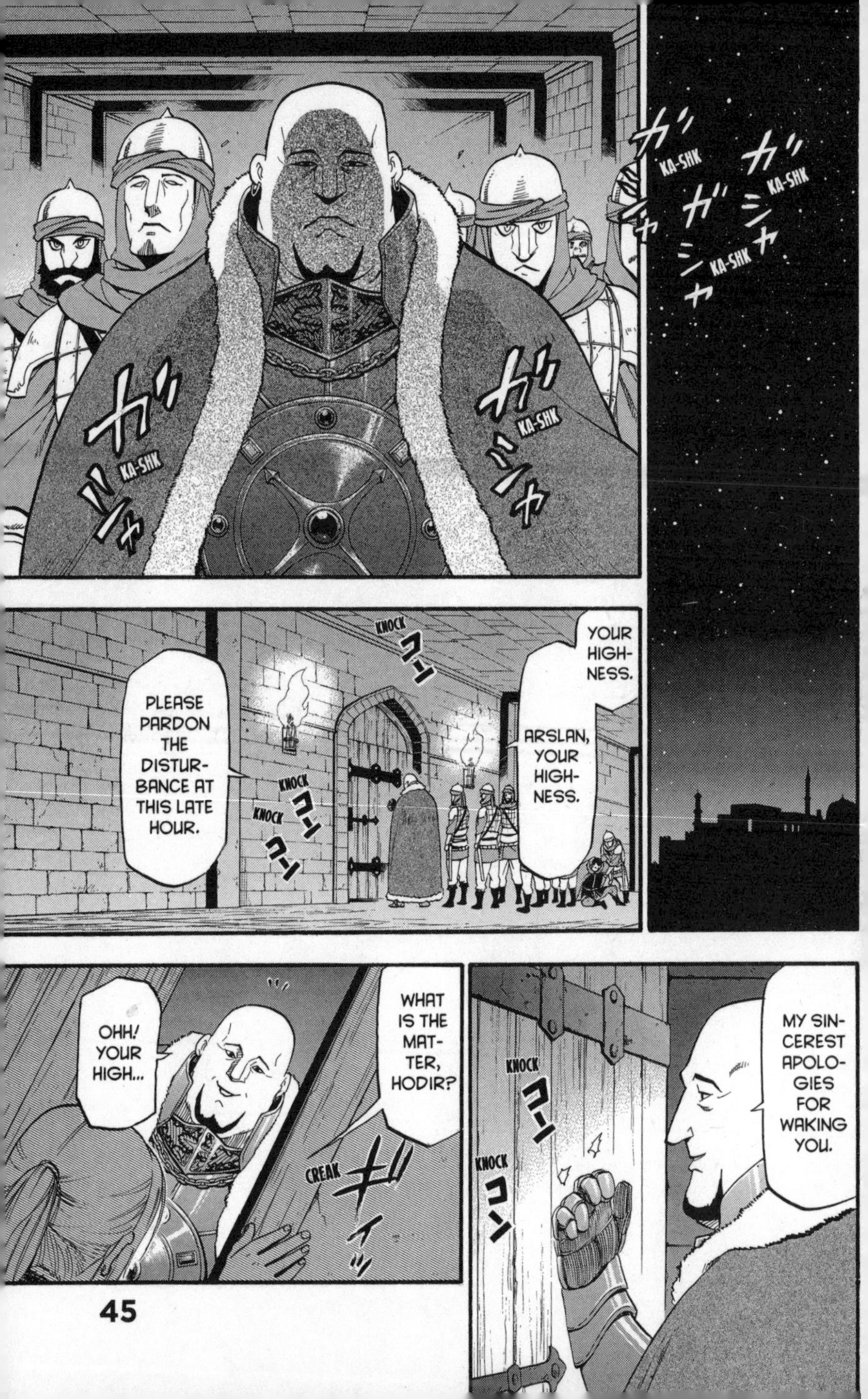
KA-SHK
KA-SHK
KA-SHK
KA-SHK
KA-SHK
YOUR HIGHNESS.
ARSLAN, YOUR HIGHNESS.
KNOCK
PLEASE PARDON THE DISTURBANCE AT THIS LATE HOUR.
KNOCK
KNOCK
MY SINCEREST APOLOGIES FOR WAKING YOU.
KNOCK
KNOCK
WHAT IS THE MATTER, HODIR?
CREAK
OHH! YOUR HIGH...

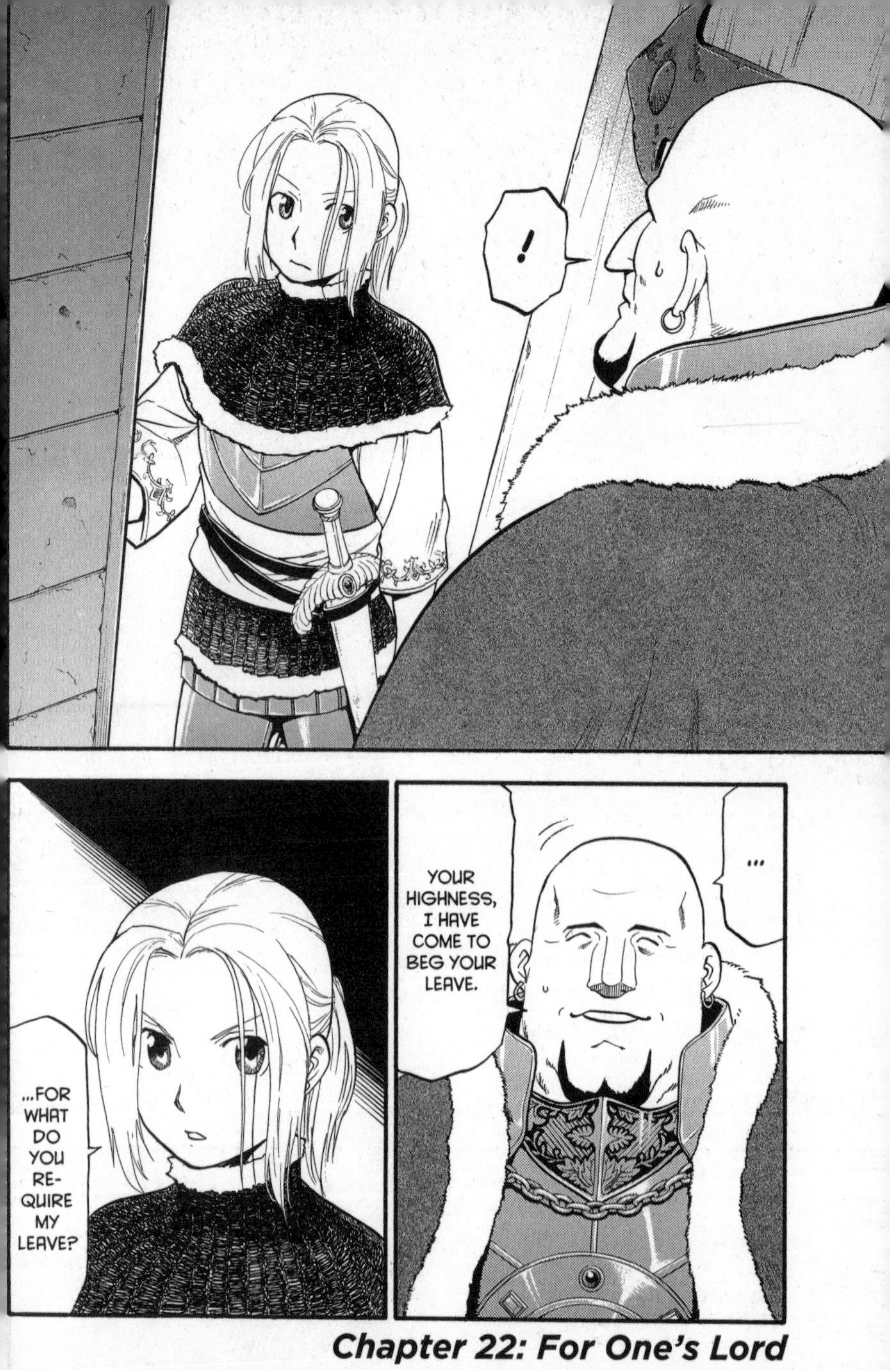
!
...
YOUR HIGHNESS, I HAVE COME TO BEG YOUR LEAVE.
...FOR WHAT DO YOU RE-QUIRE MY LEAVE?

Chapter 22: For One's Lord

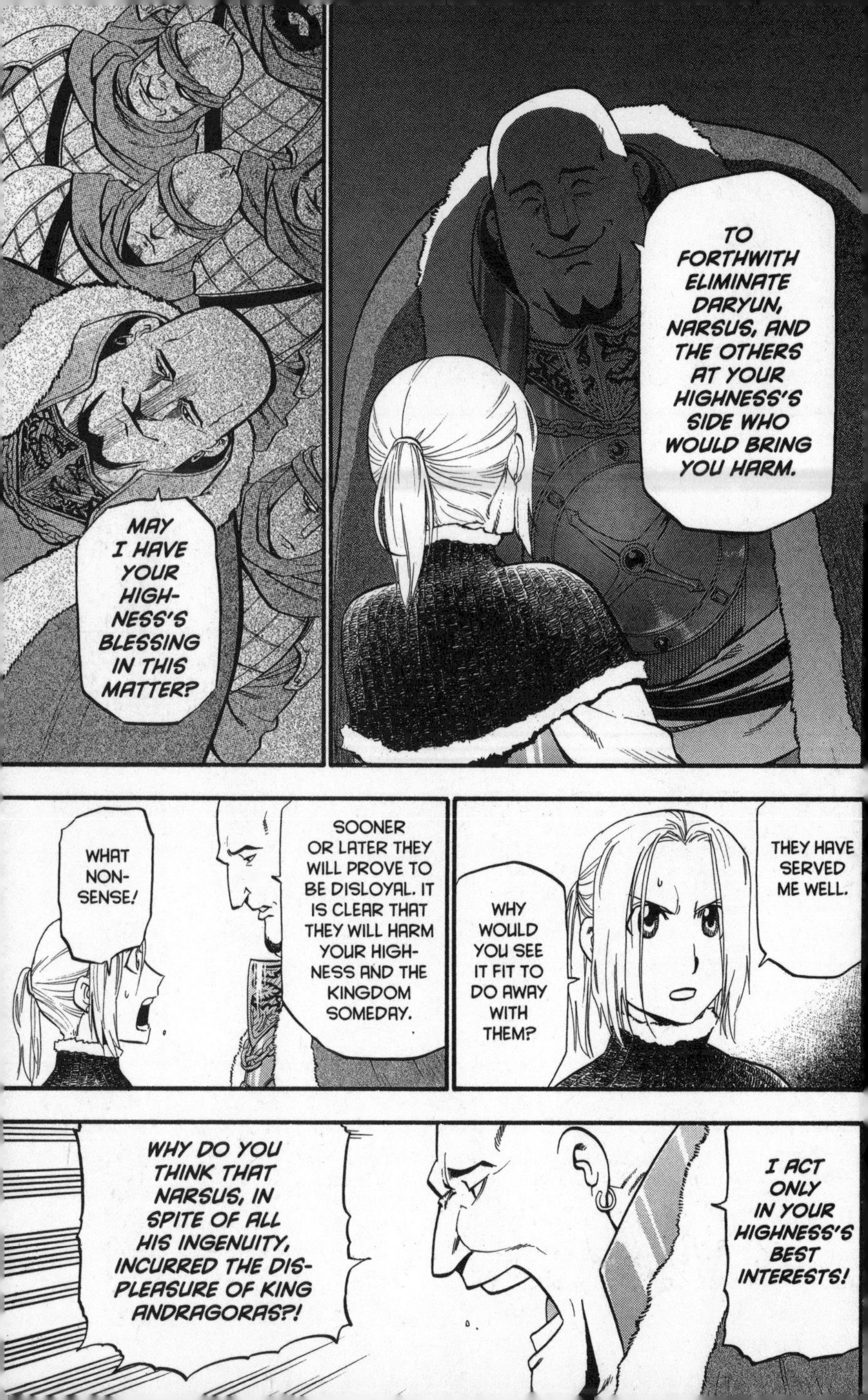
TO FORTHWITH ELIMINATE DARYUN, NARSUS, AND THE OTHERS AT YOUR HIGHNESS'S SIDE WHO WOULD BRING YOU HARM.
MAY I HAVE YOUR HIGHNESS'S BLESSING IN THIS MATTER?
THEY HAVE SERVED ME WELL.
WHY WOULD YOU SEE IT FIT TO DO AWAY WITH THEM?
SOONER OR LATER THEY WILL PROVE TO BE DISLOYAL. IT IS CLEAR THAT THEY WILL HARM YOUR HIGHNESS AND THE KINGDOM SOMEDAY.
WHAT NONSENSE!
I ACT ONLY IN YOUR HIGHNESS'S BEST INTERESTS!
WHY DO YOU THINK THAT NARSUS, IN SPITE OF ALL HIS INGENUITY, INCURRED THE DISPLEASURE OF KING ANDRAGORAS?!

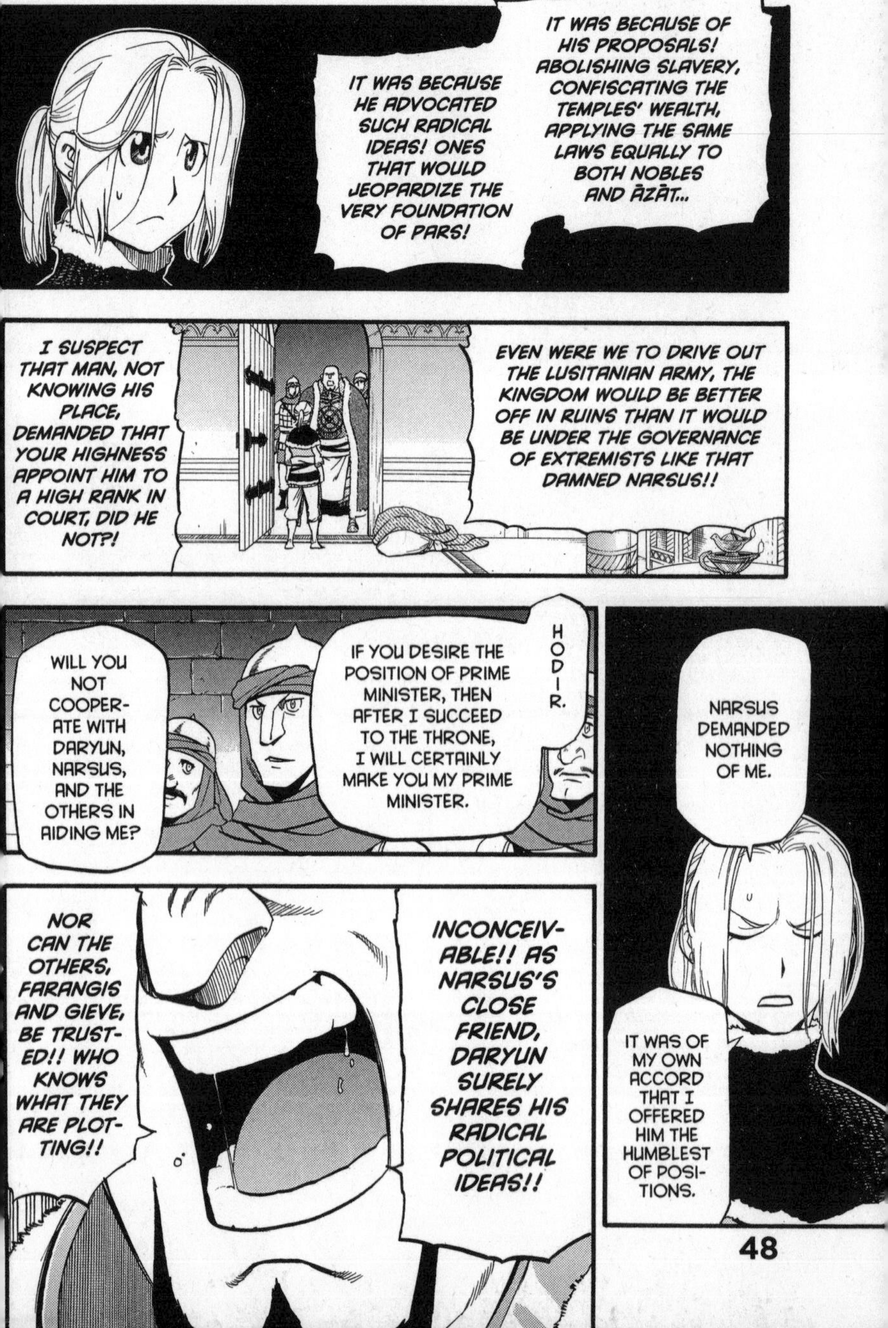
IT WAS BECAUSE OF HIS PROPOSALS! ABOLISHING SLAVERY, CONFISCATING THE TEMPLES' WEALTH, APPLYING THE SAME LAWS EQUALLY TO BOTH NOBLES AND ĀZĀT...
IT WAS BECAUSE HE ADVOCATED SUCH RADICAL IDEAS! ONES THAT WOULD JEOPARDIZE THE VERY FOUNDATION OF PARS!
EVEN WERE WE TO DRIVE OUT THE LUSITANIAN ARMY, THE KINGDOM WOULD BE BETTER OFF IN RUINS THAN IT WOULD BE UNDER THE GOVERNANCE OF EXTREMISTS LIKE THAT DAMNED NARSUS!!
I SUSPECT THAT MAN, NOT KNOWING HIS PLACE, DEMANDED THAT YOUR HIGHNESS APPOINT HIM TO A HIGH RANK IN COURT, DID HE NOT?!
NARSUS DEMANDED NOTHING OF ME.
IT WAS OF MY OWN ACCORD THAT I OFFERED HIM THE HUMBLEST OF POSITIONS.
HODIR.
IF YOU DESIRE THE POSITION OF PRIME MINISTER, THEN AFTER I SUCCEED TO THE THRONE, I WILL CERTAINLY MAKE YOU MY PRIME MINISTER.
WILL YOU NOT COOPERATE WITH DARYUN, NARSUS, AND THE OTHERS IN AIDING ME?
INCONCEIVABLE!! AS NARSUS'S CLOSE FRIEND, DARYUN SURELY SHARES HIS RADICAL POLITICAL IDEAS!!
NOR CAN THE OTHERS, FARANGIS AND GIEVE, BE TRUSTED!! WHO KNOWS WHAT THEY ARE PLOTTING!!

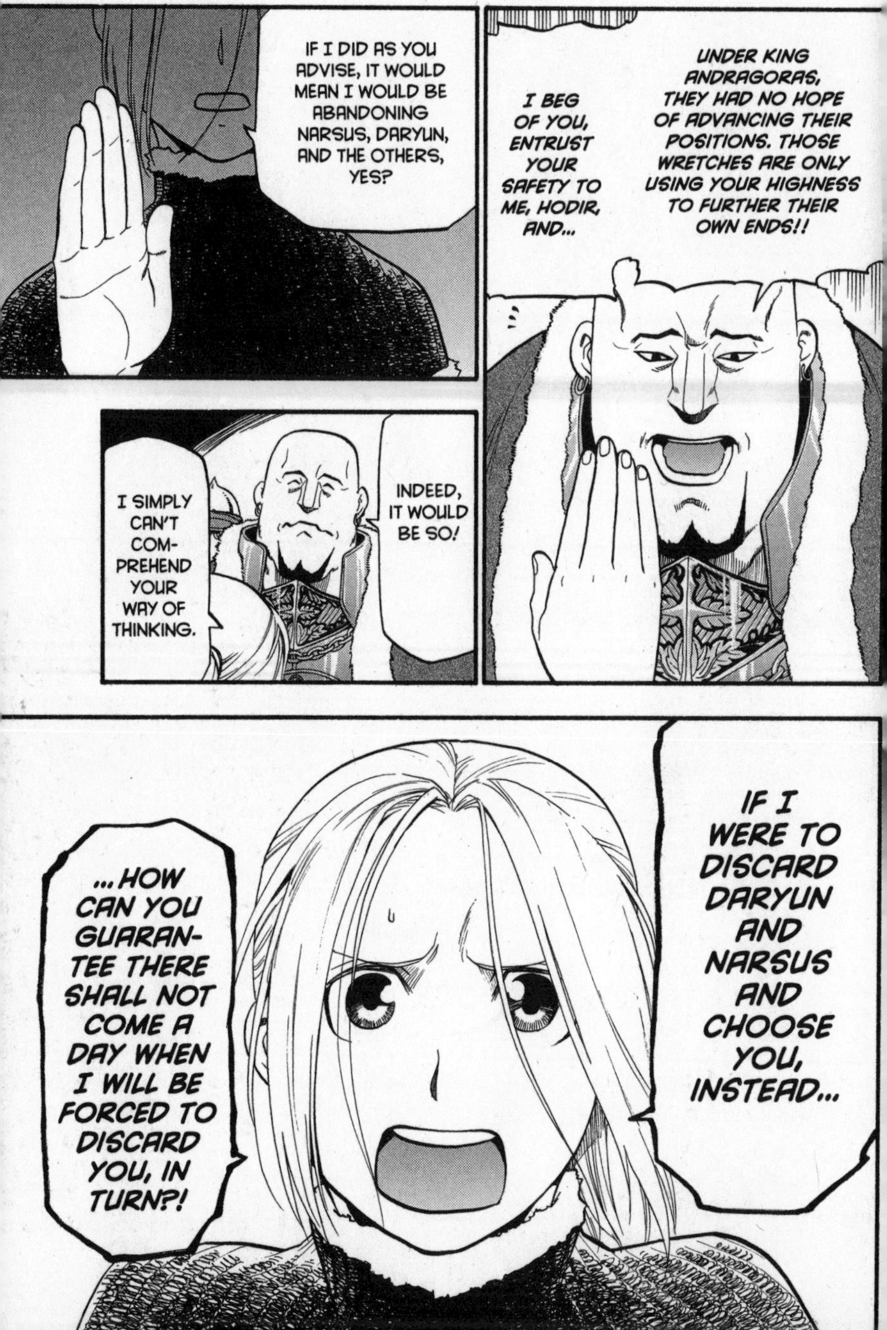
UNDER KING ANDRAGORAS, THEY HAD NO HOPE OF ADVANCING THEIR POSITIONS. THOSE WRETCHES ARE ONLY USING YOUR HIGHNESS TO FURTHER THEIR OWN ENDS!!
I BEG OF YOU, ENTRUST YOUR SAFETY TO ME, HODIR, AND...
IF I DID AS YOU ADVISE, IT WOULD MEAN I WOULD BE ABANDONING NARSUS, DARYUN, AND THE OTHERS, YES?
INDEED, IT WOULD BE SO!
I SIMPLY CAN'T COM-PREHEND YOUR WAY OF THINKING.
IF I WERE TO DISCARD DARYUN AND NARSUS AND CHOOSE YOU, INSTEAD...
...HOW CAN YOU GUARAN-TEE THERE SHALL NOT COME A DAY WHEN I WILL BE FORCED TO DISCARD YOU, IN TURN?!

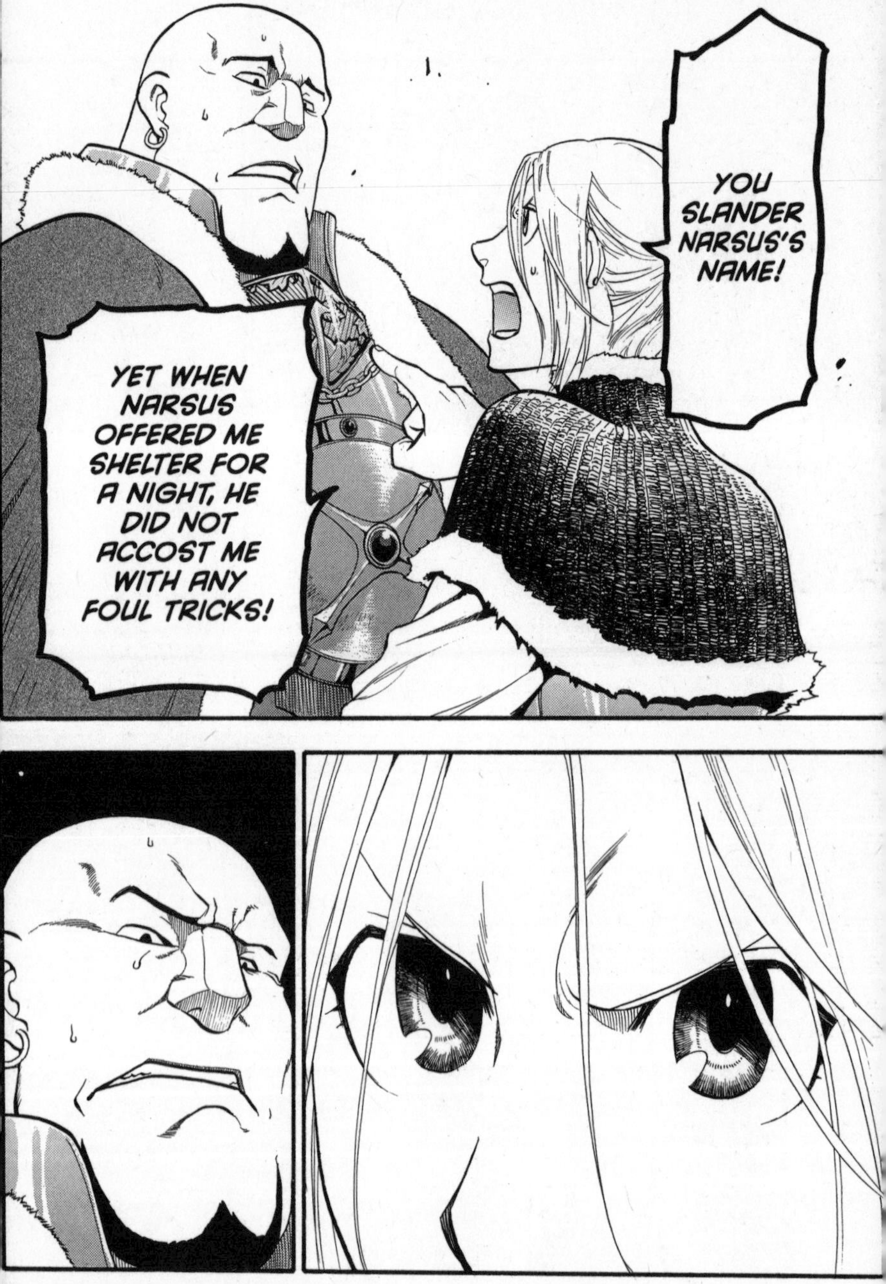
YOU SLANDER NARSUS'S NAME!
YET WHEN NARSUS OFFERED ME SHELTER FOR A NIGHT, HE DID NOT ACCOST ME WITH ANY FOUL TRICKS!

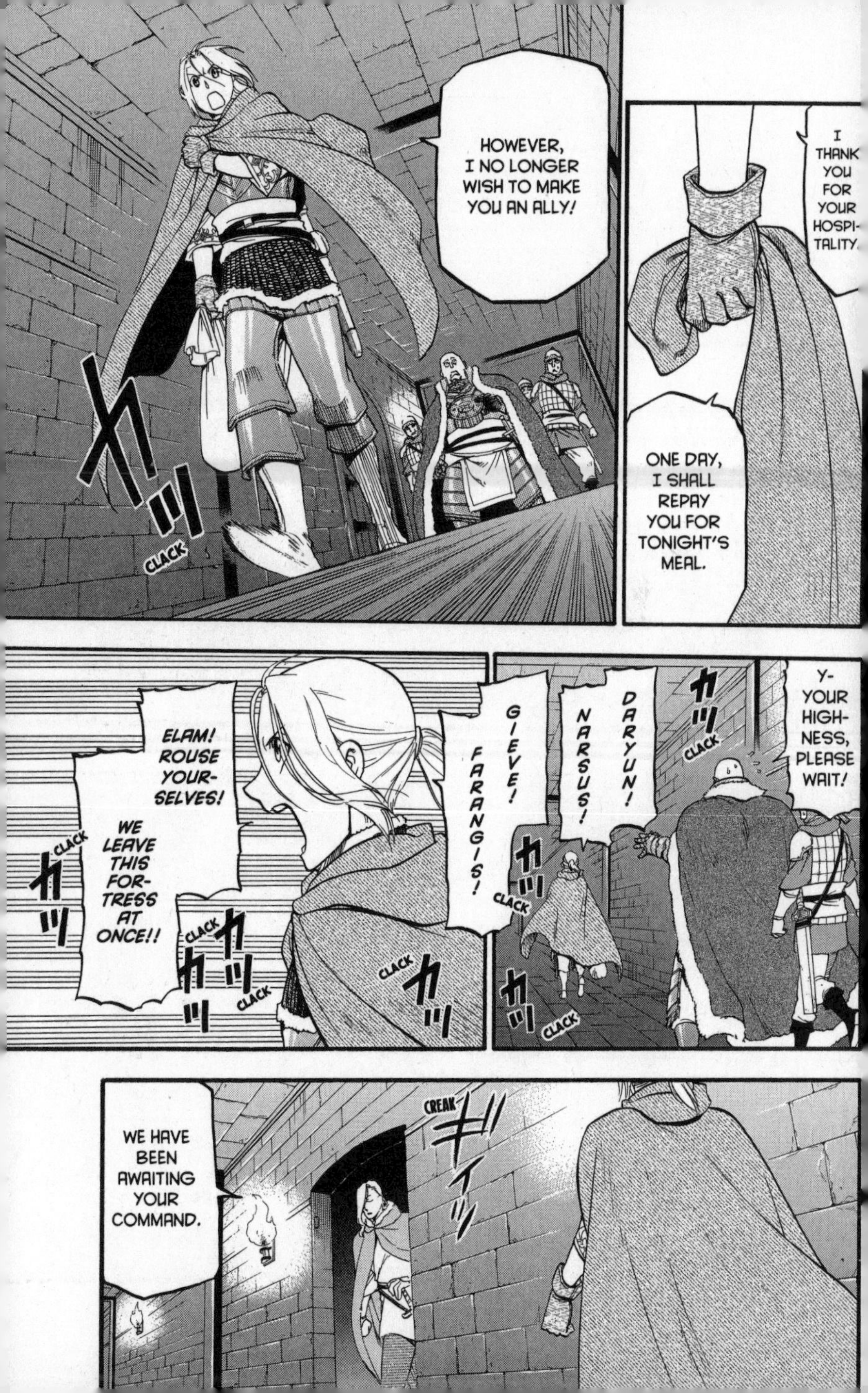
I THANK YOU FOR YOUR HOSPITALITY.
ONE DAY, I SHALL REPAY YOU FOR TONIGHT'S MEAL.
HOWEVER, I NO LONGER WISH TO MAKE YOU AN ALLY!
CLACK
Y-YOUR HIGHNESS, PLEASE WAIT!
CLACK
DARYUN! NARSUS!
GIEVE! FARANGIS!
CLACK
CLACK
CLACK
ELAM! ROUSE YOURSELVES!
WE LEAVE THIS FORTRESS AT ONCE!!
CLACK
CLACK
CLACK
CREAK
WE HAVE BEEN AWAITING YOUR COMMAND.

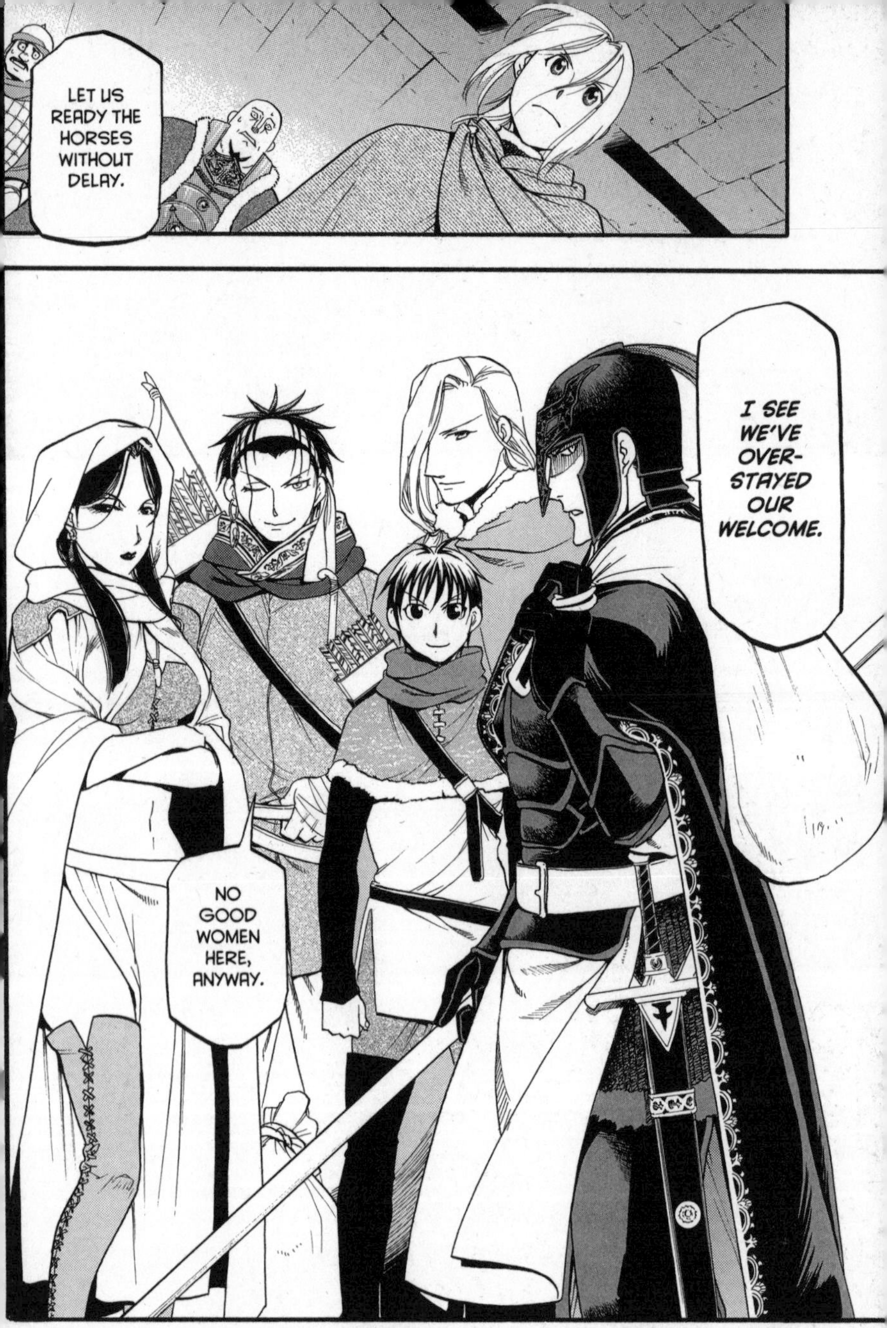
LET US READY THE HORSES WITHOUT DELAY.
I SEE WE'VE OVER-STAYED OUR WELCOME.
NO GOOD WOMEN HERE, ANYWAY.

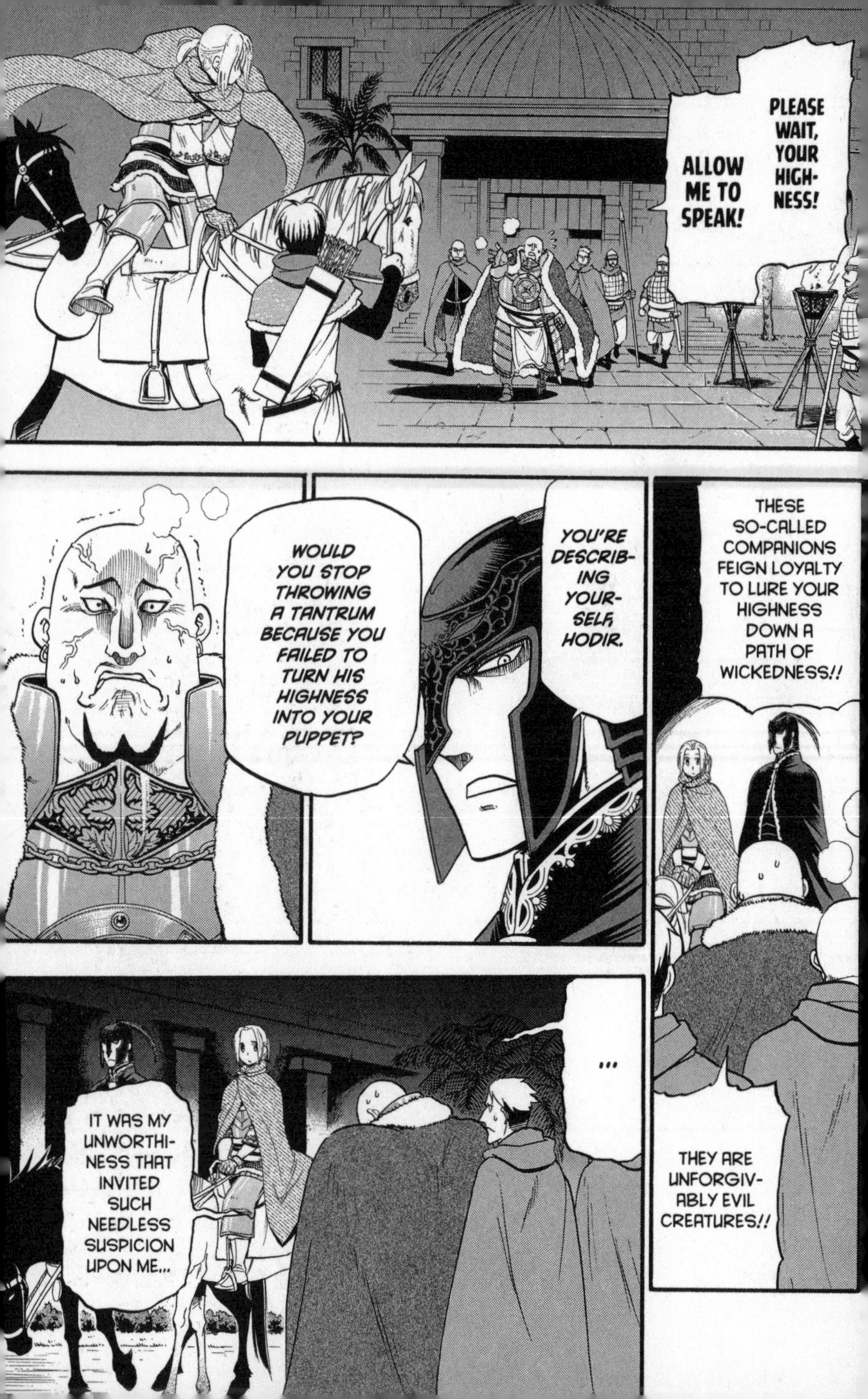
PLEASE WAIT, YOUR HIGH-NESS!
ALLOW ME TO SPEAK!
THESE SO-CALLED COMPANIONS FEIGN LOYALTY TO LURE YOUR HIGHNESS DOWN A PATH OF WICKEDNESS!!
THEY ARE UNFORGIV-ABLY EVIL CREATURES!!
YOU'RE DESCRIB-ING YOUR-SELF, HODIR.
WOULD YOU STOP THROWING A TANTRUM BECAUSE YOU FAILED TO TURN HIS HIGHNESS INTO YOUR PUPPET?
...
IT WAS MY UNWORTHI-NESS THAT INVITED SUCH NEEDLESS SUSPICION UPON ME...

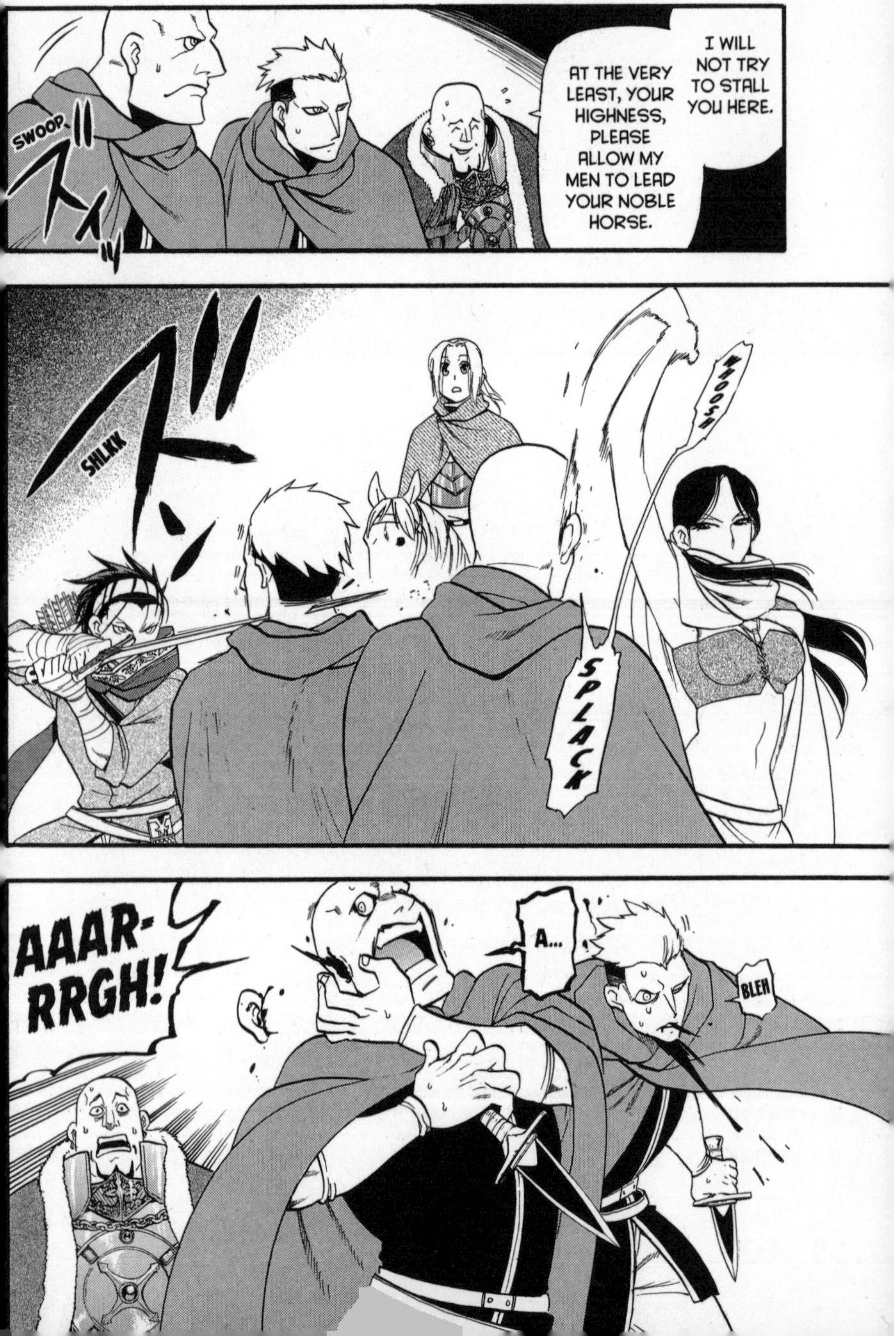
I WILL NOT TRY TO STALL YOU HERE.
AT THE VERY LEAST, YOUR HIGHNESS, PLEASE ALLOW MY MEN TO LEAD YOUR NOBLE HORSE.
SWOOP
WHOOSH
SPLACK
SHLKK
BLEH
A...
AAAR-RRGH!

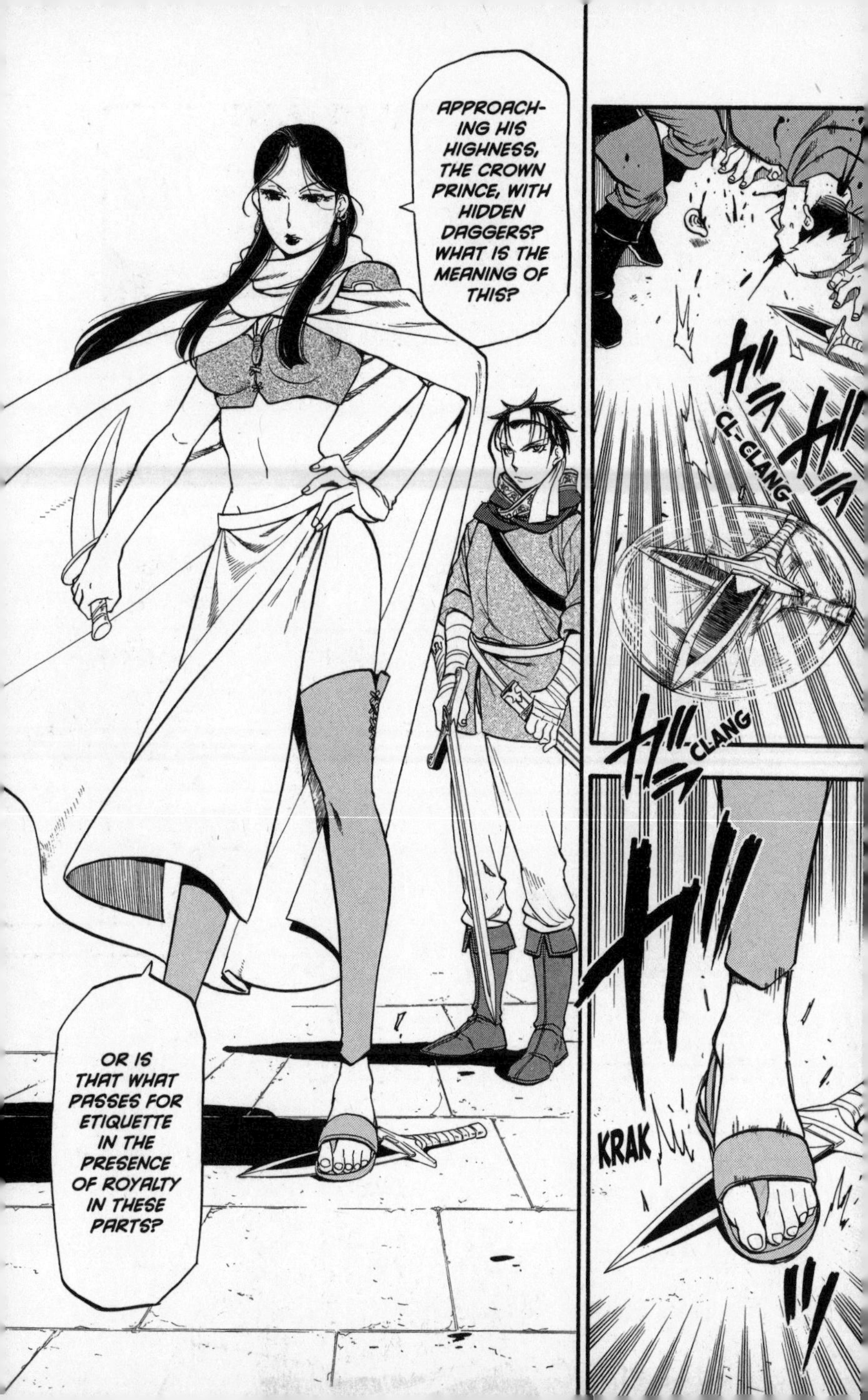
CL-CLANG
CLANG
KRAK
APPROACHING HIS HIGHNESS, THE CROWN PRINCE, WITH HIDDEN DAGGERS? WHAT IS THE MEANING OF THIS?
OR IS THAT WHAT PASSES FOR ETIQUETTE IN THE PRESENCE OF ROYALTY IN THESE PARTS?

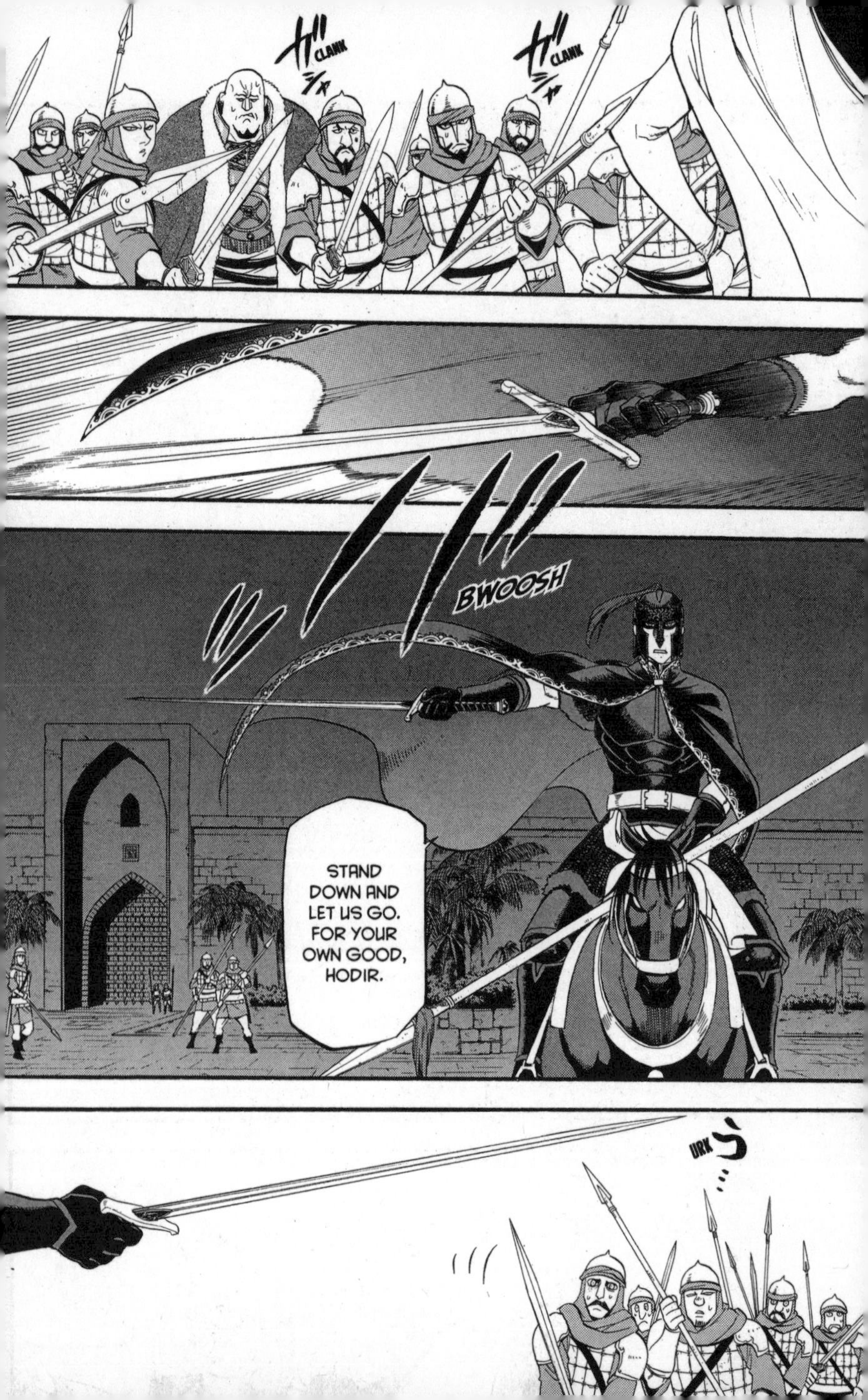
ガシャ
CLANK
ガシャ
CLANK
BWOOSH
STAND DOWN AND LET US GO. FOR YOUR OWN GOOD, HODIR.
う…
URK

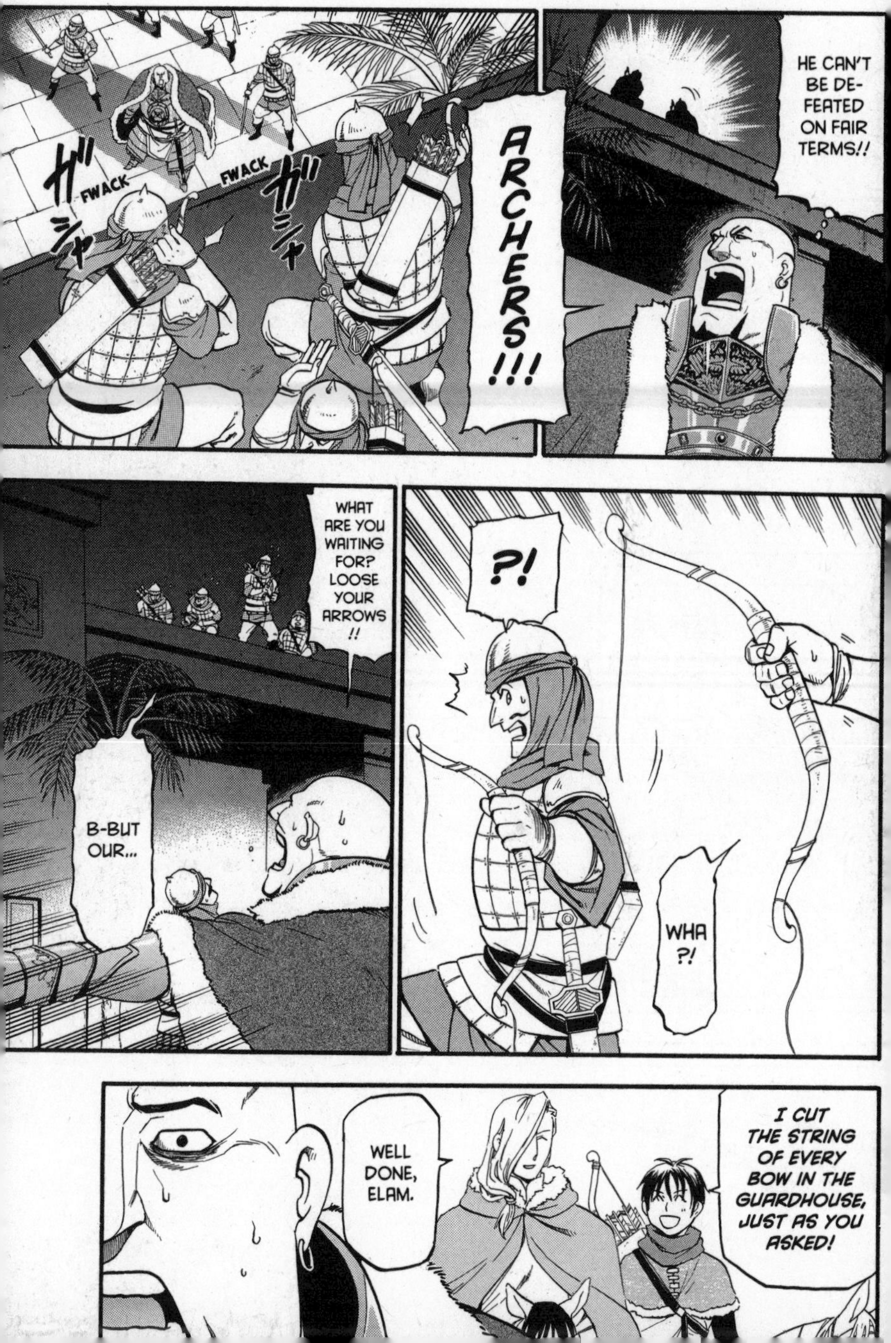
HE CAN'T BE DE-FEATED ON FAIR TERMS!!
ARCHERS!!!
ガシャ
FWACK
ガシャ
FWACK
?!
WHA ?!
WHAT ARE YOU WAITING FOR? LOOSE YOUR ARROWS!!
B-BUT OUR...
I CUT THE STRING OF EVERY BOW IN THE GUARDHOUSE, JUST AS YOU ASKED!
WELL DONE, ELAM.

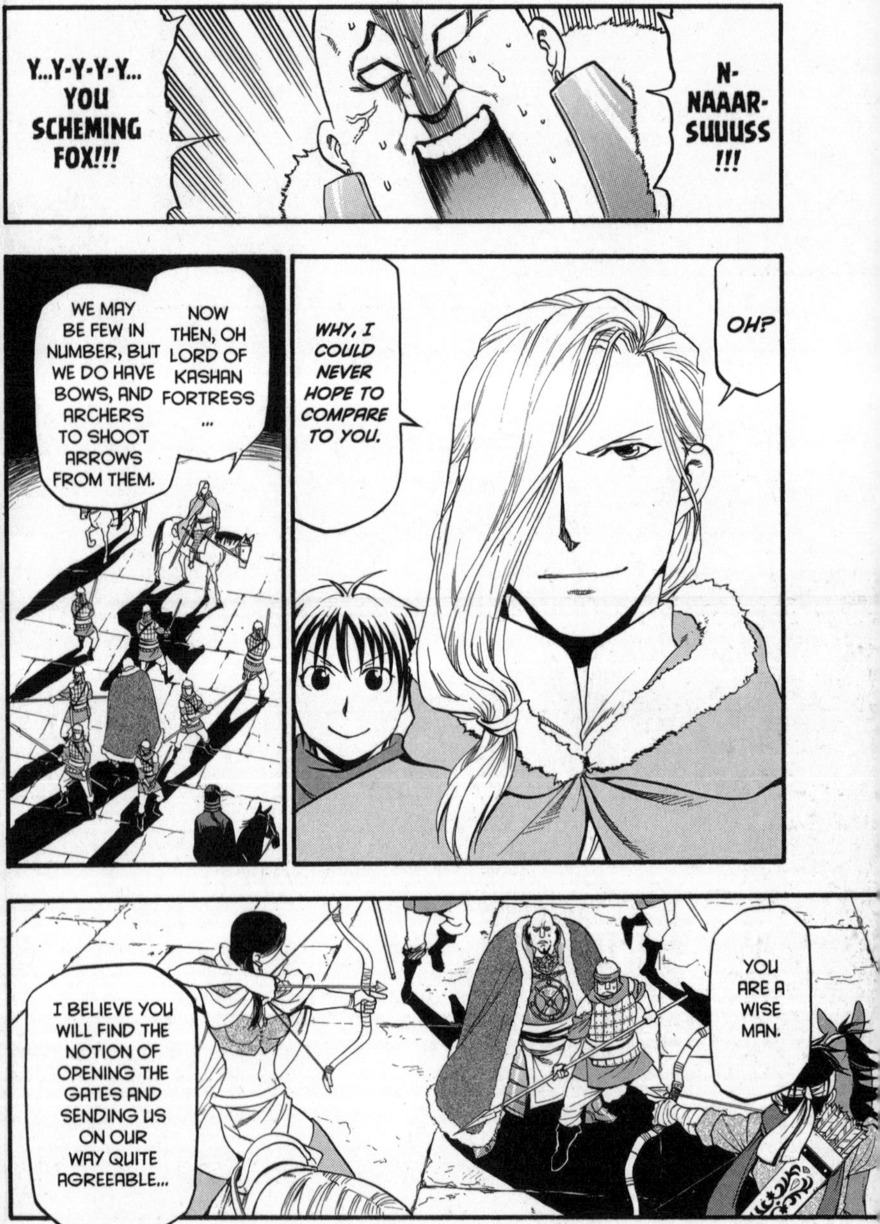
N-NAAAR-SUUUSS!!!
Y...Y-Y-Y-Y... YOU SCHEMING FOX!!!
OH?
WHY, I COULD NEVER HOPE TO COMPARE TO YOU.
NOW THEN, OH LORD OF KASHAN FORTRESS...
WE MAY BE FEW IN NUMBER, BUT WE DO HAVE BOWS, AND ARCHERS TO SHOOT ARROWS FROM THEM.
YOU ARE A WISE MAN.
I BELIEVE YOU WILL FIND THE NOTION OF OPENING THE GATES AND SENDING US ON OUR WAY QUITE AGREEABLE...

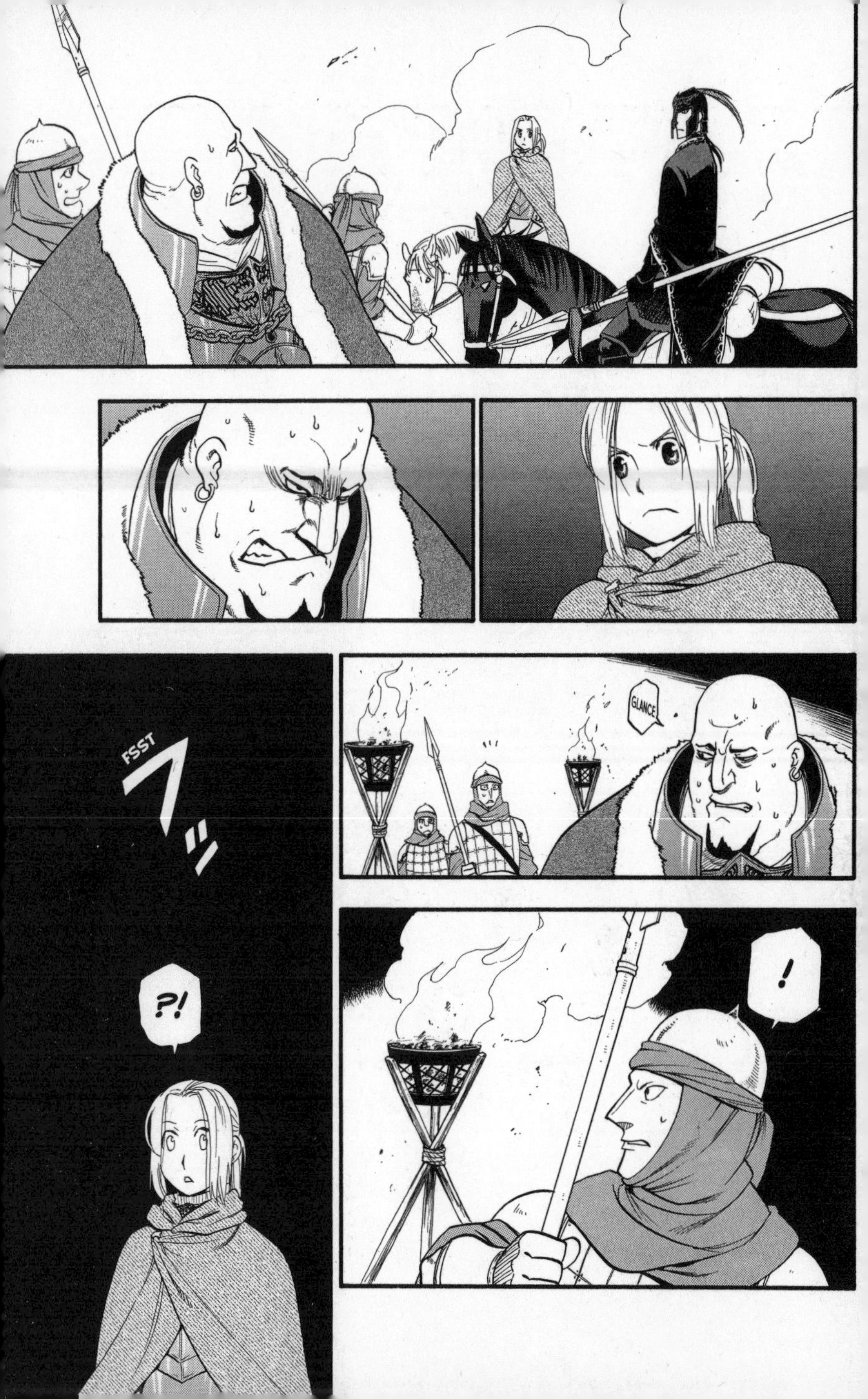
GLANCE
!
FSST
?!

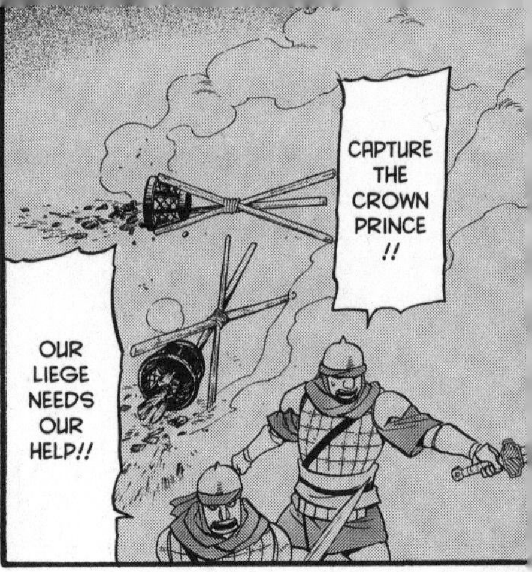
CAPTURE THE CROWN PRINCE !!
OUR LIEGE NEEDS OUR HELP!!

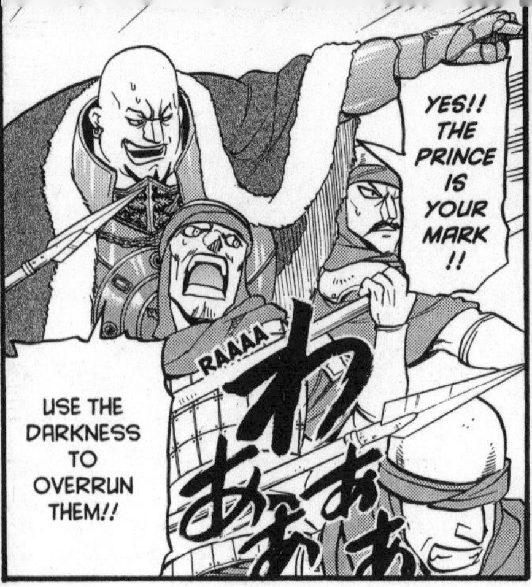
YES!! THE PRINCE IS YOUR MARK !!
RAAAA
わあああ
USE THE DARKNESS TO OVERRUN THEM!!

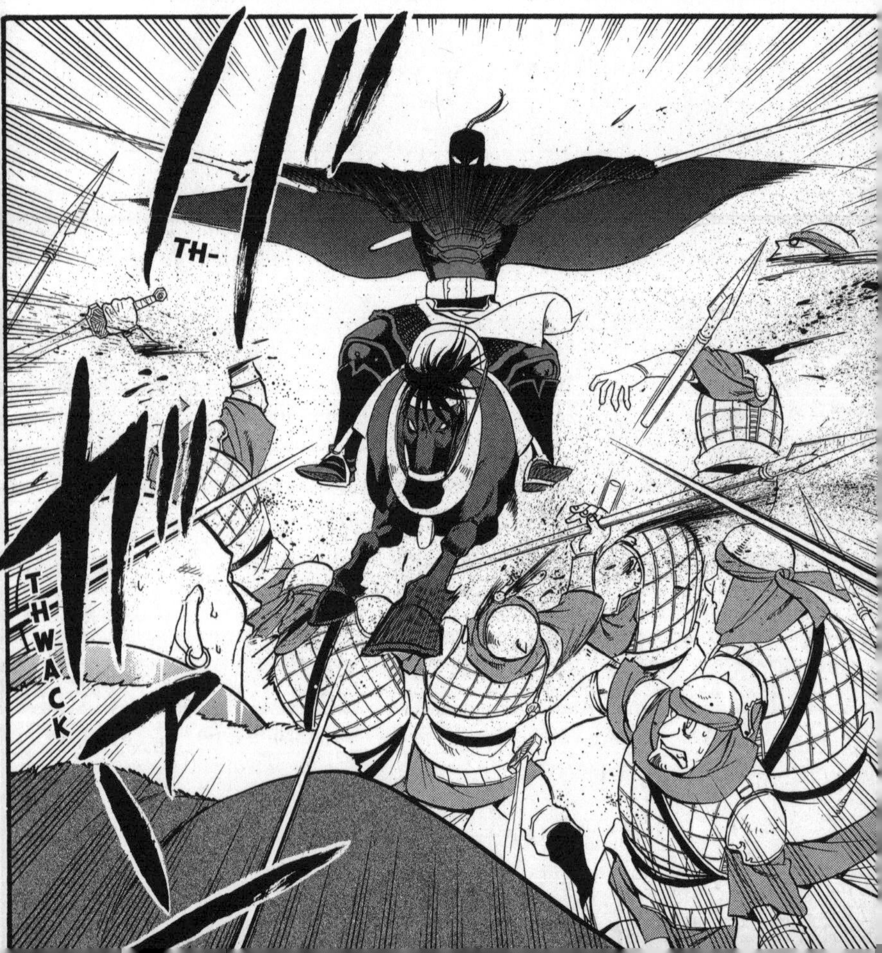
TH-
THWACK

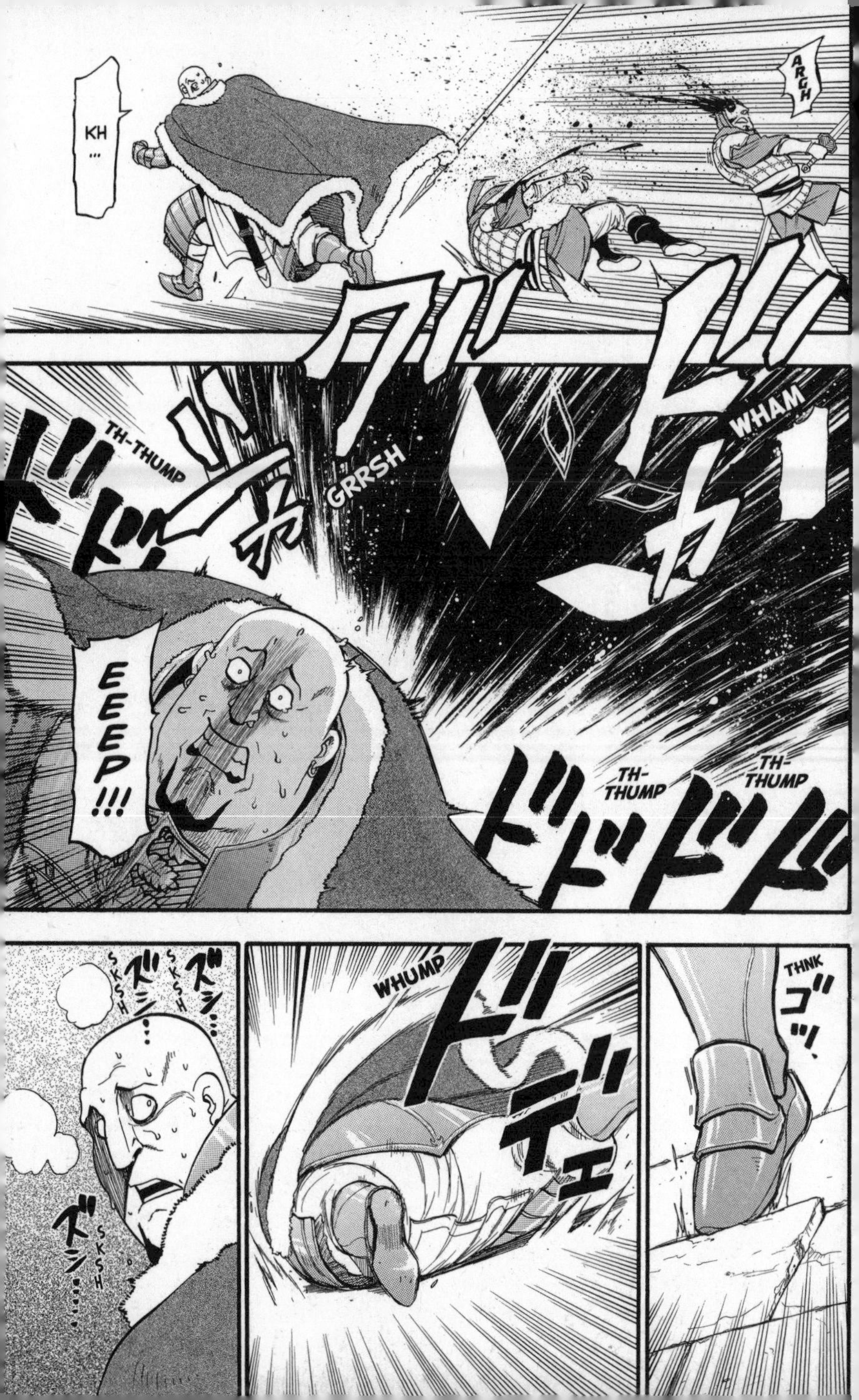
ARGH
KH ...
WHAM
GRRSH
TH-THUMP
EEEEP!!!
TH-THUMP
TH-THUMP
THNK
WHUMP
SKSH
SKSH
SKSH

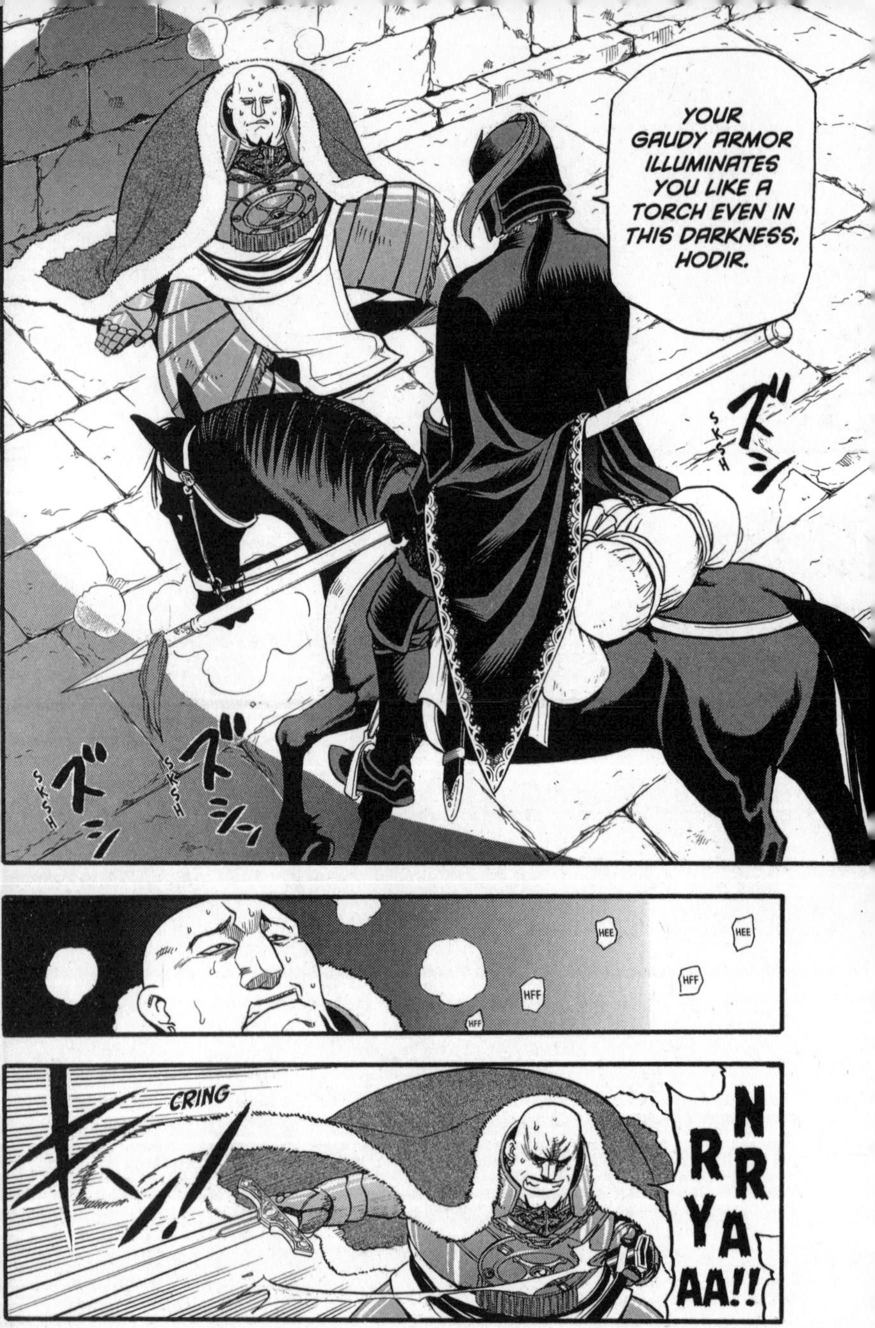
YOUR GAUDY ARMOR ILLUMINATES YOU LIKE A TORCH EVEN IN THIS DARKNESS, HODIR.
SKSH
SKSH
SKSH
HEE
HFF
HEE
HFF
HFF
NNRRYAAA!!
CRING

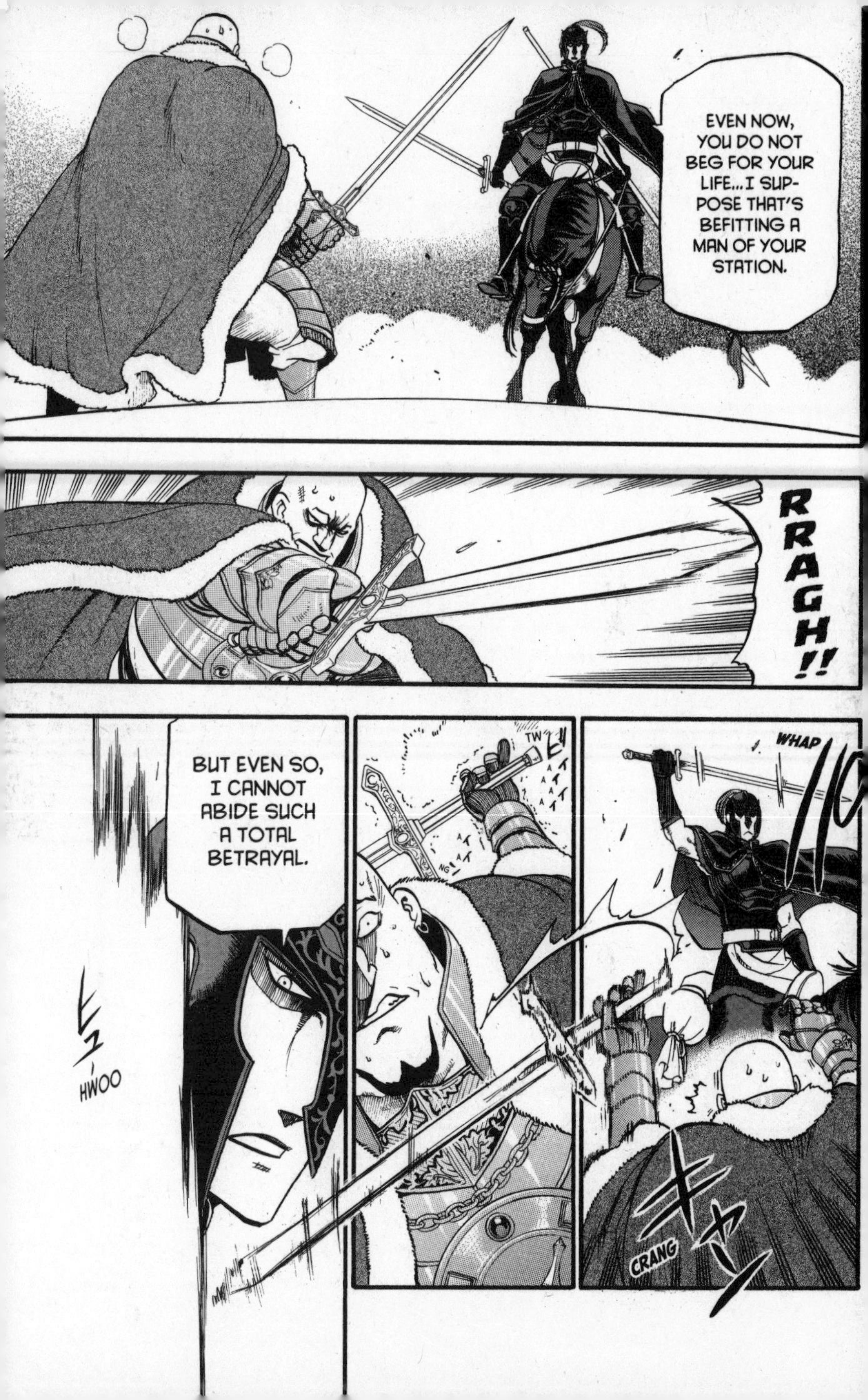
EVEN NOW, YOU DO NOT BEG FOR YOUR LIFE...I SUP-POSE THAT'S BEFITTING A MAN OF YOUR STATION.
RRAGH!!
WHAP
CRANG
TW
NG
BUT EVEN SO, I CANNOT ABIDE SUCH A TOTAL BETRAYAL.
HWOO

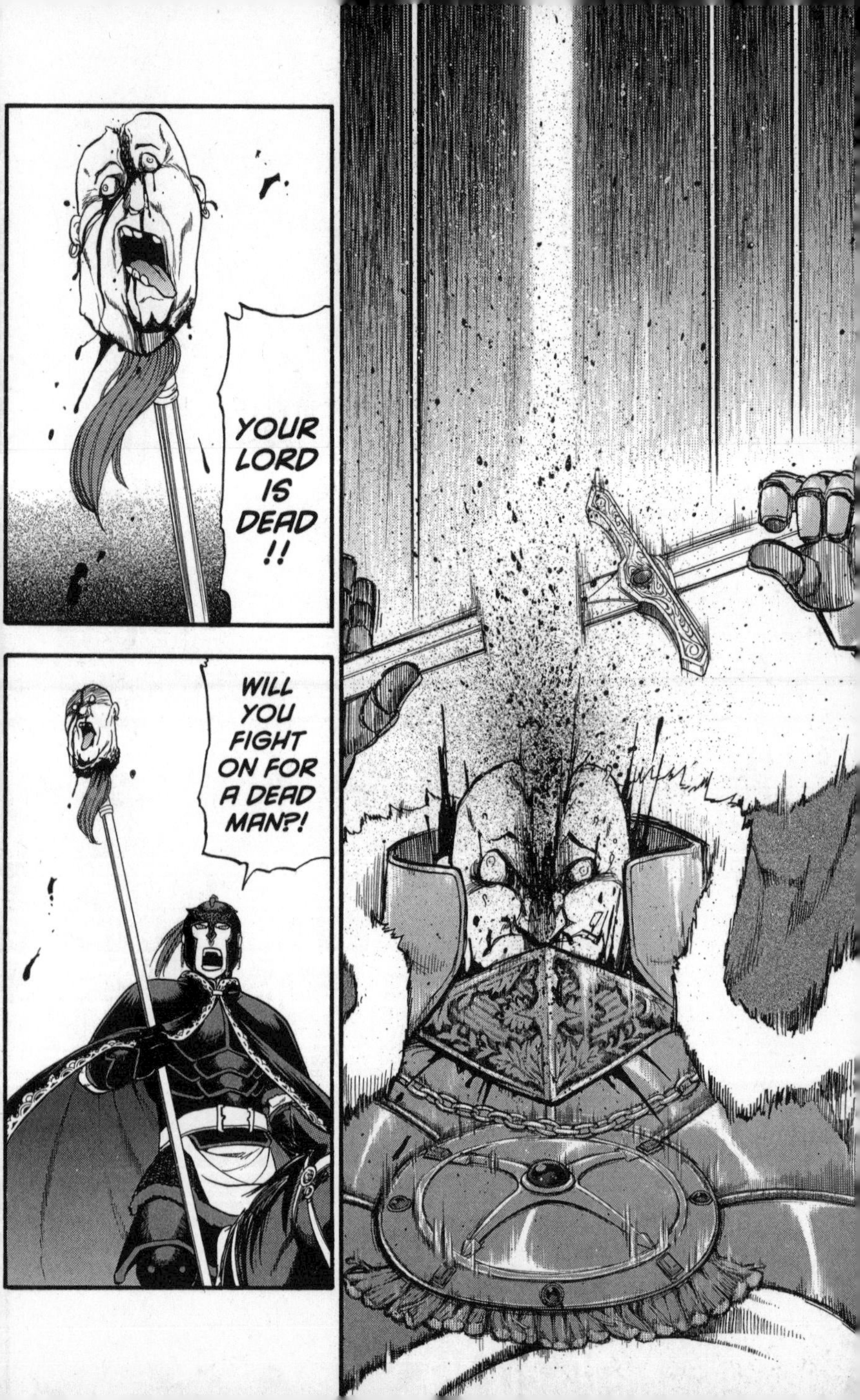
YOUR LORD IS DEAD!!
WILL YOU FIGHT ON FOR A DEAD MAN?!

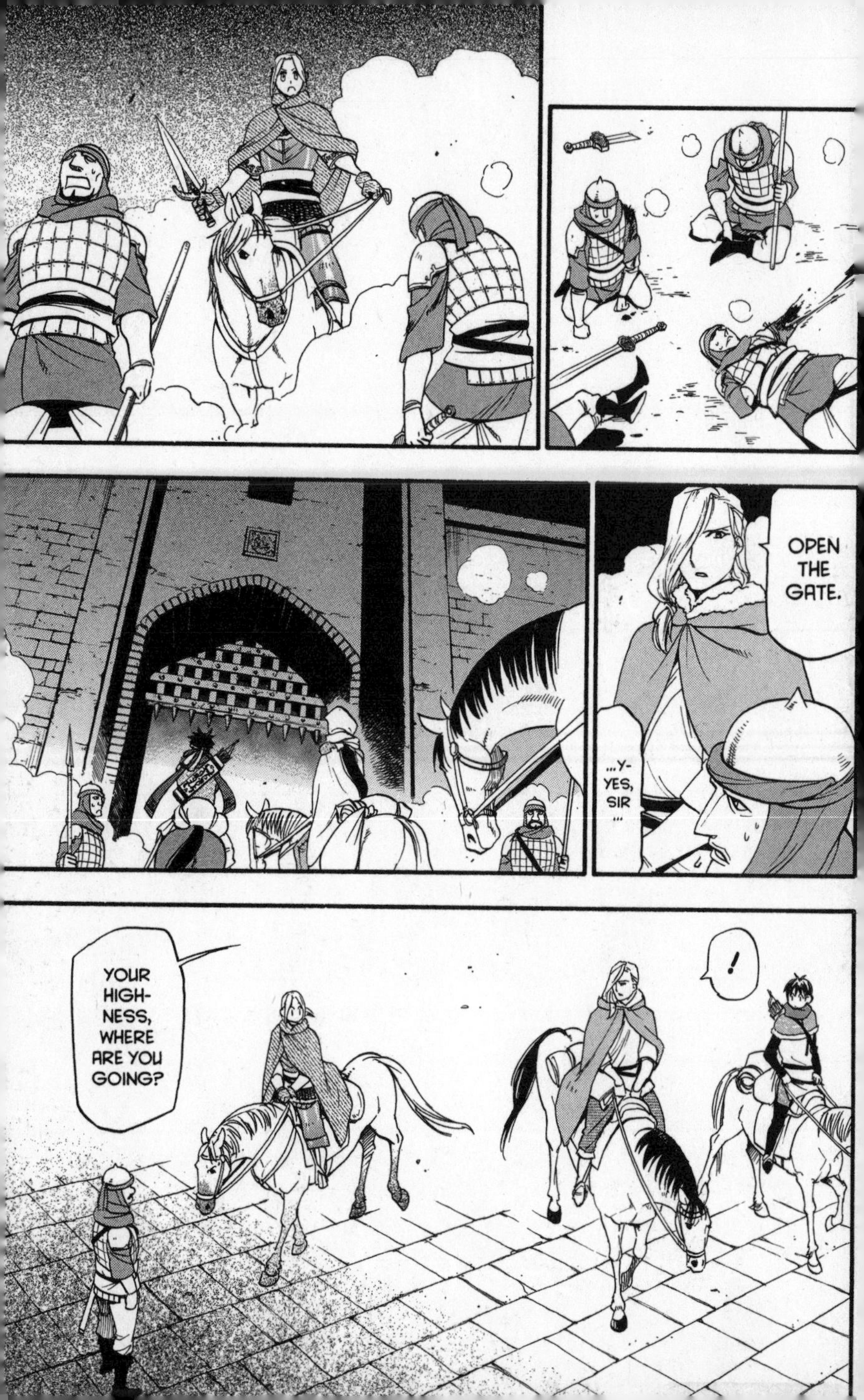
OPEN THE GATE.
...Y-YES, SIR...
!
YOUR HIGH-NESS, WHERE ARE YOU GOING?

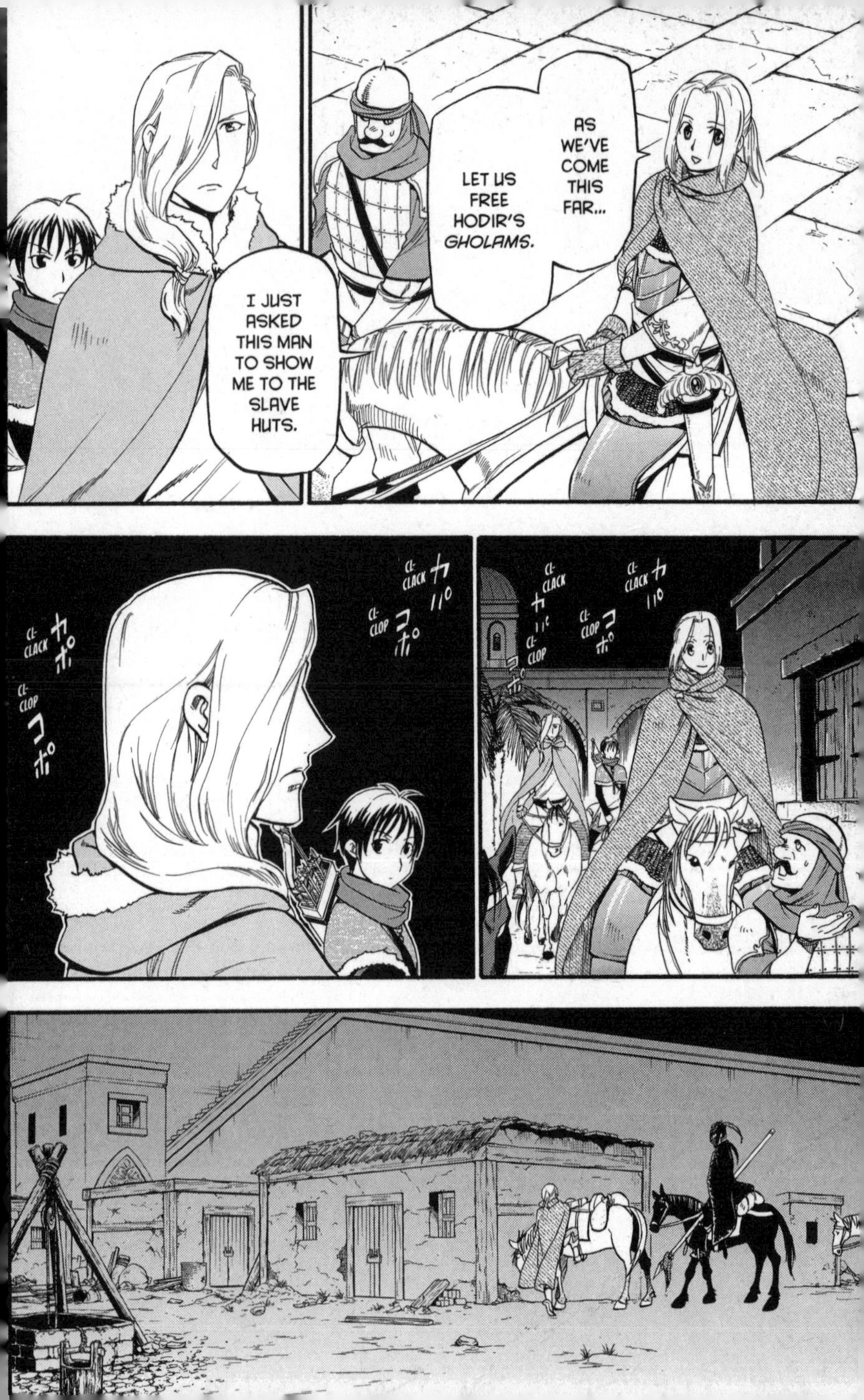
AS WE'VE COME THIS FAR...
LET US FREE HODIR'S *GHOLAMS.*
I JUST ASKED THIS MAN TO SHOW ME TO THE SLAVE HUTS.
CL-CLACK
CL-CLACK
CL-CLOP
CL-CLOP
CL-CLACK
CL-CLOP
CL-CLACK
CL-CLOP

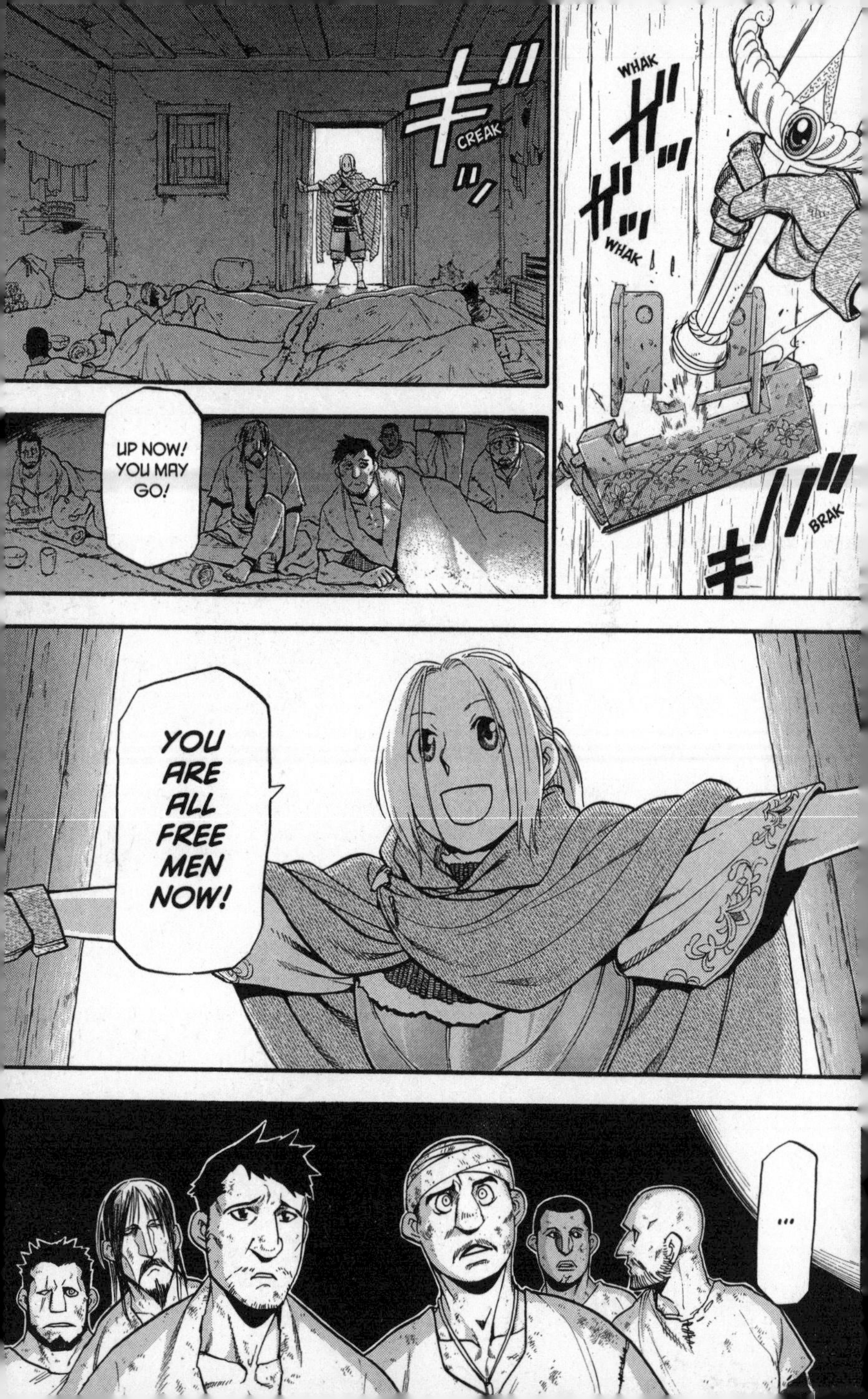
WHAK
WHAK
BRAK
CREAK
UP NOW! YOU MAY GO!
YOU ARE ALL FREE MEN NOW!
...

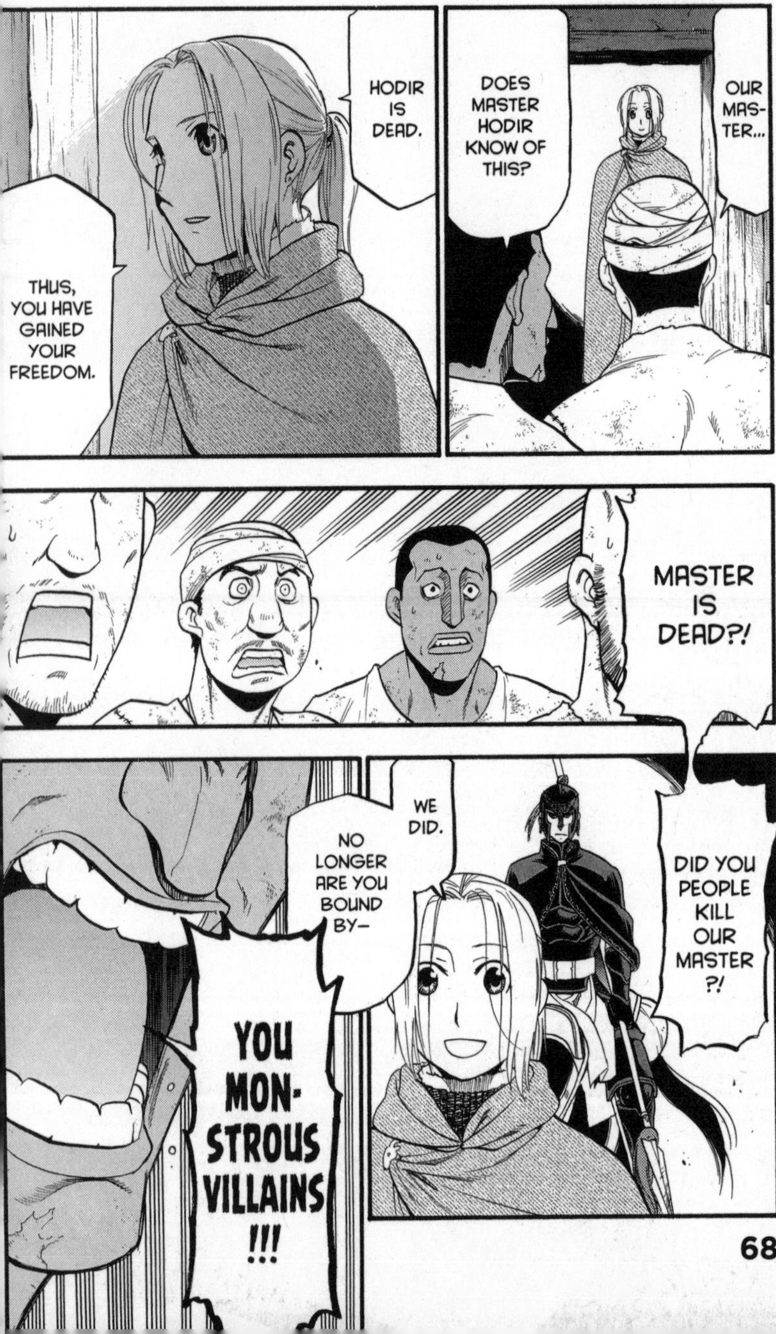
OUR MASTER...
DOES MASTER HODIR KNOW OF THIS?
HODIR IS DEAD.
THUS, YOU HAVE GAINED YOUR FREEDOM.
MASTER IS DEAD?!
DID YOU PEOPLE KILL OUR MASTER?!
WE DID.
NO LONGER ARE YOU BOUND BY—
YOU MONSTROUS VILLAINS!!!

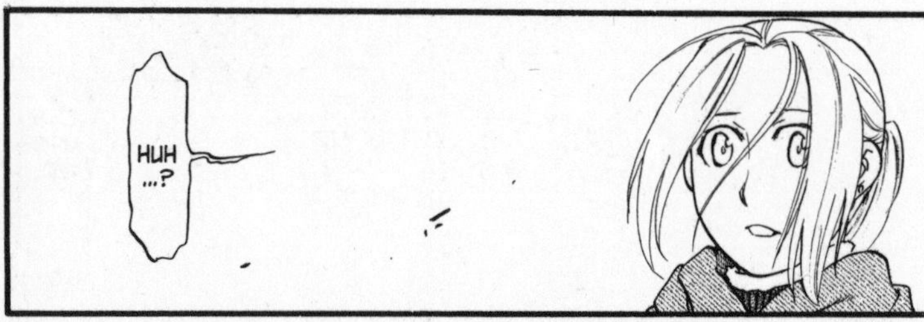
HUH ...?

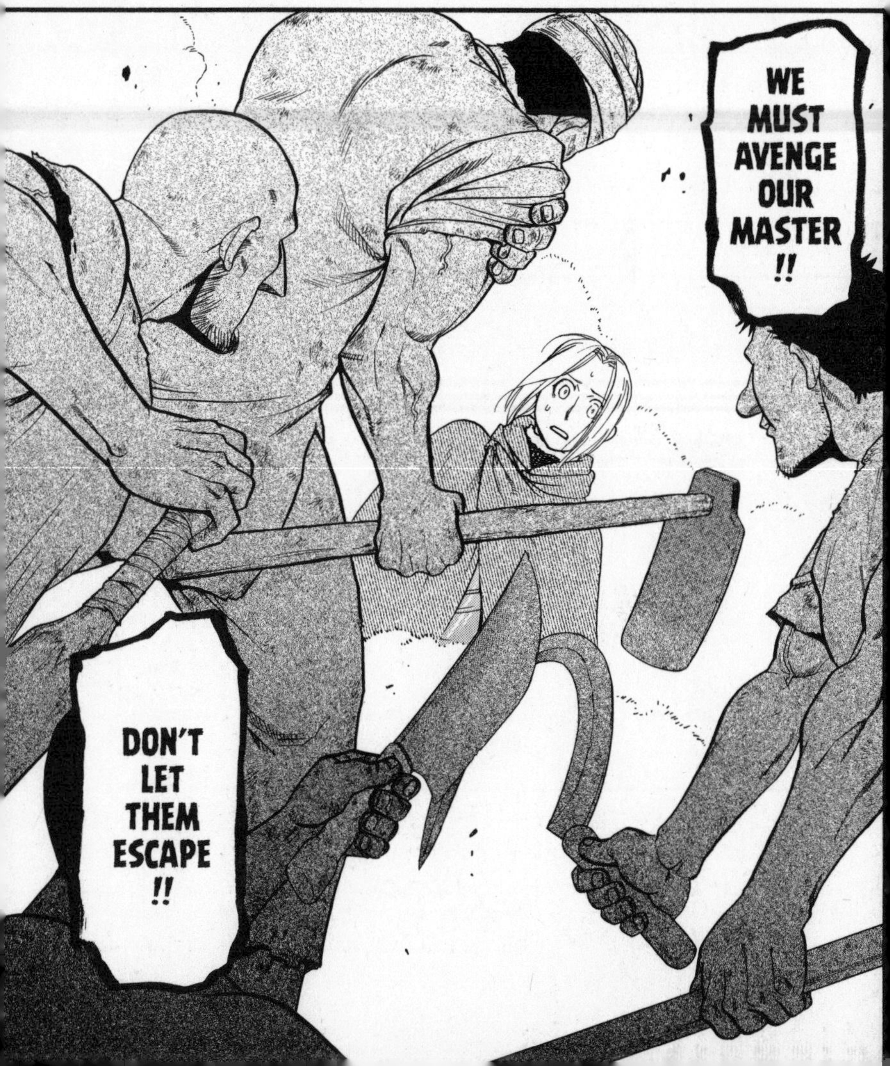
WE MUST AVENGE OUR MASTER !!
DON'T LET THEM ESCAPE !!

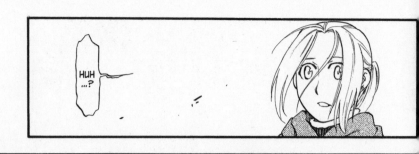

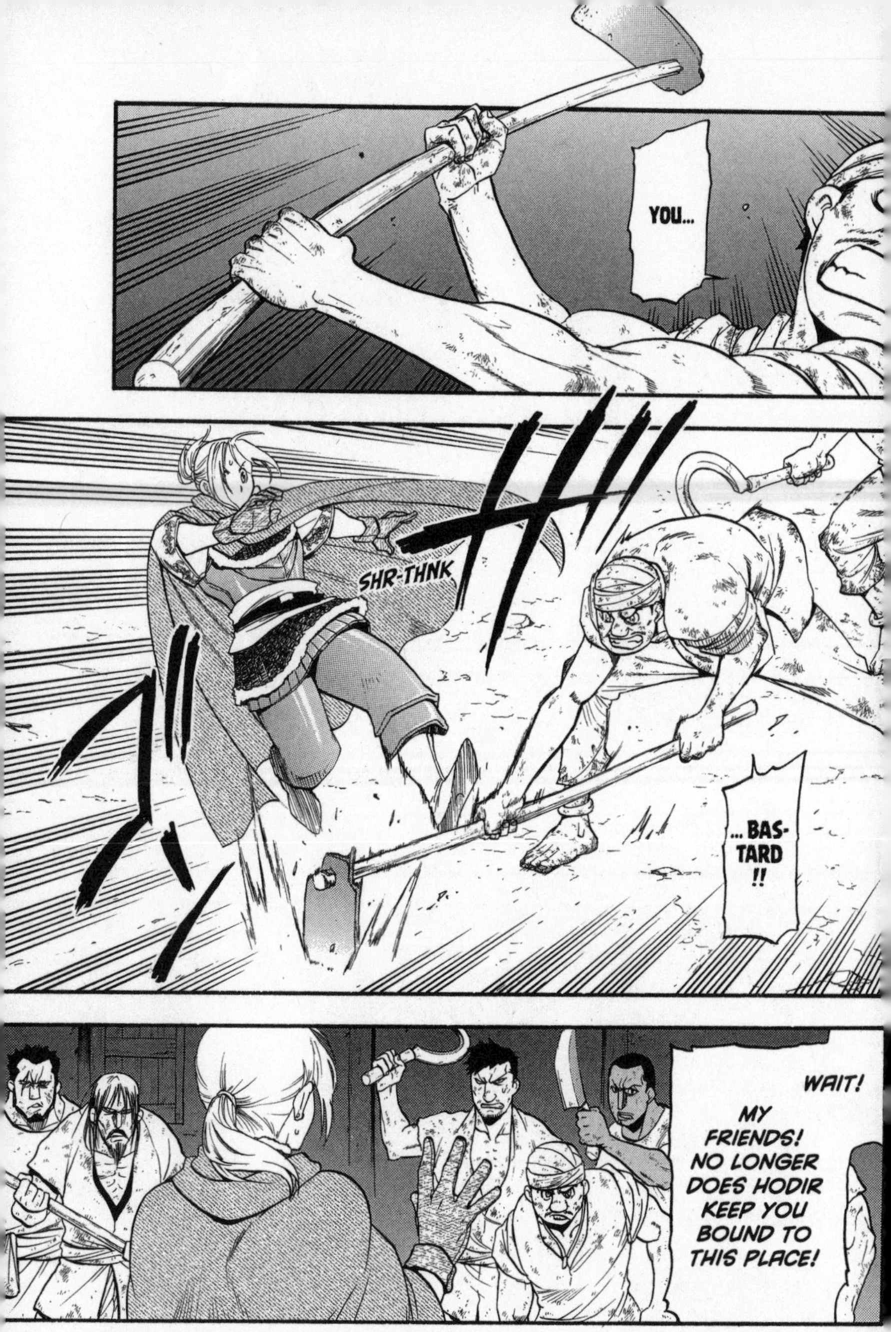

YOU...
SHR-THNK
... BAS-TARD !!
WAIT!
MY FRIENDS! NO LONGER DOES HODIR KEEP YOU BOUND TO THIS PLACE!

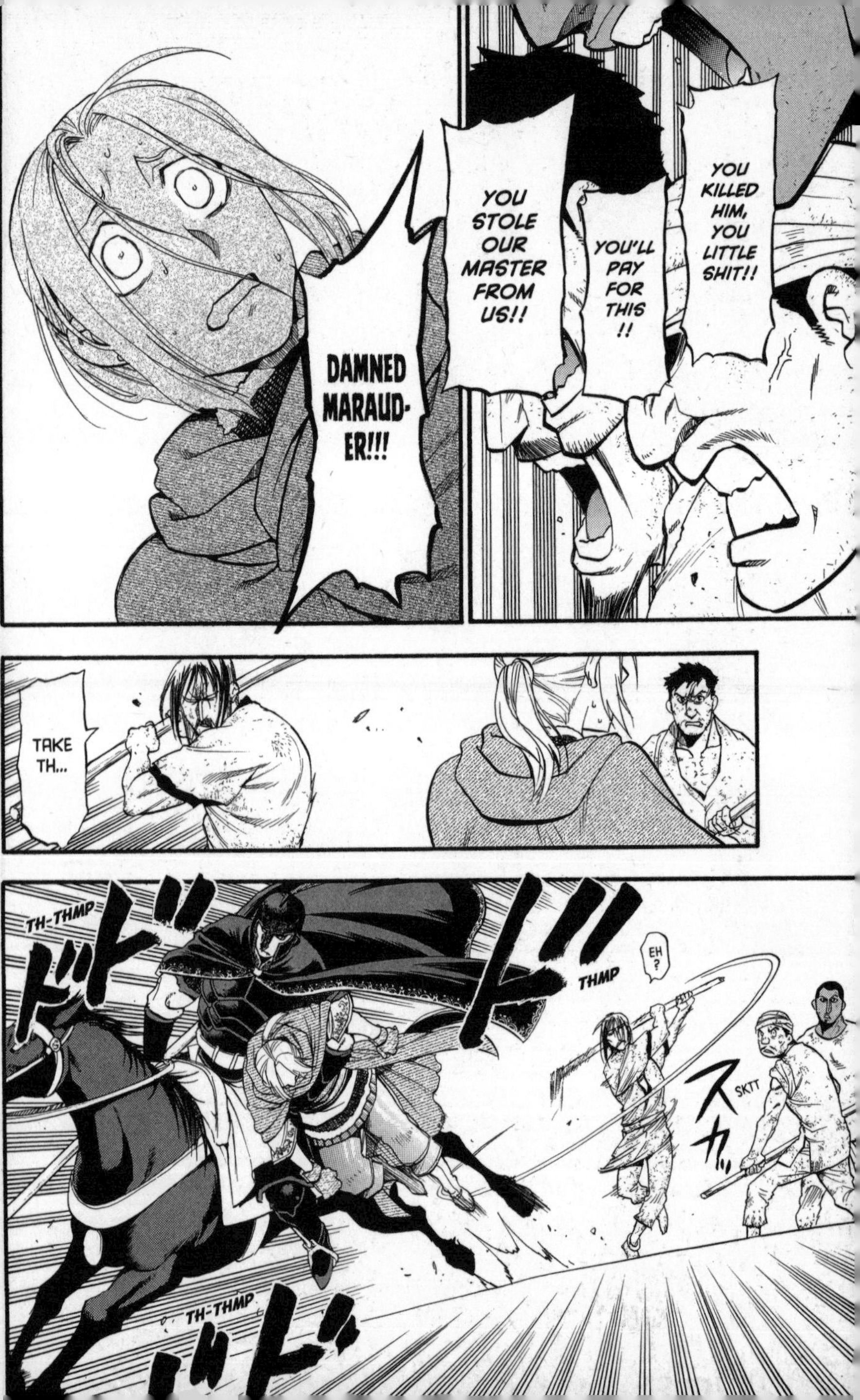
YOU KILLED HIM, YOU LITTLE SHIT!!
YOU'LL PAY FOR THIS!!
YOU STOLE OUR MASTER FROM US!!
DAMNED MARAUD-ER!!!
TAKE TH...
EH?
SKTT
THMP
TH-THMP
TH-THMP

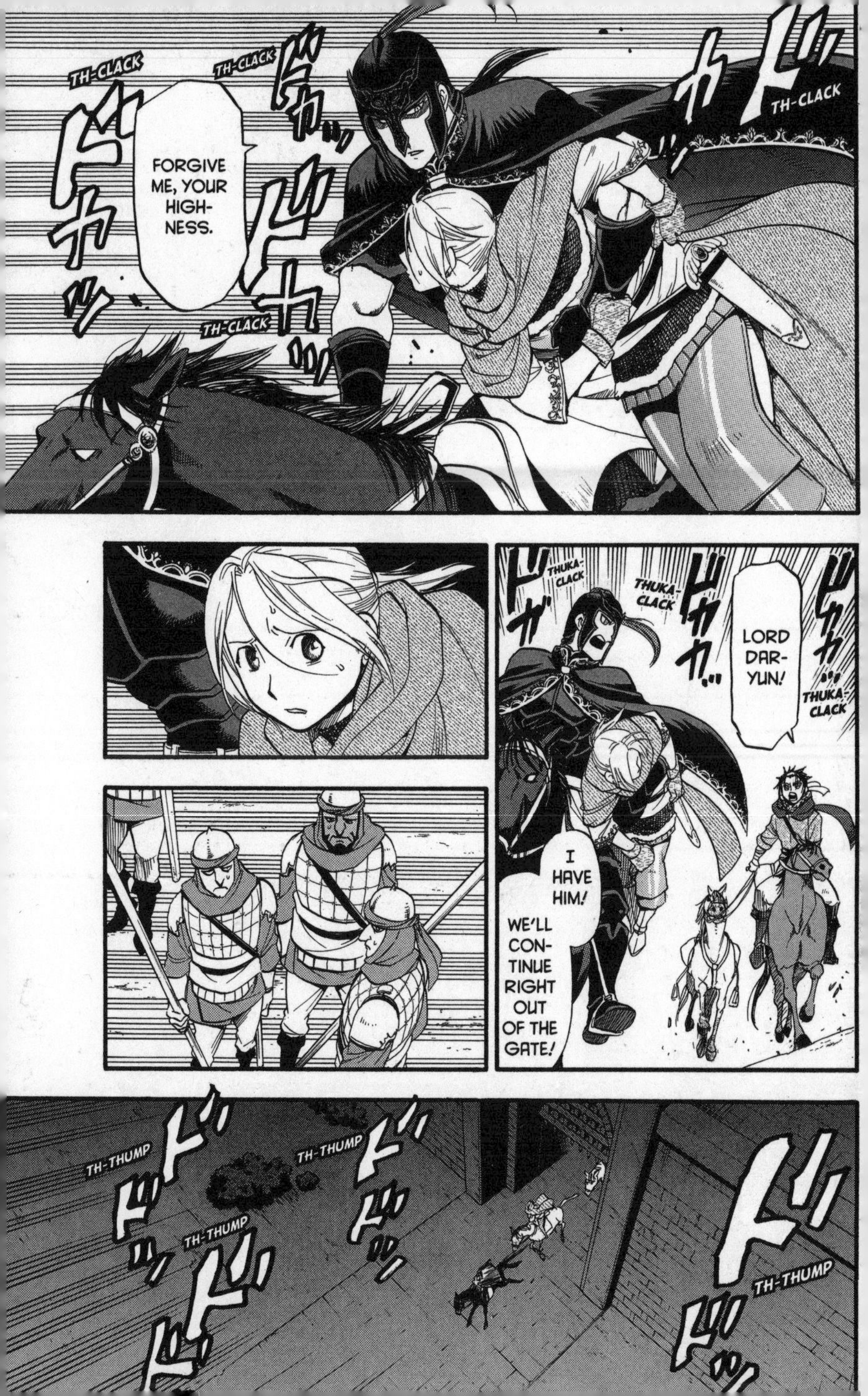
TH-CLACK
TH-CLACK
FORGIVE ME, YOUR HIGH-NESS.
TH-CLACK
TH-CLACK
THUKA-CLACK
LORD DAR-YUN!
THUKA-CLACK
THUKA-CLACK
I HAVE HIM!
WE'LL CON-TINUE RIGHT OUT OF THE GATE!
TH-THUMP
TH-THUMP
TH-THUMP
TH-THUMP

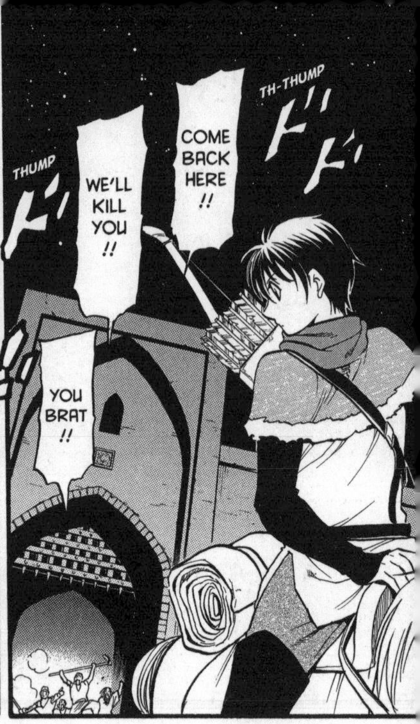
TH-THUMP
COME BACK HERE !!
WE'LL KILL YOU !!
THUMP
YOU BRAT !!

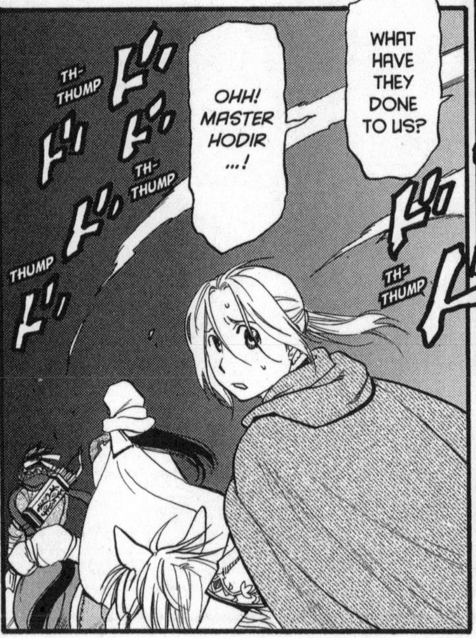
TH-THUMP
WHAT HAVE THEY DONE TO US?
OHH! MASTER HODIR ...!
TH-THUMP
TH-THUMP
THUMP

Chapter 23:The Site of Justice

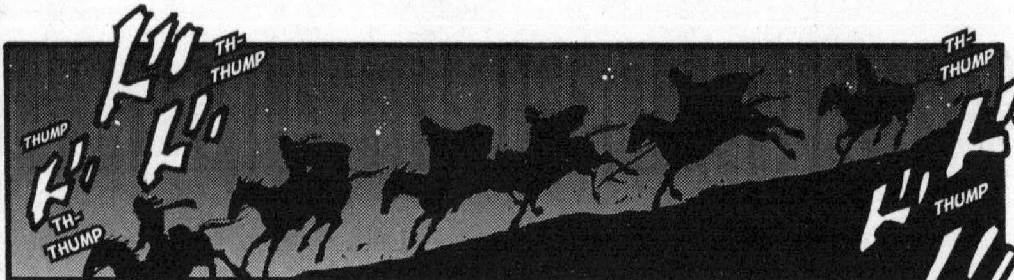
TH-THUMP
THUMP
TH-THUMP
THUMP
TH-THUMP

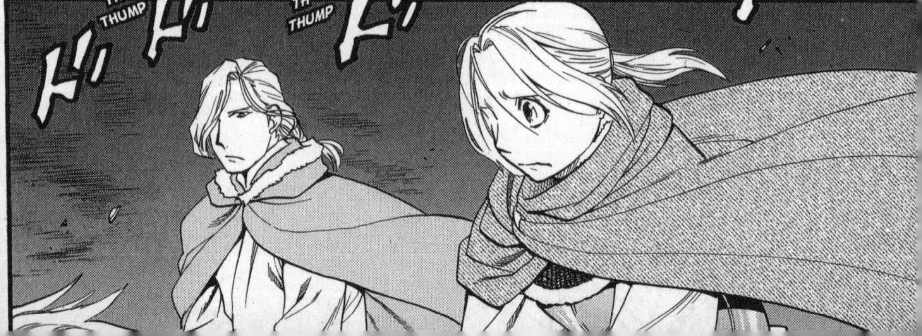
TH-THUMP
TH-THUMP

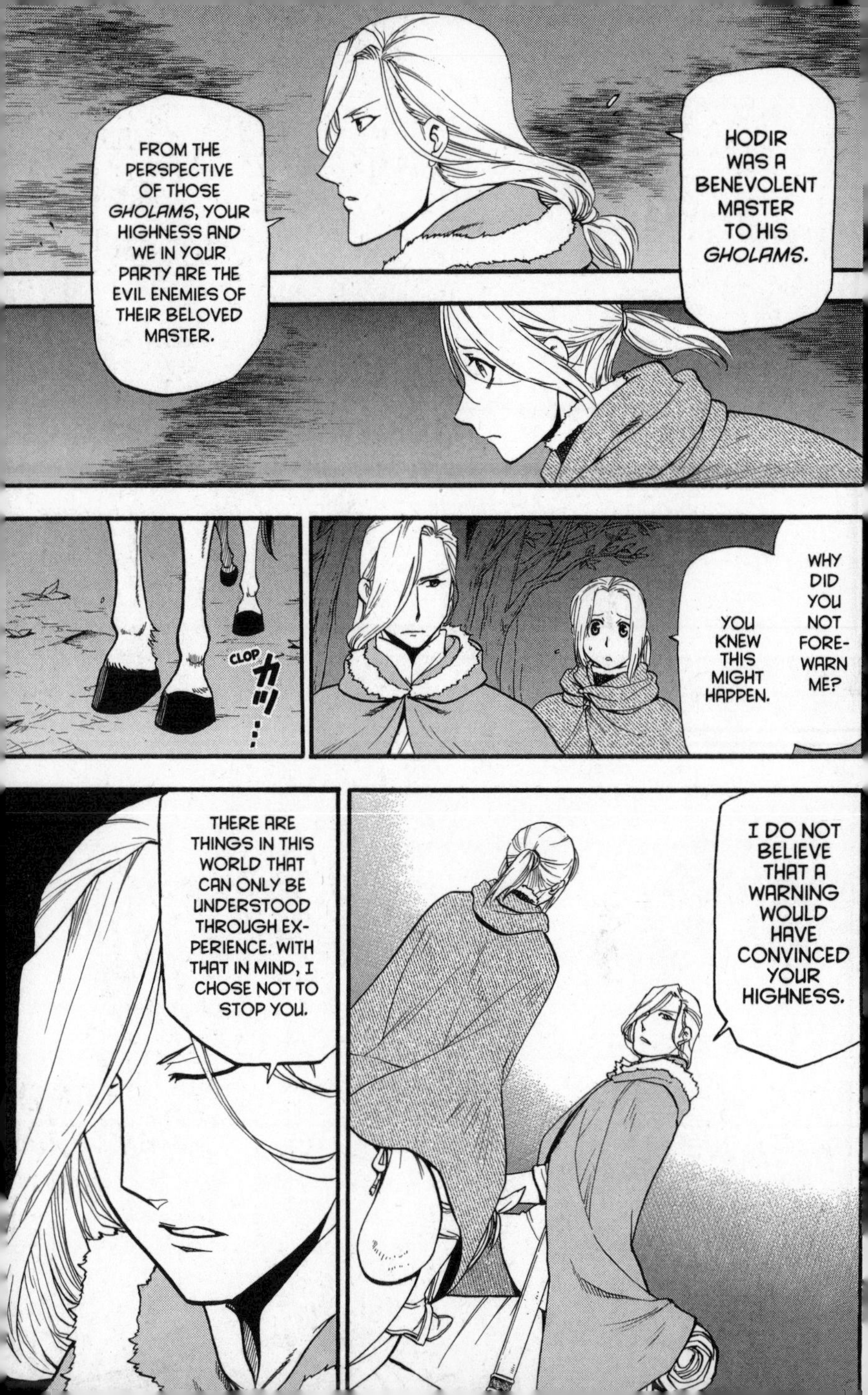
HODIR WAS A BENEVOLENT MASTER TO HIS *GHOLAMS*.
FROM THE PERSPECTIVE OF THOSE *GHOLAMS*, YOUR HIGHNESS AND WE IN YOUR PARTY ARE THE EVIL ENEMIES OF THEIR BELOVED MASTER.
WHY DID YOU NOT FORE-WARN ME?
YOU KNEW THIS MIGHT HAPPEN.
CLOP
カツ…
I DO NOT BELIEVE THAT A WARNING WOULD HAVE CONVINCED YOUR HIGHNESS.
THERE ARE THINGS IN THIS WORLD THAT CAN ONLY BE UNDERSTOOD THROUGH EX-PERIENCE. WITH THAT IN MIND, I CHOSE NOT TO STOP YOU.

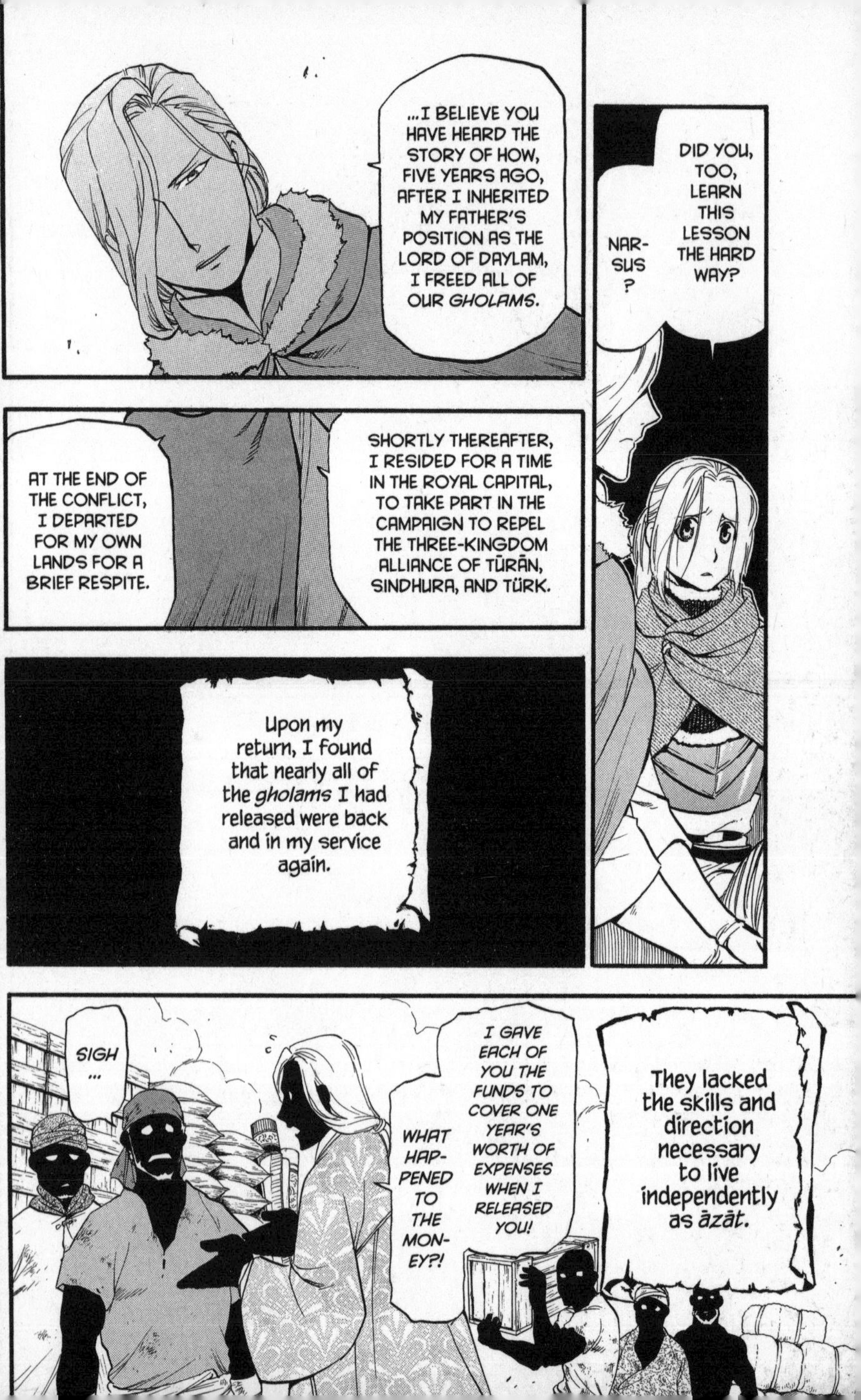
NARSUS?
DID YOU, TOO, LEARN THIS LESSON THE HARD WAY?
...I BELIEVE YOU HAVE HEARD THE STORY OF HOW, FIVE YEARS AGO, AFTER I INHERITED MY FATHER'S POSITION AS THE LORD OF DAYLAM, I FREED ALL OF OUR *GHOLAMS*.
SHORTLY THEREAFTER, I RESIDED FOR A TIME IN THE ROYAL CAPITAL, TO TAKE PART IN THE CAMPAIGN TO REPEL THE THREE-KINGDOM ALLIANCE OF TŪRĀN, SINDHURA, AND TÜRK.
AT THE END OF THE CONFLICT, I DEPARTED FOR MY OWN LANDS FOR A BRIEF RESPITE.
Upon my return, I found that nearly all of the *gholams* I had released were back and in my service again.
They lacked the skills and direction necessary to live independently as *āzāt*.
I GAVE EACH OF YOU THE FUNDS TO COVER ONE YEAR'S WORTH OF EXPENSES WHEN I RELEASED YOU!
WHAT HAPPENED TO THE MONEY?!
SIGH...

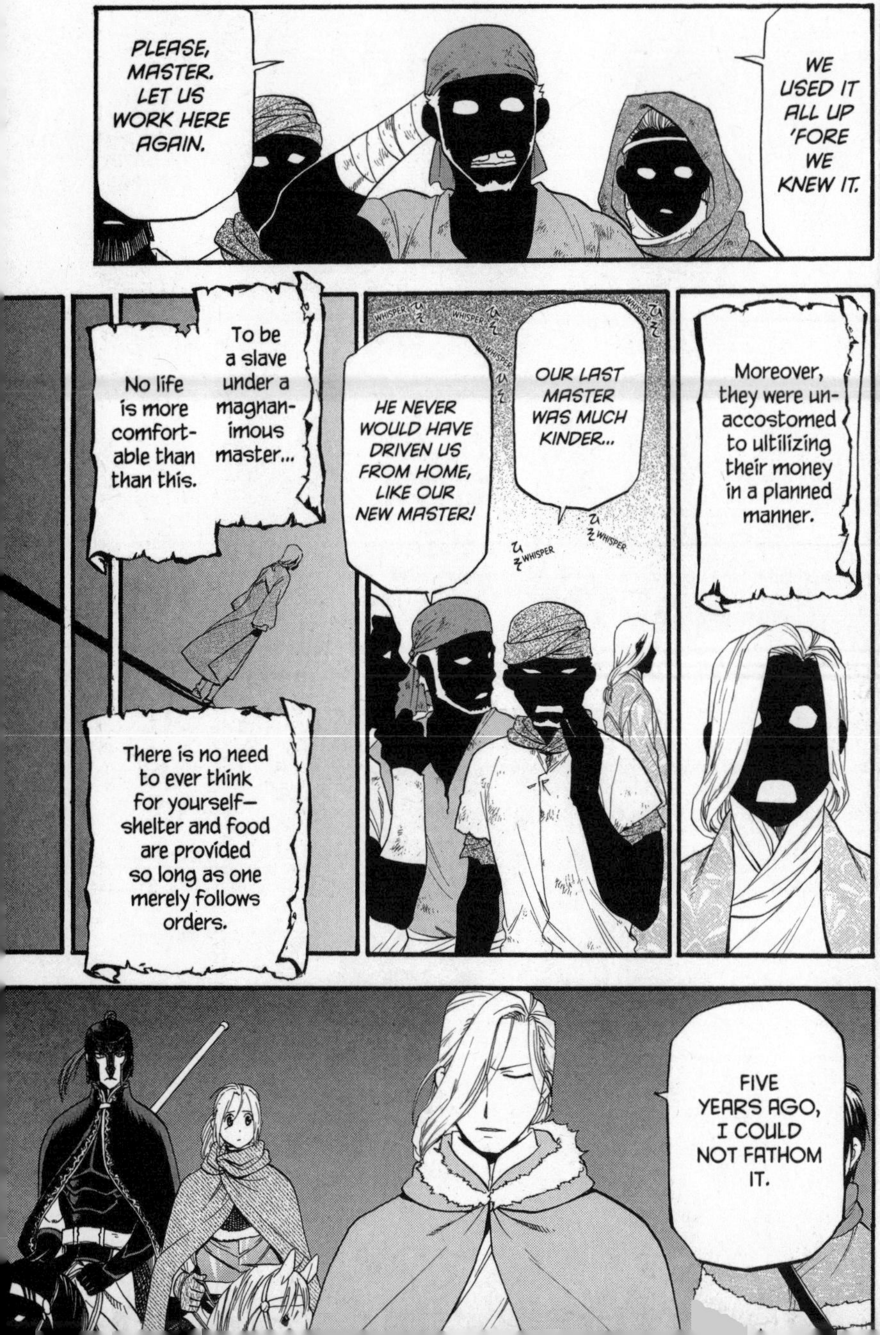
WE USED IT ALL UP 'FORE WE KNEW IT.
PLEASE, MASTER. LET US WORK HERE AGAIN.
Moreover, they were un-accostomed to ultilizing their money in a planned manner.
WHISPER
WHISPER
WHISPER
WHISPER
OUR LAST MASTER WAS MUCH KINDER...
HE NEVER WOULD HAVE DRIVEN US FROM HOME, LIKE OUR NEW MASTER!
WHISPER
WHISPER
To be a slave under a magnan-imous master...
No life is more comfort-able than than this.
There is no need to ever think for yourself—shelter and food are provided so long as one merely follows orders.
FIVE YEARS AGO, I COULD NOT FATHOM IT.

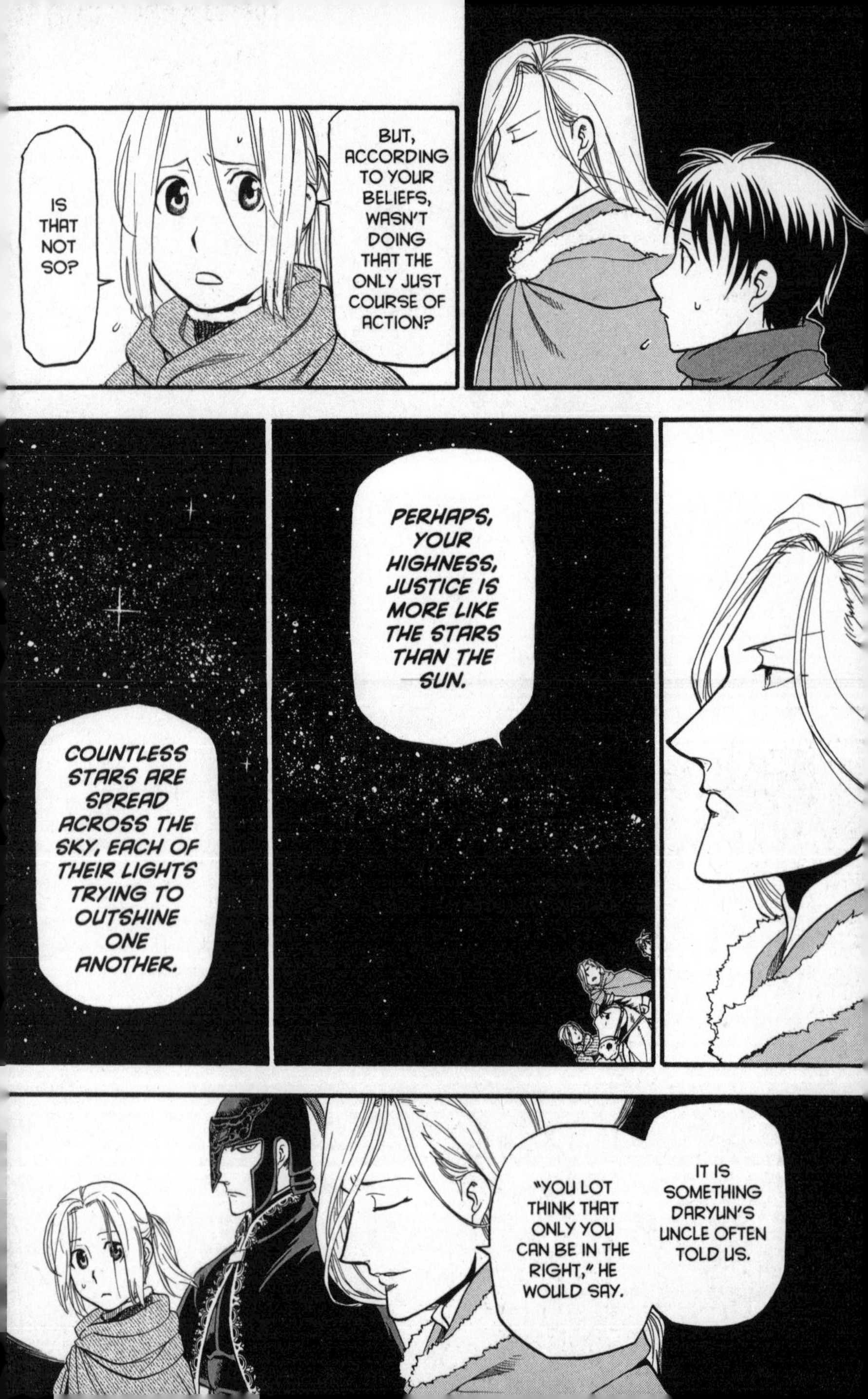
BUT, ACCORDING TO YOUR BELIEFS, WASN'T DOING THAT THE ONLY JUST COURSE OF ACTION?
IS THAT NOT SO?
PERHAPS, YOUR HIGHNESS, JUSTICE IS MORE LIKE THE STARS THAN THE SUN.
COUNTLESS STARS ARE SPREAD ACROSS THE SKY, EACH OF THEIR LIGHTS TRYING TO OUTSHINE ONE ANOTHER.
IT IS SOMETHING DARYUN'S UNCLE OFTEN TOLD US.
"YOU LOT THINK THAT ONLY YOU CAN BE IN THE RIGHT," HE WOULD SAY.

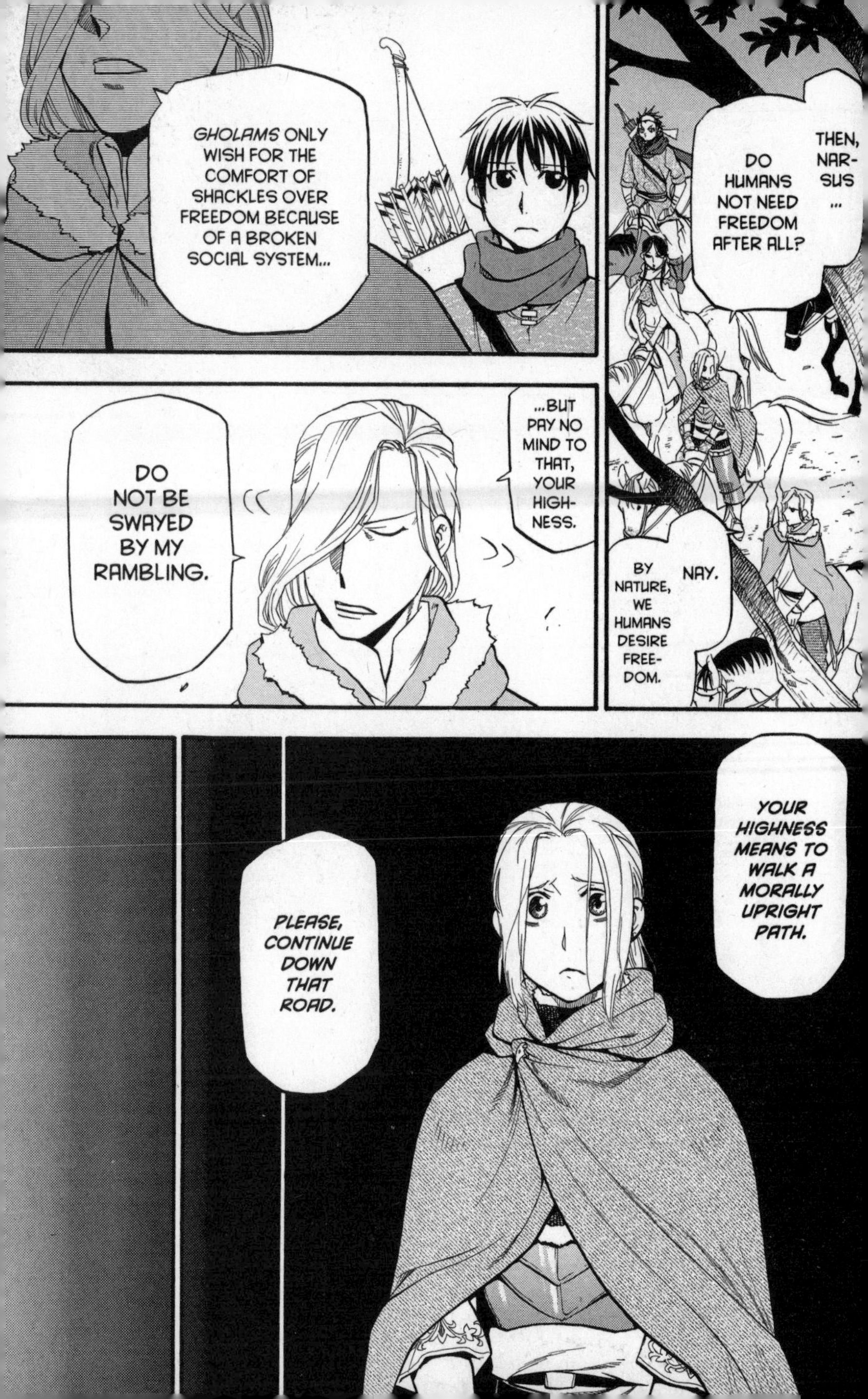
THEN, NARSUS...
DO HUMANS NOT NEED FREEDOM AFTER ALL?
NAY.
BY NATURE, WE HUMANS DESIRE FREEDOM.
GHOLAMS ONLY WISH FOR THE COMFORT OF SHACKLES OVER FREEDOM BECAUSE OF A BROKEN SOCIAL SYSTEM...
...BUT PAY NO MIND TO THAT, YOUR HIGHNESS.
DO NOT BE SWAYED BY MY RAMBLING.
YOUR HIGHNESS MEANS TO WALK A MORALLY UPRIGHT PATH.
PLEASE, CONTINUE DOWN THAT ROAD.

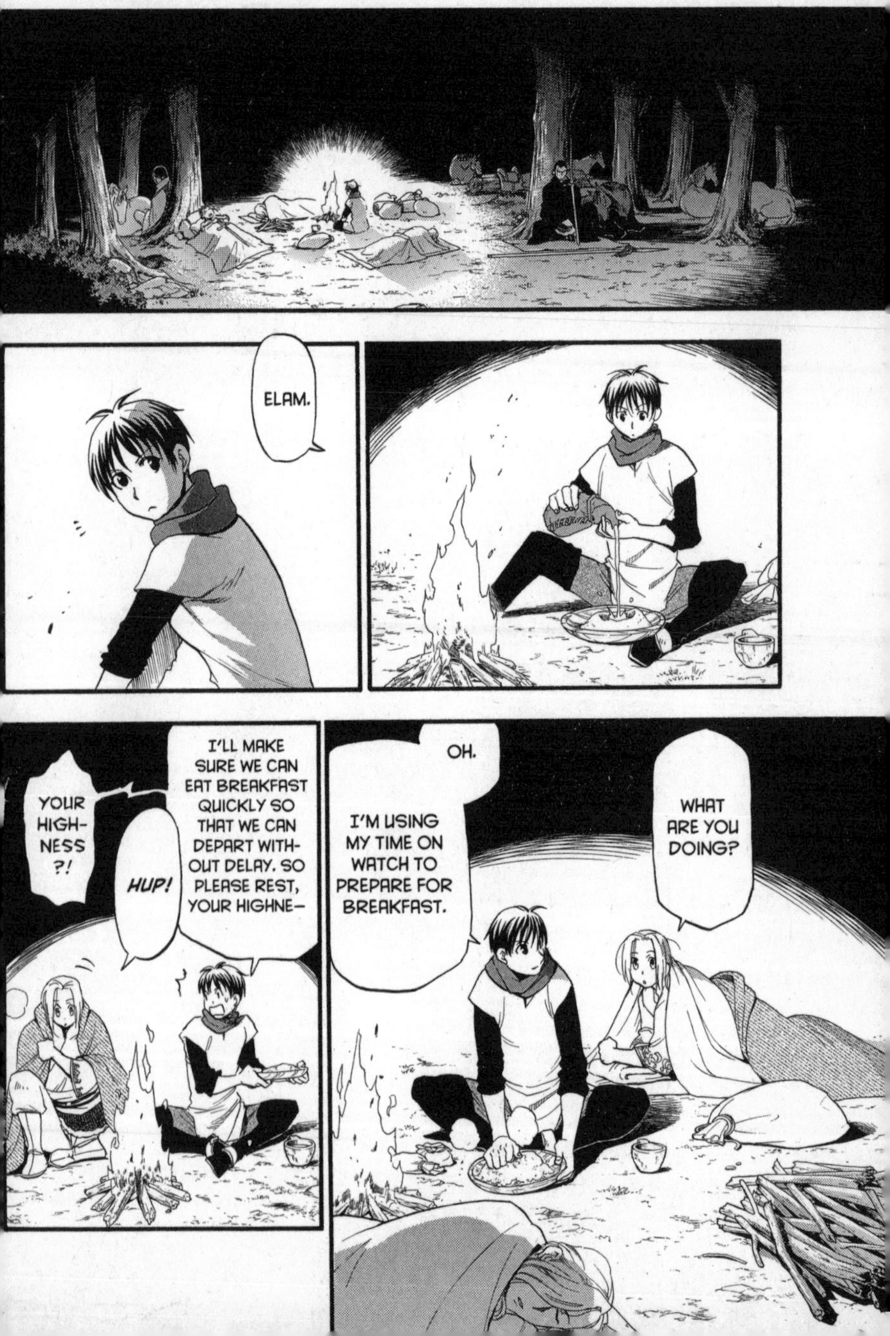
ELAM.
WHAT ARE YOU DOING?
OH.
I'M USING MY TIME ON WATCH TO PREPARE FOR BREAKFAST.
I'LL MAKE SURE WE CAN EAT BREAKFAST QUICKLY SO THAT WE CAN DEPART WITH-OUT DELAY. SO PLEASE REST, YOUR HIGHNE—
HUP!
YOUR HIGH-NESS ?!

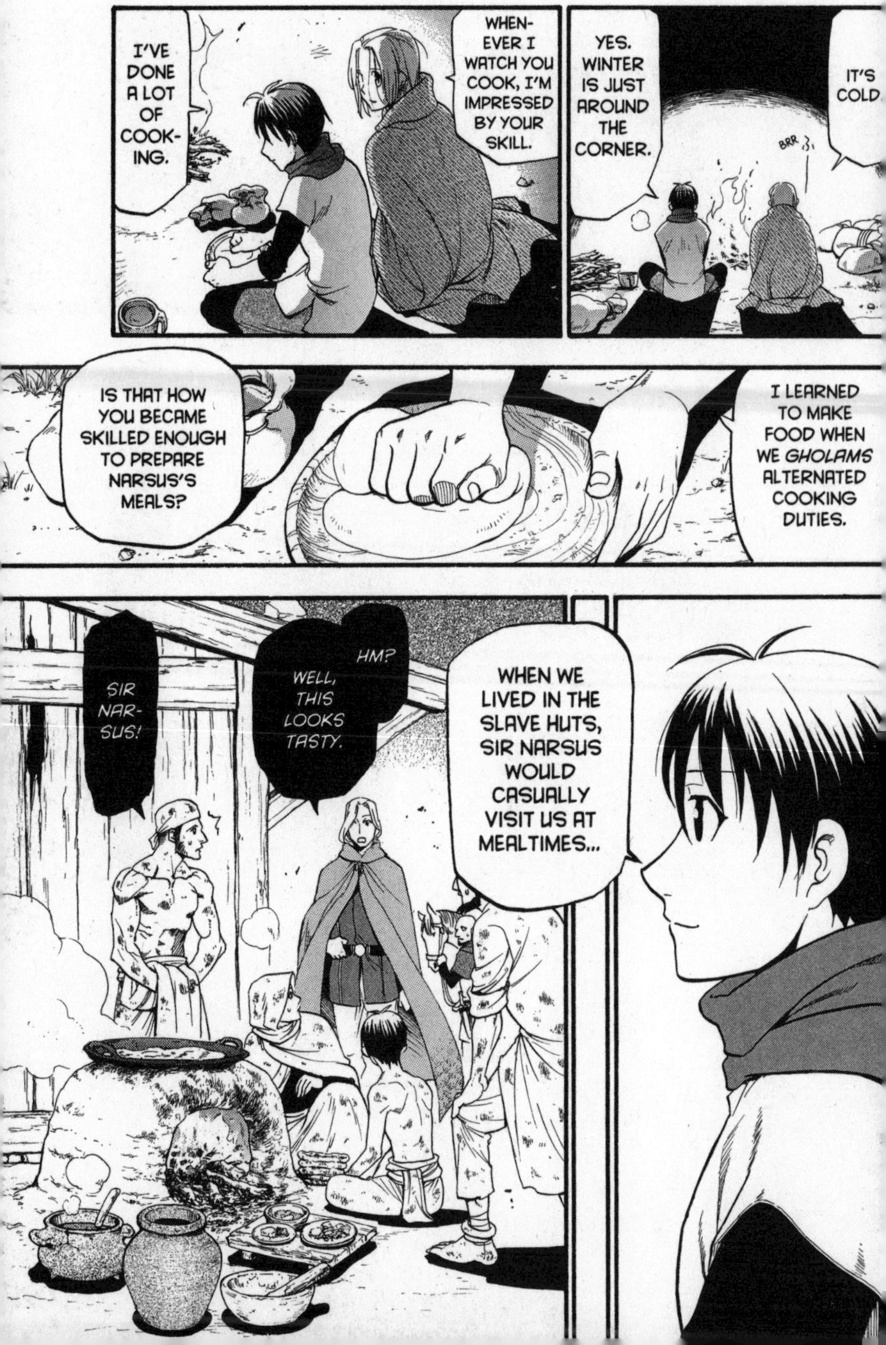
IT'S COLD.
BRR
YES. WINTER IS JUST AROUND THE CORNER.
WHEN-EVER I WATCH YOU COOK, I'M IMPRESSED BY YOUR SKILL.
I'VE DONE A LOT OF COOK-ING.
IS THAT HOW YOU BECAME SKILLED ENOUGH TO PREPARE NARSUS'S MEALS?
I LEARNED TO MAKE FOOD WHEN WE *GHOLAMS* ALTERNATED COOKING DUTIES.
WHEN WE LIVED IN THE SLAVE HUTS, SIR NARSUS WOULD CASUALLY VISIT US AT MEALTIMES...
SIR NAR-SUS!
HM? WELL, THIS LOOKS TASTY.

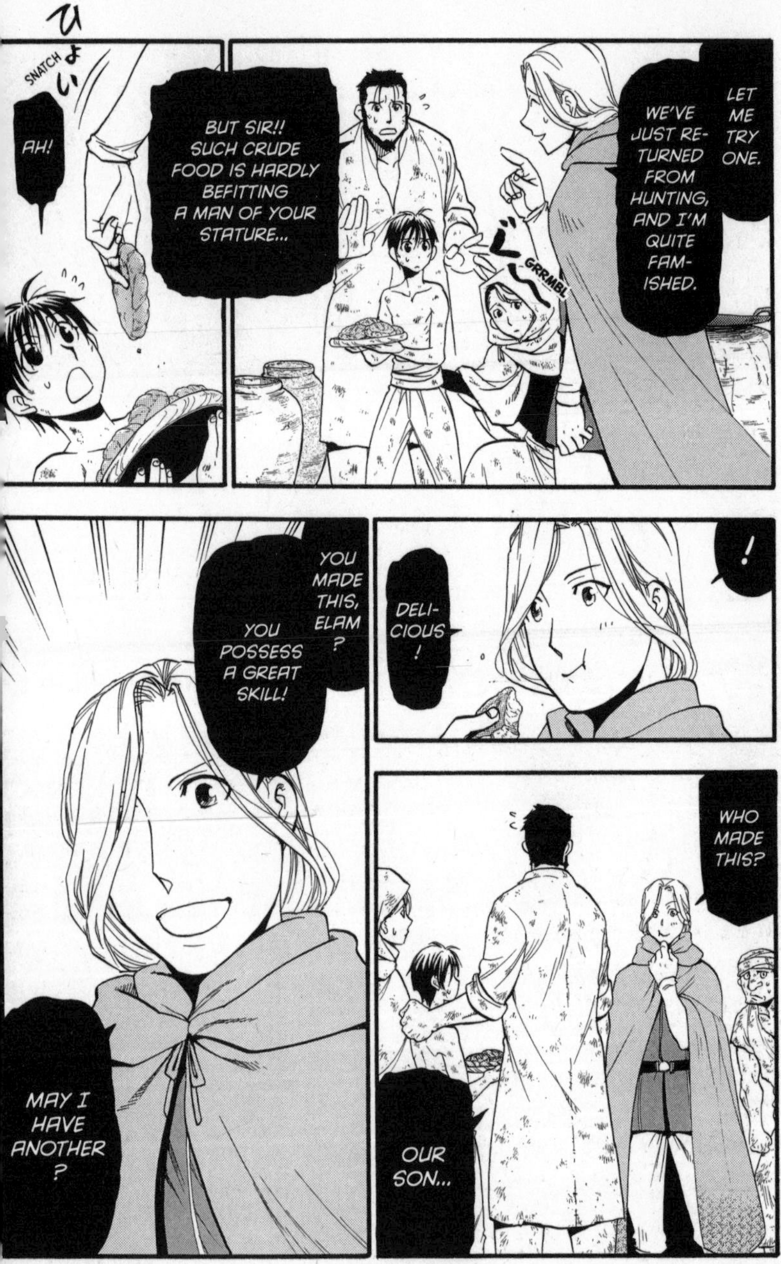
LET ME TRY ONE.
WE'VE JUST RE-TURNED FROM HUNTING, AND I'M QUITE FAM-ISHED.
じ〜
GRRMBL
BUT SIR!! SUCH CRUDE FOOD IS HARDLY BEFITTING A MAN OF YOUR STATURE...
ひょい
SNATCH
AH!
!
DELI-CIOUS!
WHO MADE THIS?
OUR SON...
YOU MADE THIS, ELAM?
YOU POSSESS A GREAT SKILL!
MAY I HAVE ANOTHER?

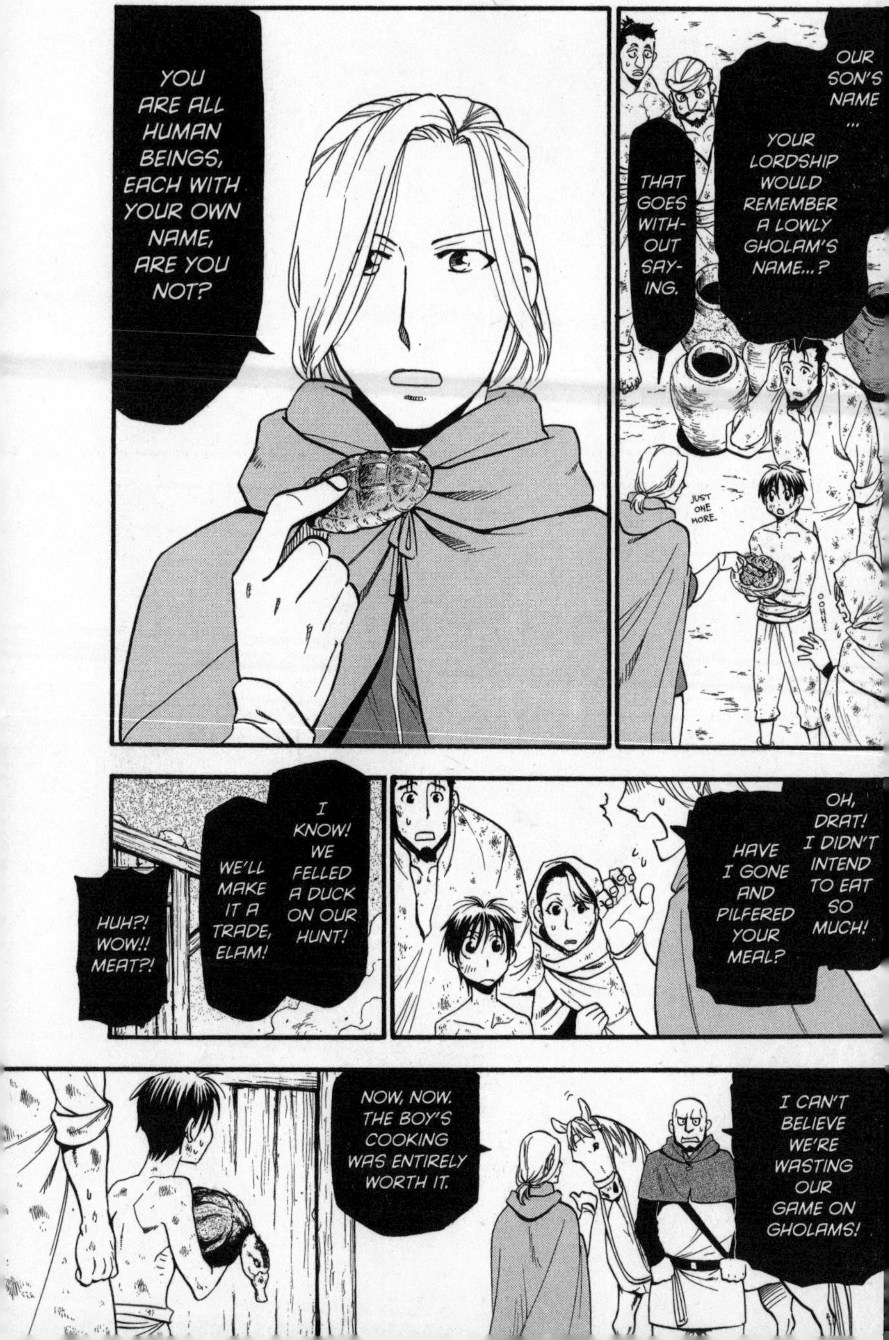
OUR SON'S NAME ... YOUR LORDSHIP WOULD REMEMBER A LOWLY GHOLAM'S NAME...?
THAT GOES WITH-OUT SAY-ING.
JUST ONE MORE.
OOHH...
YOU ARE ALL HUMAN BEINGS, EACH WITH YOUR OWN NAME, ARE YOU NOT?
OH, DRAT! I DIDN'T INTEND TO EAT SO MUCH!
HAVE I GONE AND PILFERED YOUR MEAL?
I KNOW! WE FELLED A DUCK ON OUR HUNT!
WE'LL MAKE IT A TRADE, ELAM!
HUH?! WOW!! MEAT?!
I CAN'T BELIEVE WE'RE WASTING OUR GAME ON GHOLAMS!
NOW, NOW. THE BOY'S COOKING WAS ENTIRELY WORTH IT.

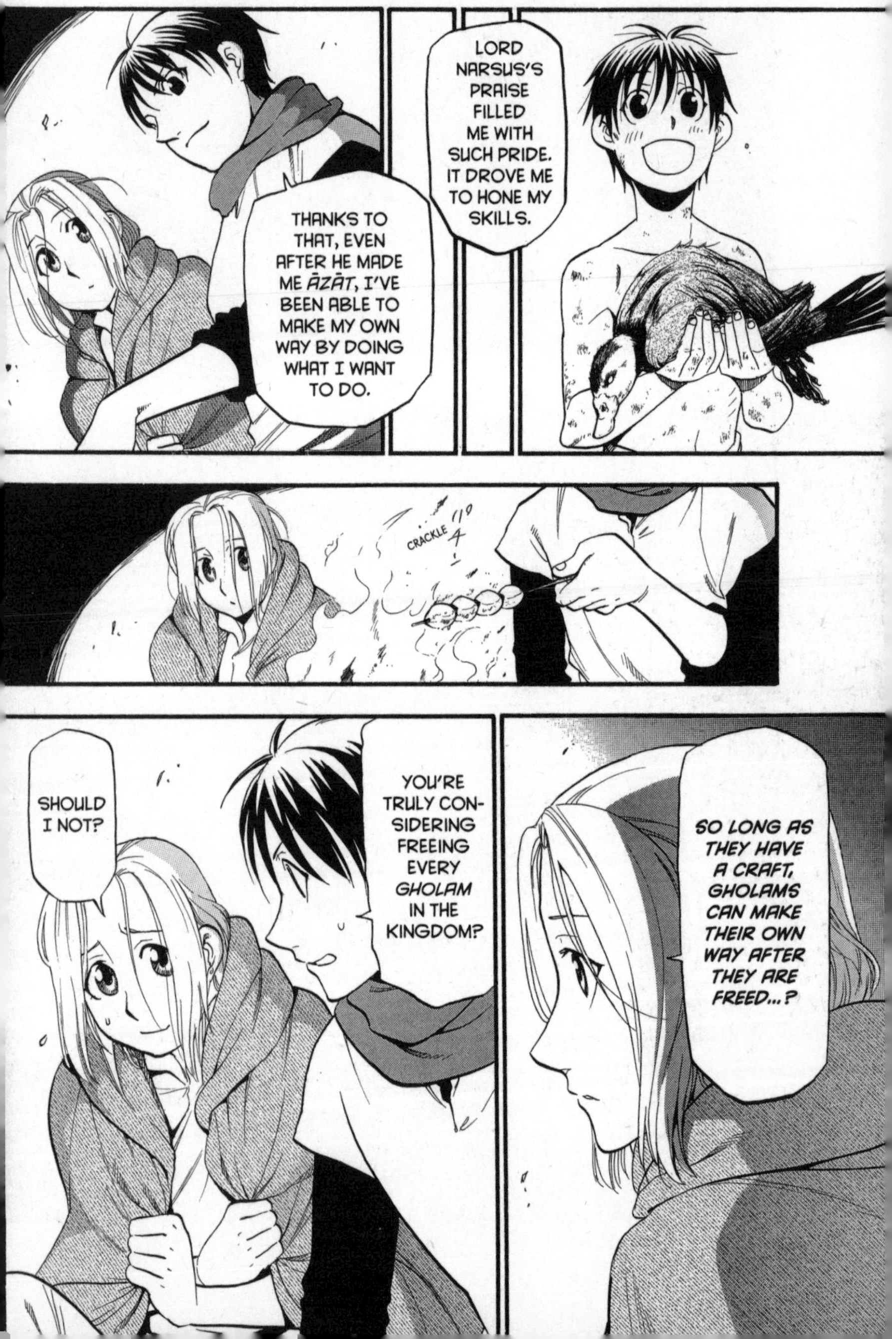
LORD NARSUS'S PRAISE FILLED ME WITH SUCH PRIDE. IT DROVE ME TO HONE MY SKILLS.
THANKS TO THAT, EVEN AFTER HE MADE ME *ĀZĀT*, I'VE BEEN ABLE TO MAKE MY OWN WAY BY DOING WHAT I WANT TO DO.
CRACKLE
SO LONG AS THEY HAVE A CRAFT, GHOLAMS CAN MAKE THEIR OWN WAY AFTER THEY ARE FREED...?
YOU'RE TRULY CON-SIDERING FREEING EVERY *GHOLAM* IN THE KINGDOM?
SHOULD I NOT?

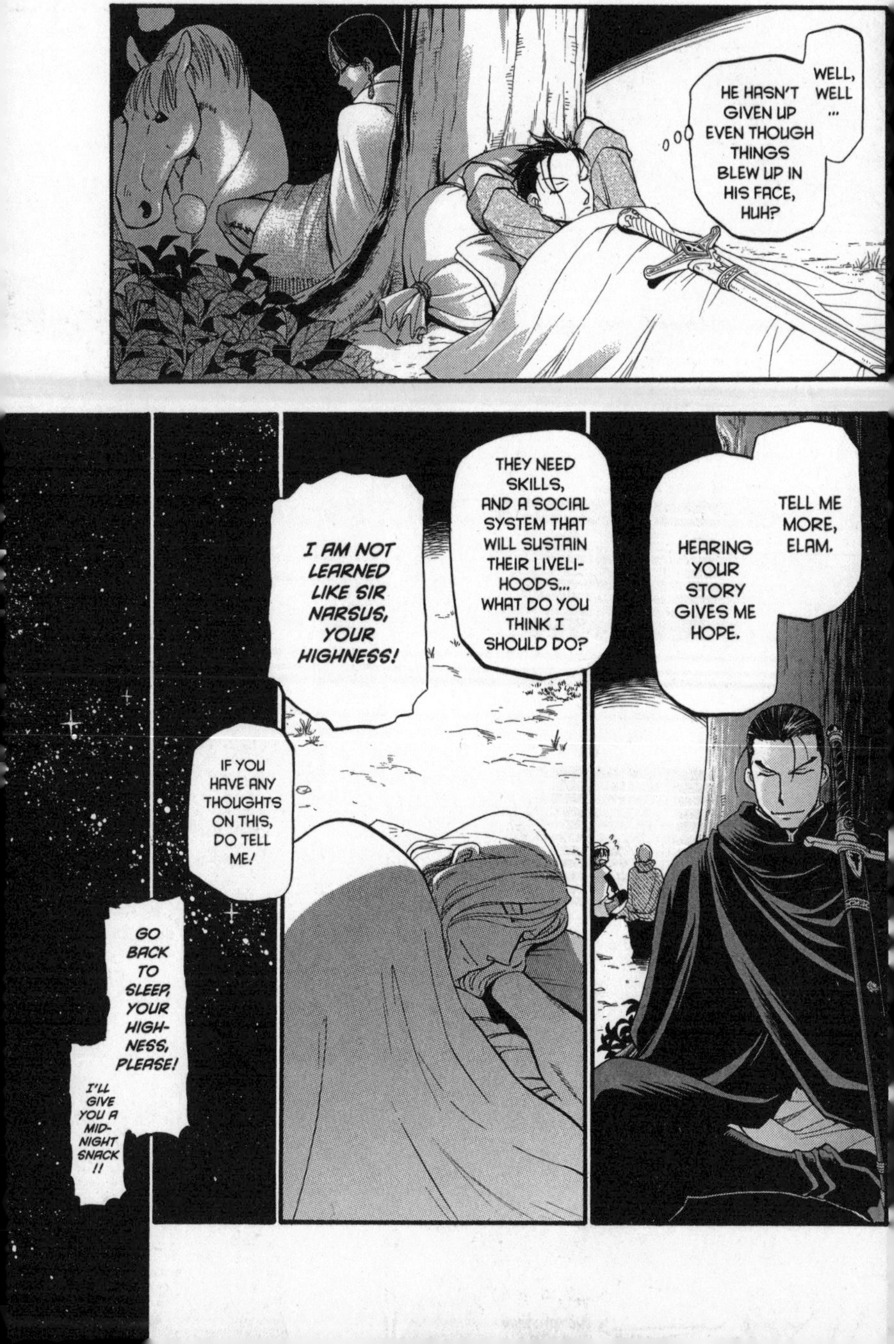
WELL, WELL ...
HE HASN'T GIVEN UP EVEN THOUGH THINGS BLEW UP IN HIS FACE, HUH?
TELL ME MORE, ELAM.
HEARING YOUR STORY GIVES ME HOPE.
THEY NEED SKILLS, AND A SOCIAL SYSTEM THAT WILL SUSTAIN THEIR LIVELI-HOODS... WHAT DO YOU THINK I SHOULD DO?
I AM NOT LEARNED LIKE SIR NARSUS, YOUR HIGHNESS!
IF YOU HAVE ANY THOUGHTS ON THIS, DO TELL ME!
GO BACK TO SLEEP, YOUR HIGH-NESS, PLEASE!
I'LL GIVE YOU A MID-NIGHT SNACK !!

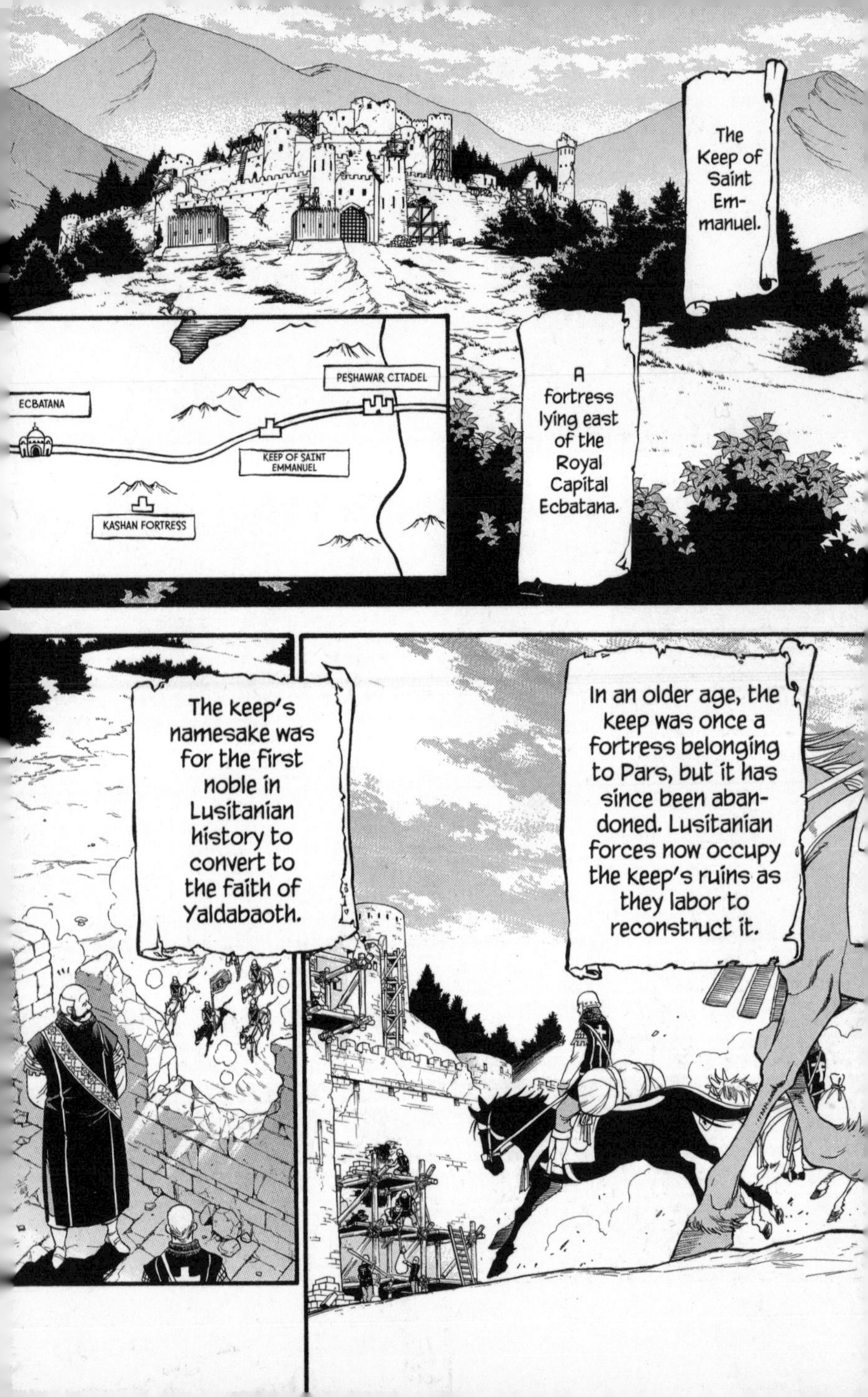
The Keep of Saint Emmanuel.
A fortress lying east of the Royal Capital Ecbatana.
PESHAWAR CITADEL
ECBATANA
KEEP OF SAINT EMMANUEL
KASHAN FORTRESS
In an older age, the keep was once a fortress belonging to Pars, but it has since been abandoned. Lusitanian forces now occupy the keep's ruins as they labor to reconstruct it.
The keep's namesake was for the first noble in Lusitanian history to convert to the faith of Yaldabaoth.

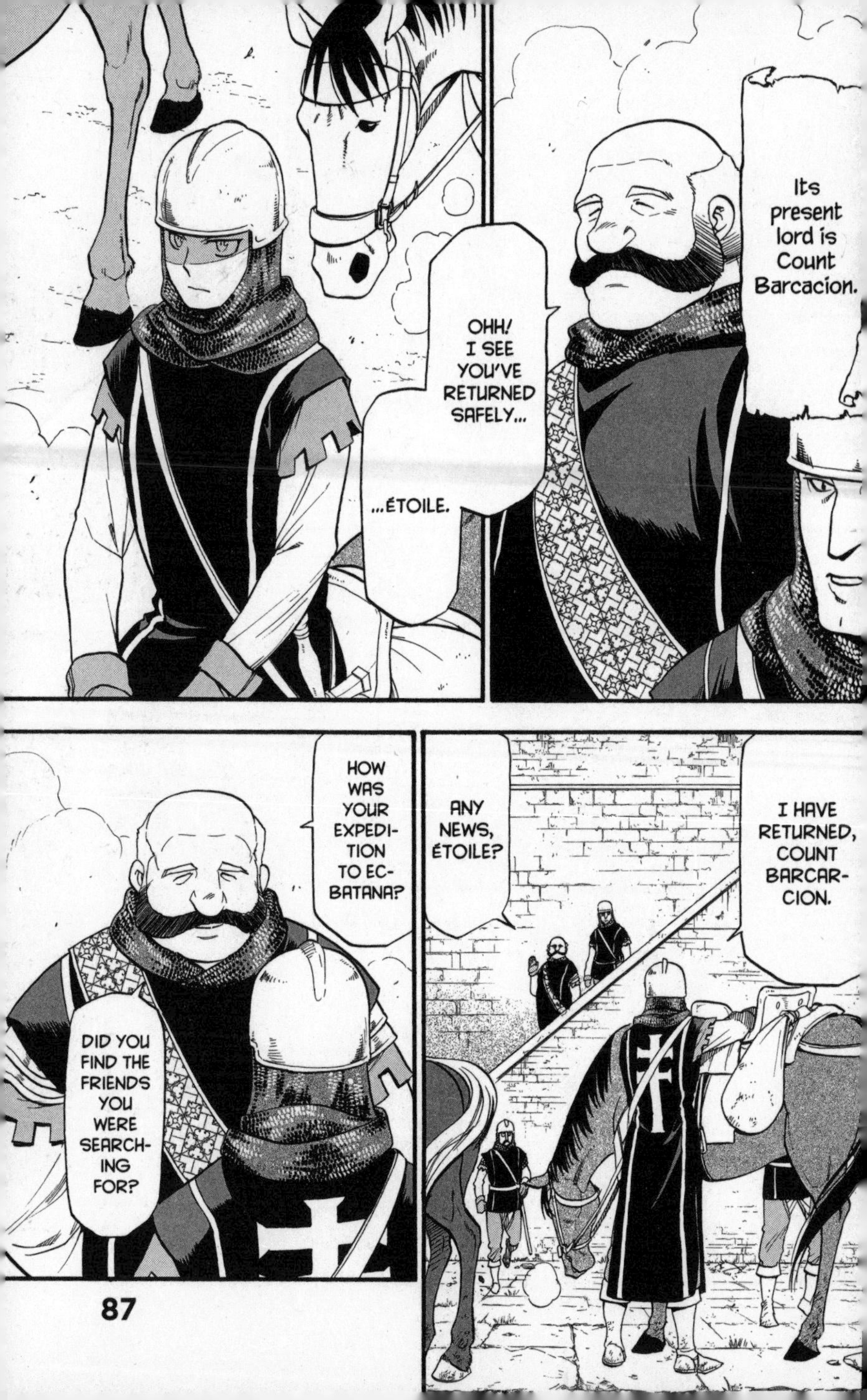
Its present lord is Count Barcacion.
OHH! I SEE YOU'VE RETURNED SAFELY...
...ÉTOILE.
I HAVE RETURNED, COUNT BARCARCION.
ANY NEWS, ÉTOILE?
HOW WAS YOUR EXPEDITION TO ECBATANA?
DID YOU FIND THE FRIENDS YOU WERE SEARCHING FOR?

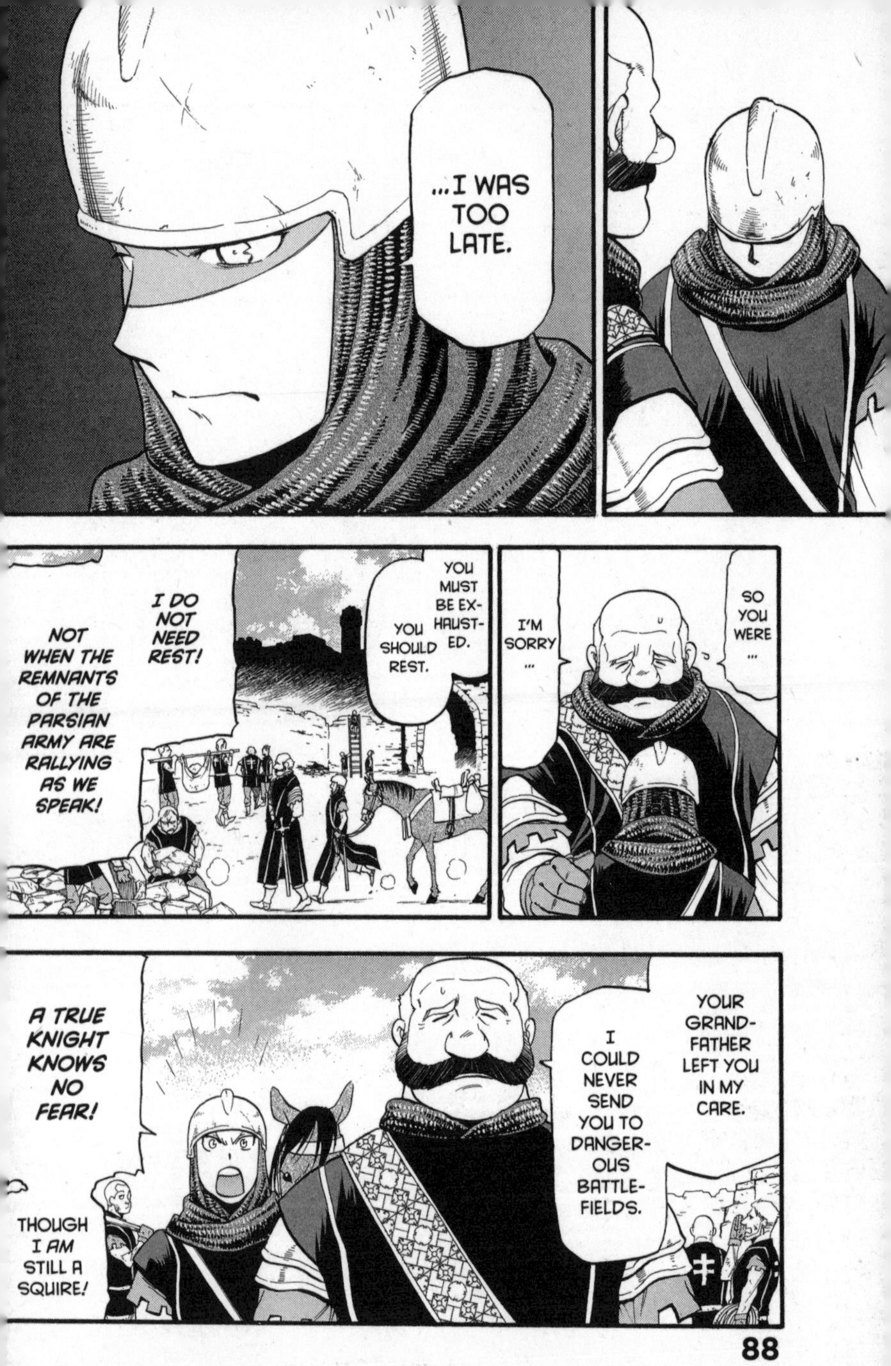
...I WAS TOO LATE.
SO YOU WERE ...
I'M SORRY ...
YOU MUST BE EXHAUSTED.
YOU SHOULD REST.
I DO NOT NEED REST!
NOT WHEN THE REMNANTS OF THE PARSIAN ARMY ARE RALLYING AS WE SPEAK!
YOUR GRANDFATHER LEFT YOU IN MY CARE.
I COULD NEVER SEND YOU TO DANGEROUS BATTLEFIELDS.
A TRUE KNIGHT KNOWS NO FEAR!
THOUGH I AM STILL A SQUIRE!

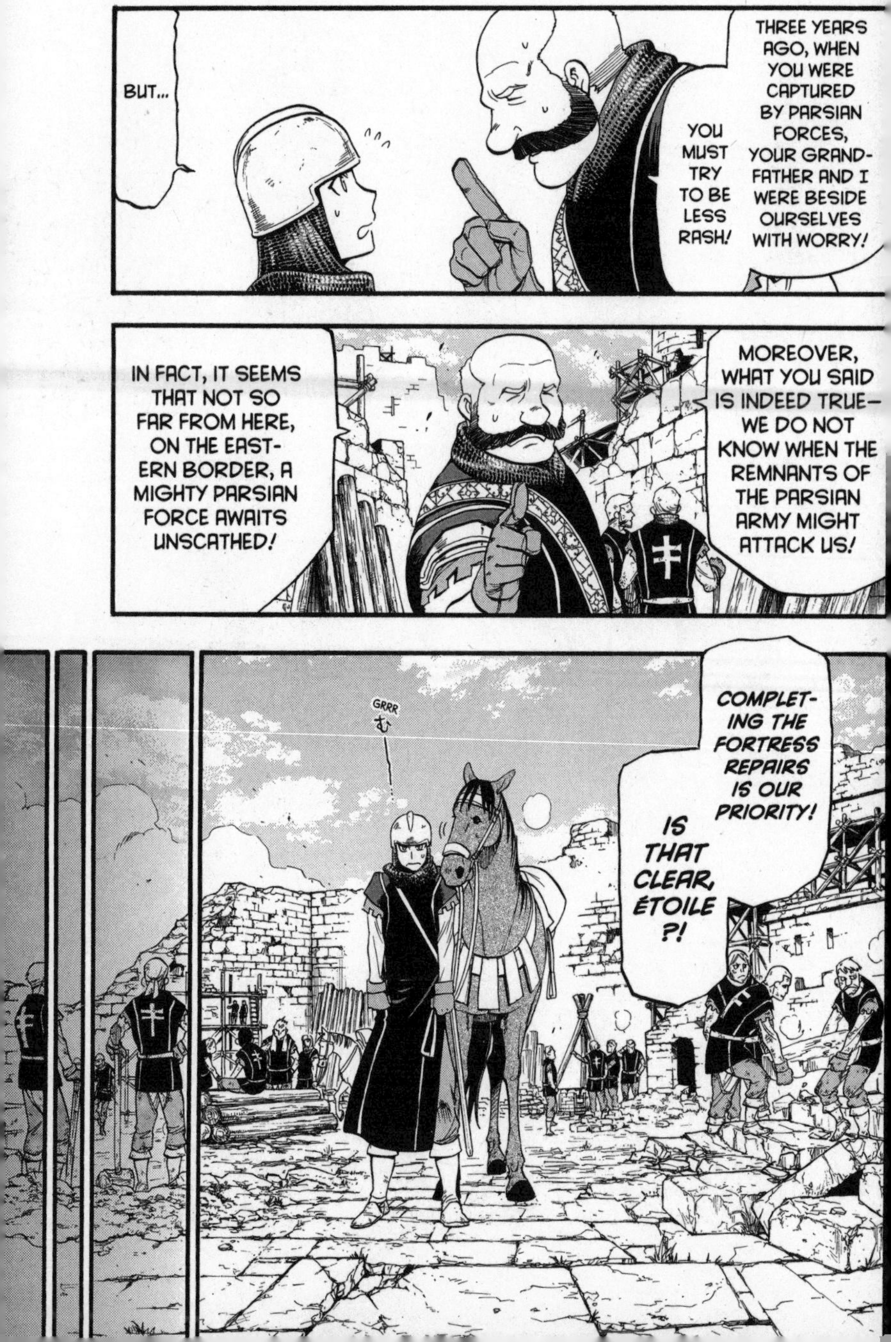
THREE YEARS AGO, WHEN YOU WERE CAPTURED BY PARSIAN FORCES, YOUR GRAND-FATHER AND I WERE BESIDE OURSELVES WITH WORRY!
YOU MUST TRY TO BE LESS RASH!
BUT...
MOREOVER, WHAT YOU SAID IS INDEED TRUE—WE DO NOT KNOW WHEN THE REMNANTS OF THE PARSIAN ARMY MIGHT ATTACK US!
IN FACT, IT SEEMS THAT NOT SO FAR FROM HERE, ON THE EAST-ERN BORDER, A MIGHTY PARSIAN FORCE AWAITS UNSCATHED!
COMPLET-ING THE FORTRESS REPAIRS IS OUR PRIORITY!
IS THAT CLEAR, ÉTOILE ?!
GRRR
む

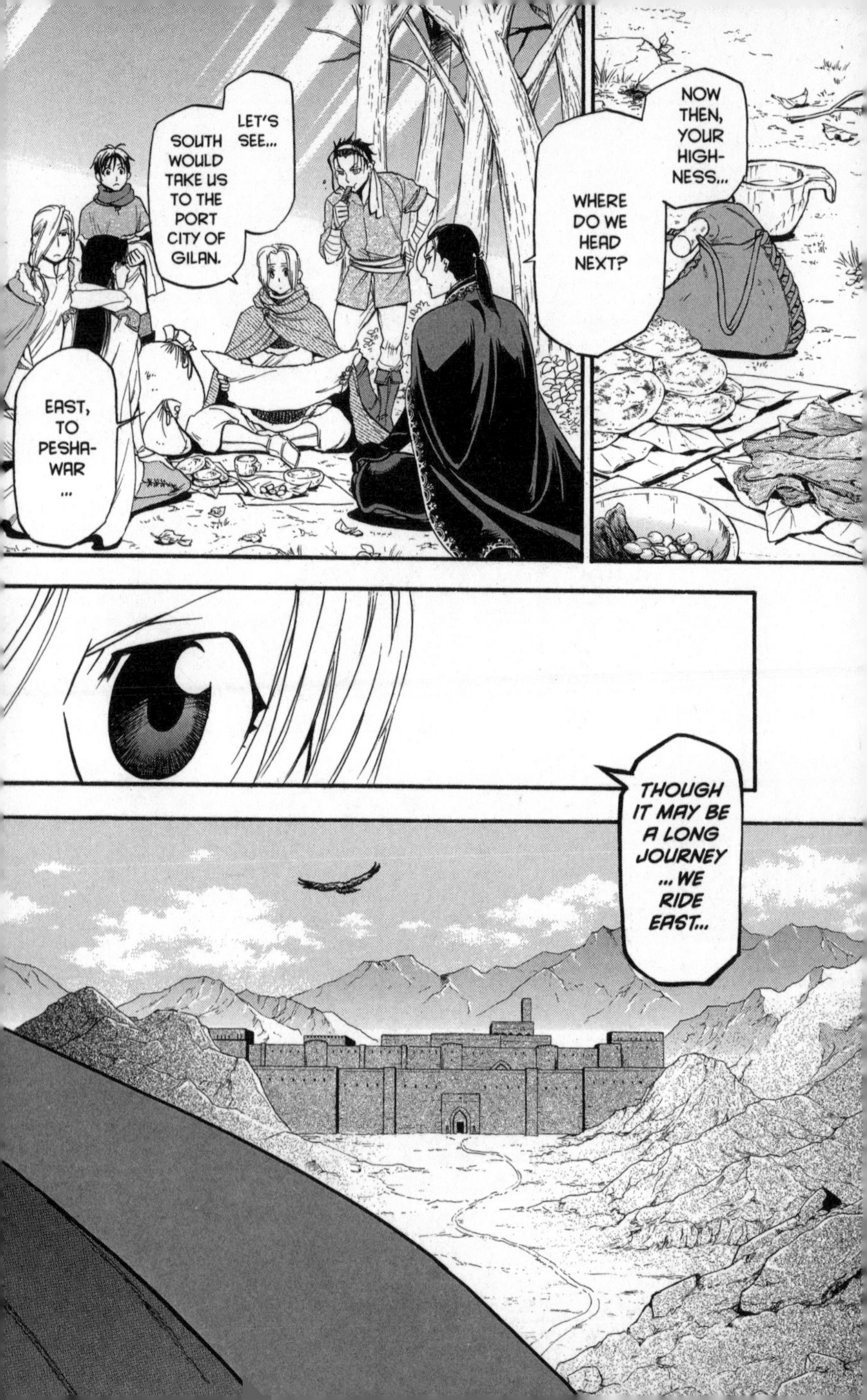
NOW THEN, YOUR HIGHNESS...
WHERE DO WE HEAD NEXT?
LET'S SEE... SOUTH WOULD TAKE US TO THE PORT CITY OF GILAN.
EAST, TO PESHAWAR ...
THOUGH IT MAY BE A LONG JOURNEY ... WE RIDE EAST...

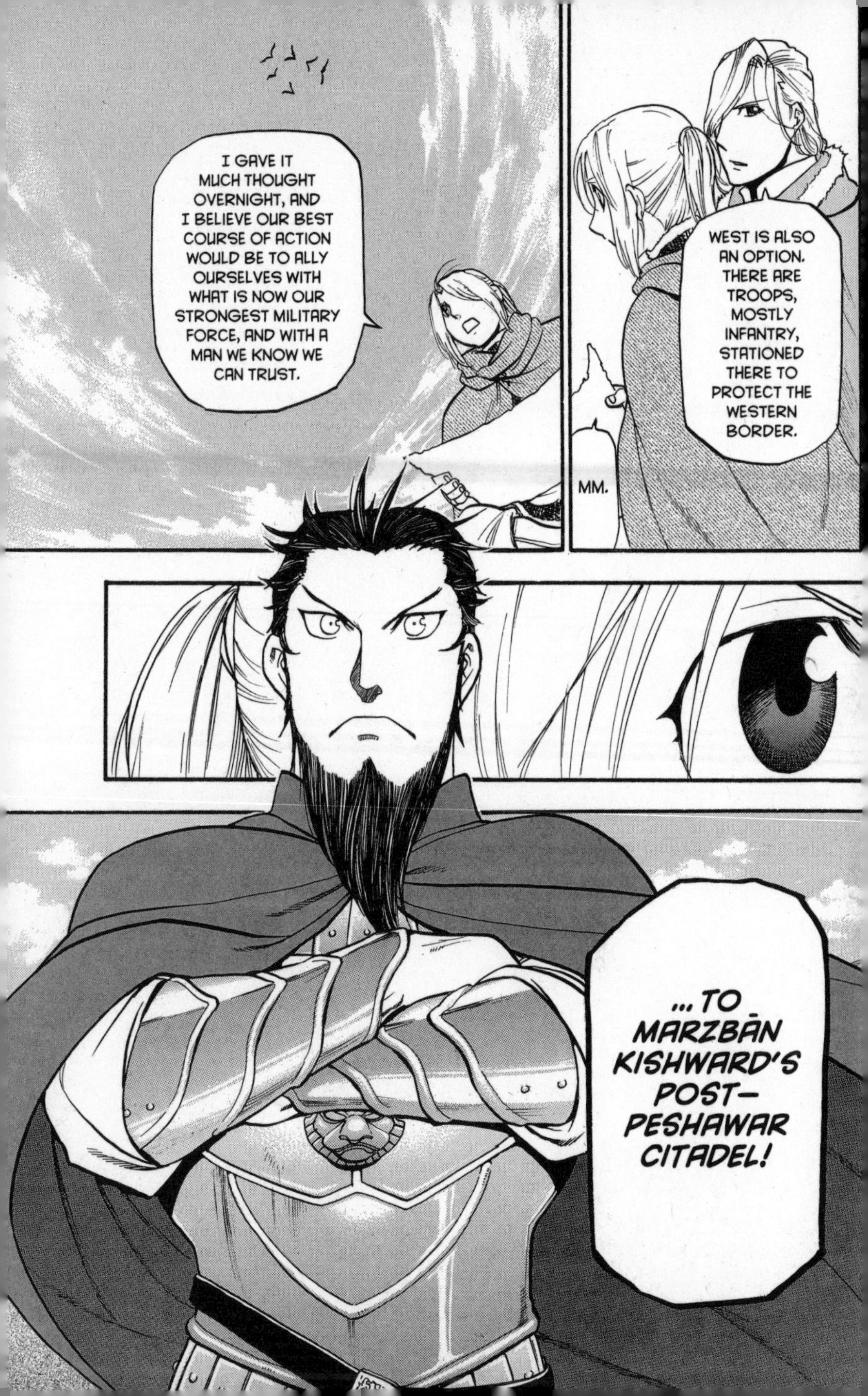
WEST IS ALSO AN OPTION. THERE ARE TROOPS, MOSTLY INFANTRY, STATIONED THERE TO PROTECT THE WESTERN BORDER.
MM.
I GAVE IT MUCH THOUGHT OVERNIGHT, AND I BELIEVE OUR BEST COURSE OF ACTION WOULD BE TO ALLY OURSELVES WITH WHAT IS NOW OUR STRONGEST MILITARY FORCE, AND WITH A MAN WE KNOW WE CAN TRUST.
...TO MARZBĀN KISHWARD'S POST— PESHAWAR CITADEL!

THE HEROIC LEGEND OF
ARSLAN

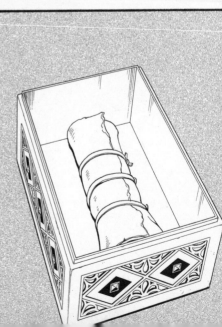

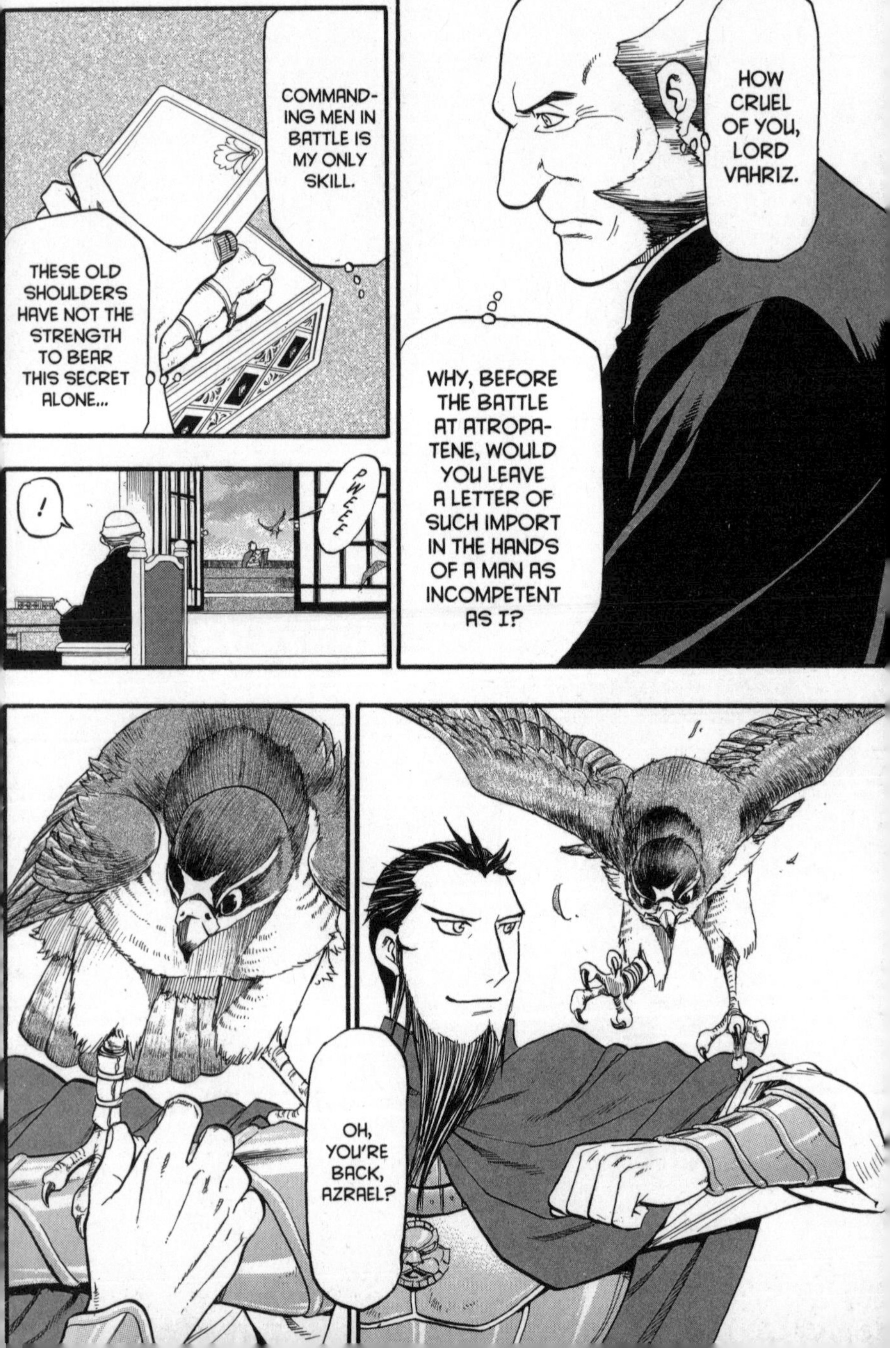
HOW CRUEL OF YOU, LORD VAHRIZ.
WHY, BEFORE THE BATTLE AT ATROPA-TENE, WOULD YOU LEAVE A LETTER OF SUCH IMPORT IN THE HANDS OF A MAN AS INCOMPETENT AS I?
COMMAND-ING MEN IN BATTLE IS MY ONLY SKILL.
THESE OLD SHOULDERS HAVE NOT THE STRENGTH TO BEAR THIS SECRET ALONE...
PWEEEE
!
OH, YOU'RE BACK, AZRAEL?

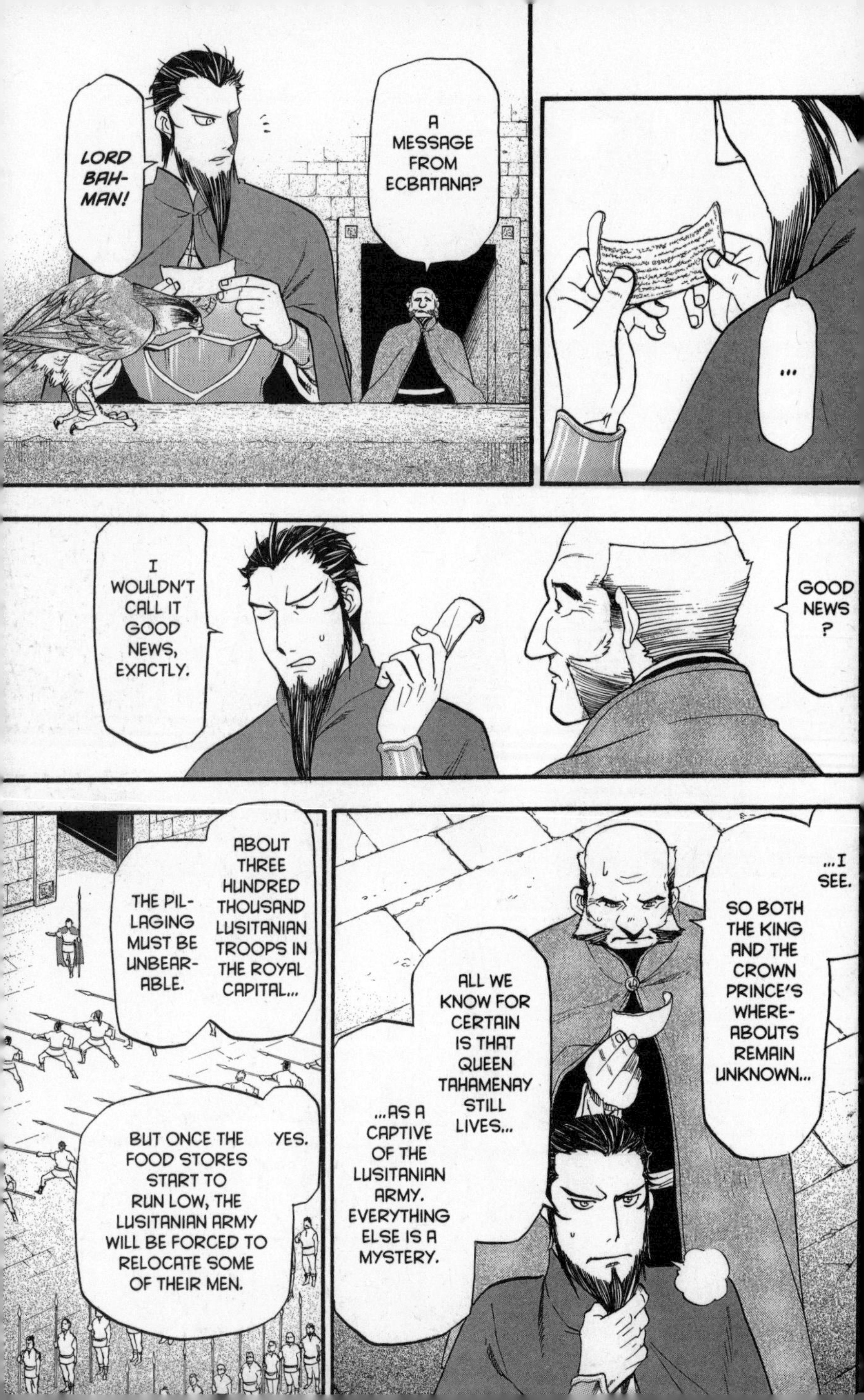
...
A MESSAGE FROM ECBATANA?
LORD BAH-MAN!
GOOD NEWS?
I WOULDN'T CALL IT GOOD NEWS, EXACTLY.
...I SEE.
SO BOTH THE KING AND THE CROWN PRINCE'S WHERE-ABOUTS REMAIN UNKNOWN...
ALL WE KNOW FOR CERTAIN IS THAT QUEEN TAHAMENAY STILL LIVES...
...AS A CAPTIVE OF THE LUSITANIAN ARMY. EVERYTHING ELSE IS A MYSTERY.
ABOUT THREE HUNDRED THOUSAND LUSITANIAN TROOPS IN THE ROYAL CAPITAL...
THE PIL-LAGING MUST BE UNBEAR-ABLE.
YES.
BUT ONCE THE FOOD STORES START TO RUN LOW, THE LUSITANIAN ARMY WILL BE FORCED TO RELOCATE SOME OF THEIR MEN.

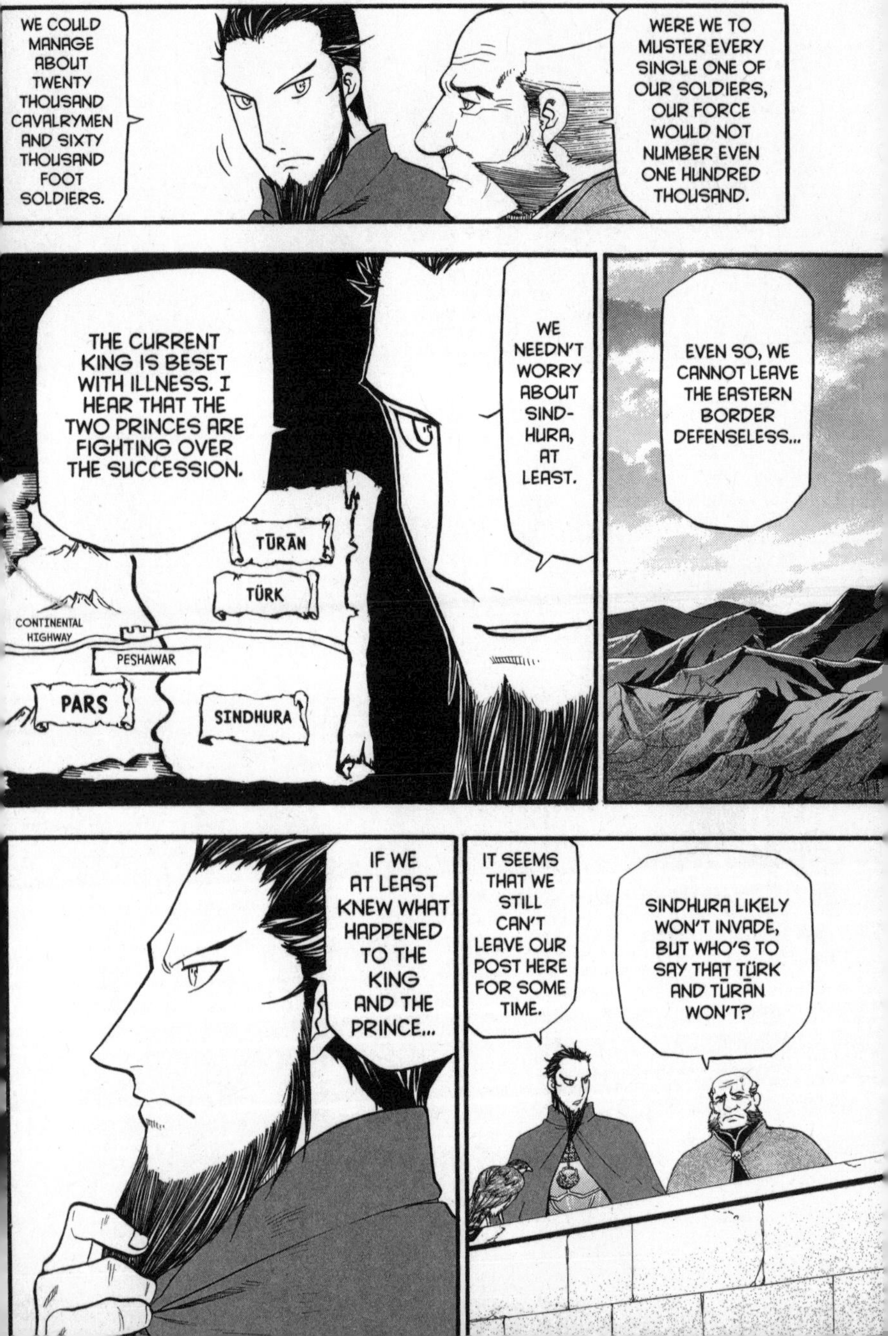
WERE WE TO MUSTER EVERY SINGLE ONE OF OUR SOLDIERS, OUR FORCE WOULD NOT NUMBER EVEN ONE HUNDRED THOUSAND.
WE COULD MANAGE ABOUT TWENTY THOUSAND CAVALRYMEN AND SIXTY THOUSAND FOOT SOLDIERS.
EVEN SO, WE CANNOT LEAVE THE EASTERN BORDER DEFENSELESS...
WE NEEDN'T WORRY ABOUT SINDHURA, AT LEAST.
THE CURRENT KING IS BESET WITH ILLNESS. I HEAR THAT THE TWO PRINCES ARE FIGHTING OVER THE SUCCESSION.
TŪRĀN
TÜRK
CONTINENTAL HIGHWAY
PESHAWAR
PARS
SINDHURA
SINDHURA LIKELY WON'T INVADE, BUT WHO'S TO SAY THAT TÜRK AND TŪRĀN WON'T?
IT SEEMS THAT WE STILL CAN'T LEAVE OUR POST HERE FOR SOME TIME.
IF WE AT LEAST KNEW WHAT HAPPENED TO THE KING AND THE PRINCE...

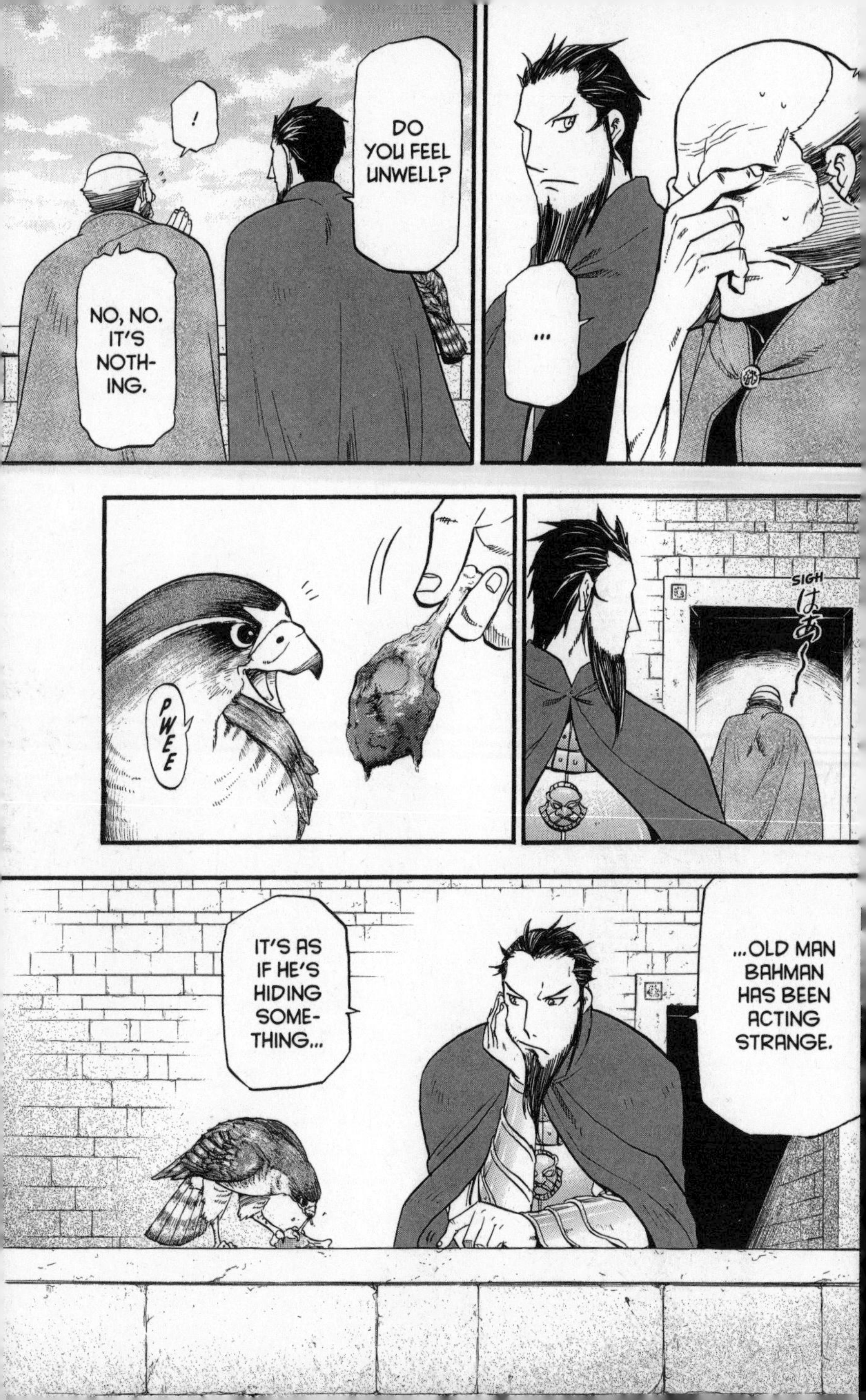
...
DO YOU FEEL UNWELL?
!
NO, NO. IT'S NOTH-ING.
SIGH はあ~
PWEE
...OLD MAN BAHMAN HAS BEEN ACTING STRANGE.
IT'S AS IF HE'S HIDING SOME-THING...

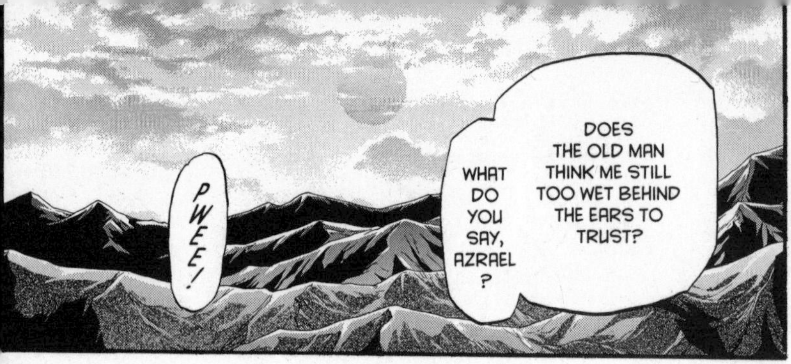
DOES THE OLD MAN THINK ME STILL TOO WET BEHIND THE EARS TO TRUST?
WHAT DO YOU SAY, AZRAEL?
PWEE!

Chapter 24: Hand of the Devil

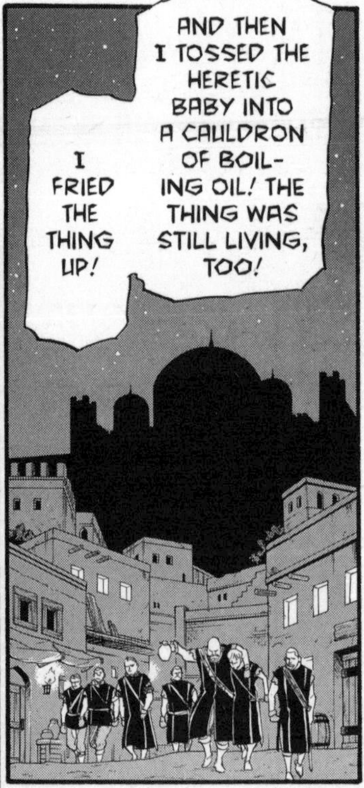
AND THEN I TOSSED THE HERETIC BABY INTO A CAULDRON OF BOIL-ING OIL! THE THING WAS STILL LIVING, TOO!
I FRIED THE THING UP!

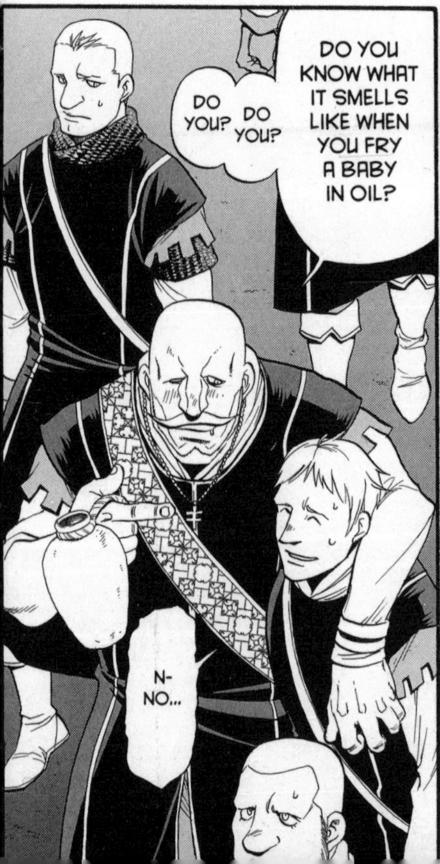
DO YOU KNOW WHAT IT SMELLS LIKE WHEN YOU FRY A BABY IN OIL?
DO YOU? DO YOU?
N-NO...

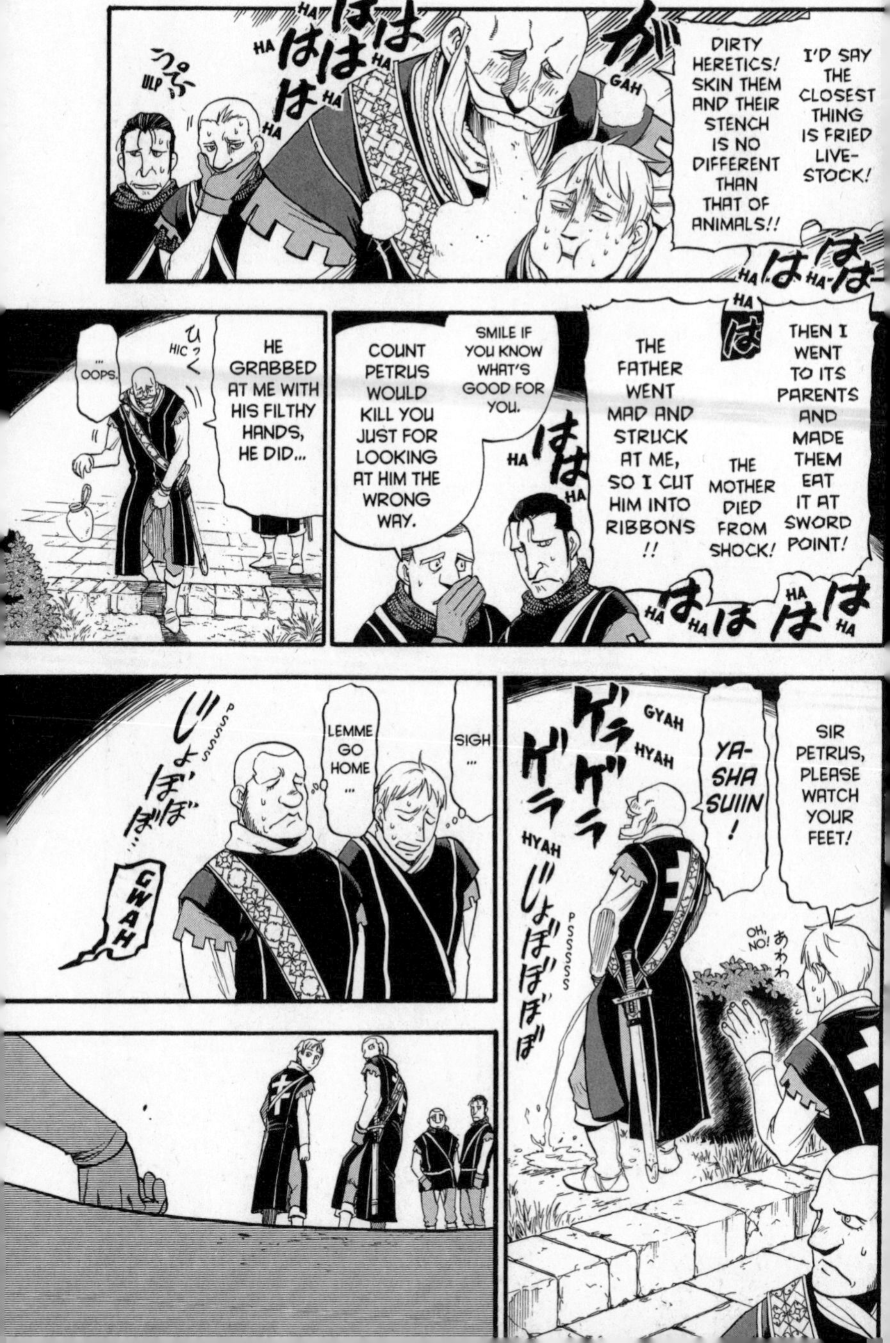
I'D SAY THE CLOSEST THING IS FRIED LIVE-STOCK!
DIRTY HERETICS! SKIN THEM AND THEIR STENCH IS NO DIFFERENT THAN THAT OF ANIMALS!!
が GAH
ははははは HA HA HA HA HA
うっぷ ULP
ははは HA HA- HA
THEN I WENT TO ITS PARENTS AND MADE THEM EAT IT AT SWORD POINT!
THE MOTHER DIED FROM SHOCK!
THE FATHER WENT MAD AND STRUCK AT ME, SO I CUT HIM INTO RIBBONS!!
ははは HA HA HA HA HA
SMILE IF YOU KNOW WHAT'S GOOD FOR YOU.
はは HA HA
COUNT PETRUS WOULD KILL YOU JUST FOR LOOKING AT HIM THE WRONG WAY.
HE GRABBED AT ME WITH HIS FILTHY HANDS, HE DID...
ひっく HIC
... OOPS.
SIR PETRUS, PLEASE WATCH YOUR FEET!
YA-SHA SUIIN!
ゲラゲラゲラ GYAH HYAH HYAH
じょぼぼぼぼ PSSSSS
OH, NO! あわわ
SIGH ...
LEMME GO HOME ...
じょぼぼぼ… PSSSSS
GWAH

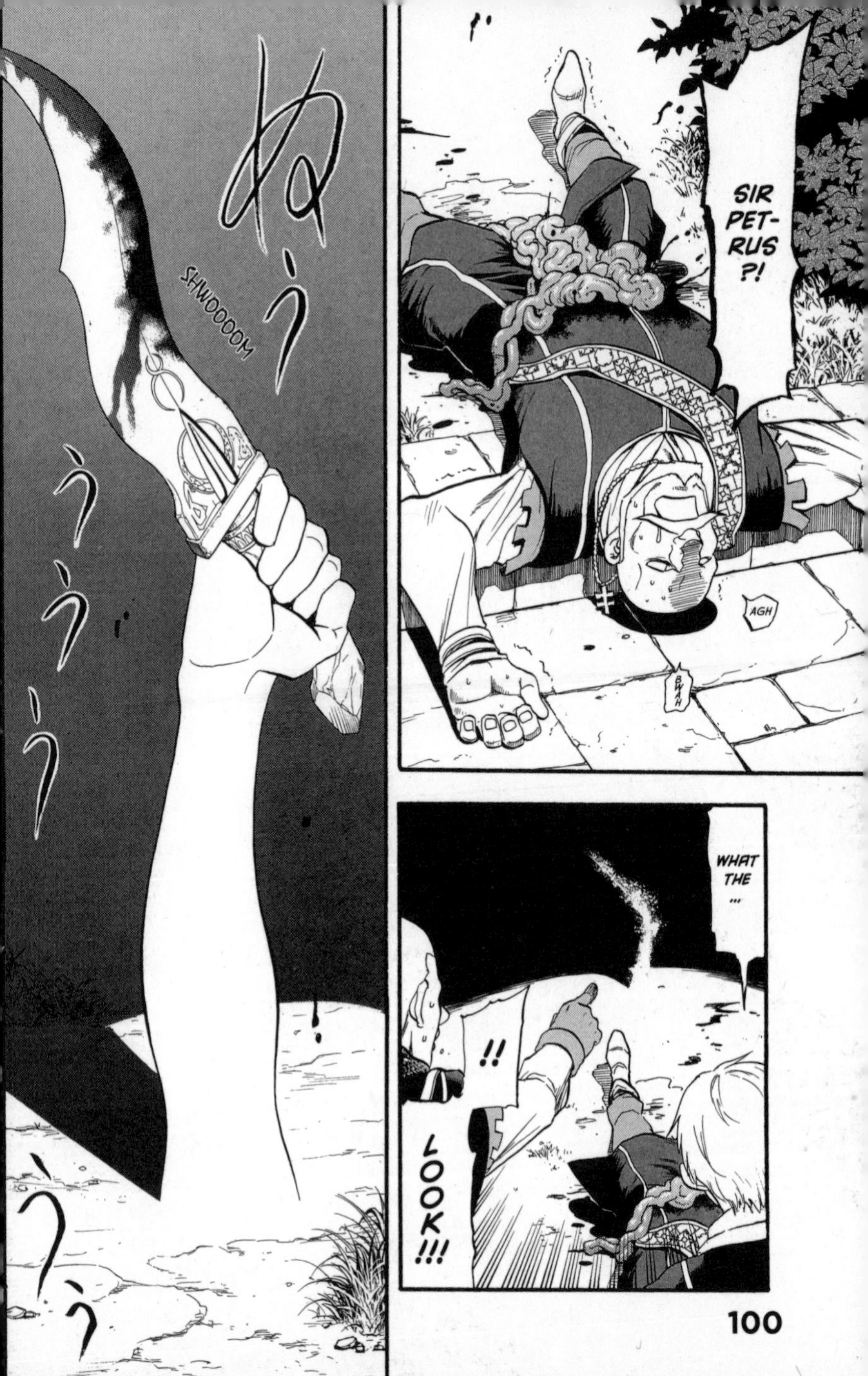
SIR PETRUS?!
AGH
BWAH
WHAT THE ...
!!
LOOK!!!
SHWOOOOM

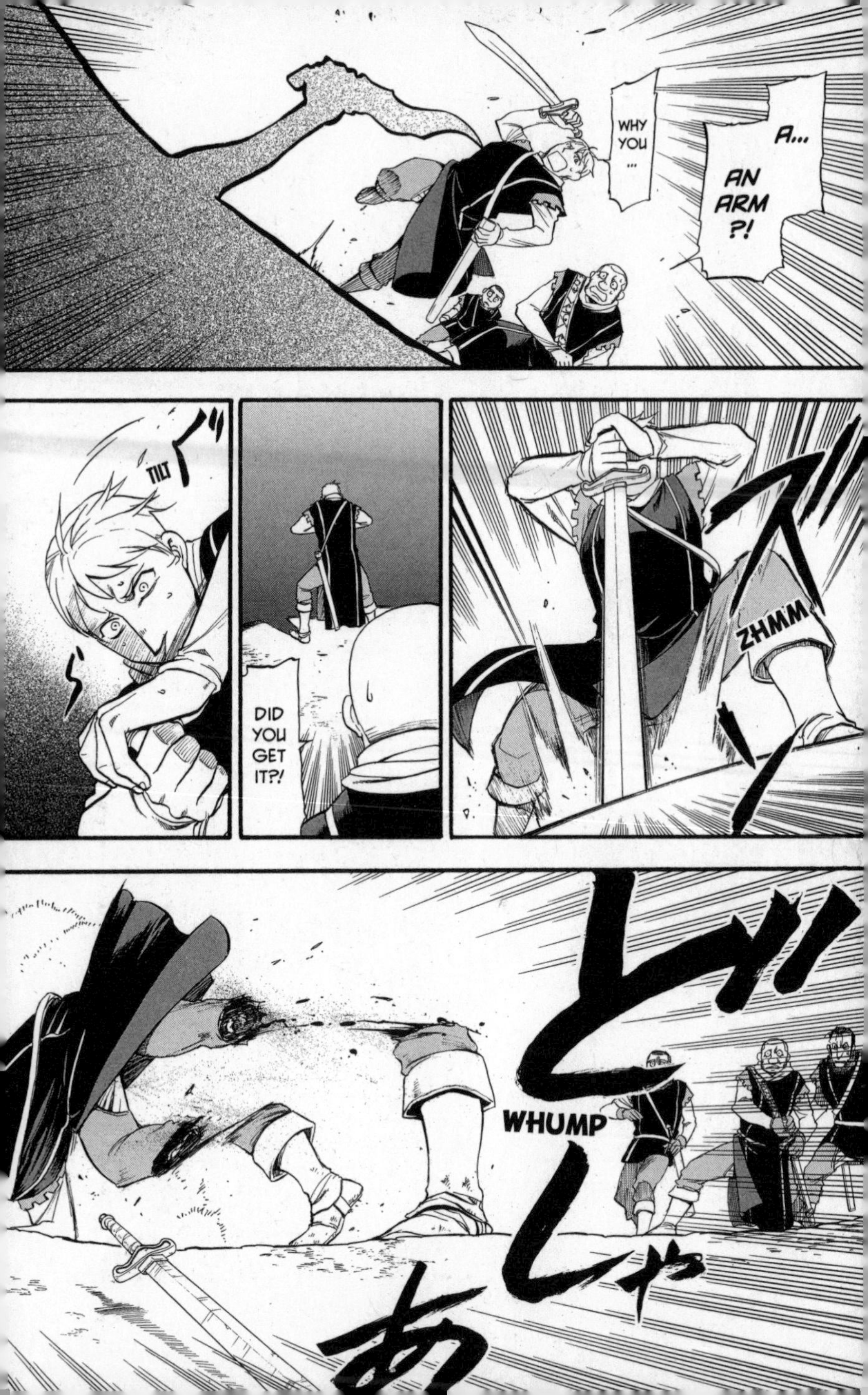
A... AN ARM?!
WHY YOU ...
ZHMM
DID YOU GET IT?!
TILT
WHUMP

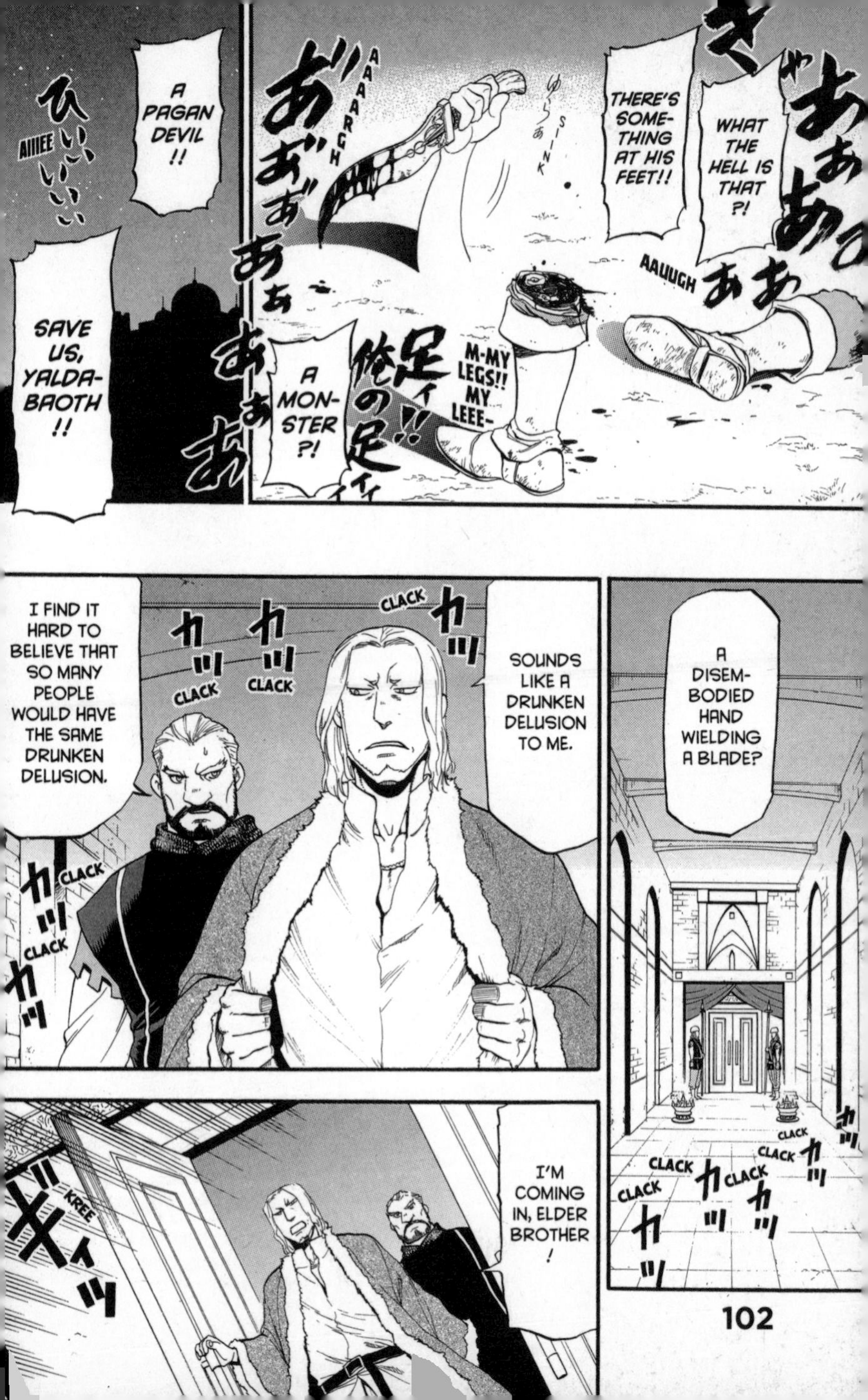
AAUGH
WHAT THE HELL IS THAT?!
THERE'S SOMETHING AT HIS FEET!!
SIIINK
M-MY LEGS!! MY LEEE-
A MONSTER?!
AAAARGH
A PAGAN DEVIL!!
AIIIEE
SAVE US, YALDABAOTH!!
A DISEMBODIED HAND WIELDING A BLADE?
CLACK
CLACK
CLACK
CLACK
CLACK
SOUNDS LIKE A DRUNKEN DELUSION TO ME.
CLACK
CLACK
I FIND IT HARD TO BELIEVE THAT SO MANY PEOPLE WOULD HAVE THE SAME DRUNKEN DELUSION.
CLACK
CLACK
I'M COMING IN, ELDER BROTHER!
KREE

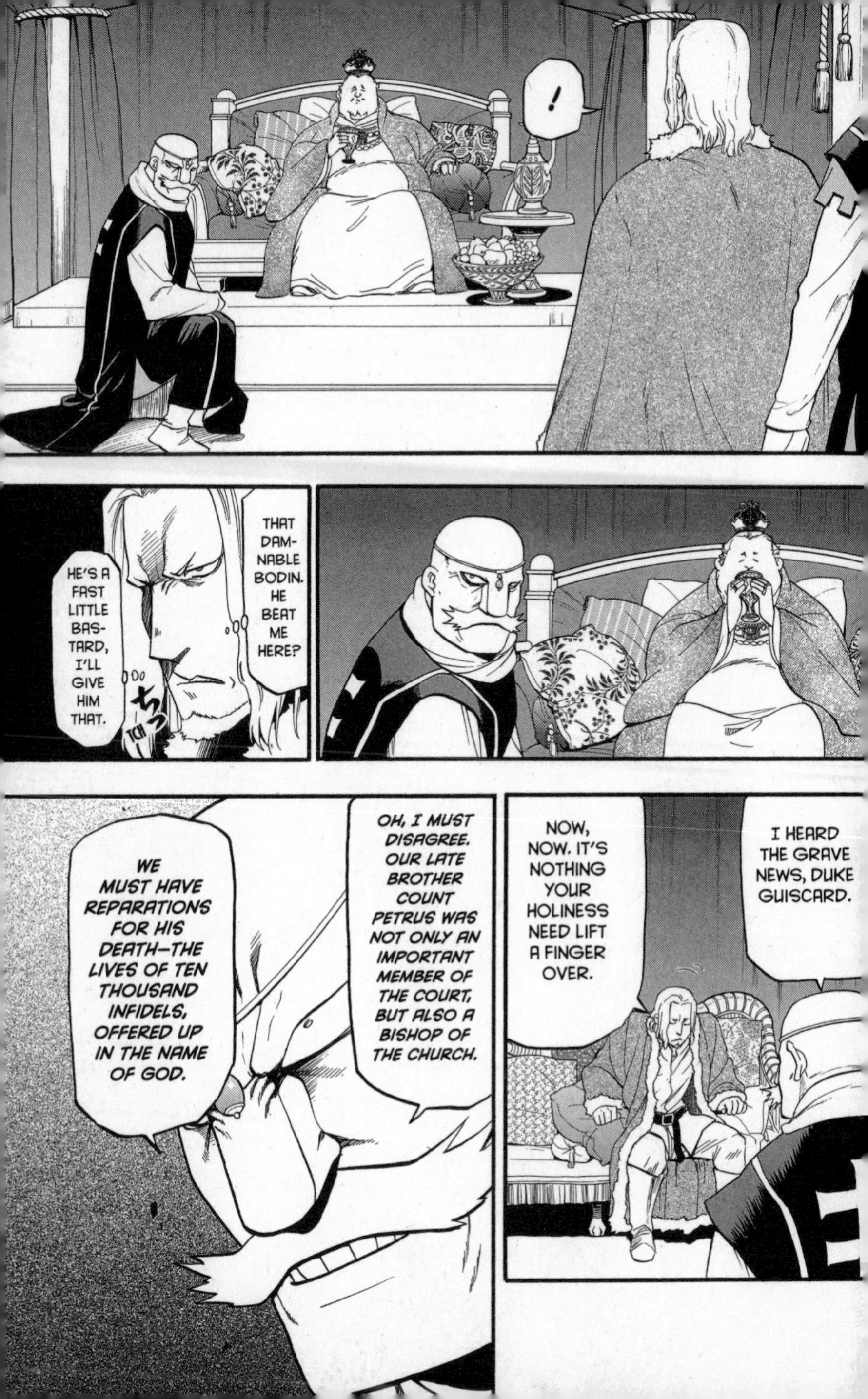
!
THAT DAMNABLE BODIN. HE BEAT ME HERE?
HE'S A FAST LITTLE BASTARD, I'LL GIVE HIM THAT.
TCH
I HEARD THE GRAVE NEWS, DUKE GUISCARD.
NOW, NOW. IT'S NOTHING YOUR HOLINESS NEED LIFT A FINGER OVER.
OH, I MUST DISAGREE. OUR LATE BROTHER COUNT PETRUS WAS NOT ONLY AN IMPORTANT MEMBER OF THE COURT, BUT ALSO A BISHOP OF THE CHURCH.
WE MUST HAVE REPARATIONS FOR HIS DEATH—THE LIVES OF TEN THOUSAND INFIDELS, OFFERED UP IN THE NAME OF GOD.

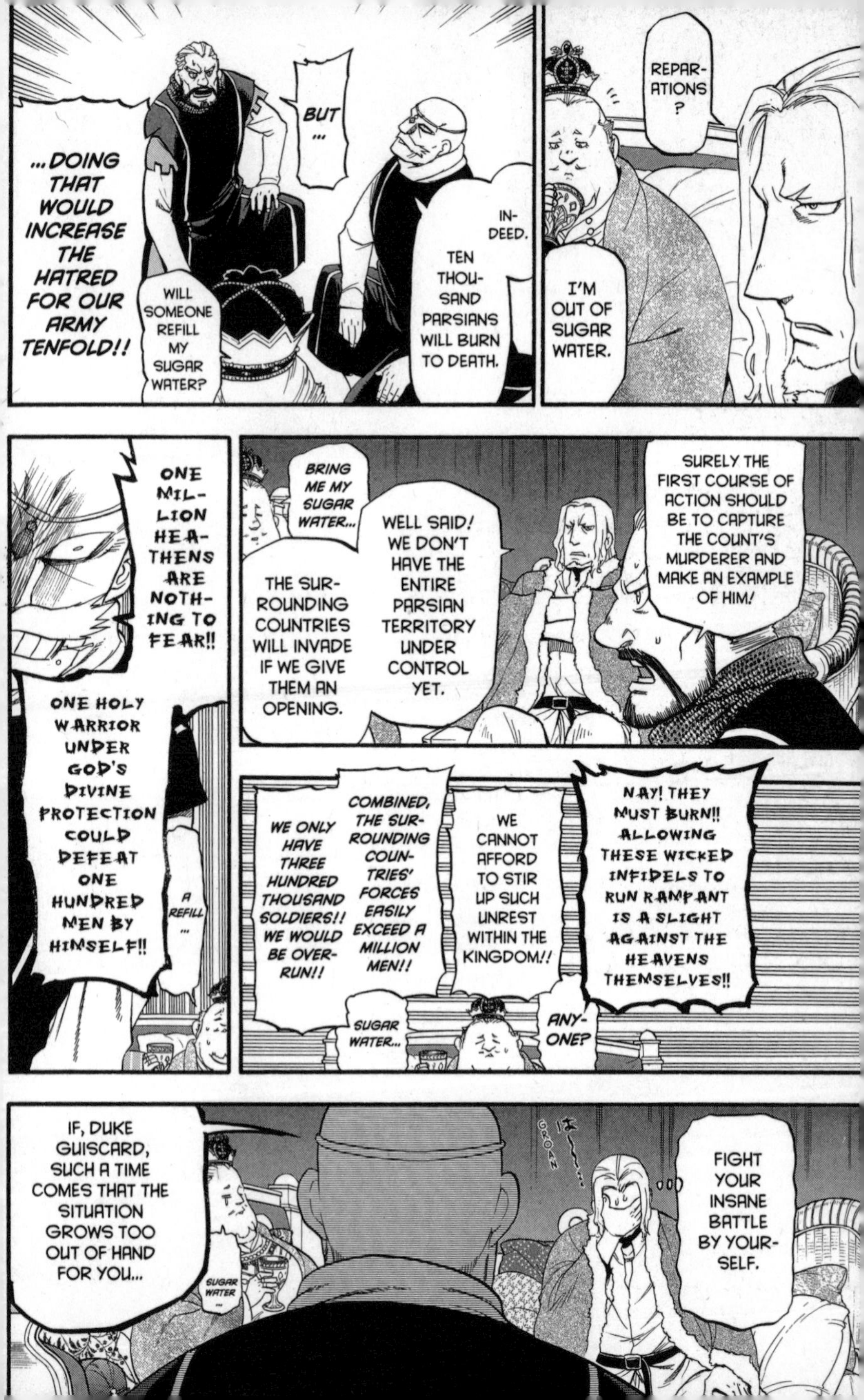
REPARATIONS?
I'M OUT OF SUGAR WATER.
INDEED. TEN THOUSAND PARSIANS WILL BURN TO DEATH.
BUT...
...DOING THAT WOULD INCREASE THE HATRED FOR OUR ARMY TENFOLD!!
WILL SOMEONE REFILL MY SUGAR WATER?
SURELY THE FIRST COURSE OF ACTION SHOULD BE TO CAPTURE THE COUNT'S MURDERER AND MAKE AN EXAMPLE OF HIM!
WELL SAID! WE DON'T HAVE THE ENTIRE PARSIAN TERRITORY UNDER CONTROL YET.
BRING ME MY SUGAR WATER...
THE SURROUNDING COUNTRIES WILL INVADE IF WE GIVE THEM AN OPENING.
NAY! THEY MUST BURN!! ALLOWING THESE WICKED INFIDELS TO RUN RAMPANT IS A SLIGHT AGAINST THE HEAVENS THEMSELVES!!
ANYONE?
WE CANNOT AFFORD TO STIR UP SUCH UNREST WITHIN THE KINGDOM!!
COMBINED, THE SURROUNDING COUNTRIES' FORCES EASILY EXCEED A MILLION MEN!!
WE ONLY HAVE THREE HUNDRED THOUSAND SOLDIERS!! WE WOULD BE OVERRUN!!
SUGAR WATER...
ONE MILLION HEATHENS ARE NOTHING TO FEAR!!
ONE HOLY WARRIOR UNDER GOD'S DIVINE PROTECTION COULD DEFEAT ONE HUNDRED MEN BY HIMSELF!!
A REFILL...
FIGHT YOUR INSANE BATTLE BY YOURSELF.
GROAN
SUGAR WATER...
IF, DUKE GUISCARD, SUCH A TIME COMES THAT THE SITUATION GROWS TOO OUT OF HAND FOR YOU...

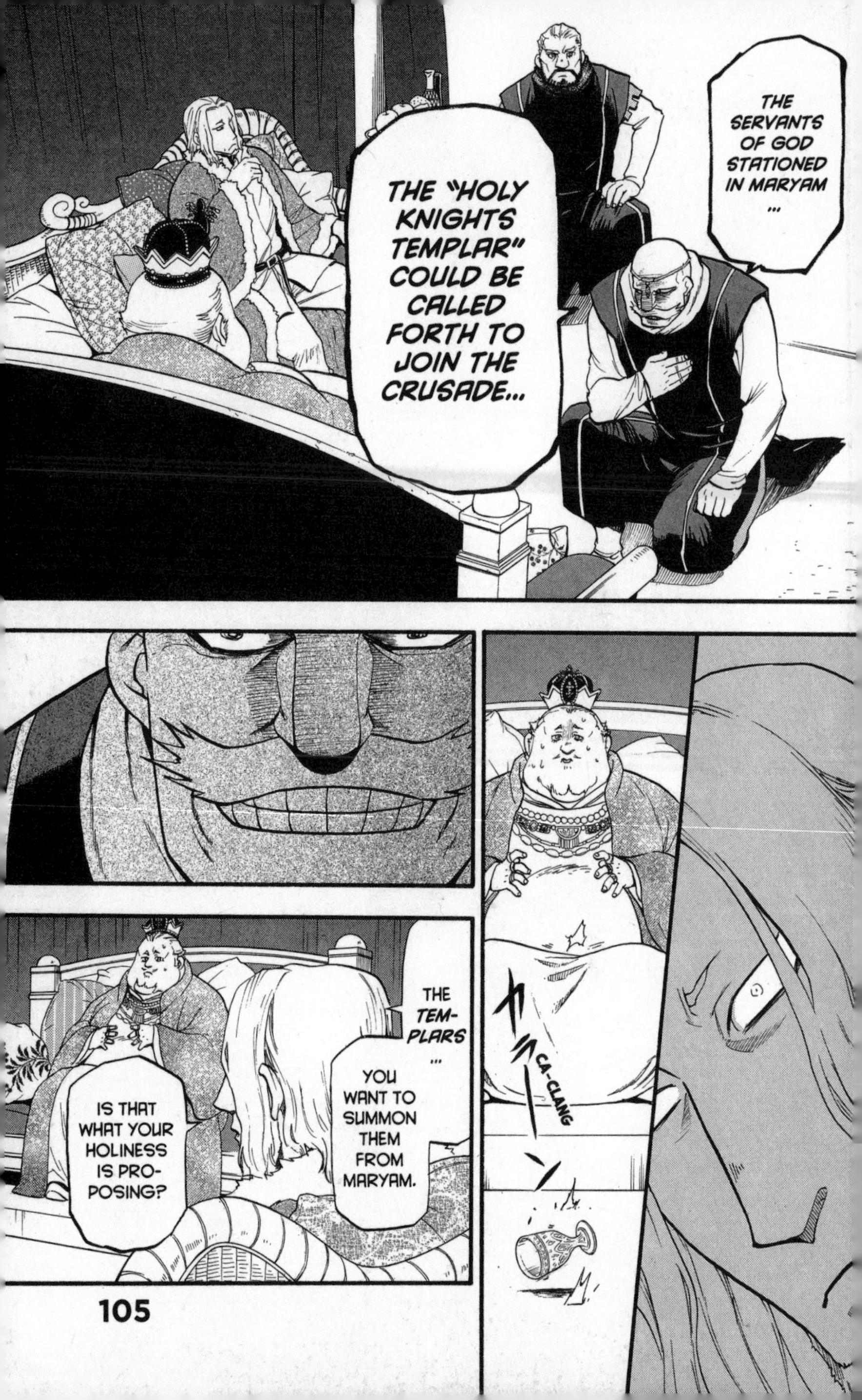
THE SERVANTS OF GOD STATIONED IN MARYAM ...
THE "HOLY KNIGHTS TEMPLAR" COULD BE CALLED FORTH TO JOIN THE CRUSADE...
CA-CLANG
THE TEMPLARS ...
YOU WANT TO SUMMON THEM FROM MARYAM.
IS THAT WHAT YOUR HOLINESS IS PROPOSING?

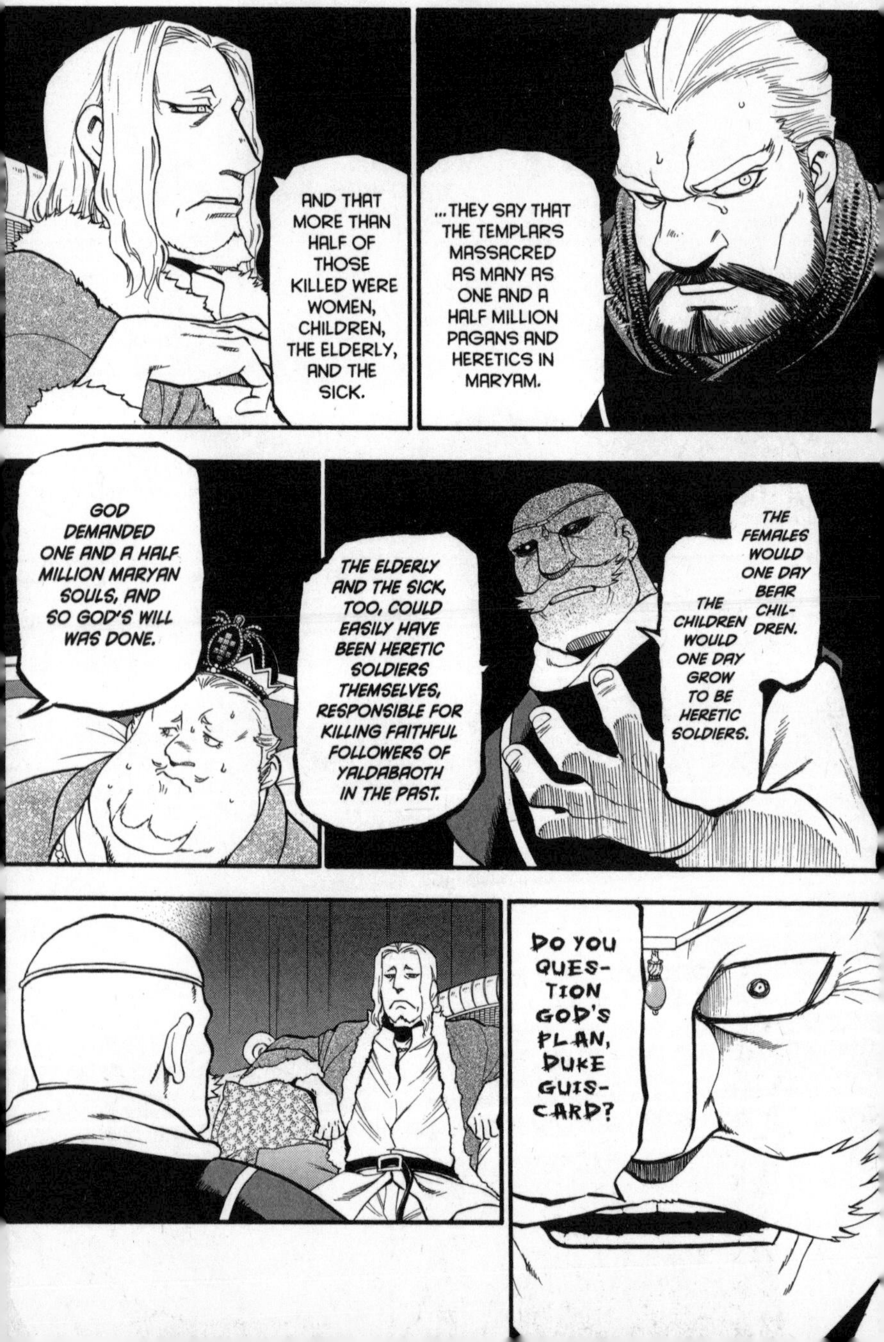
...THEY SAY THAT THE TEMPLARS MASSACRED AS MANY AS ONE AND A HALF MILLION PAGANS AND HERETICS IN MARYAM.
AND THAT MORE THAN HALF OF THOSE KILLED WERE WOMEN, CHILDREN, THE ELDERLY, AND THE SICK.
THE FEMALES WOULD ONE DAY BEAR CHIL-DREN.
THE CHILDREN WOULD ONE DAY GROW TO BE HERETIC SOLDIERS.
THE ELDERLY AND THE SICK, TOO, COULD EASILY HAVE BEEN HERETIC SOLDIERS THEMSELVES, RESPONSIBLE FOR KILLING FAITHFUL FOLLOWERS OF YALDABAOTH IN THE PAST.
GOD DEMANDED ONE AND A HALF MILLION MARYAN SOULS, AND SO GOD'S WILL WAS DONE.
DO YOU QUES-TION GOD'S PLAN, DUKE GUIS-CARD?

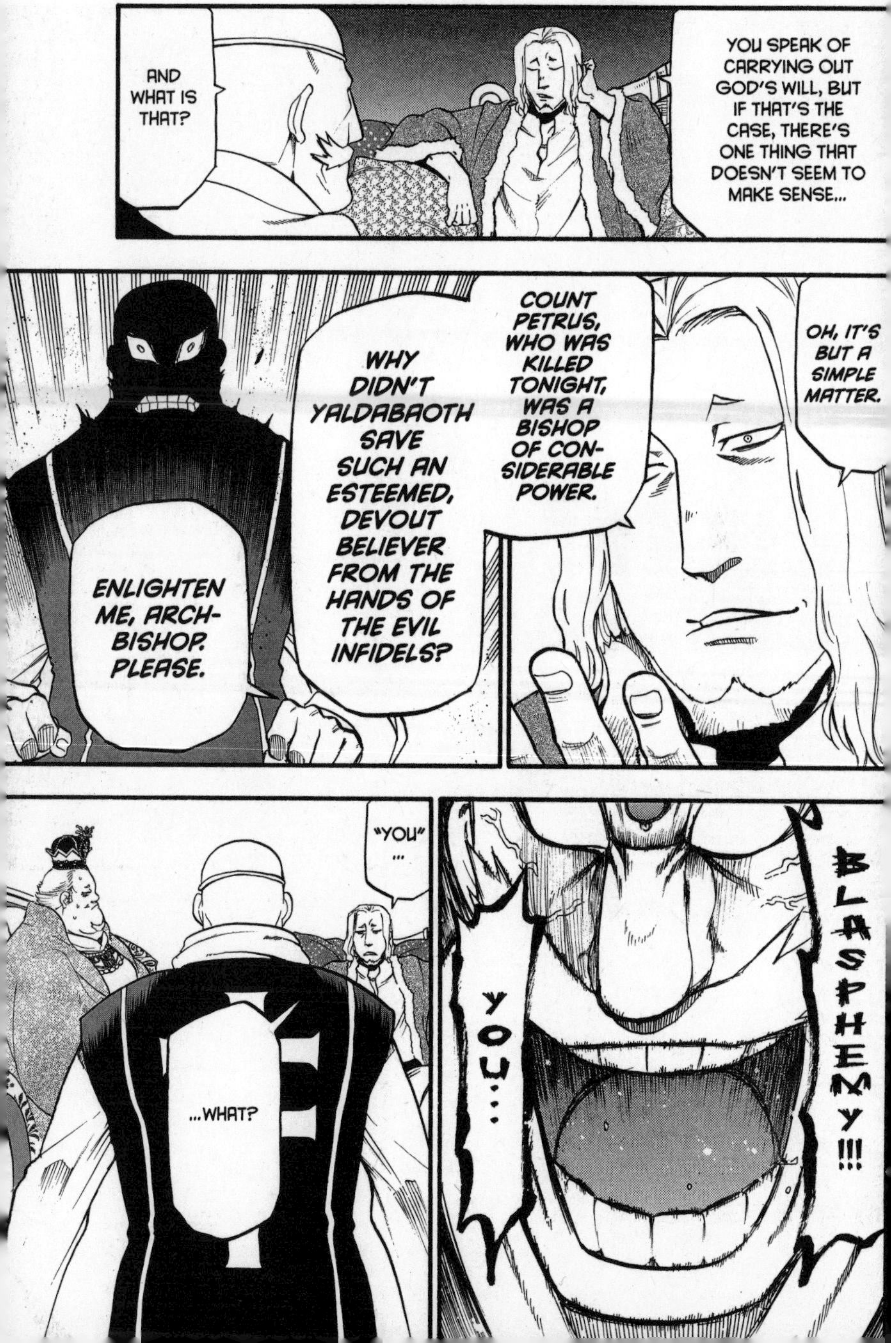
YOU SPEAK OF CARRYING OUT GOD'S WILL, BUT IF THAT'S THE CASE, THERE'S ONE THING THAT DOESN'T SEEM TO MAKE SENSE...
AND WHAT IS THAT?
OH, IT'S BUT A SIMPLE MATTER.
COUNT PETRUS, WHO WAS KILLED TONIGHT, WAS A BISHOP OF CONSIDERABLE POWER.
WHY DIDN'T YALDABAOTH SAVE SUCH AN ESTEEMED, DEVOUT BELIEVER FROM THE HANDS OF THE EVIL INFIDELS?
ENLIGHTEN ME, ARCHBISHOP. PLEASE.
BLASPHEMY!!!
YOU...
"YOU" ...
...WHAT?

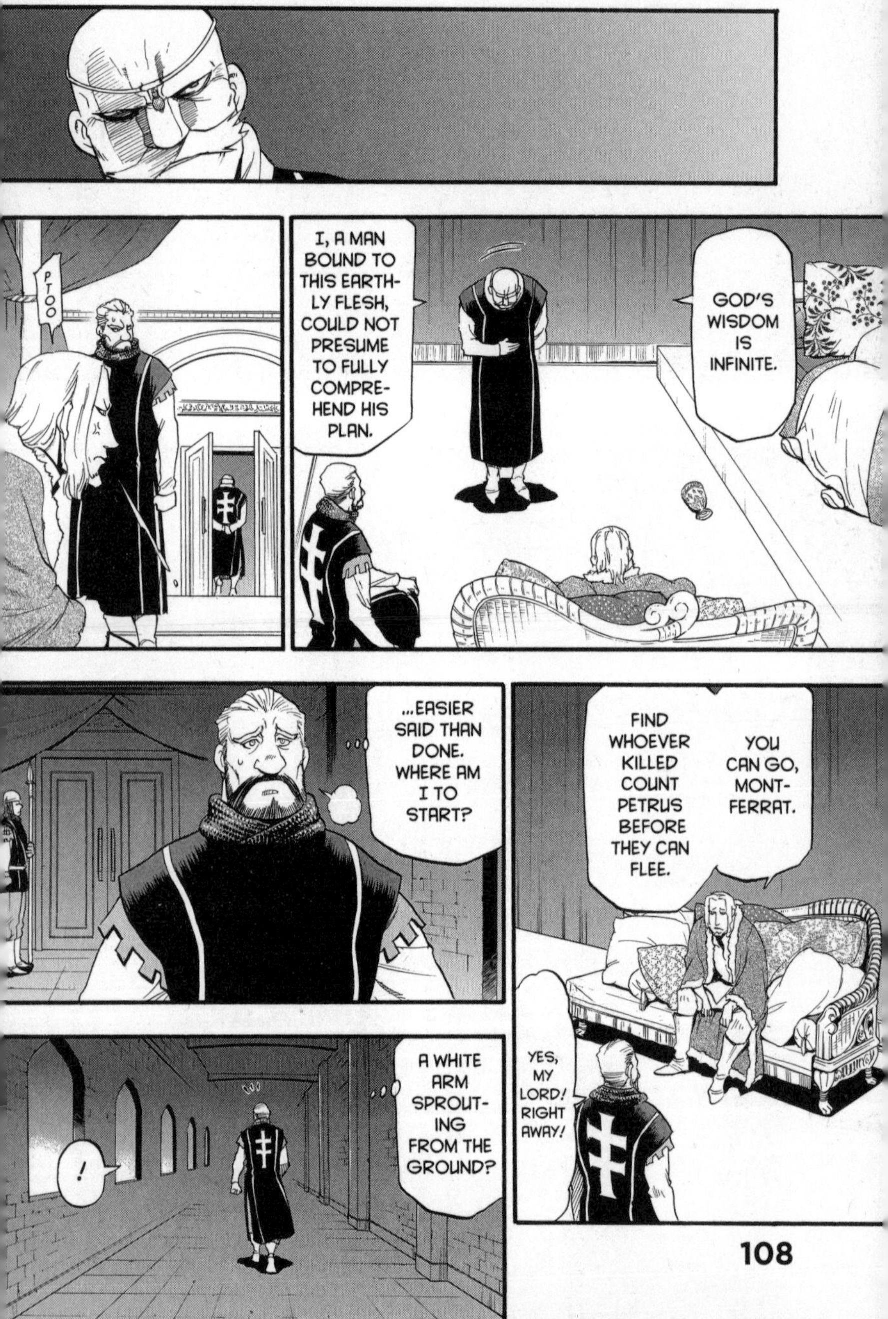
GOD'S WISDOM IS INFINITE.
I, A MAN BOUND TO THIS EARTHLY FLESH, COULD NOT PRESUME TO FULLY COMPREHEND HIS PLAN.
PTOO
YOU CAN GO, MONTFERRAT.
FIND WHOEVER KILLED COUNT PETRUS BEFORE THEY CAN FLEE.
YES, MY LORD! RIGHT AWAY!
...EASIER SAID THAN DONE. WHERE AM I TO START?
A WHITE ARM SPROUTING FROM THE GROUND?
!

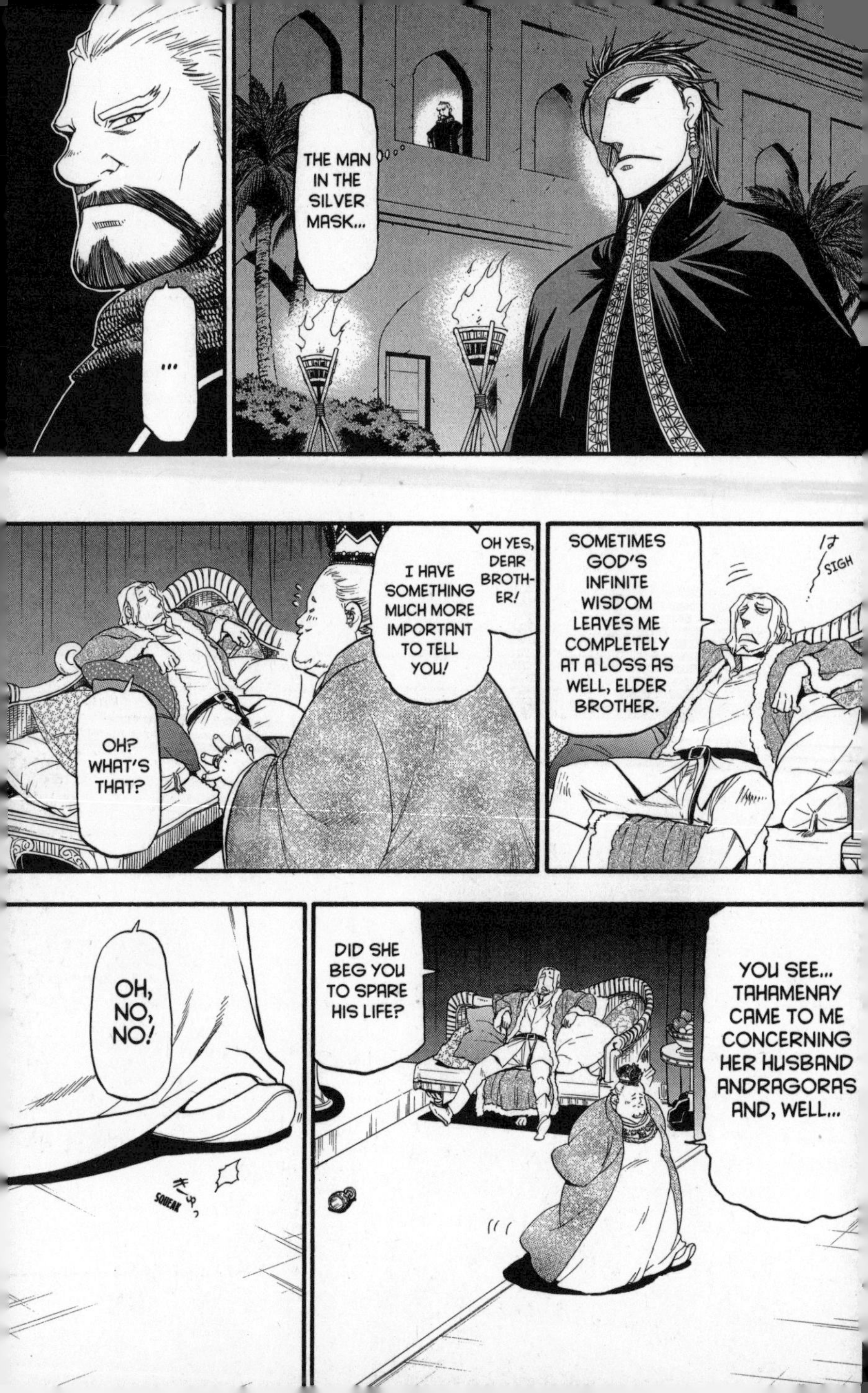
THE MAN IN THE SILVER MASK...
...
SIGH
SOMETIMES GOD'S INFINITE WISDOM LEAVES ME COMPLETELY AT A LOSS AS WELL, ELDER BROTHER.
OH YES, DEAR BROTH-ER!
I HAVE SOMETHING MUCH MORE IMPORTANT TO TELL YOU!
OH? WHAT'S THAT?
YOU SEE... TAHAMENAY CAME TO ME CONCERNING HER HUSBAND ANDRAGORAS AND, WELL...
DID SHE BEG YOU TO SPARE HIS LIFE?
OH, NO, NO!
SQUEAK

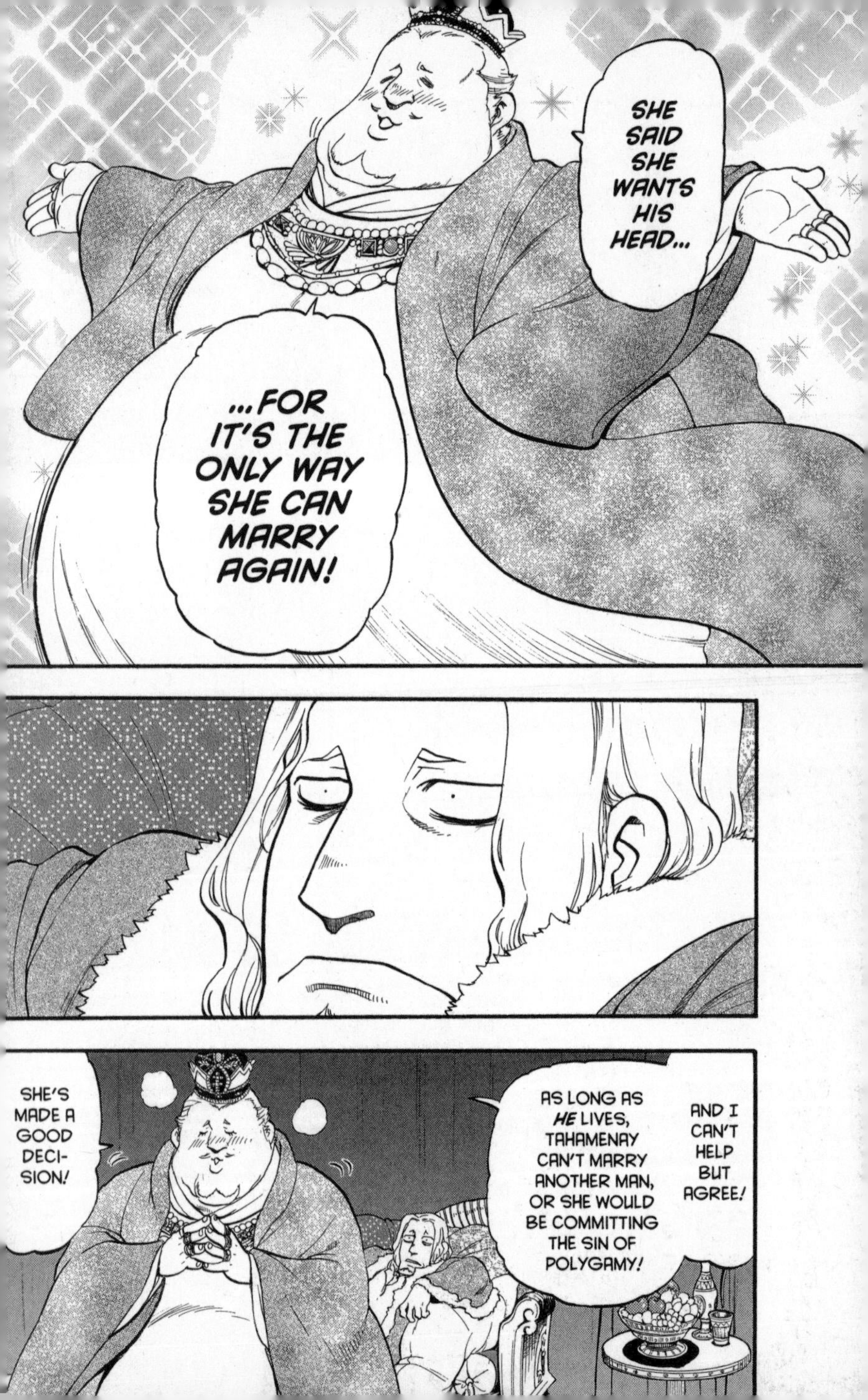
SHE SAID SHE WANTS HIS HEAD...
...FOR IT'S THE ONLY WAY SHE CAN MARRY AGAIN!
AND I CAN'T HELP BUT AGREE!
AS LONG AS *HE* LIVES, TAHAMENAY CAN'T MARRY ANOTHER MAN, OR SHE WOULD BE COMMITTING THE SIN OF POLYGAMY!
SHE'S MADE A GOOD DECI-SION!

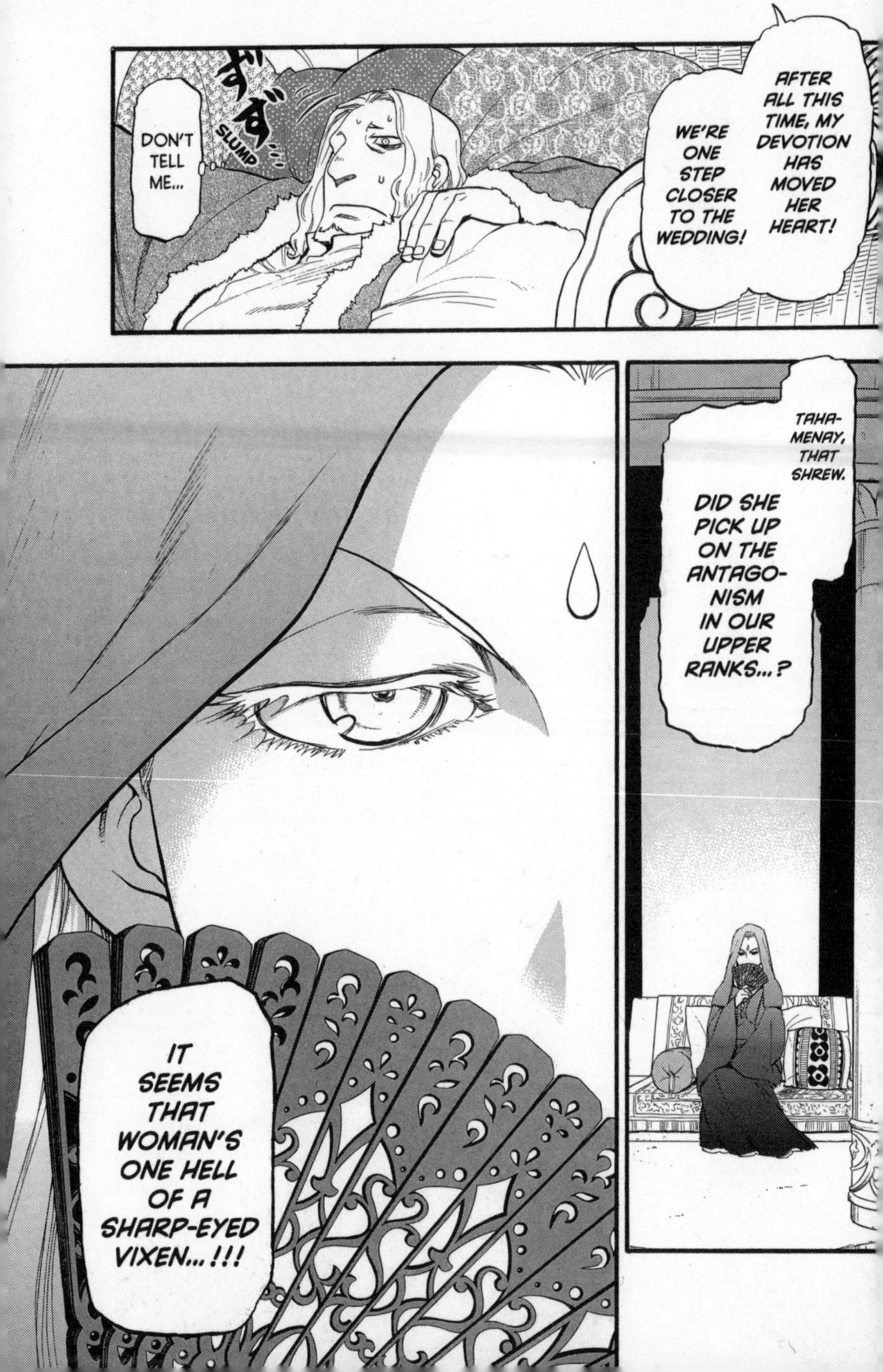
AFTER ALL THIS TIME, MY DEVOTION HAS MOVED HER HEART!
WE'RE ONE STEP CLOSER TO THE WEDDING!
SLUMP
DON'T TELL ME...
TAHAMENAY, THAT SHREW.
DID SHE PICK UP ON THE ANTAGONISM IN OUR UPPER RANKS...?
IT SEEMS THAT WOMAN'S ONE HELL OF A SHARP-EYED VIXEN...!!!

THE HEROIC LEGEND OF
ARSLAN

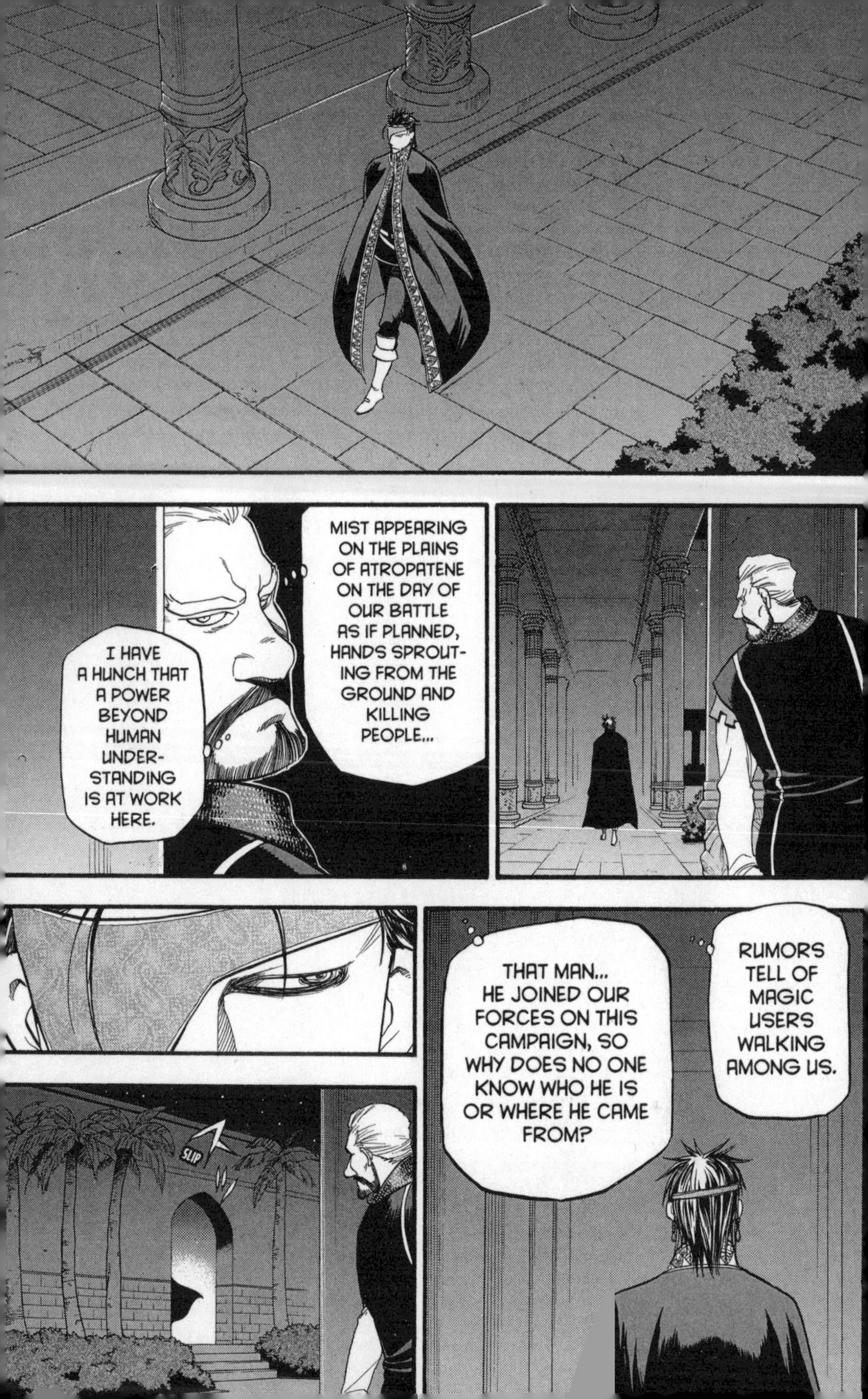
MIST APPEARING ON THE PLAINS OF ATROPATENE ON THE DAY OF OUR BATTLE AS IF PLANNED, HANDS SPROUTING FROM THE GROUND AND KILLING PEOPLE...
I HAVE A HUNCH THAT A POWER BEYOND HUMAN UNDERSTANDING IS AT WORK HERE.
RUMORS TELL OF MAGIC USERS WALKING AMONG US.
THAT MAN... HE JOINED OUR FORCES ON THIS CAMPAIGN, SO WHY DOES NO ONE KNOW WHO HE IS OR WHERE HE CAME FROM?
SLIP

WHERE
DID HE
GO...?!

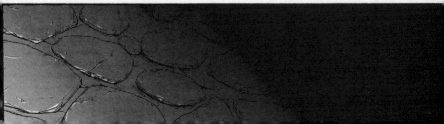

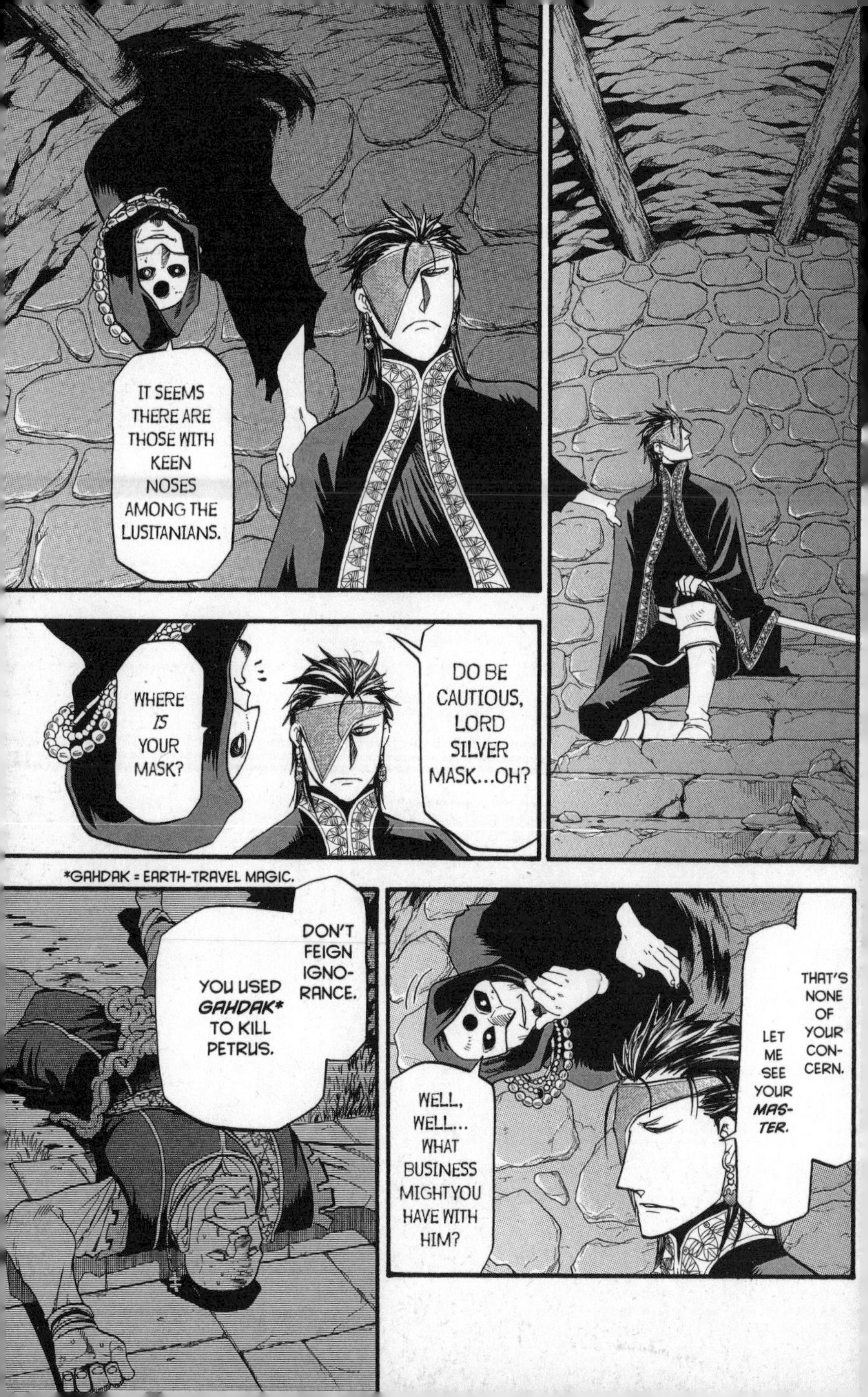
IT SEEMS THERE ARE THOSE WITH KEEN NOSES AMONG THE LUSITANIANS.
DO BE CAUTIOUS, LORD SILVER MASK...OH?
WHERE *IS* YOUR MASK?
THAT'S NONE OF YOUR CONCERN.
LET ME SEE YOUR *MASTER*.
WELL, WELL... WHAT BUSINESS MIGHT YOU HAVE WITH HIM?
DON'T FEIGN IGNORANCE.
YOU USED *GAHDAK** TO KILL PETRUS.

*GAHDAK = EARTH-TRAVEL MAGIC.

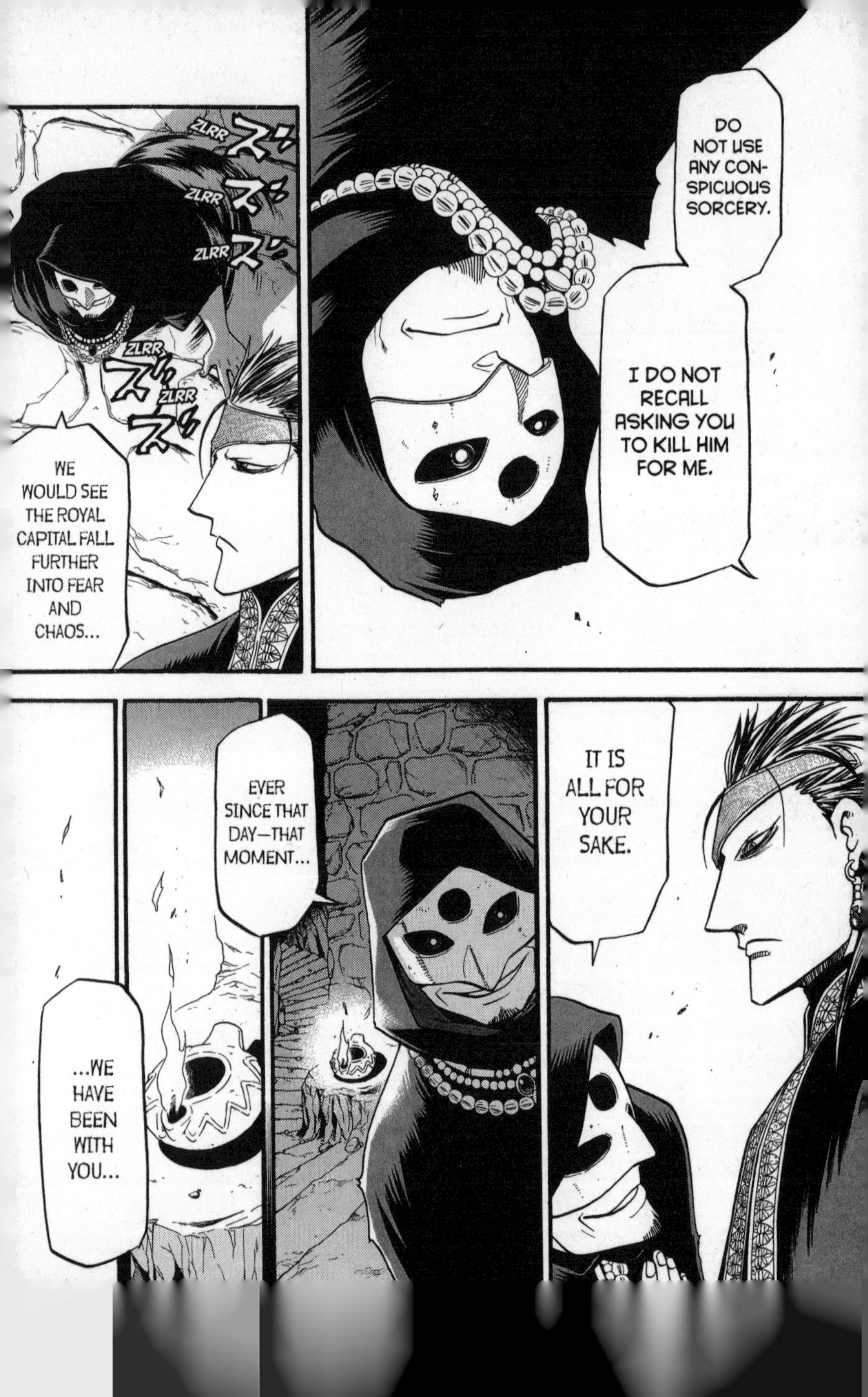
DO NOT USE ANY CON-SPICUOUS SORCERY.
I DO NOT RECALL ASKING YOU TO KILL HIM FOR ME.
ZLRR
ZLRR
ZLRR
ZLRR
ZLRR
WE WOULD SEE THE ROYAL CAPITAL FALL FURTHER INTO FEAR AND CHAOS...
IT IS ALL FOR YOUR SAKE.
EVER SINCE THAT DAY—THAT MOMENT...
...WE HAVE BEEN WITH YOU...

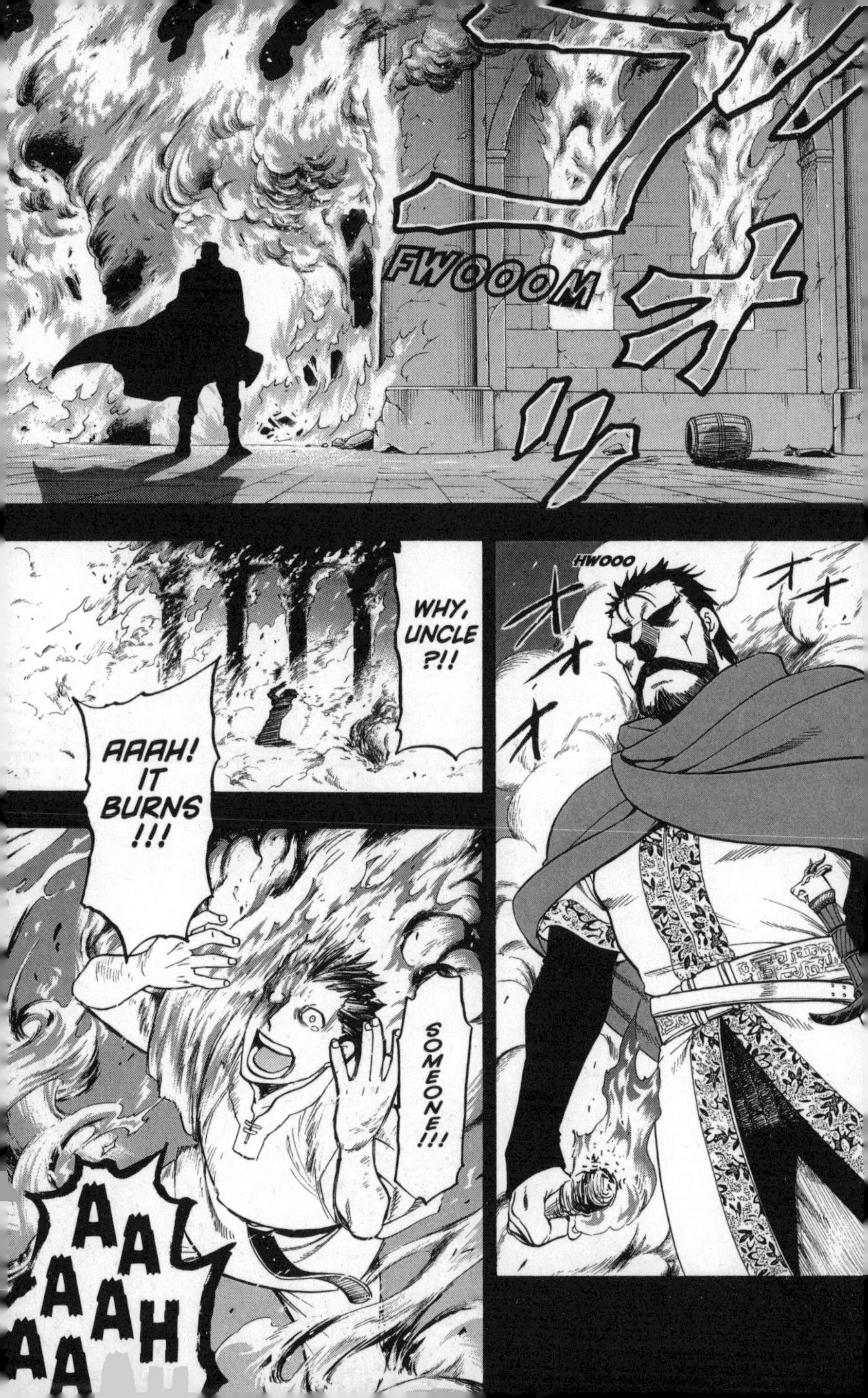
FWOOOM
HWOOO
WHY, UNCLE?!!
AAAH! IT BURNS!!!
SOMEONE!!!
AAAAAAAH

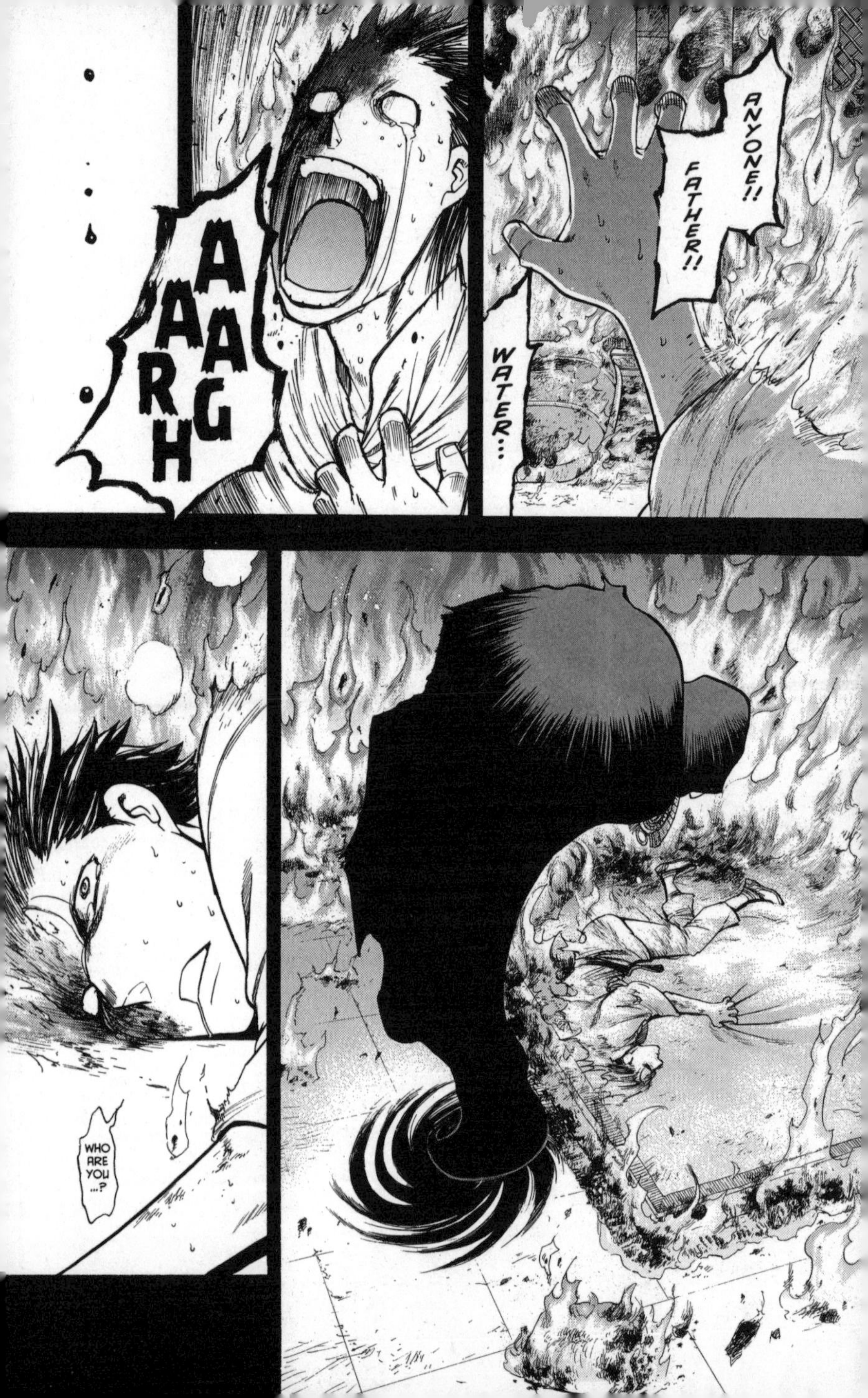
ANYONE!!
FATHER!!
WATER...
AAARGH
. . . .
WHO ARE YOU ...?

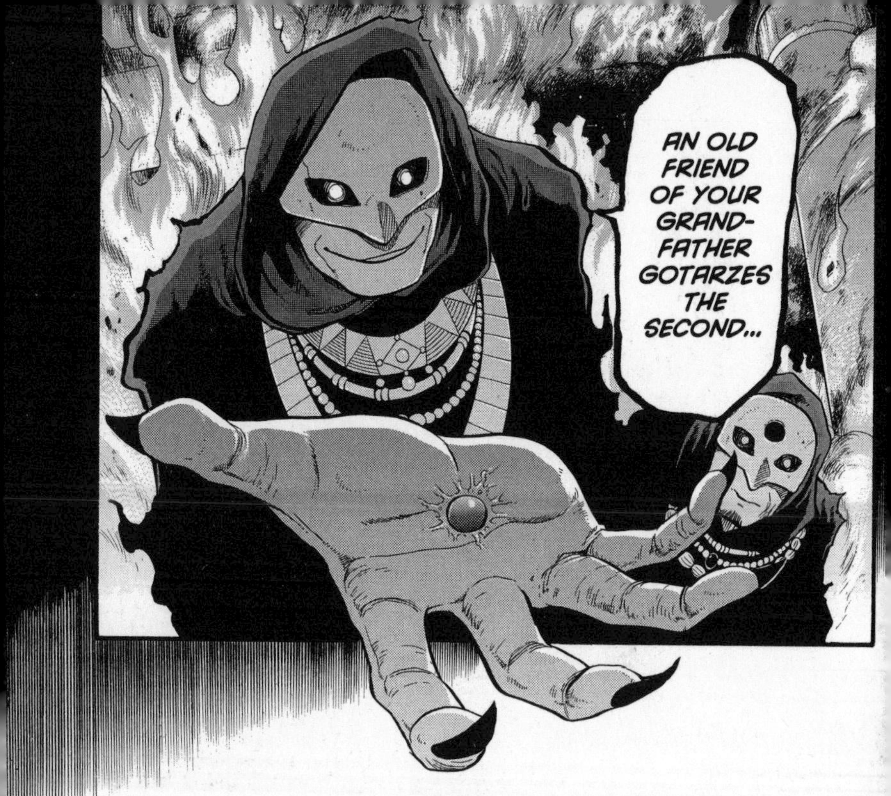
AN OLD FRIEND OF YOUR GRAND-FATHER GOTARZES THE SECOND...

Chapter 25: The Road to Peshawar

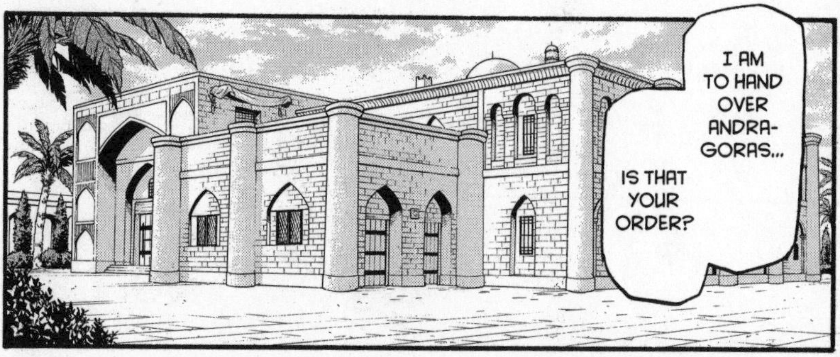
I AM TO HAND OVER ANDRA-GORAS...
IS THAT YOUR ORDER?

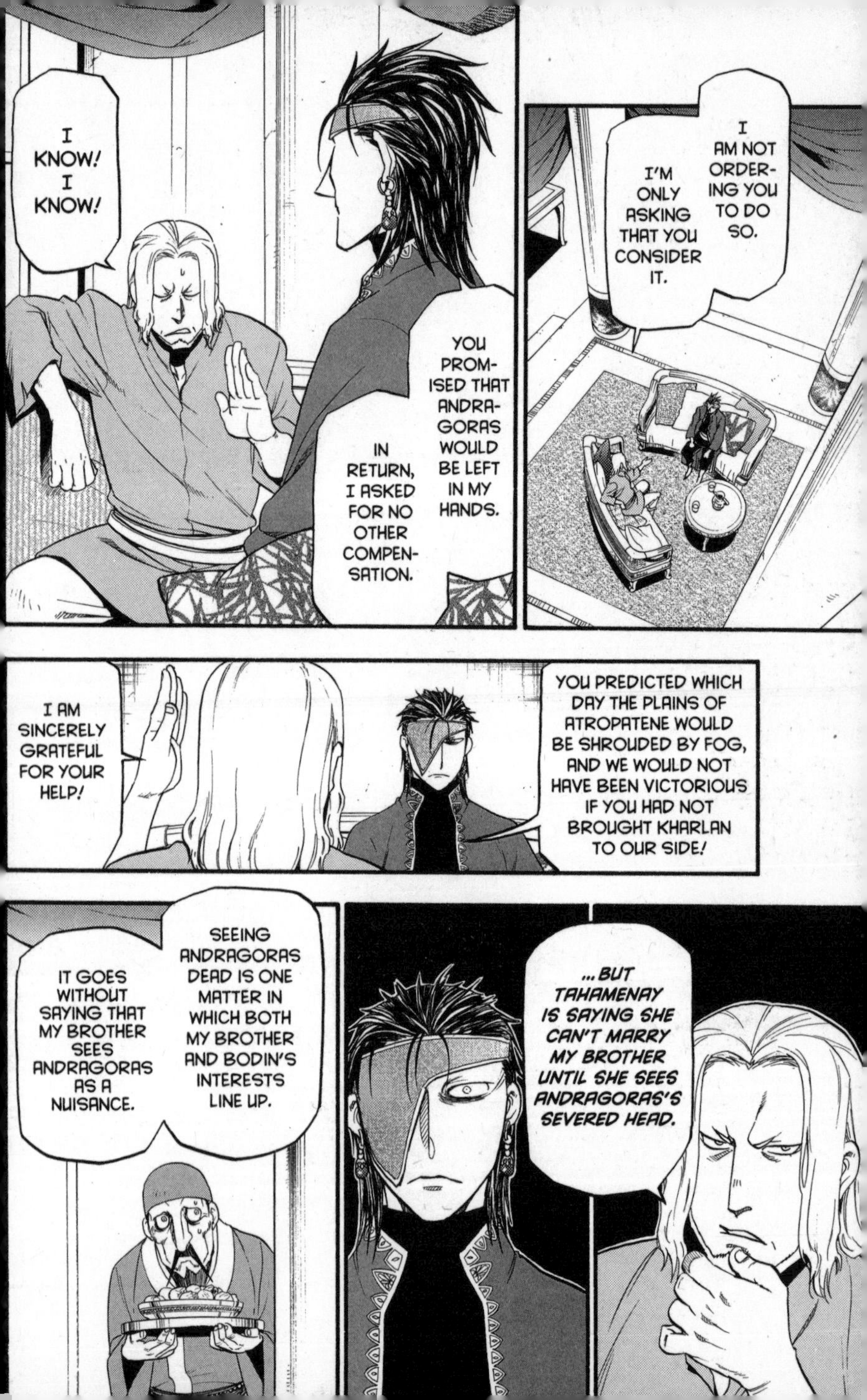
I AM NOT ORDERING YOU TO DO SO.
I'M ONLY ASKING THAT YOU CONSIDER IT.
YOU PROMISED THAT ANDRAGORAS WOULD BE LEFT IN MY HANDS.
IN RETURN, I ASKED FOR NO OTHER COMPENSATION.
I KNOW! I KNOW!
YOU PREDICTED WHICH DAY THE PLAINS OF ATROPATENE WOULD BE SHROUDED BY FOG, AND WE WOULD NOT HAVE BEEN VICTORIOUS IF YOU HAD NOT BROUGHT KHARLAN TO OUR SIDE!
I AM SINCERELY GRATEFUL FOR YOUR HELP!
...BUT TAHAMENAY IS SAYING SHE CAN'T MARRY MY BROTHER UNTIL SHE SEES ANDRAGORAS'S SEVERED HEAD.
SEEING ANDRAGORAS DEAD IS ONE MATTER IN WHICH BOTH MY BROTHER AND BODIN'S INTERESTS LINE UP.
IT GOES WITHOUT SAYING THAT MY BROTHER SEES ANDRAGORAS AS A NUISANCE.

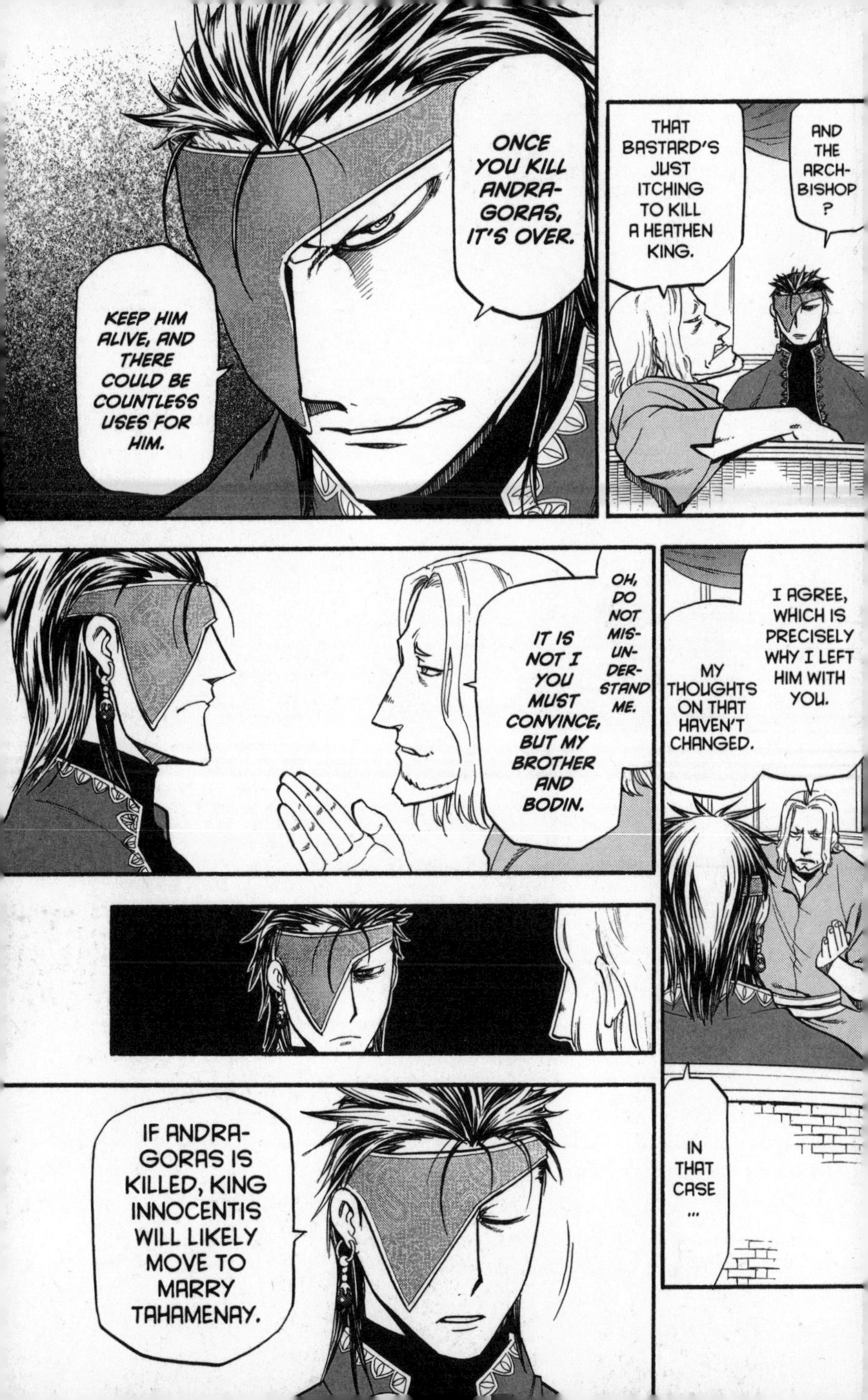
AND THE ARCH-BISHOP?
THAT BASTARD'S JUST ITCHING TO KILL A HEATHEN KING.
ONCE YOU KILL ANDRA-GORAS, IT'S OVER.
KEEP HIM ALIVE, AND THERE COULD BE COUNTLESS USES FOR HIM.
I AGREE, WHICH IS PRECISELY WHY I LEFT HIM WITH YOU.
MY THOUGHTS ON THAT HAVEN'T CHANGED.
OH, DO NOT MIS-UN-DER-STAND ME.
IT IS NOT I YOU MUST CONVINCE, BUT MY BROTHER AND BODIN.
IN THAT CASE...
IF ANDRA-GORAS IS KILLED, KING INNOCENTIS WILL LIKELY MOVE TO MARRY TAHAMENAY.

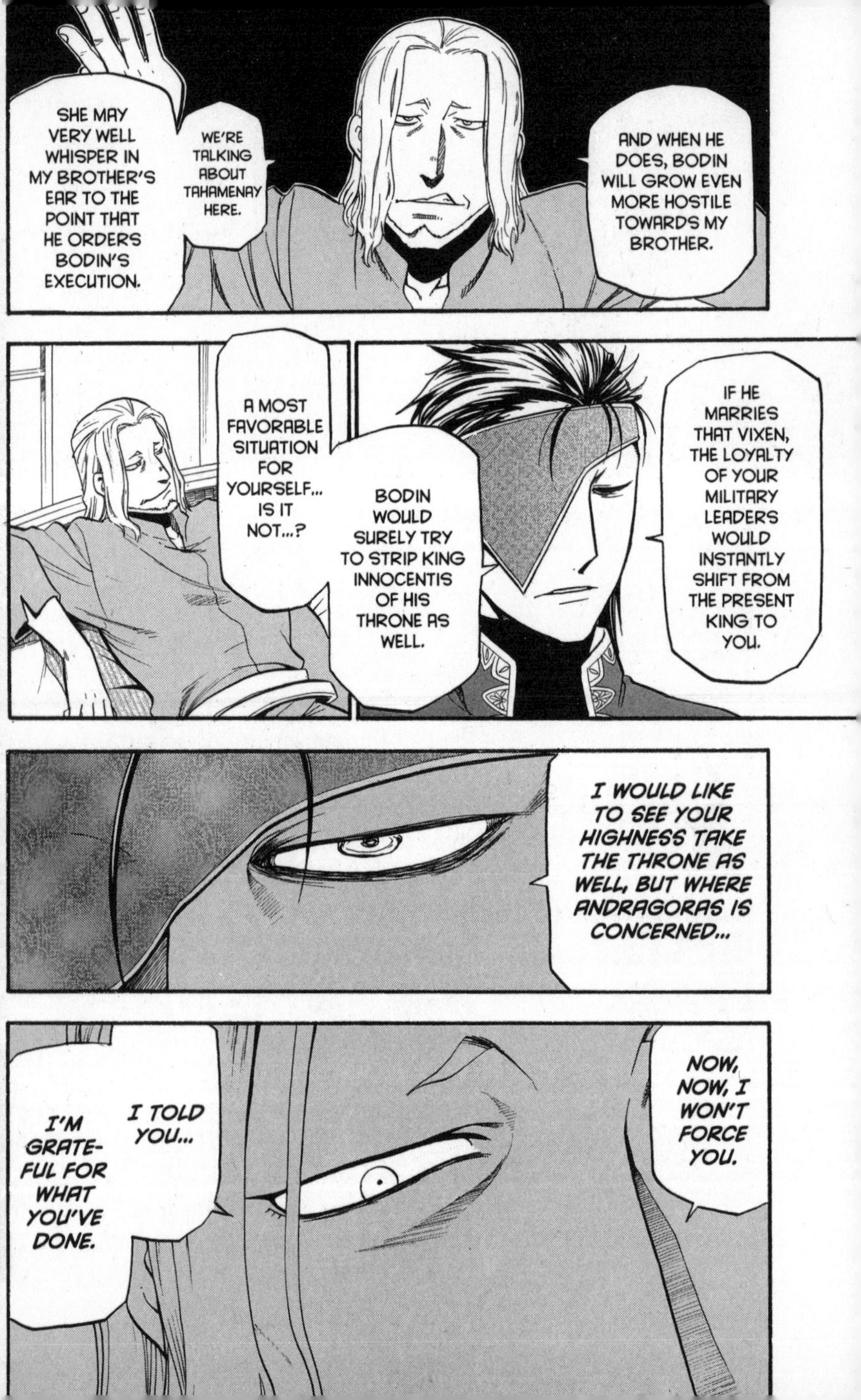
AND WHEN HE DOES, BODIN WILL GROW EVEN MORE HOSTILE TOWARDS MY BROTHER.
WE'RE TALKING ABOUT TAHAMENAY HERE.
SHE MAY VERY WELL WHISPER IN MY BROTHER'S EAR TO THE POINT THAT HE ORDERS BODIN'S EXECUTION.
IF HE MARRIES THAT VIXEN, THE LOYALTY OF YOUR MILITARY LEADERS WOULD INSTANTLY SHIFT FROM THE PRESENT KING TO YOU.
BODIN WOULD SURELY TRY TO STRIP KING INNOCENTIS OF HIS THRONE AS WELL.
A MOST FAVORABLE SITUATION FOR YOURSELF... IS IT NOT...?
I WOULD LIKE TO SEE YOUR HIGHNESS TAKE THE THRONE AS WELL, BUT WHERE ANDRAGORAS IS CONCERNED...
NOW, NOW, I WON'T FORCE YOU.
I TOLD YOU...
I'M GRATE-FUL FOR WHAT YOU'VE DONE.

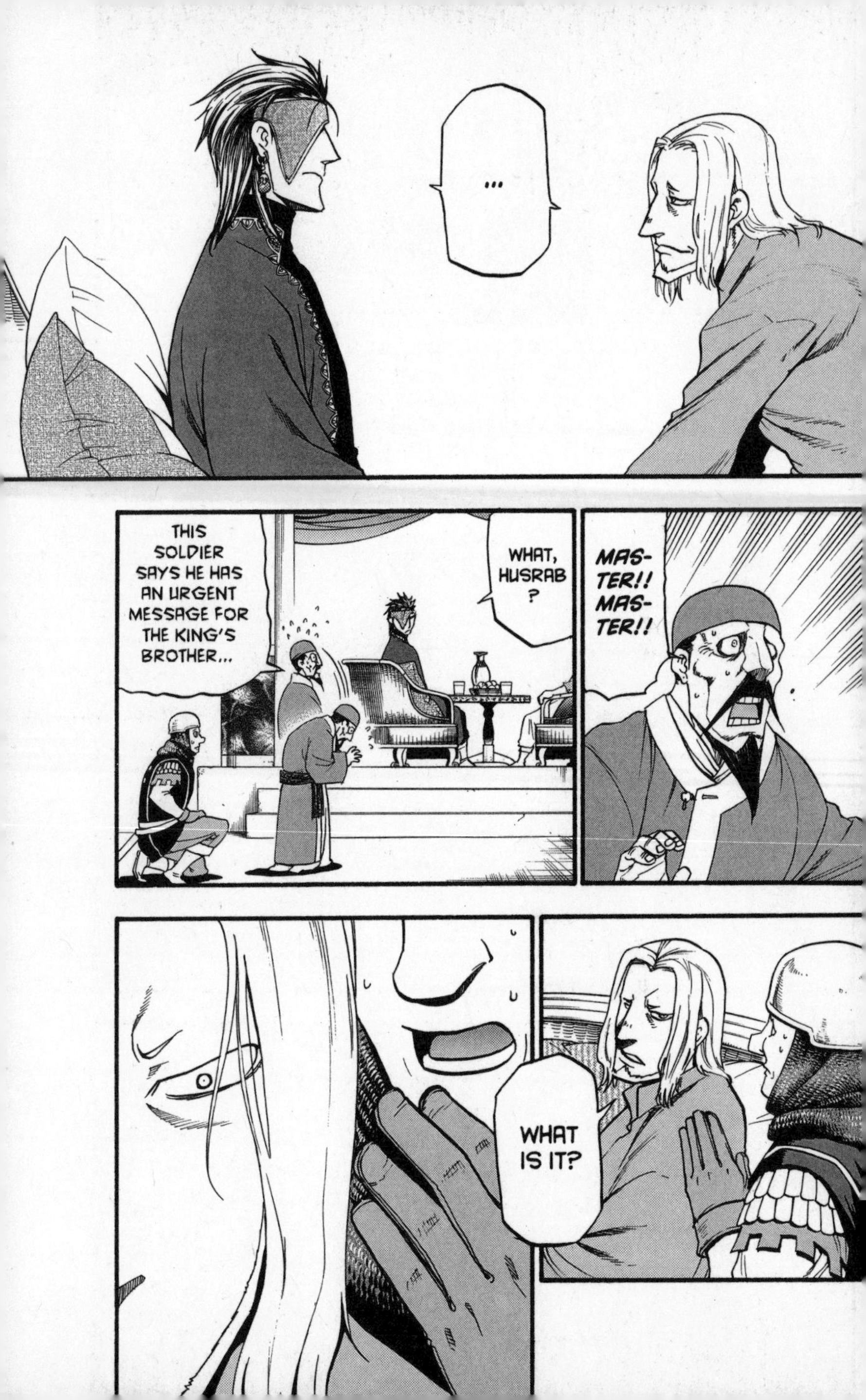
...
MAS-TER!! MAS-TER!!
WHAT, HUSRAB?
THIS SOLDIER SAYS HE HAS AN URGENT MESSAGE FOR THE KING'S BROTHER...
WHAT IS IT?

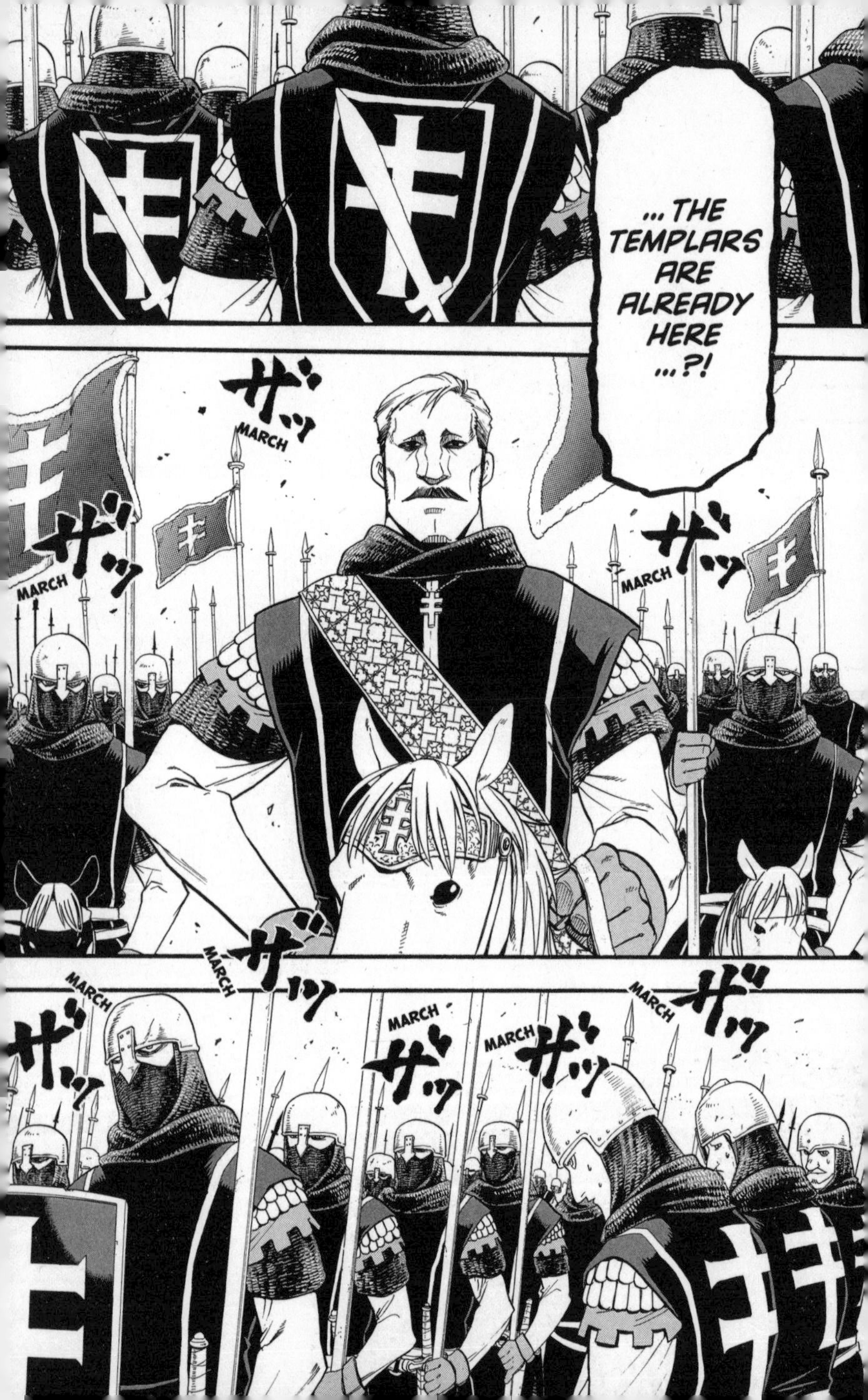
...THE TEMPLARS ARE ALREADY HERE ...?!
ザッ MARCH
ザッ MARCH
ザッ MARCH
ザッ MARCH
ザッ MARCH
ザッ MARCH
ザッ MARCH
ザッ MARCH

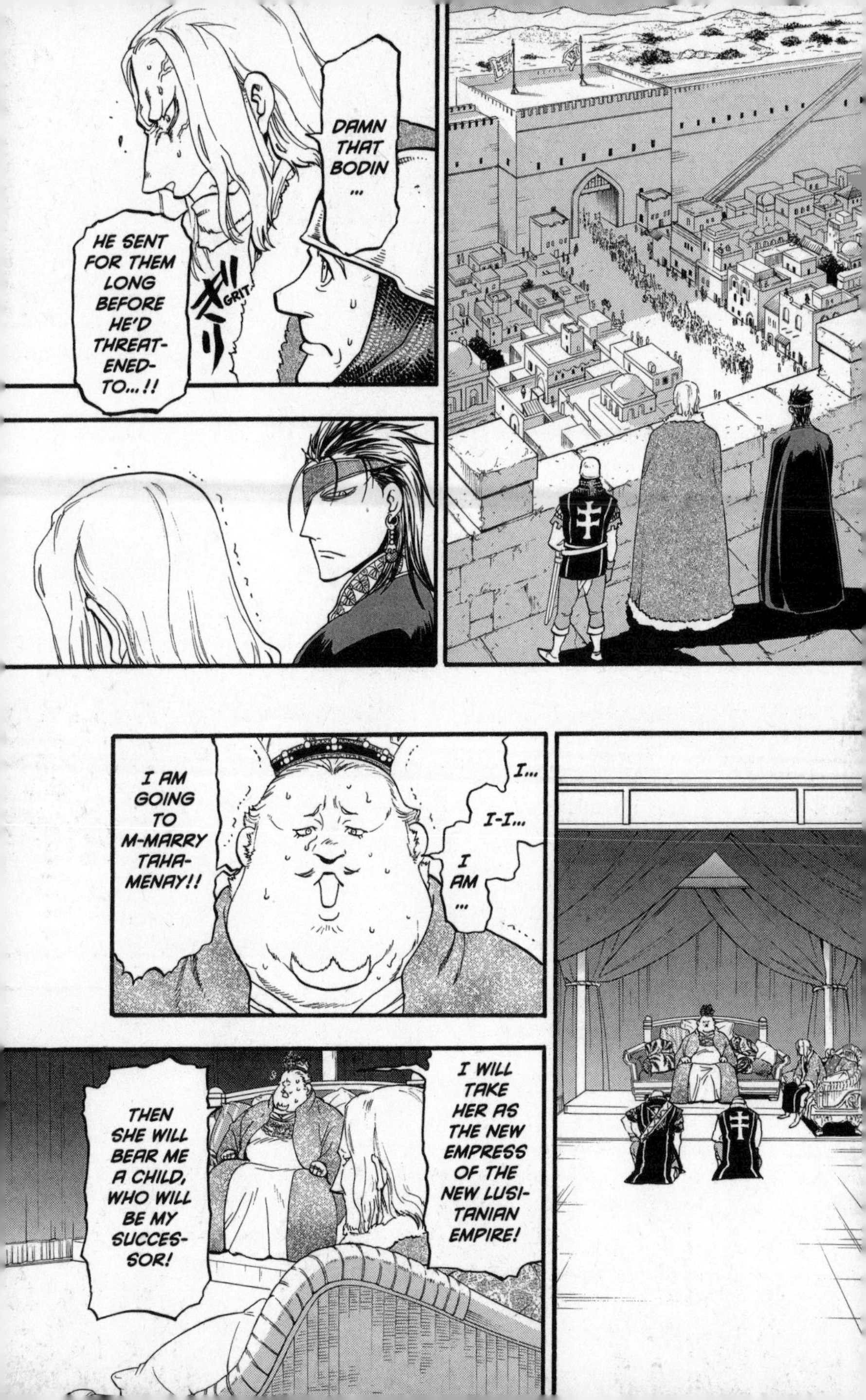
DAMN THAT BODIN ...
HE SENT FOR THEM LONG BEFORE HE'D THREAT-ENED-TO...!!
ギリ GRIT
I...
I-I...
I AM ...
I AM GOING TO M-MARRY TAHA-MENAY!!
I WILL TAKE HER AS THE NEW EMPRESS OF THE NEW LUSI-TANIAN EMPIRE!
THEN SHE WILL BEAR ME A CHILD, WHO WILL BE MY SUCCES-SOR!

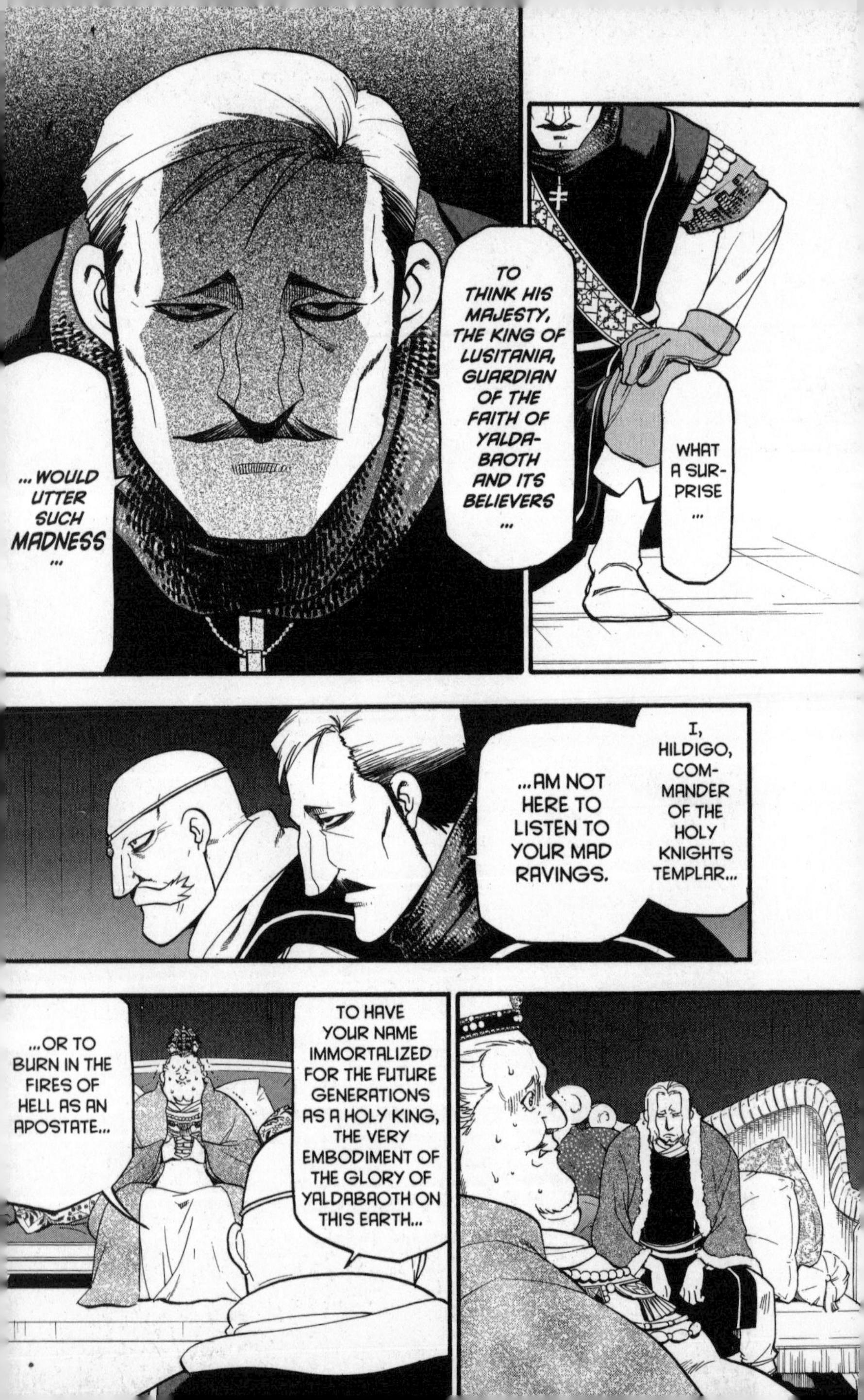
WHAT A SUR-PRISE ...
TO THINK HIS MAJESTY, THE KING OF LUSITANIA, GUARDIAN OF THE FAITH OF YALDA-BAOTH AND ITS BELIEVERS ...
... WOULD UTTER SUCH MADNESS ...
I, HILDIGO, COM-MANDER OF THE HOLY KNIGHTS TEMPLAR...
...AM NOT HERE TO LISTEN TO YOUR MAD RAVINGS.
TO HAVE YOUR NAME IMMORTALIZED FOR THE FUTURE GENERATIONS AS A HOLY KING, THE VERY EMBODIMENT OF THE GLORY OF YALDABAOTH ON THIS EARTH...
...OR TO BURN IN THE FIRES OF HELL AS AN APOSTATE...

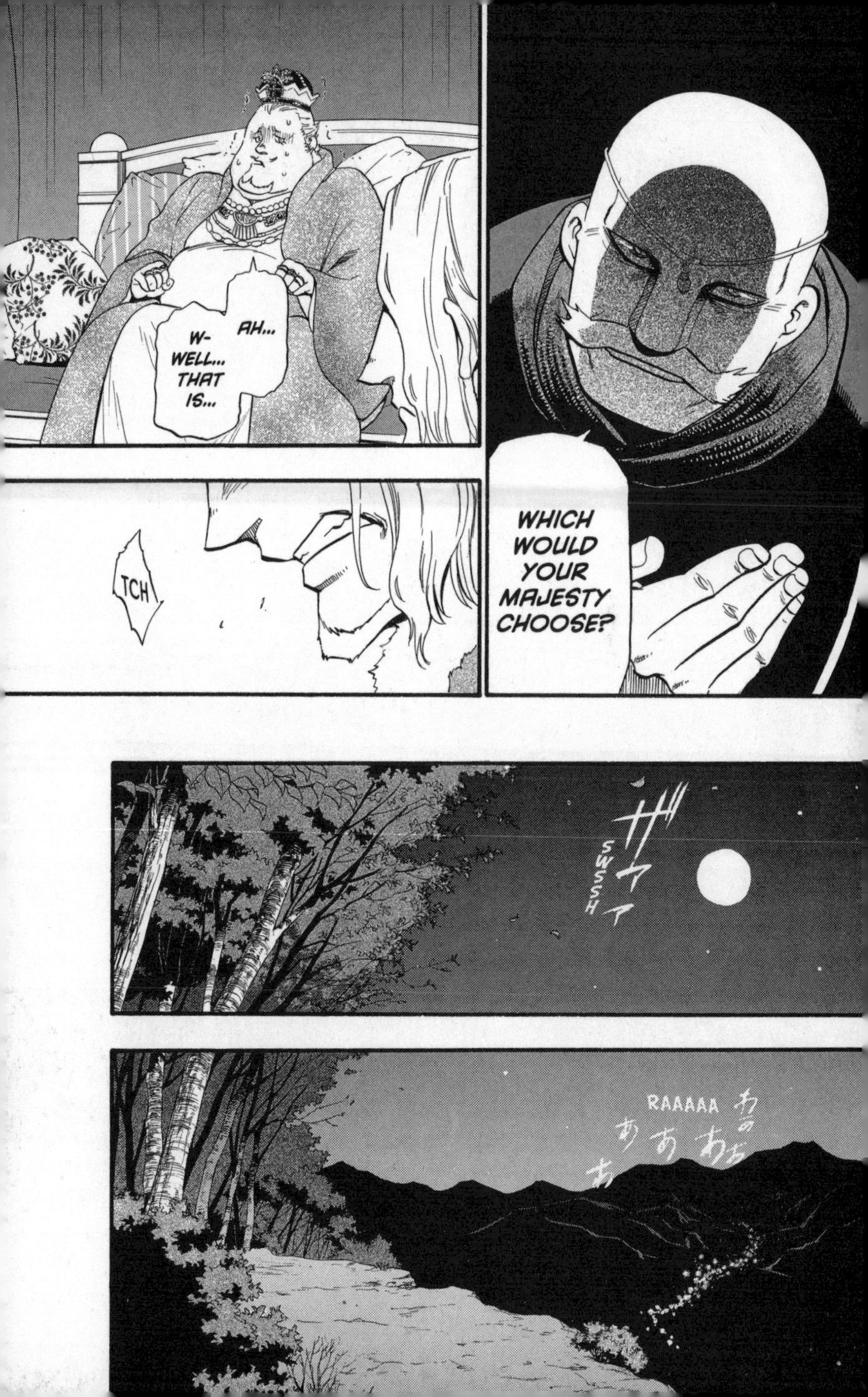
WHICH WOULD YOUR MAJESTY CHOOSE?
AH...
W-WELL... THAT IS...
TCH
SWSSH
ザァァ
RAAAAA
わぉぉあああ

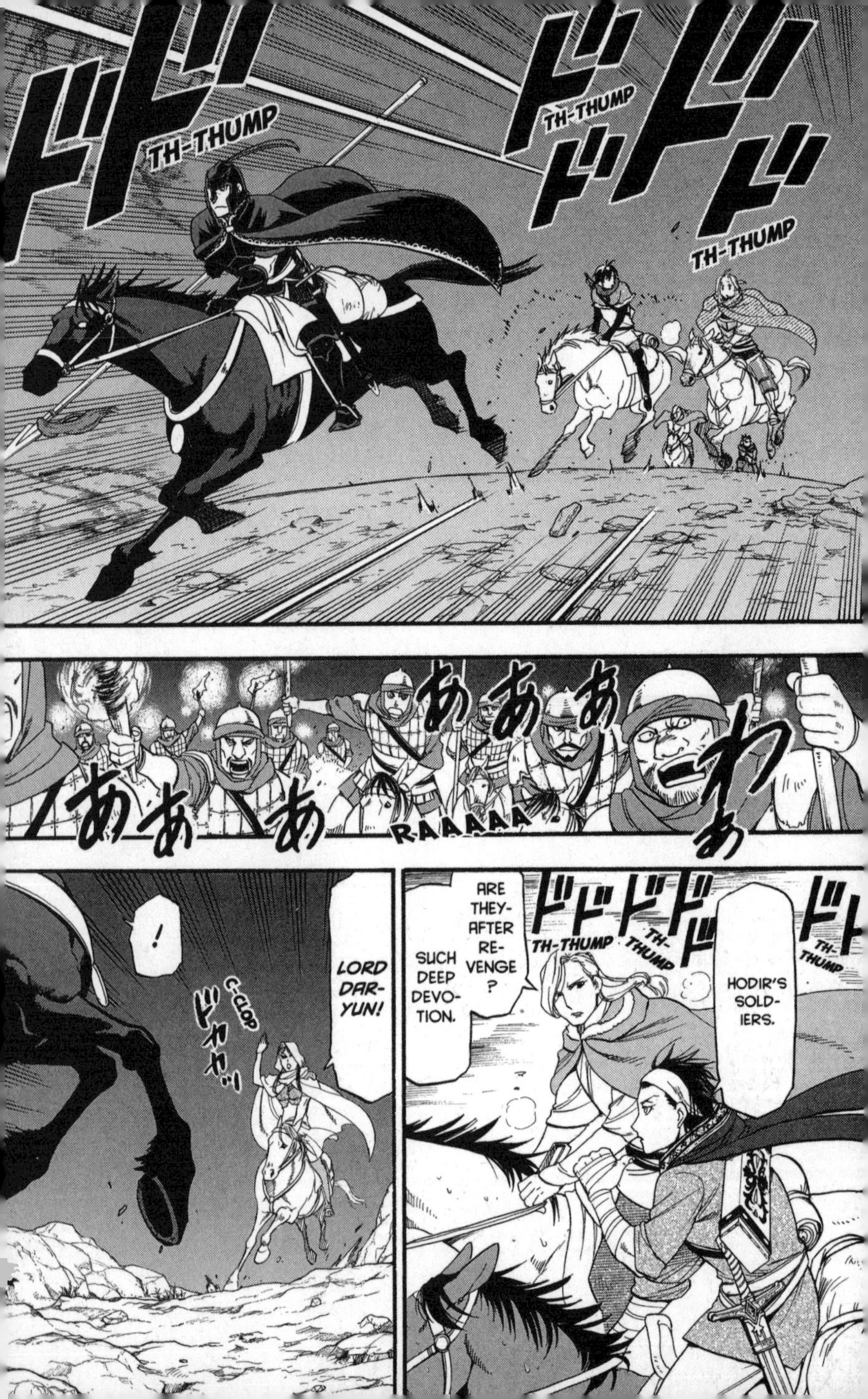

TH-THUMP
TH-THUMP
TH-THUMP
RAAAAA
TH-THUMP
TH-THUMP
TH-THUMP
HODIR'S SOLDIERS.
ARE THEY AFTER REVENGE?
SUCH DEEP DEVOTION.
LORD DARYUN!
!
C-CLOP

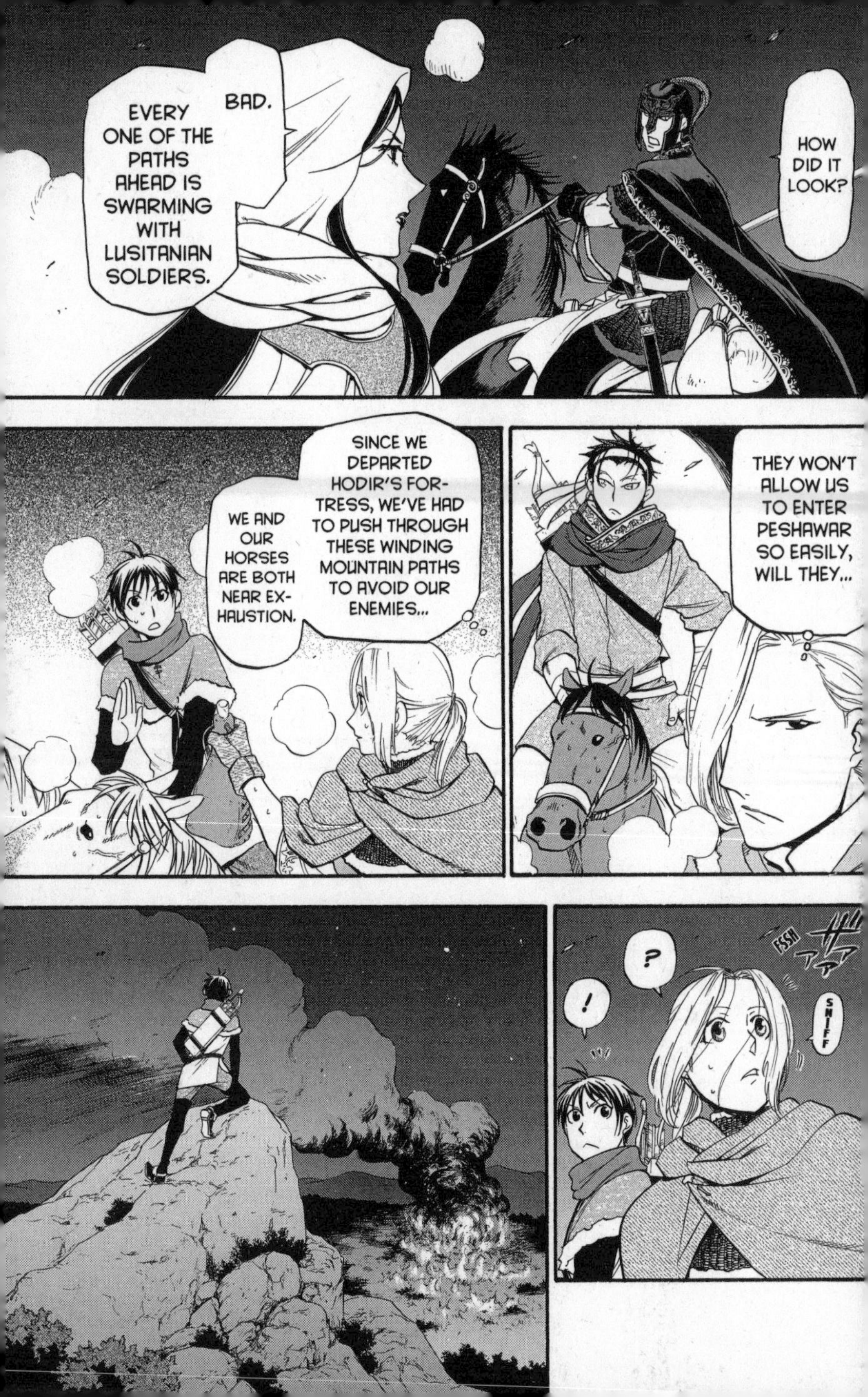
HOW DID IT LOOK?
BAD.
EVERY ONE OF THE PATHS AHEAD IS SWARMING WITH LUSITANIAN SOLDIERS.
THEY WON'T ALLOW US TO ENTER PESHAWAR SO EASILY, WILL THEY...
SINCE WE DEPARTED HODIR'S FOR-TRESS, WE'VE HAD TO PUSH THROUGH THESE WINDING MOUNTAIN PATHS TO AVOID OUR ENEMIES...
WE AND OUR HORSES ARE BOTH NEAR EX-HAUSTION.
ザアア
FSSH
SNIFF
?
!

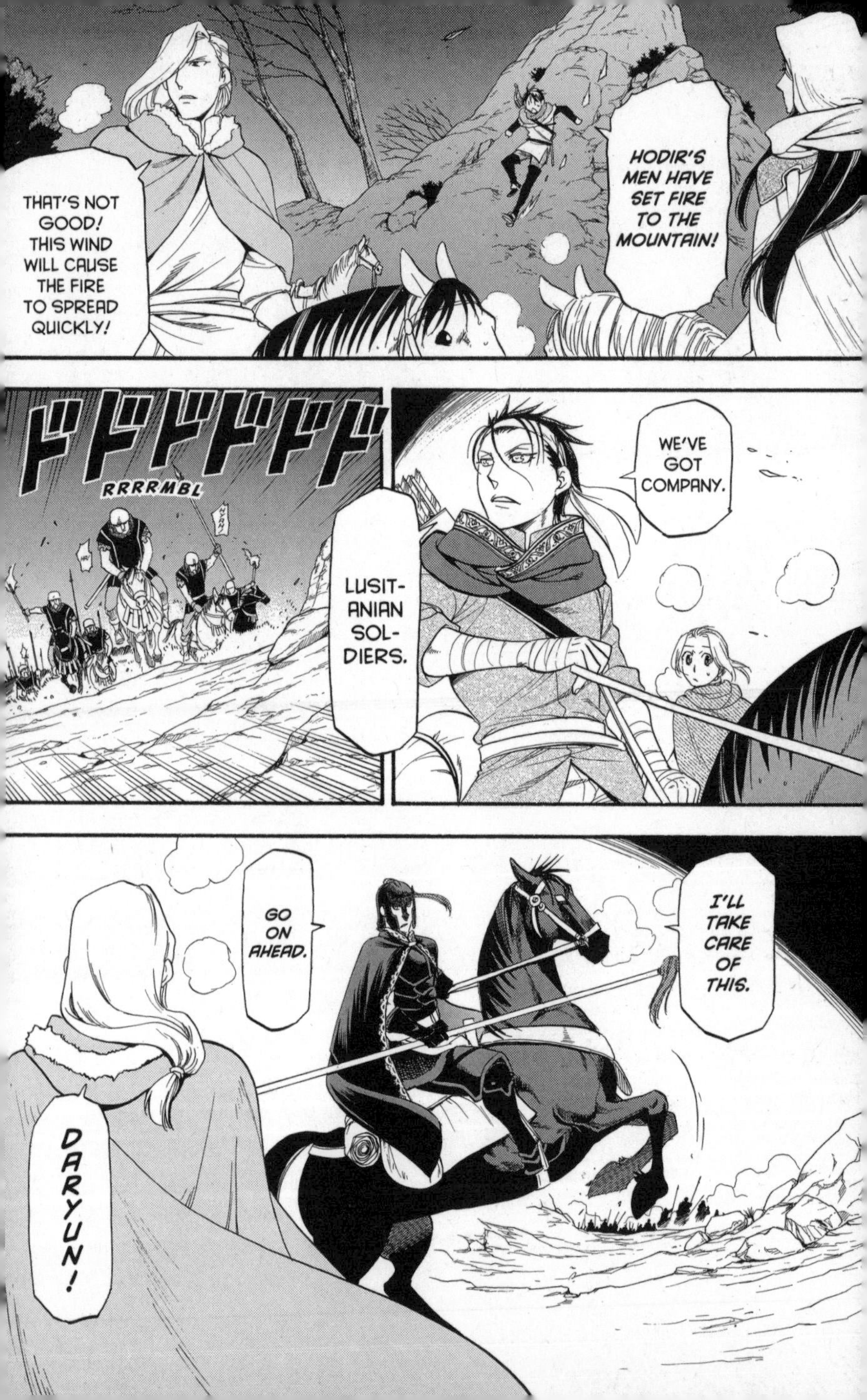
HODIR'S MEN HAVE SET FIRE TO THE MOUNTAIN!
THAT'S NOT GOOD! THIS WIND WILL CAUSE THE FIRE TO SPREAD QUICKLY!
WE'VE GOT COMPANY.
LUSIT-ANIAN SOL-DIERS.
ドドドドドド
RRRRMBL
I'LL TAKE CARE OF THIS.
GO ON AHEAD.
DARYUN!

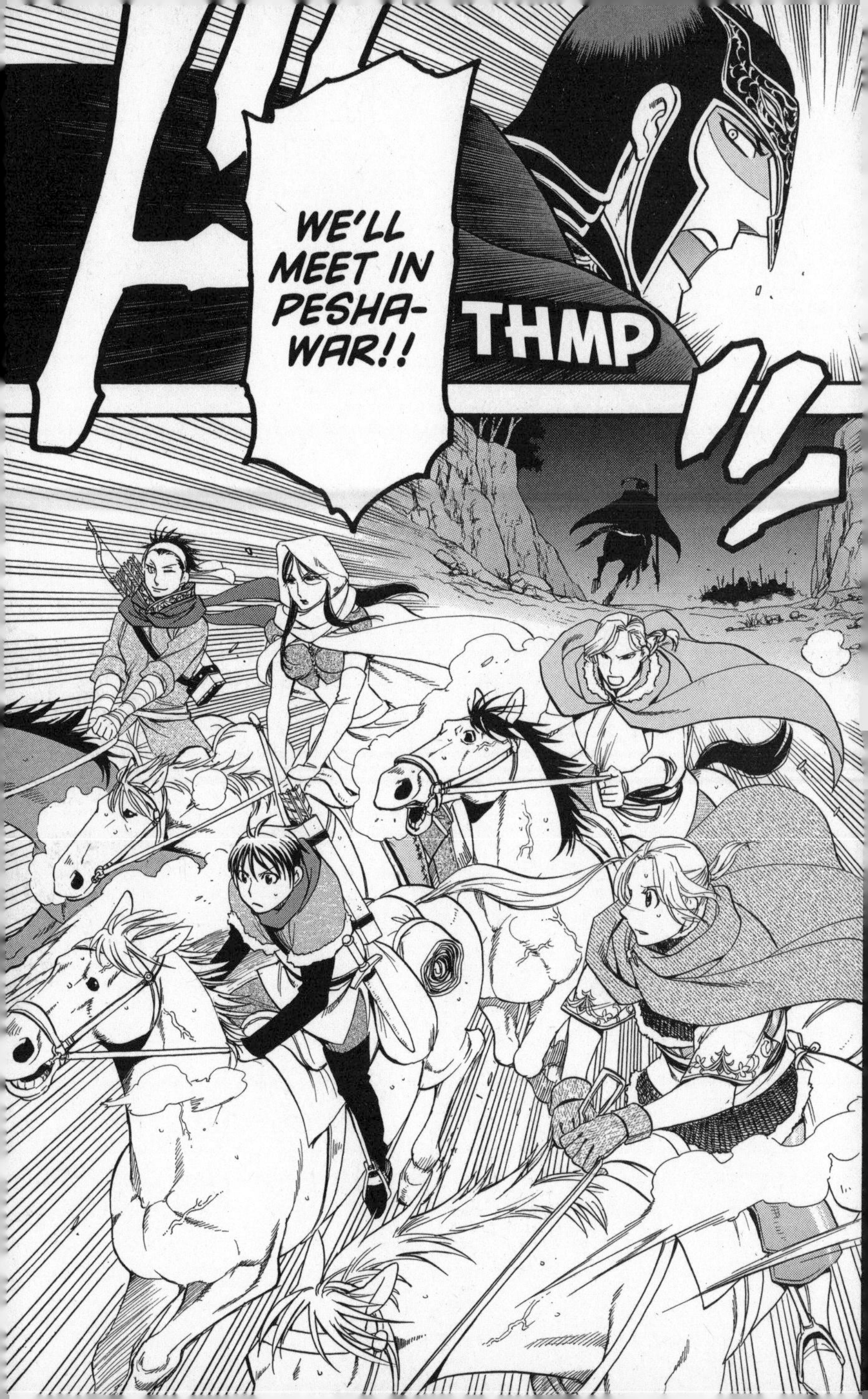
WE'LL MEET IN PESHA-WAR!!
THMP

THE HEROIC LEGEND OF
ARSLAN

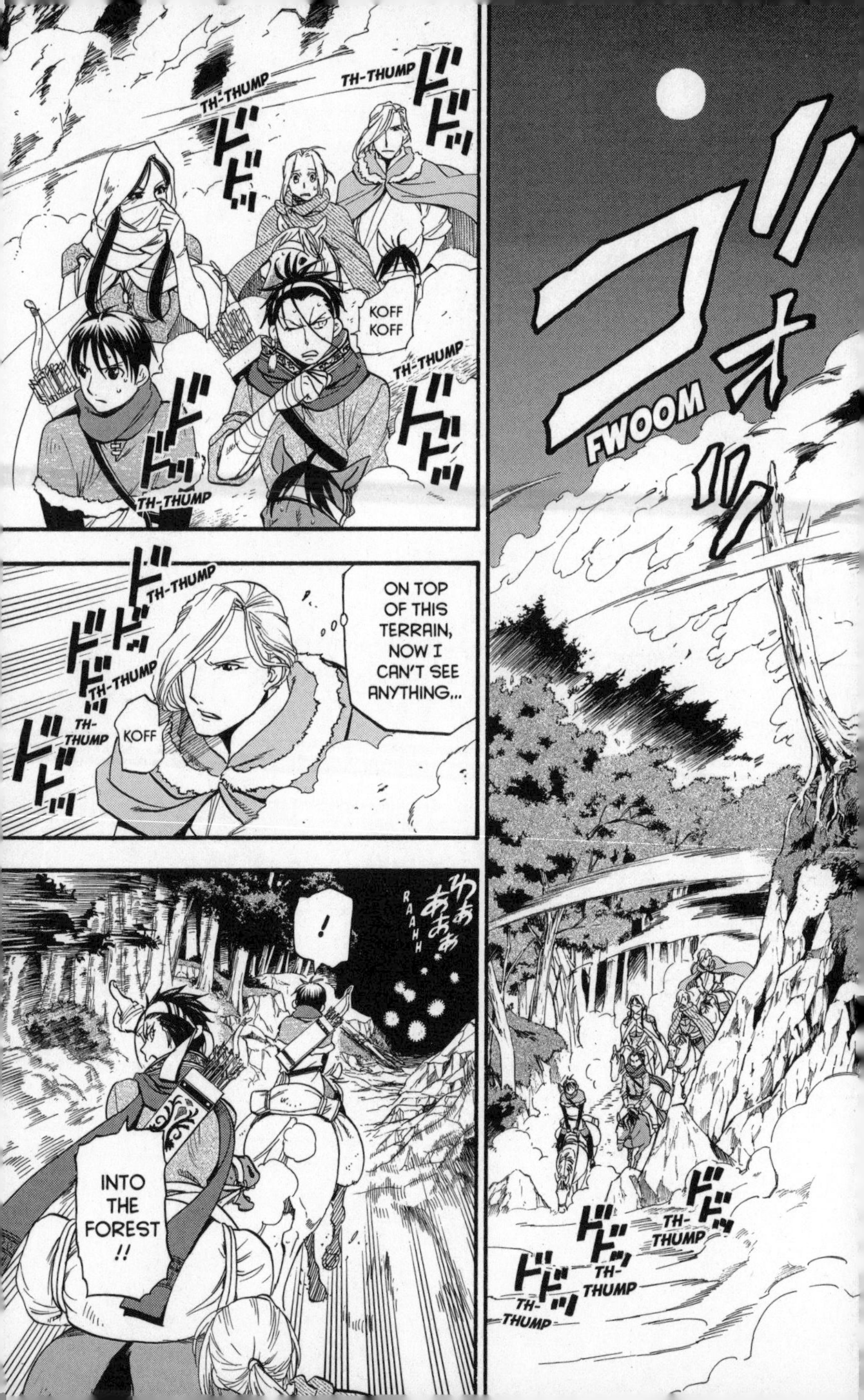
ゴオオ
FWOOM
ドドッ
TH-THUMP
ドドッ
TH-THUMP
ドドッ
TH-THUMP
ドドッ
TH-THUMP
ドドッ
TH-THUMP
KOFF KOFF
ドドッ
TH-THUMP
ドドッ
TH-THUMP
ドドッ
TH-THUMP
ドドッ
TH-THUMP
ドドッ
TH-THUMP
KOFF
ON TOP OF THIS TERRAIN, NOW I CAN'T SEE ANYTHING...
わあああ
RAAHH
!
INTO THE FOREST !!

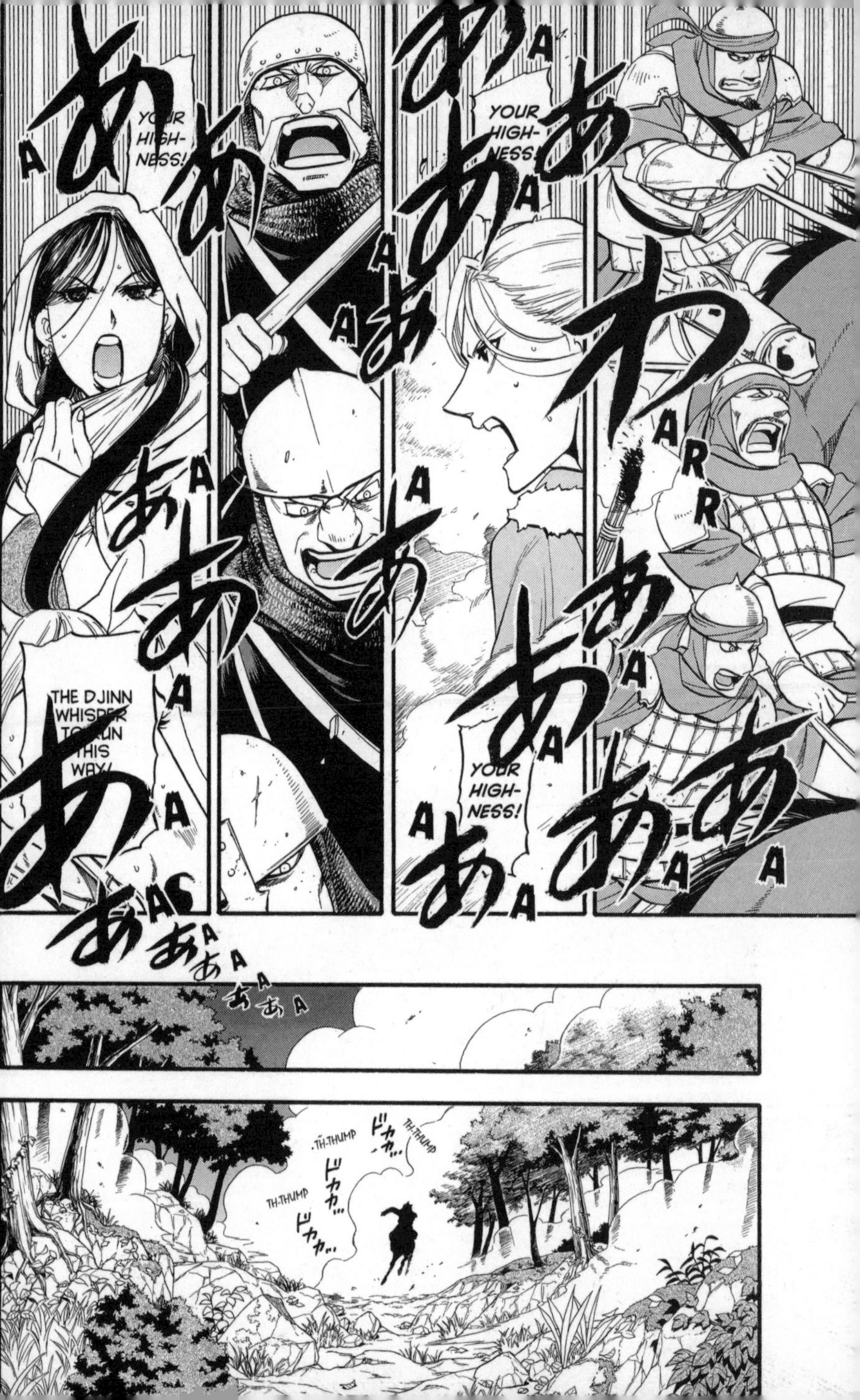

ARR
YOUR HIGH-NESS!
YOUR HIGH-NESS!
YOUR HIGH-NESS!
THE DJINN WHISPER TO RUN THIS WAY!
TH-THUMP
TH-THUMP
TH-THUMP

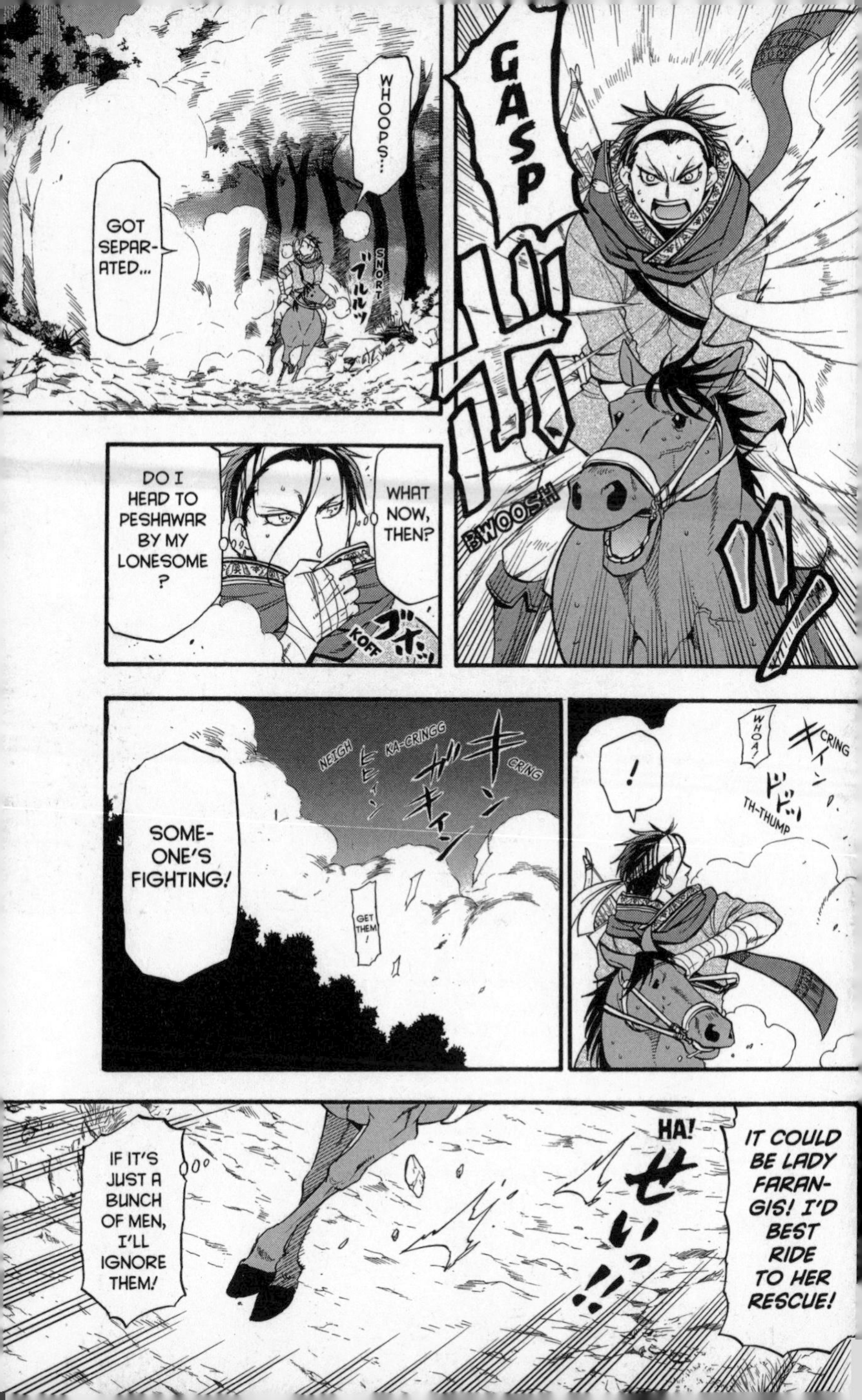
GASP
BWOOSH
WHOOPS...
GOT SEPAR-ATED...
SNORT
WHAT NOW, THEN?
DO I HEAD TO PESHAWAR BY MY LONESOME?
KOFF
WHOA!
CRING
TH-THUMP
!
SOME-ONE'S FIGHTING!
CRING
KA-CRINGG
NEIGH
GET THEM!
IT COULD BE LADY FARAN-GIS! I'D BEST RIDE TO HER RESCUE!
HA!
IF IT'S JUST A BUNCH OF MEN, I'LL IGNORE THEM!

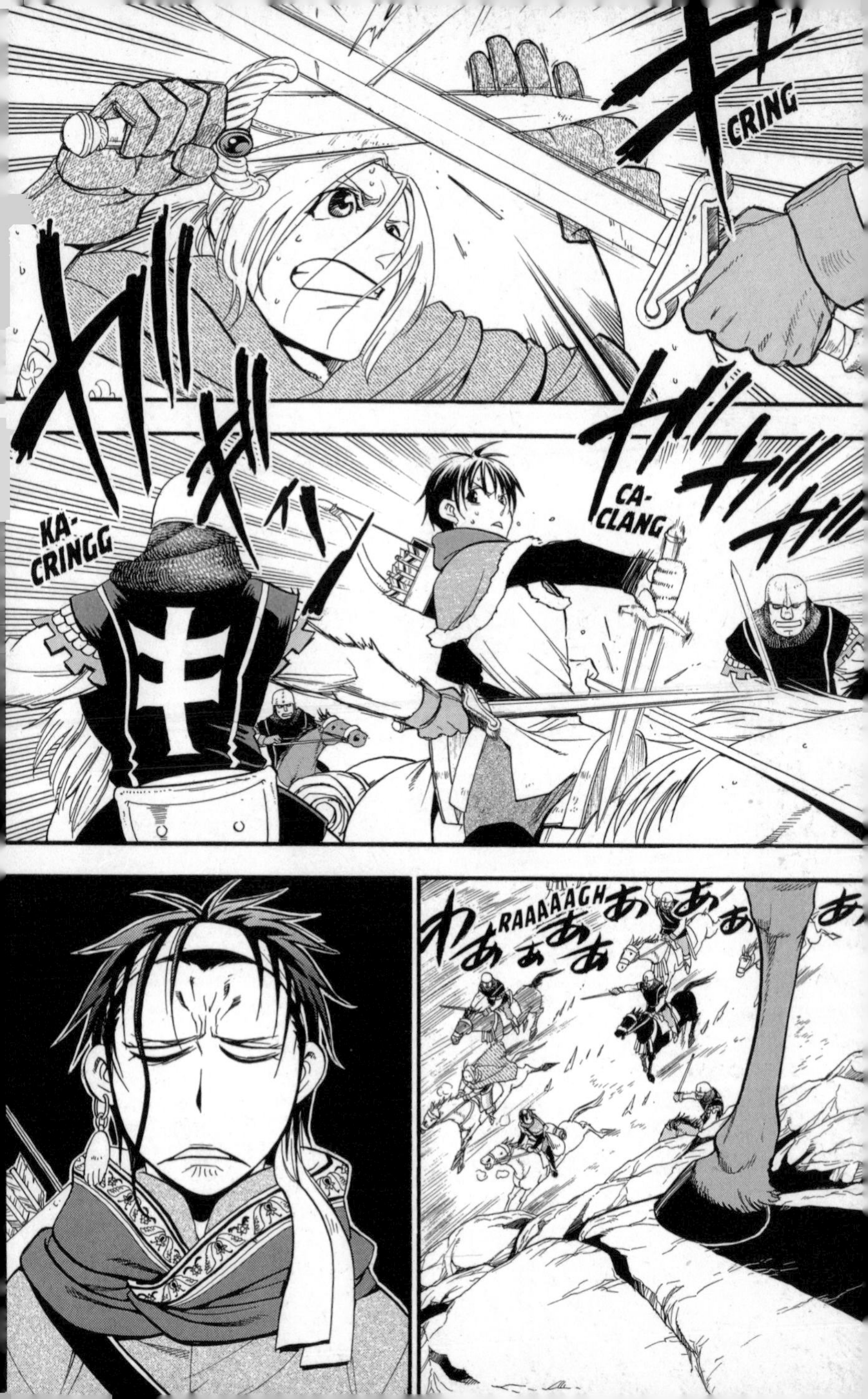
CRING
CA-CLANG
KA-CRINGG
RAAAAAGH

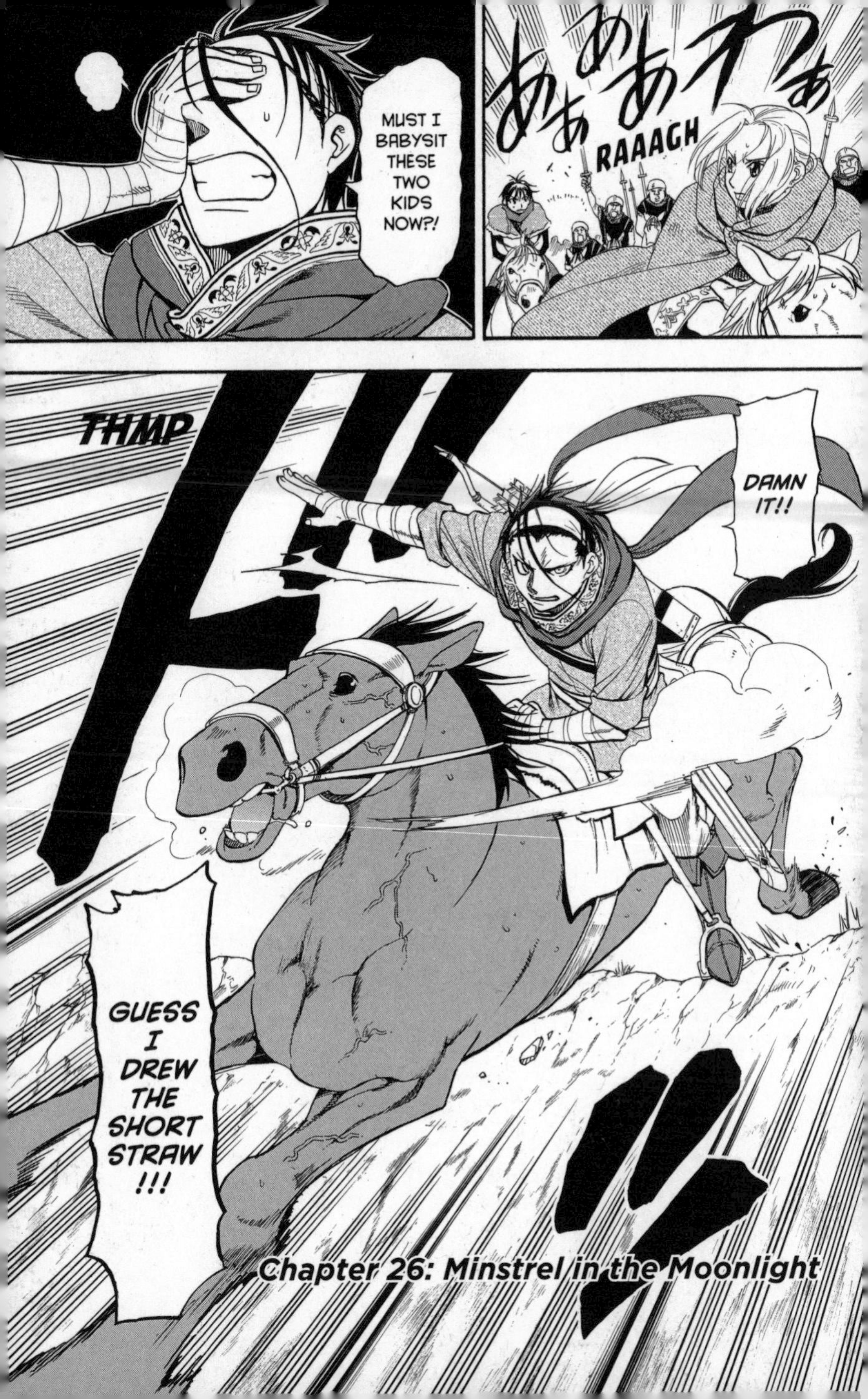
RAAAGH
MUST I BABYSIT THESE TWO KIDS NOW?!
DAMN IT!!
THMP
GUESS I DREW THE SHORT STRAW!!!
Chapter 26: Minstrel in the Moonlight

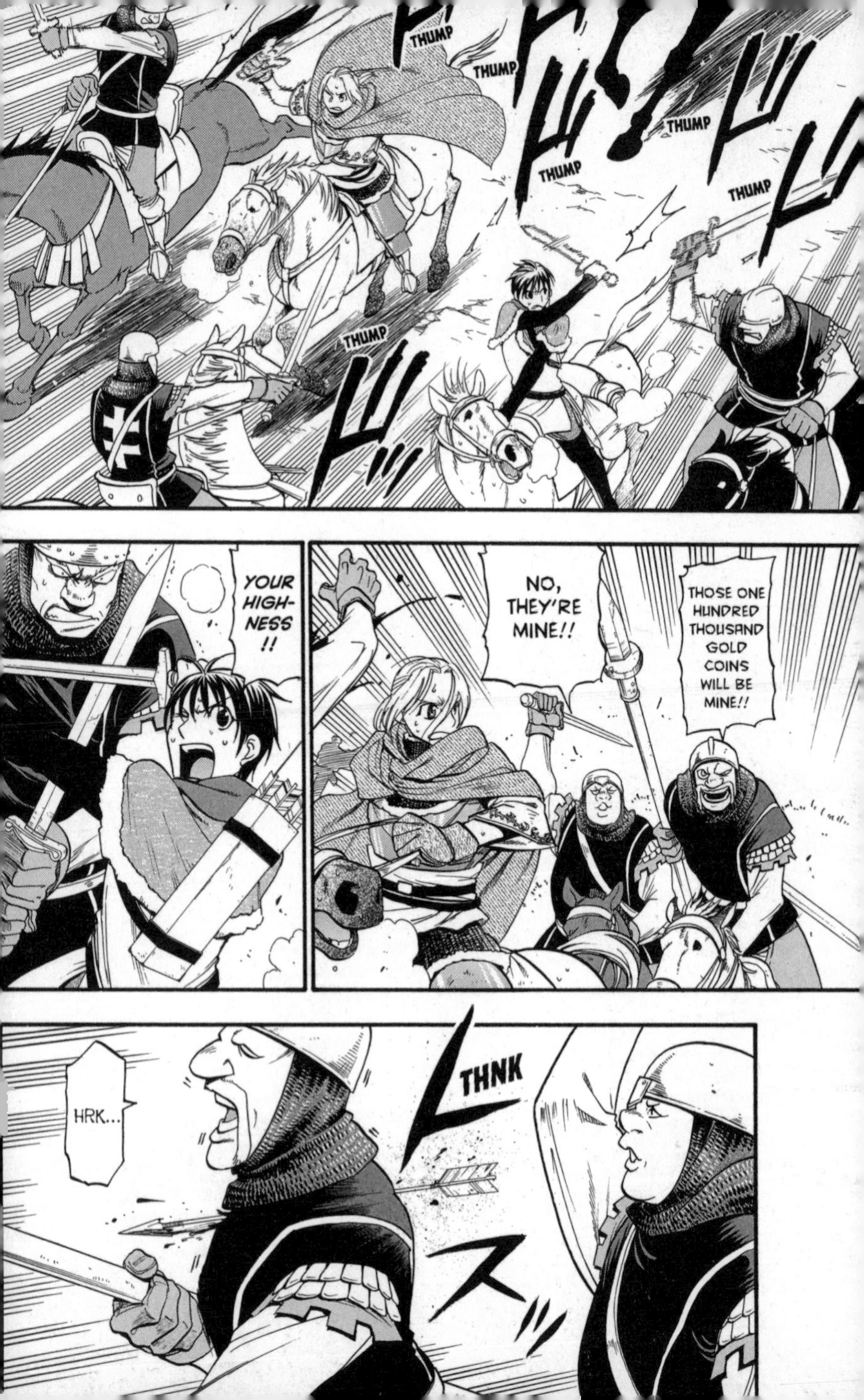
THUMP
THUMP
THUMP
THUMP
THUMP
THUMP
THOSE ONE HUNDRED THOUSAND GOLD COINS WILL BE MINE!!
NO, THEY'RE MINE!!
YOUR HIGHNESS!!
THNK
HRK...

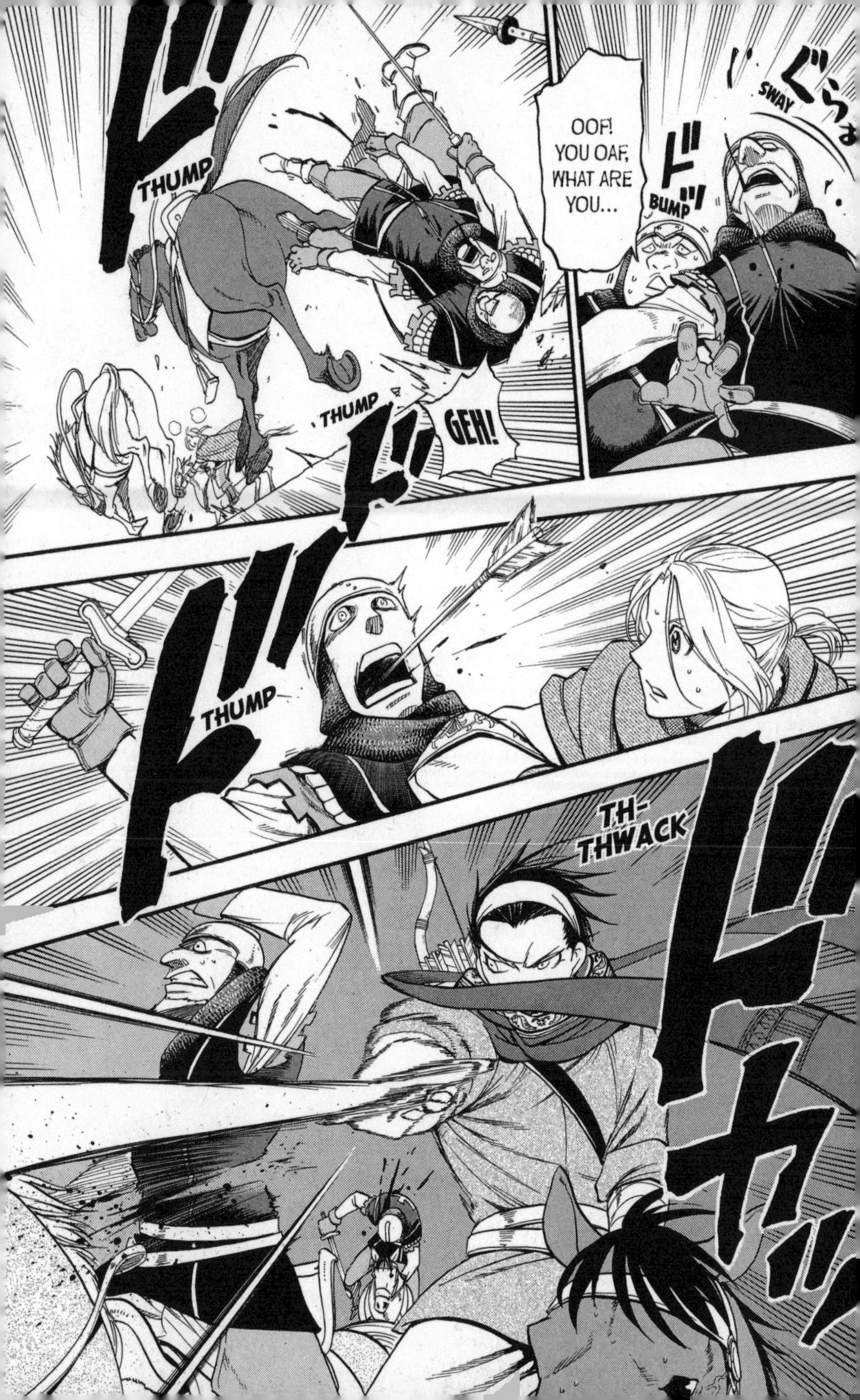
SWAY
OOF! YOU OAF, WHAT ARE YOU...
BUMP
THUMP
THUMP
GEH!
THUMP
TH-THWACK

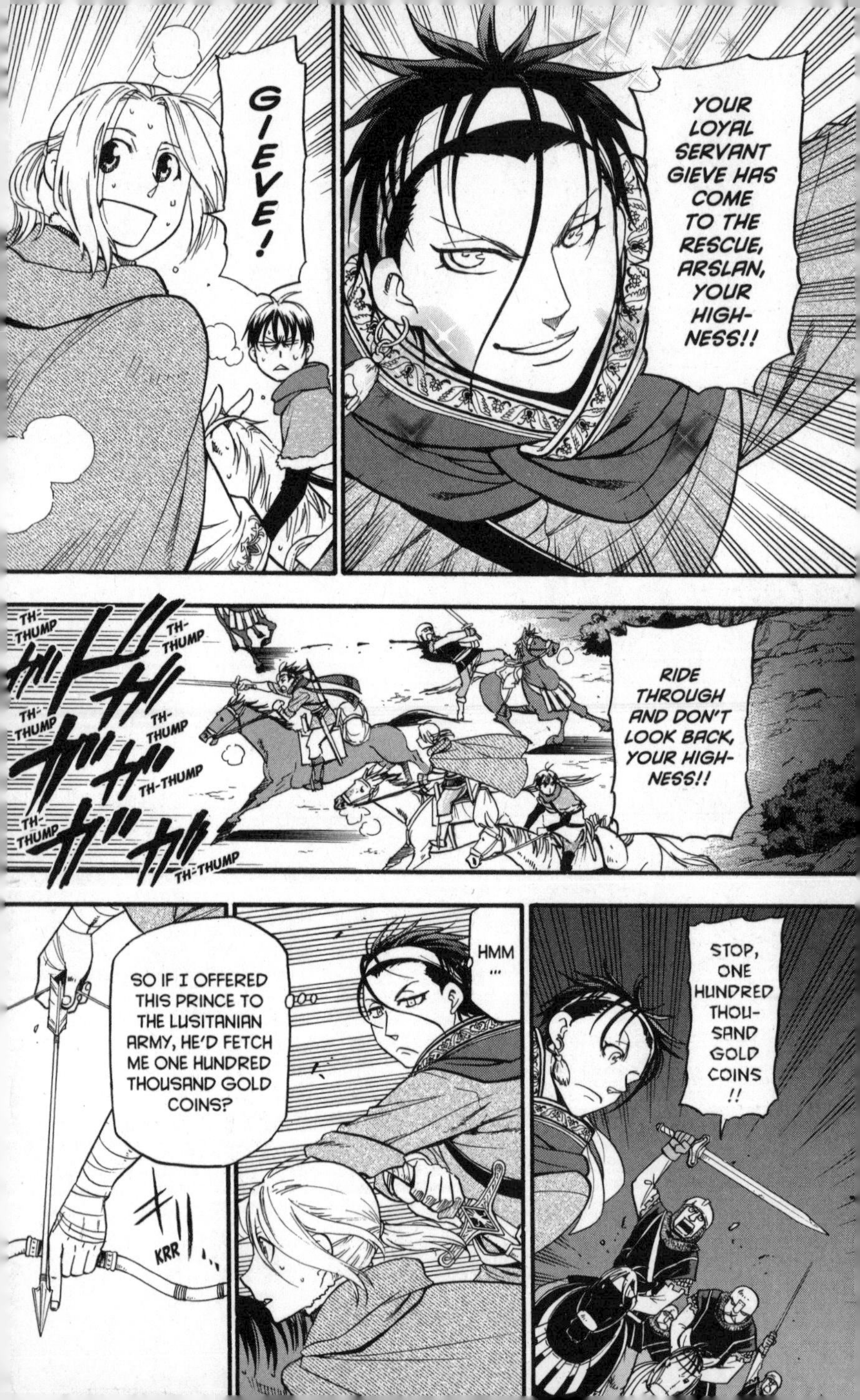

YOUR LOYAL SERVANT GIEVE HAS COME TO THE RESCUE, ARSLAN, YOUR HIGHNESS!!
GIEVE!
RIDE THROUGH AND DON'T LOOK BACK, YOUR HIGHNESS!!
TH-THUMP
TH-THUMP
TH-THUMP
TH-THUMP
TH-THUMP
TH-THUMP
TH-THUMP
STOP, ONE HUNDRED THOUSAND GOLD COINS!!
HMM ...
SO IF I OFFERED THIS PRINCE TO THE LUSITANIAN ARMY, HE'D FETCH ME ONE HUNDRED THOUSAND GOLD COINS?
KRR

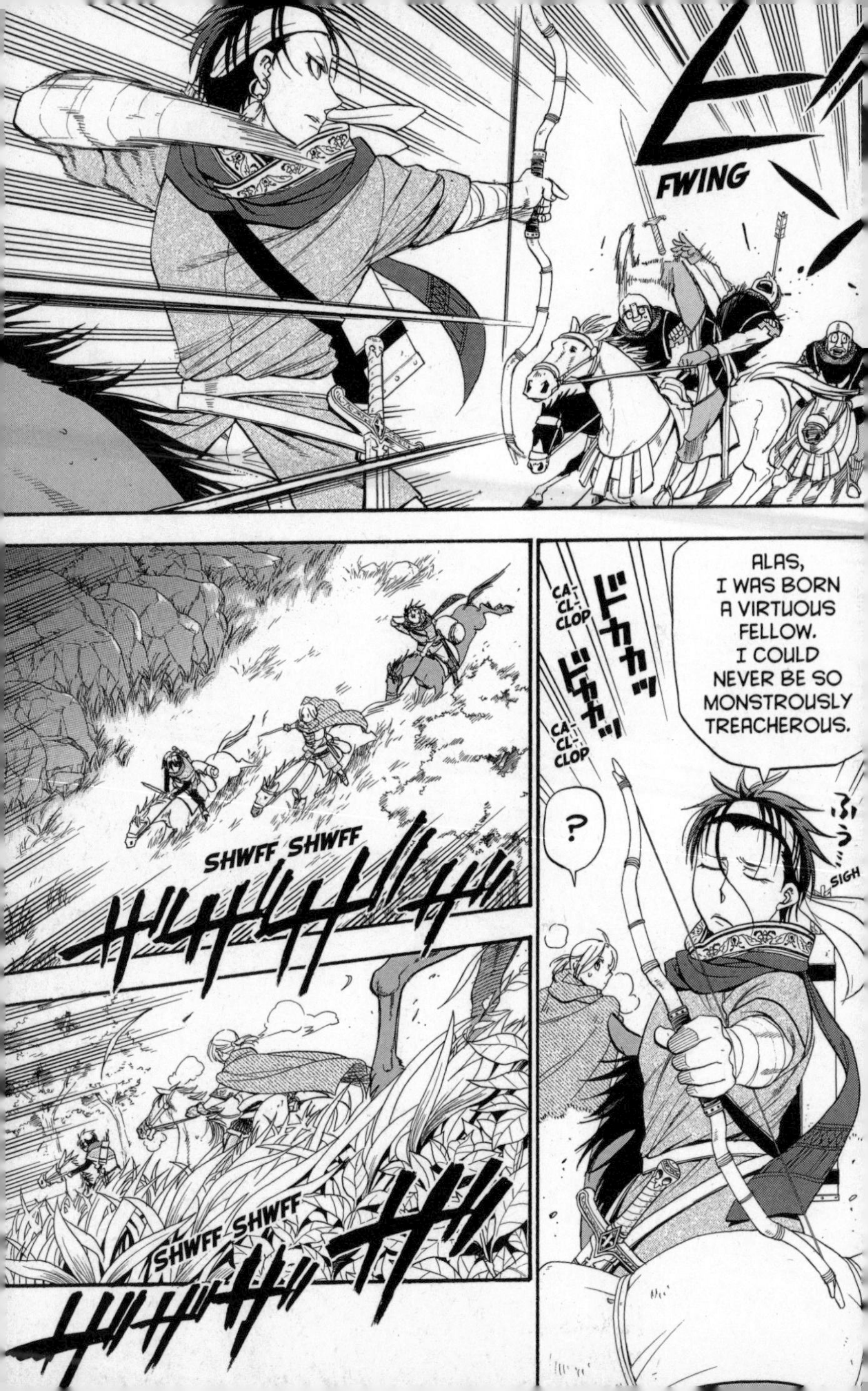
FWING
ALAS, I WAS BORN A VIRTUOUS FELLOW. I COULD NEVER BE SO MONSTROUSLY TREACHEROUS.
ふぅ
SIGH
ドカカッ
CA-CL-CLOP
ドカカッ
CA-CL-CLOP
?
SHWFF SHWFF
SHWFF SHWFF

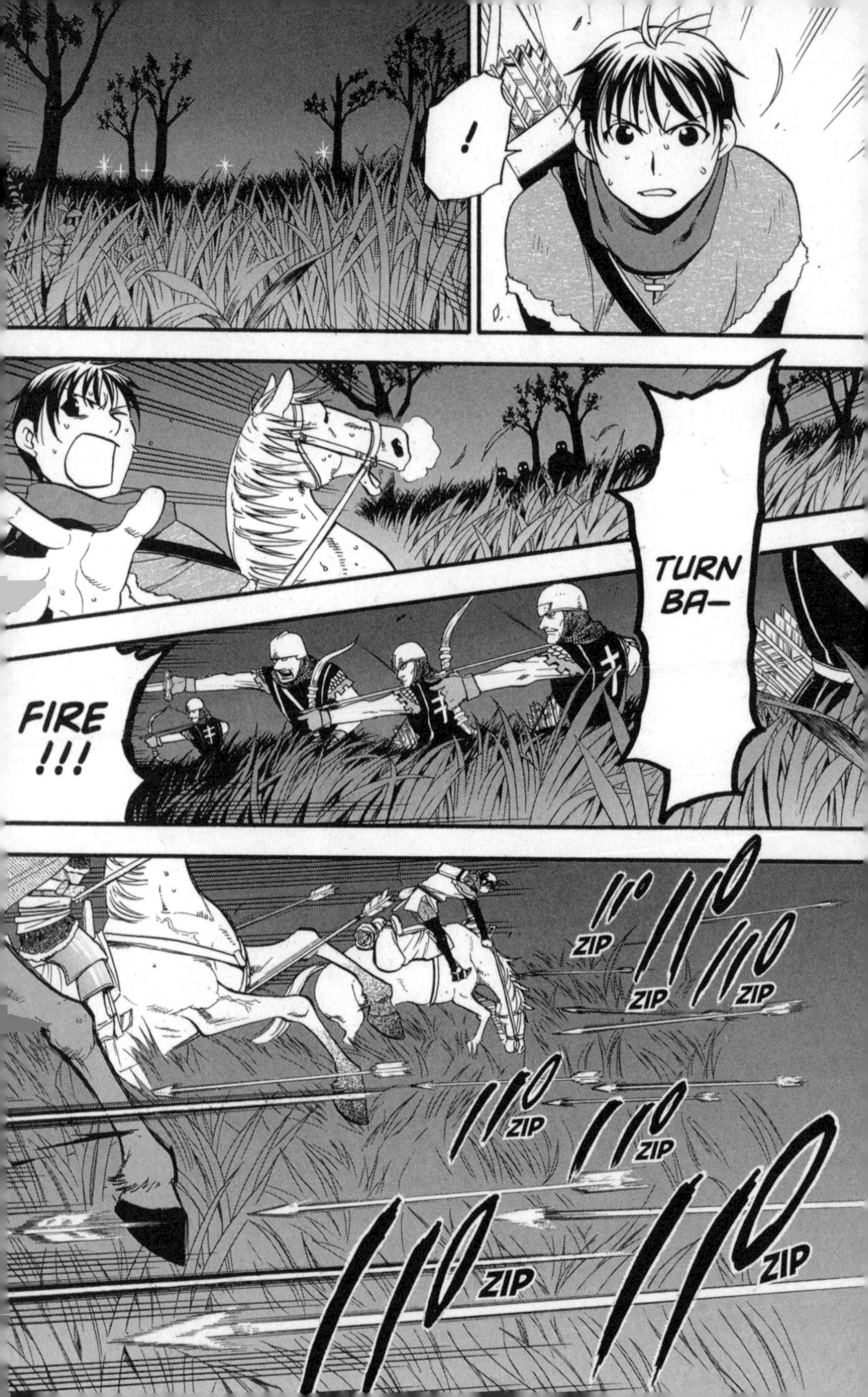
!
TURN BA—
FIRE !!!
ZIP
ZIP
ZIP
ZIP
ZIP
ZIP
ZIP

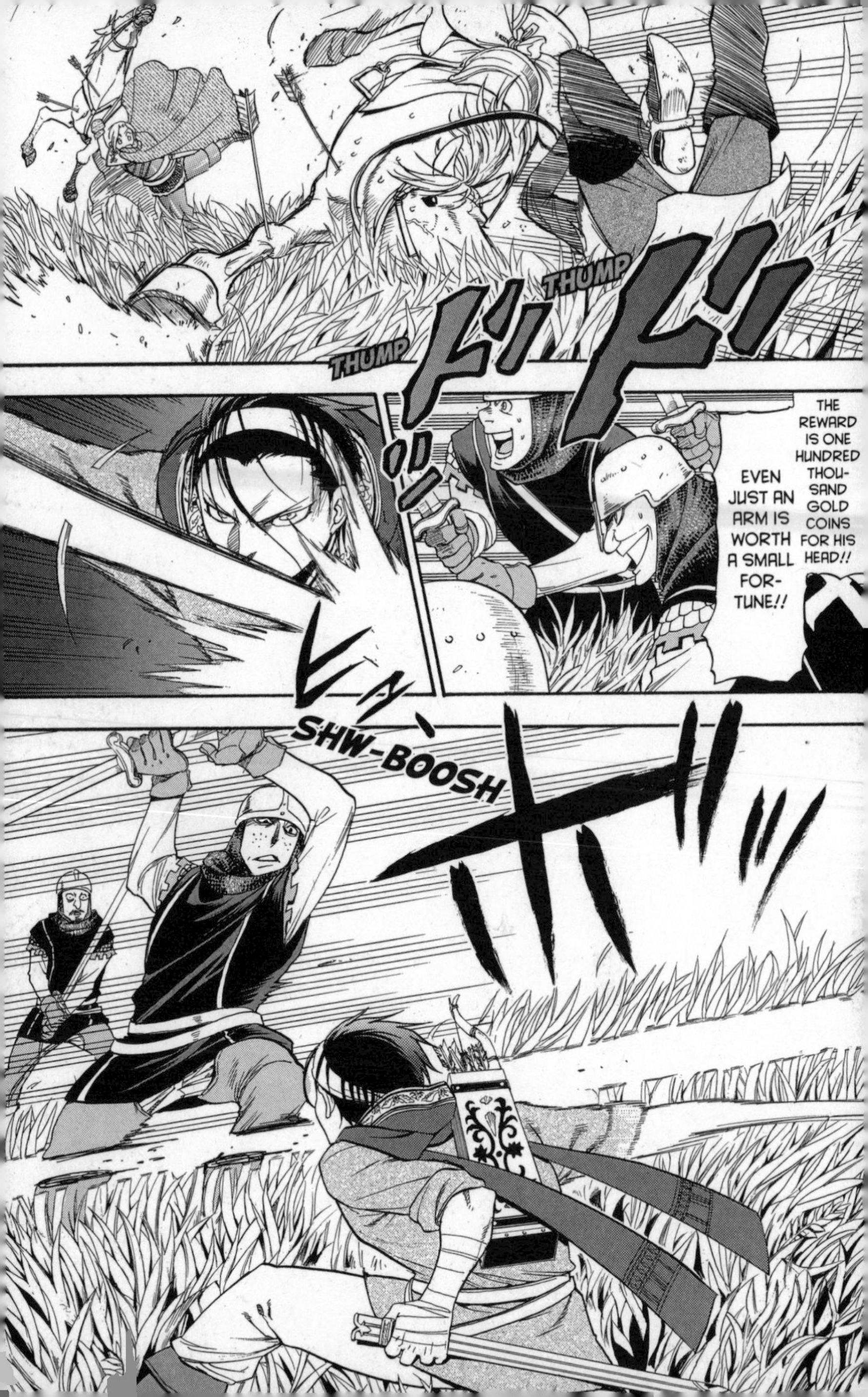
THUMP
THUMP
THE REWARD IS ONE HUNDRED THOUSAND GOLD COINS FOR HIS HEAD!!
EVEN JUST AN ARM IS WORTH A SMALL FORTUNE!!
SHW-BOOSH

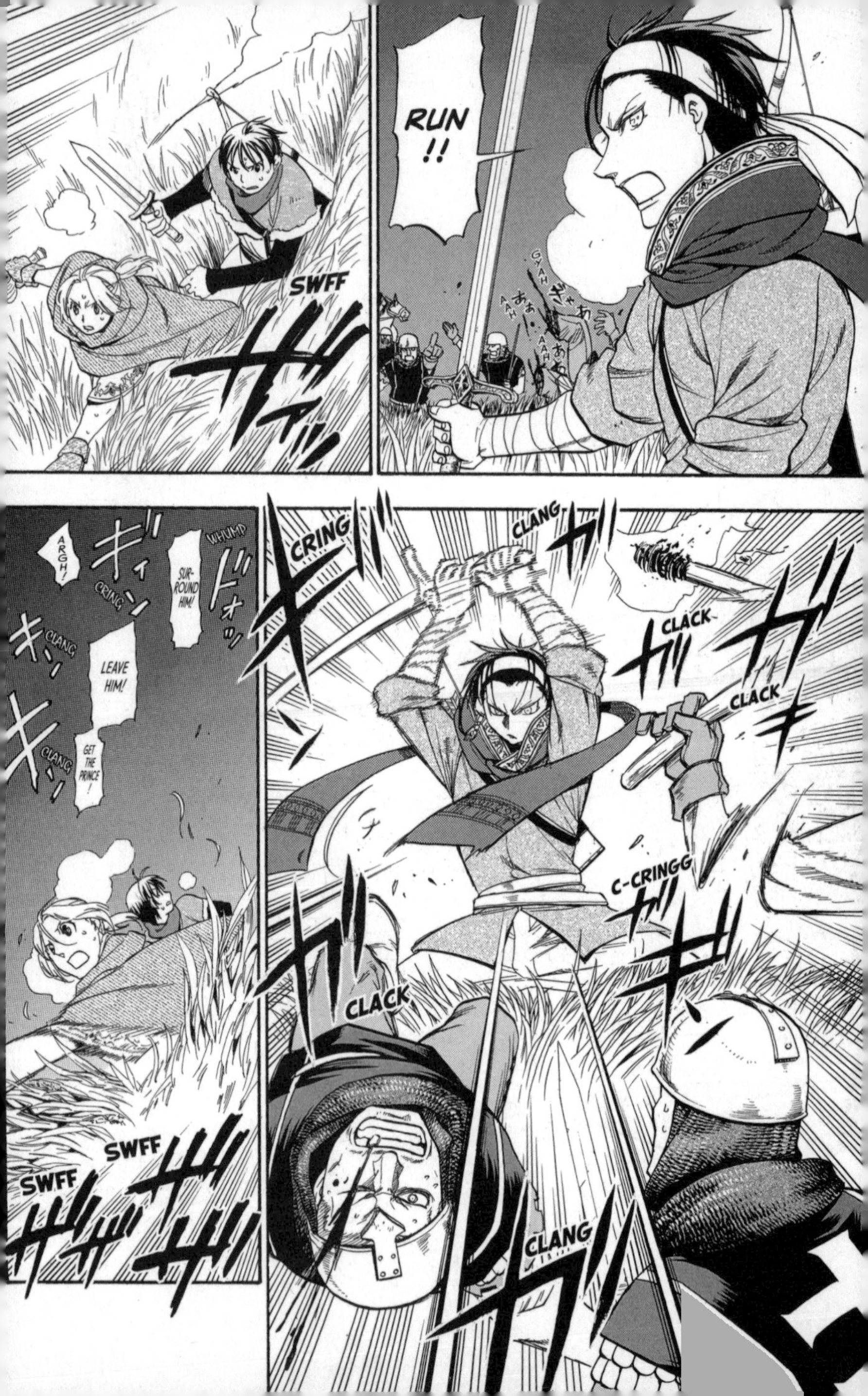
RUN !!
GYAH
AAH
AAH
SWFF
CRING
CLANG
CLACK
CLACK
C-CRINGG
CLACK
CLANG
WHUMP
SUR-ROUND HIM!
ARGH!
CRING
CLANG
LEAVE HIM!
GET THE PRINCE!
CLANG
SWFF
SWFF

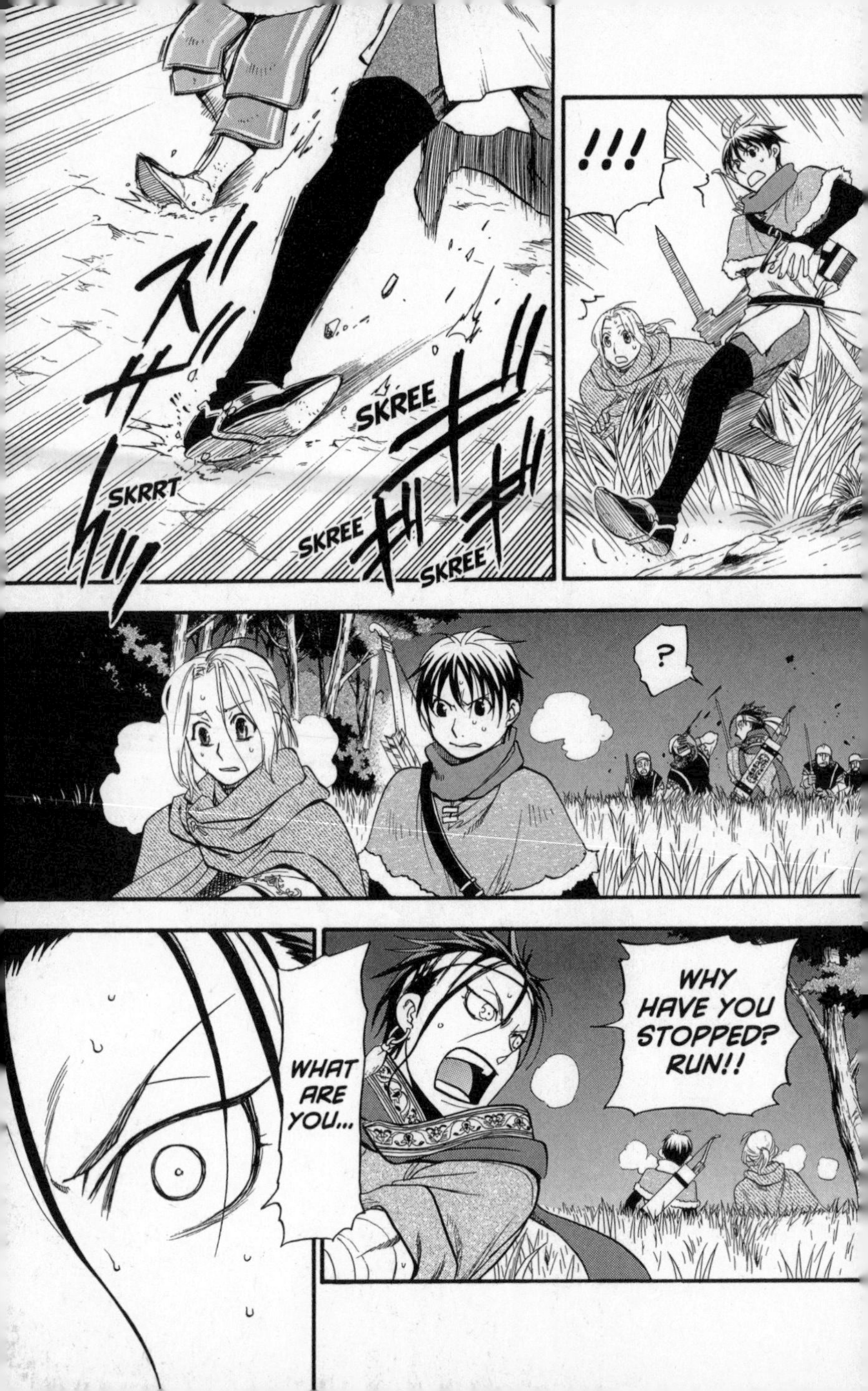
!!!
SKREE
SKREE
SKREE
SKRRT
?
WHY HAVE YOU STOPPED? RUN!!
WHAT ARE YOU...

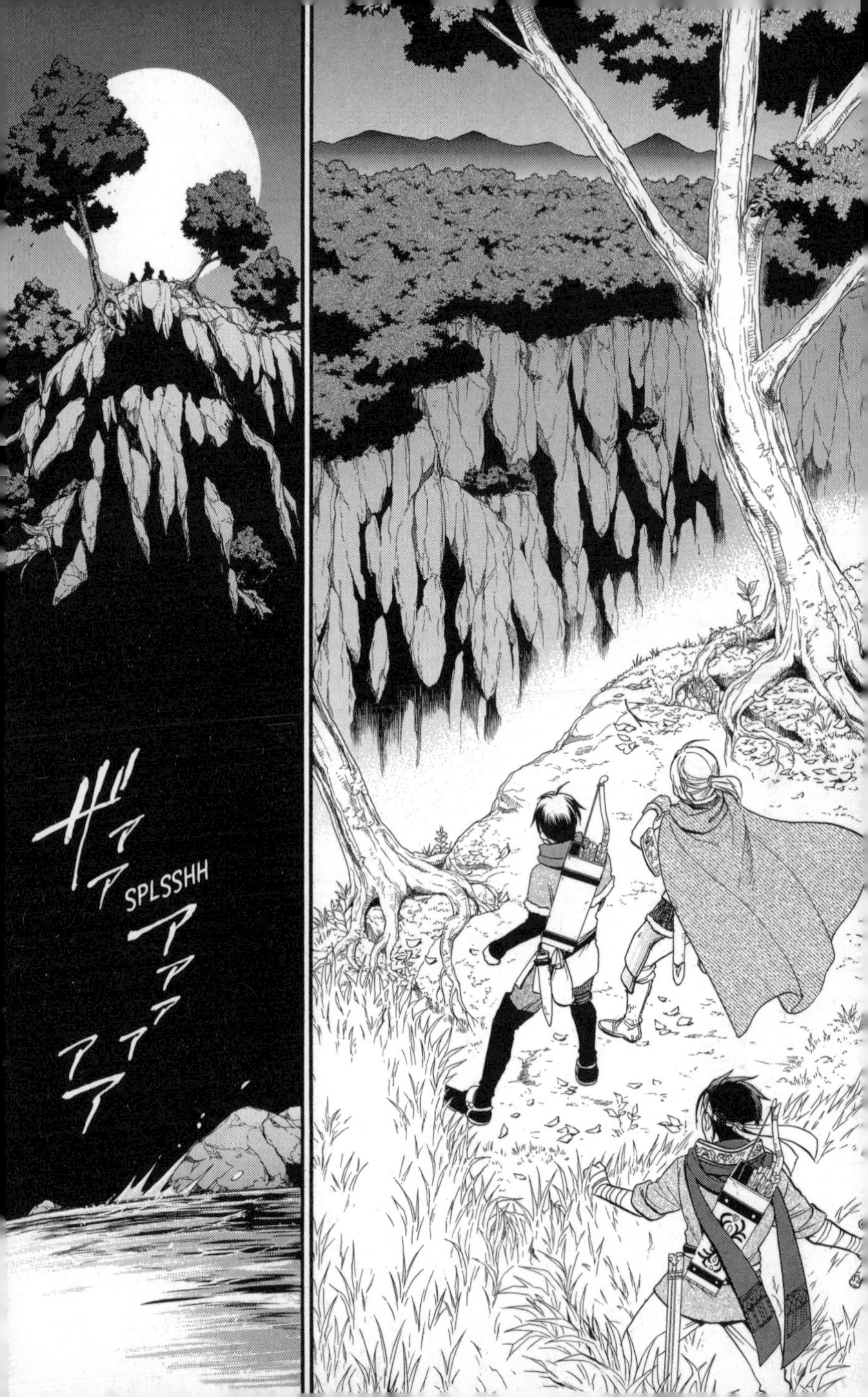
ザァアアアァアアア
SPLSSHH

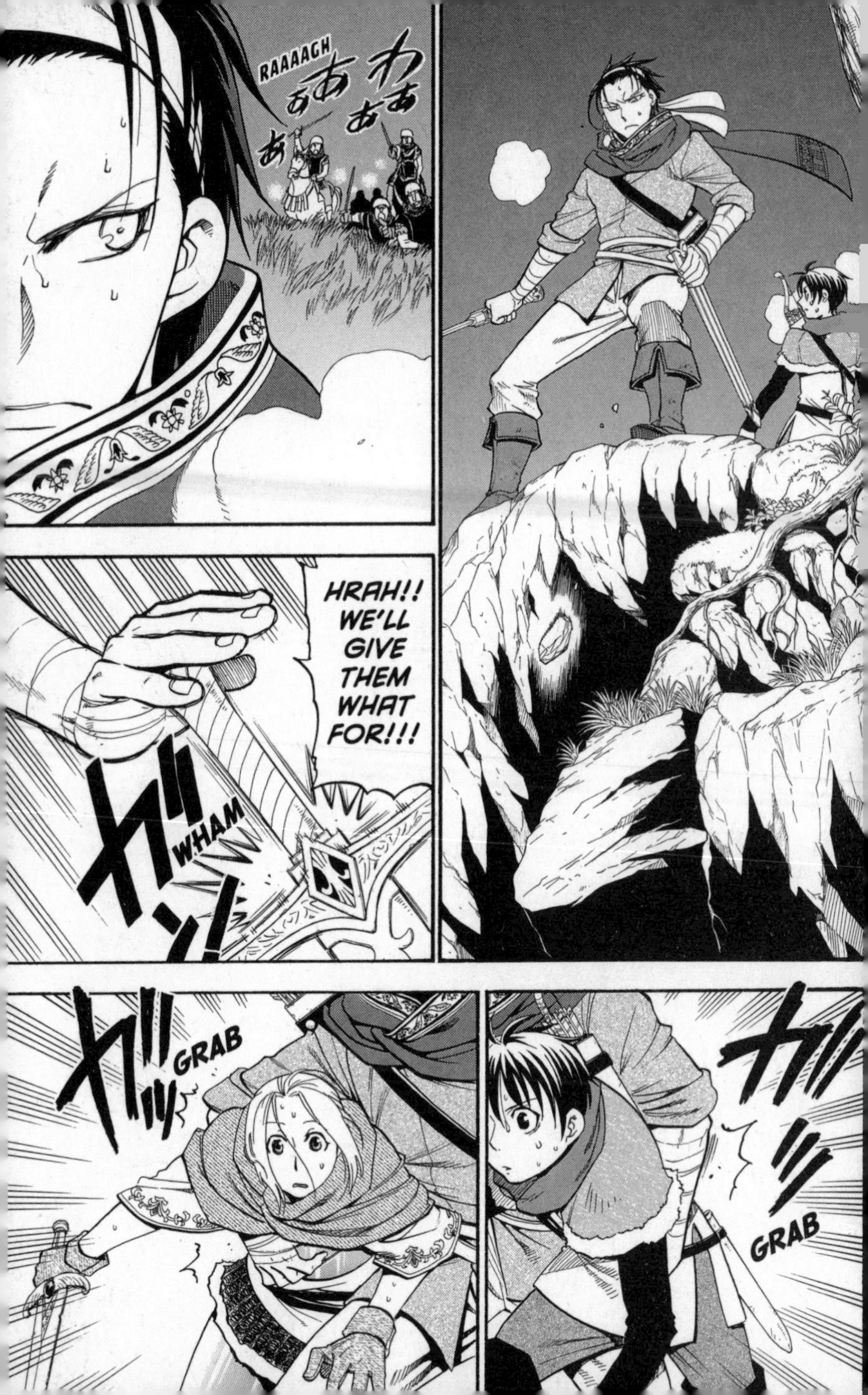
RAAAAGH
HRAH!! WE'LL GIVE THEM WHAT FOR!!!
WHAM
GRAB
GRAB

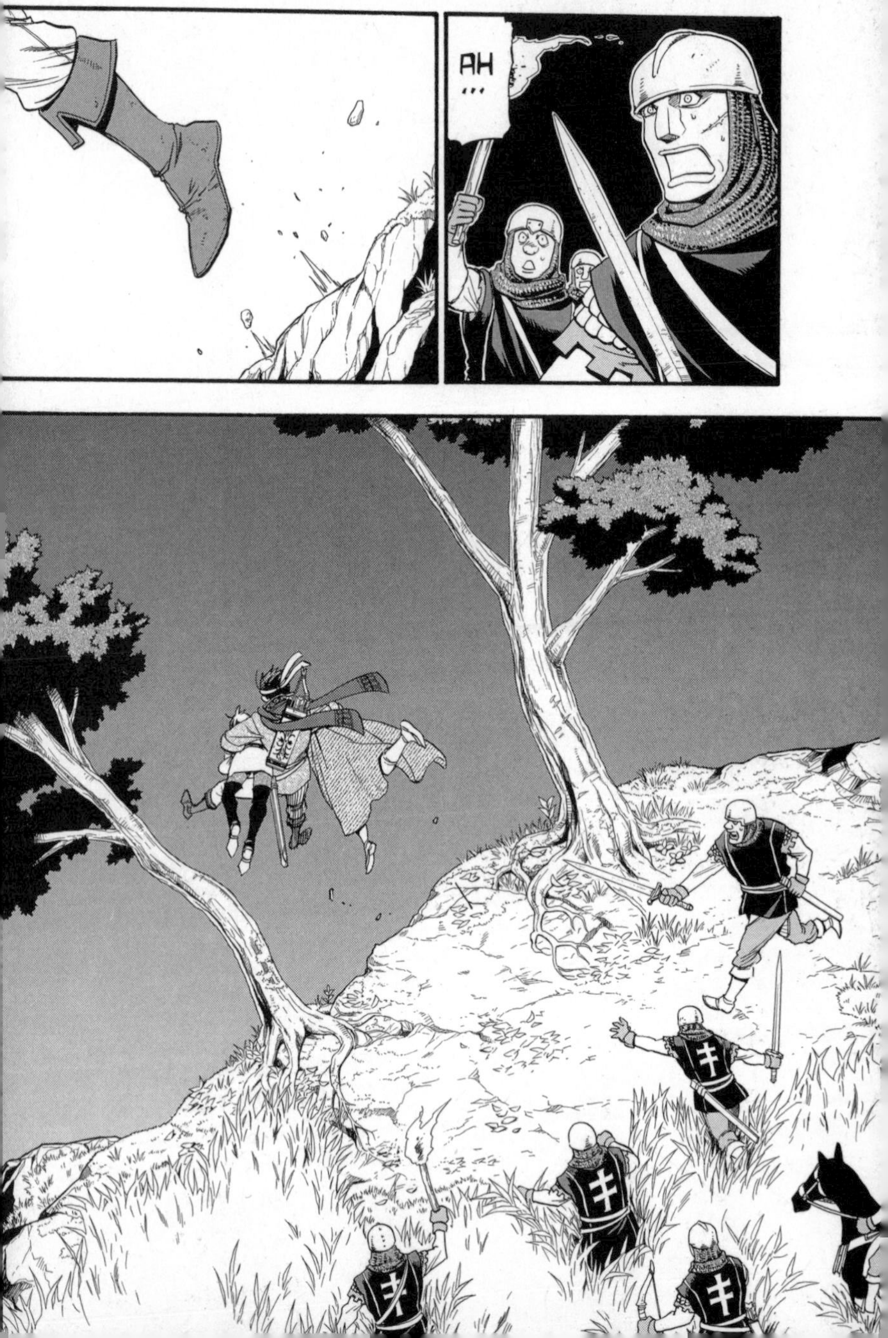
AH ...

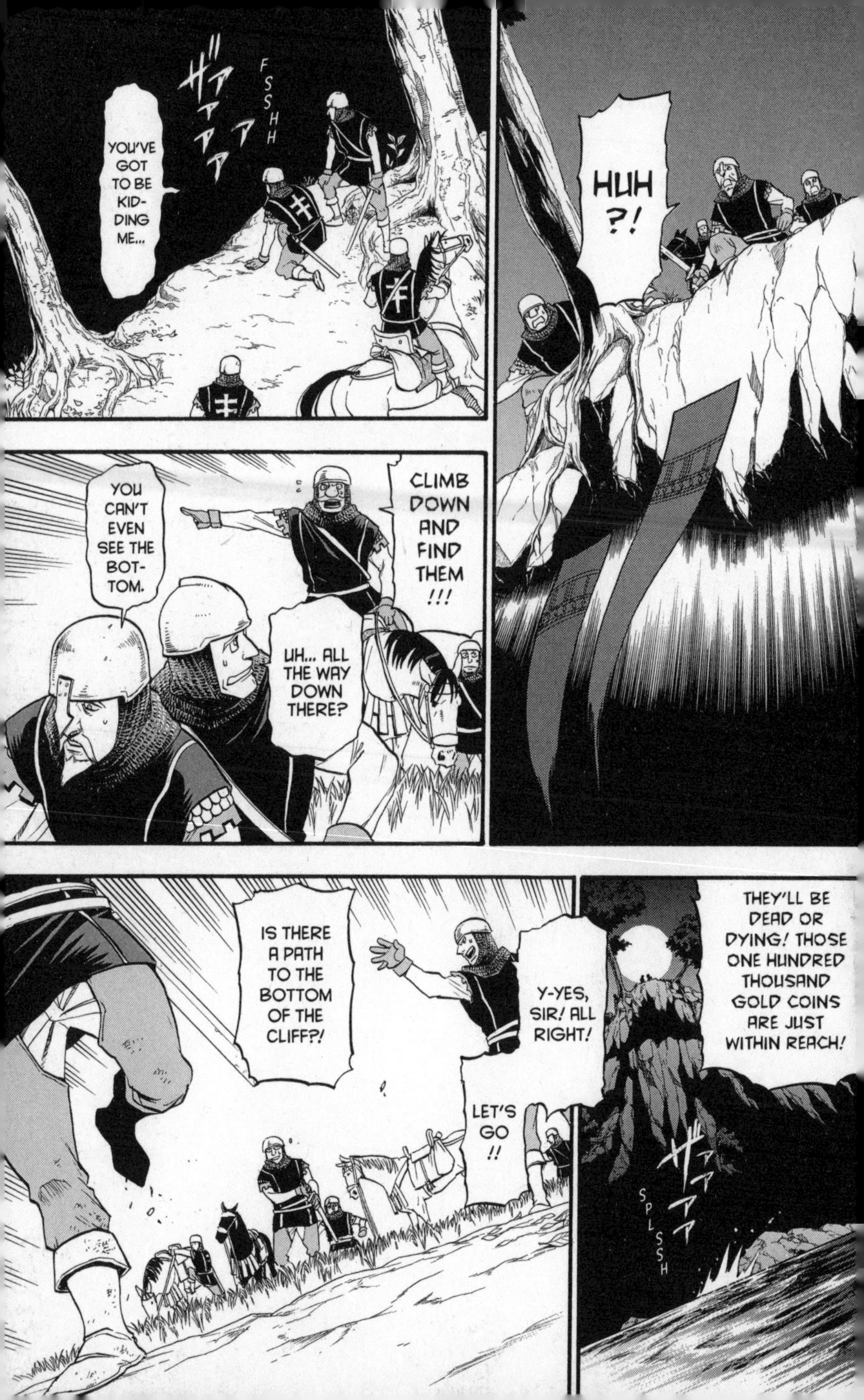
HUH?!
FSSHH
YOU'VE GOT TO BE KIDDING ME...
CLIMB DOWN AND FIND THEM!!!
YOU CAN'T EVEN SEE THE BOTTOM.
UH... ALL THE WAY DOWN THERE?
THEY'LL BE DEAD OR DYING! THOSE ONE HUNDRED THOUSAND GOLD COINS ARE JUST WITHIN REACH!
SPLSSH
Y-YES, SIR! ALL RIGHT!
IS THERE A PATH TO THE BOTTOM OF THE CLIFF?!
LET'S GO!!

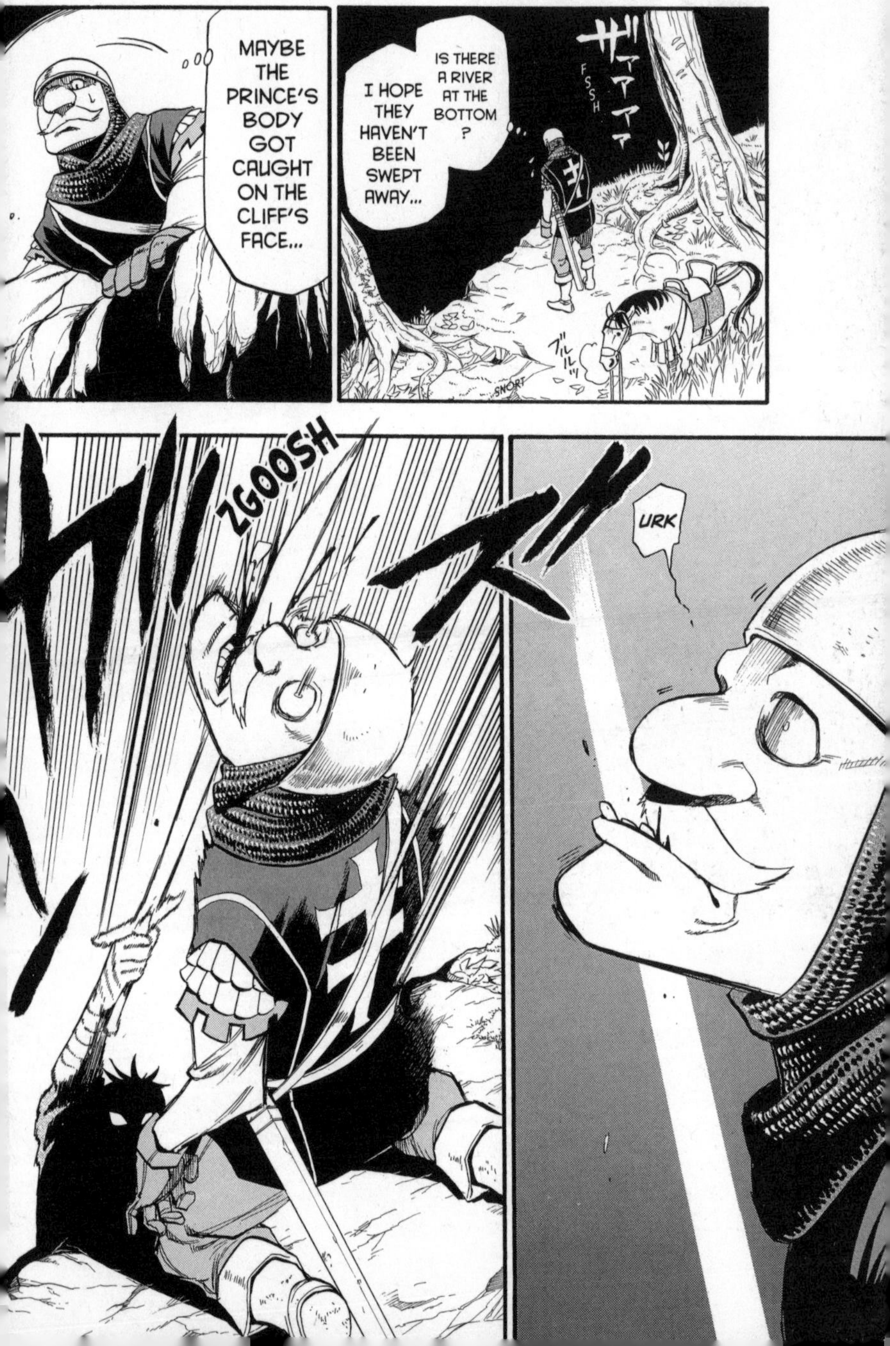
ザァァァ
FSSH
IS THERE A RIVER AT THE BOTTOM?
I HOPE THEY HAVEN'T BEEN SWEPT AWAY...
ブルルッ
SNORT
MAYBE THE PRINCE'S BODY GOT CAUGHT ON THE CLIFF'S FACE...
URK
ZGOOSH

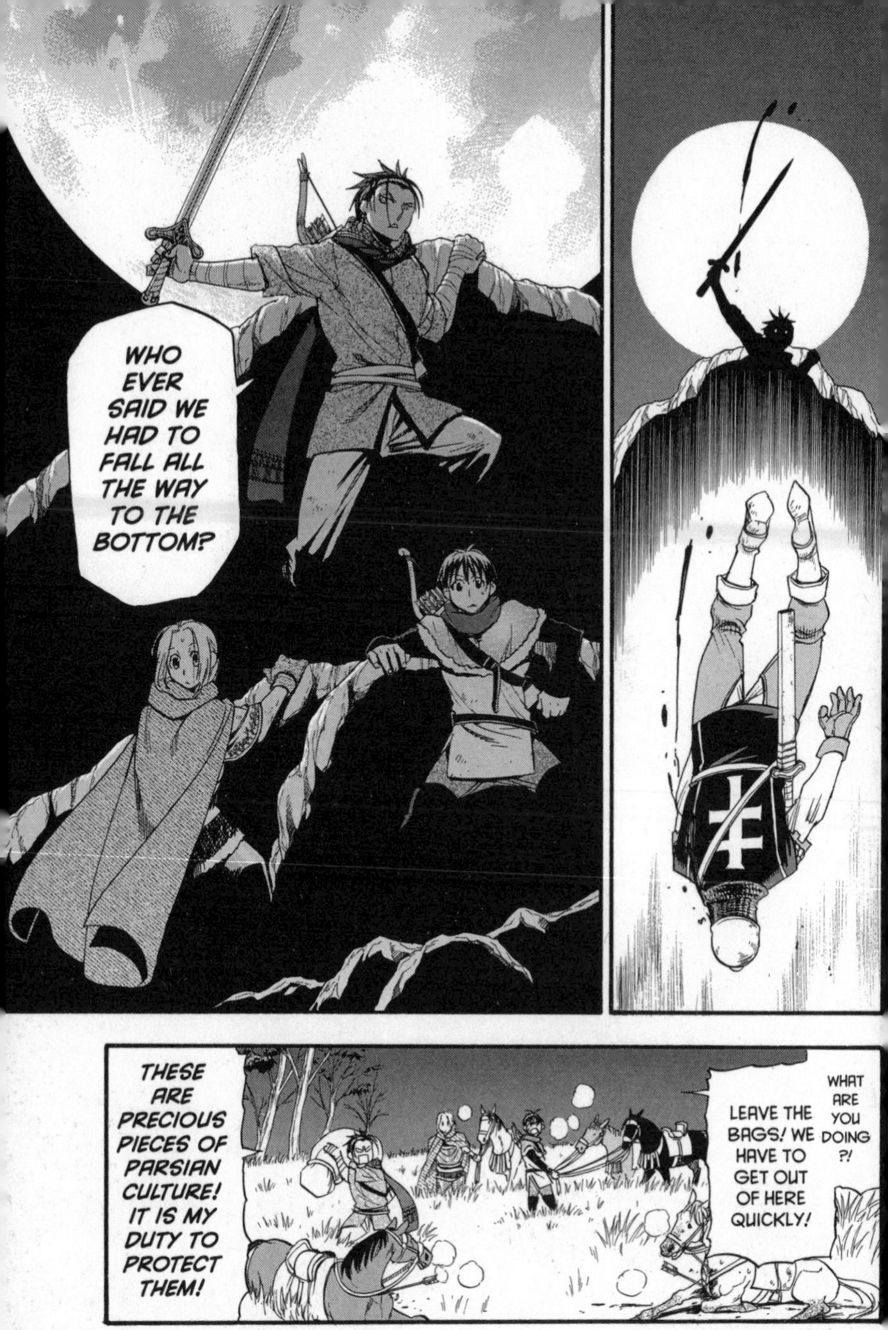
WHO EVER SAID WE HAD TO FALL ALL THE WAY TO THE BOTTOM?
WHAT ARE YOU DOING?!
LEAVE THE BAGS! WE HAVE TO GET OUT OF HERE QUICKLY!
THESE ARE PRECIOUS PIECES OF PARSIAN CULTURE! IT IS MY DUTY TO PROTECT THEM!

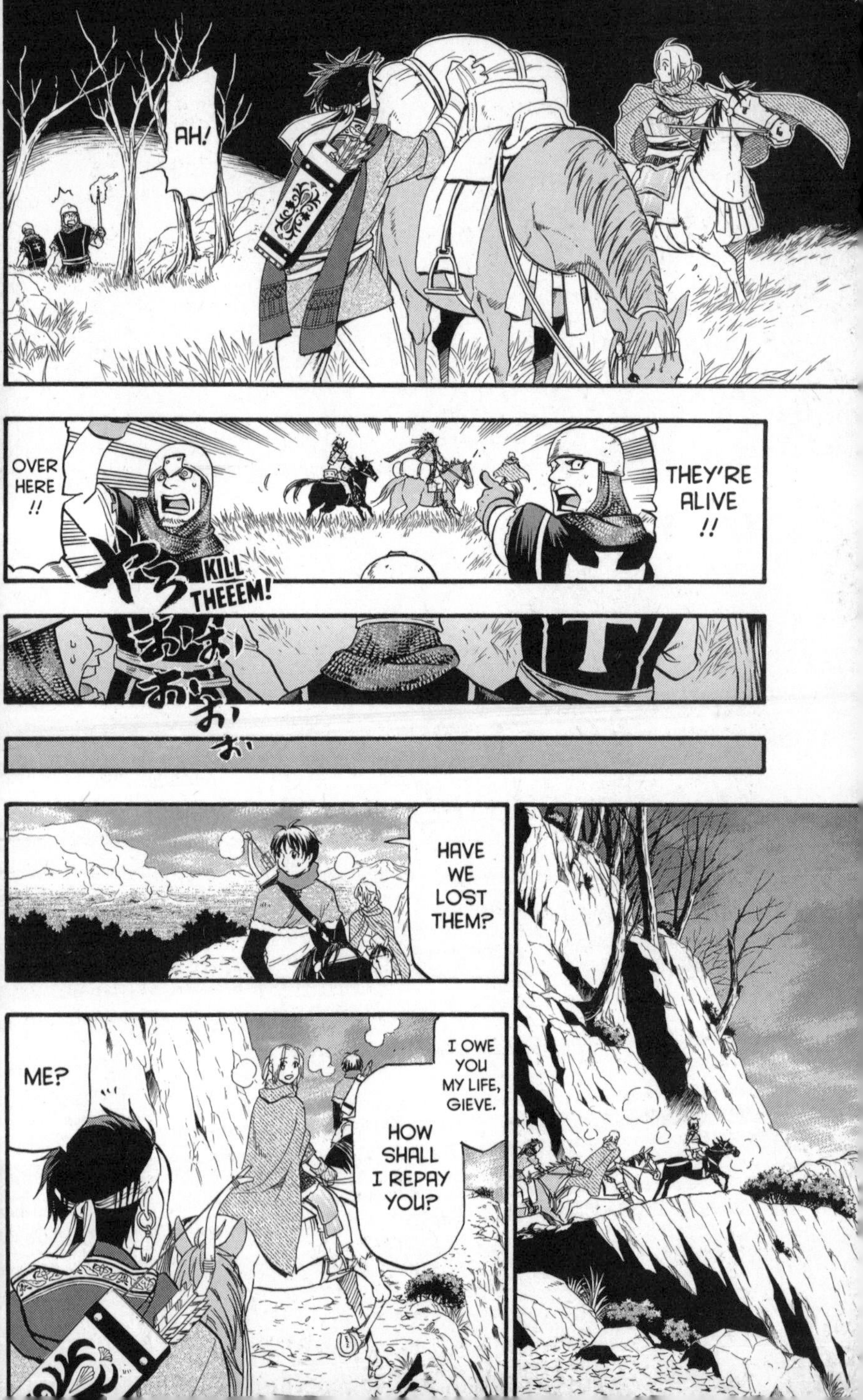
AH!
THEY'RE ALIVE !!
OVER HERE !!
KILL THEEEM!
HAVE WE LOST THEM?
I OWE YOU MY LIFE, GIEVE.
HOW SHALL I REPAY YOU?
ME?

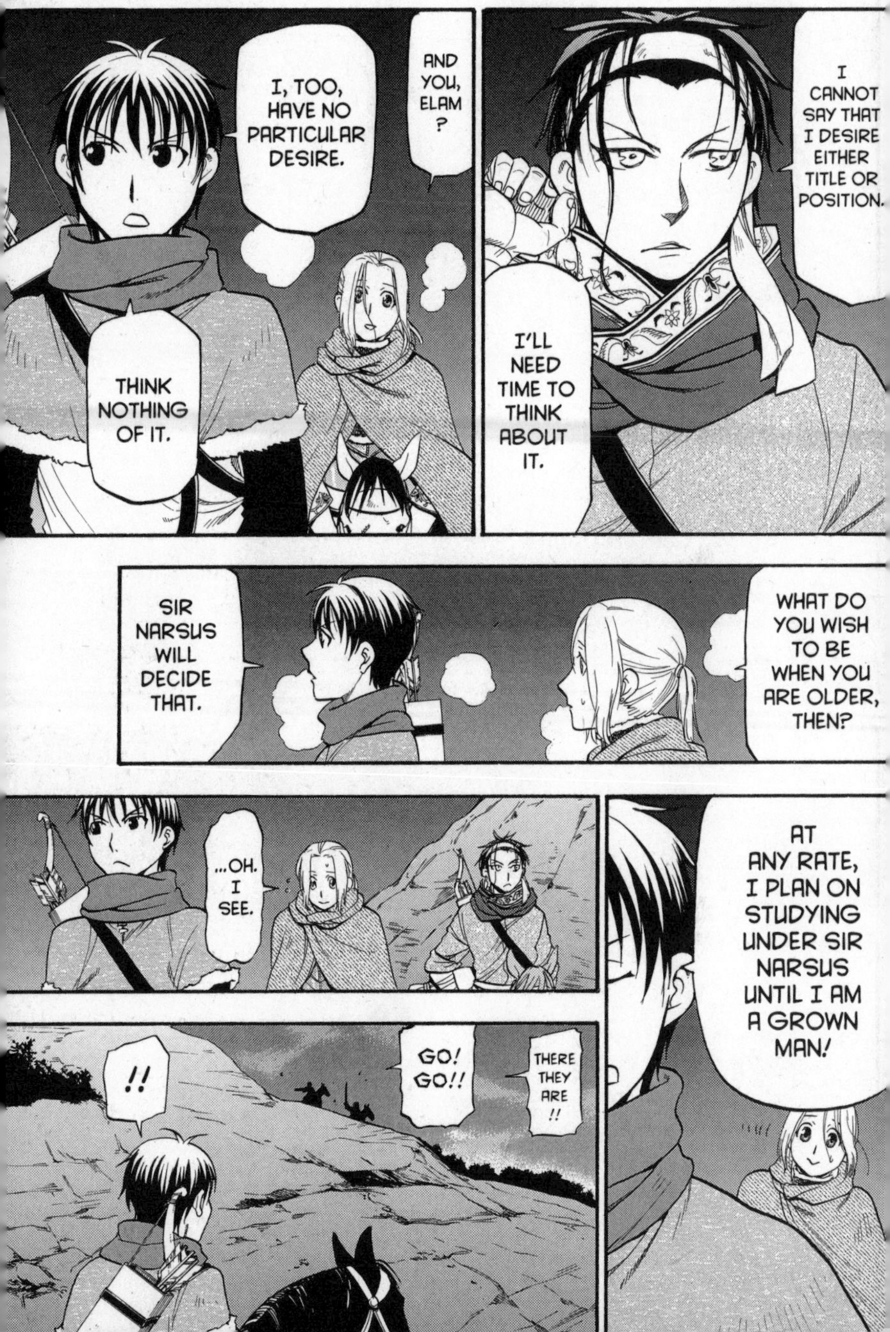
I CANNOT SAY THAT I DESIRE EITHER TITLE OR POSITION.
I'LL NEED TIME TO THINK ABOUT IT.
AND YOU, ELAM?
I, TOO, HAVE NO PARTICULAR DESIRE.
THINK NOTHING OF IT.
WHAT DO YOU WISH TO BE WHEN YOU ARE OLDER, THEN?
SIR NARSUS WILL DECIDE THAT.
AT ANY RATE, I PLAN ON STUDYING UNDER SIR NARSUS UNTIL I AM A GROWN MAN!
...OH. I SEE.
THERE THEY ARE!!
GO! GO!!
!!

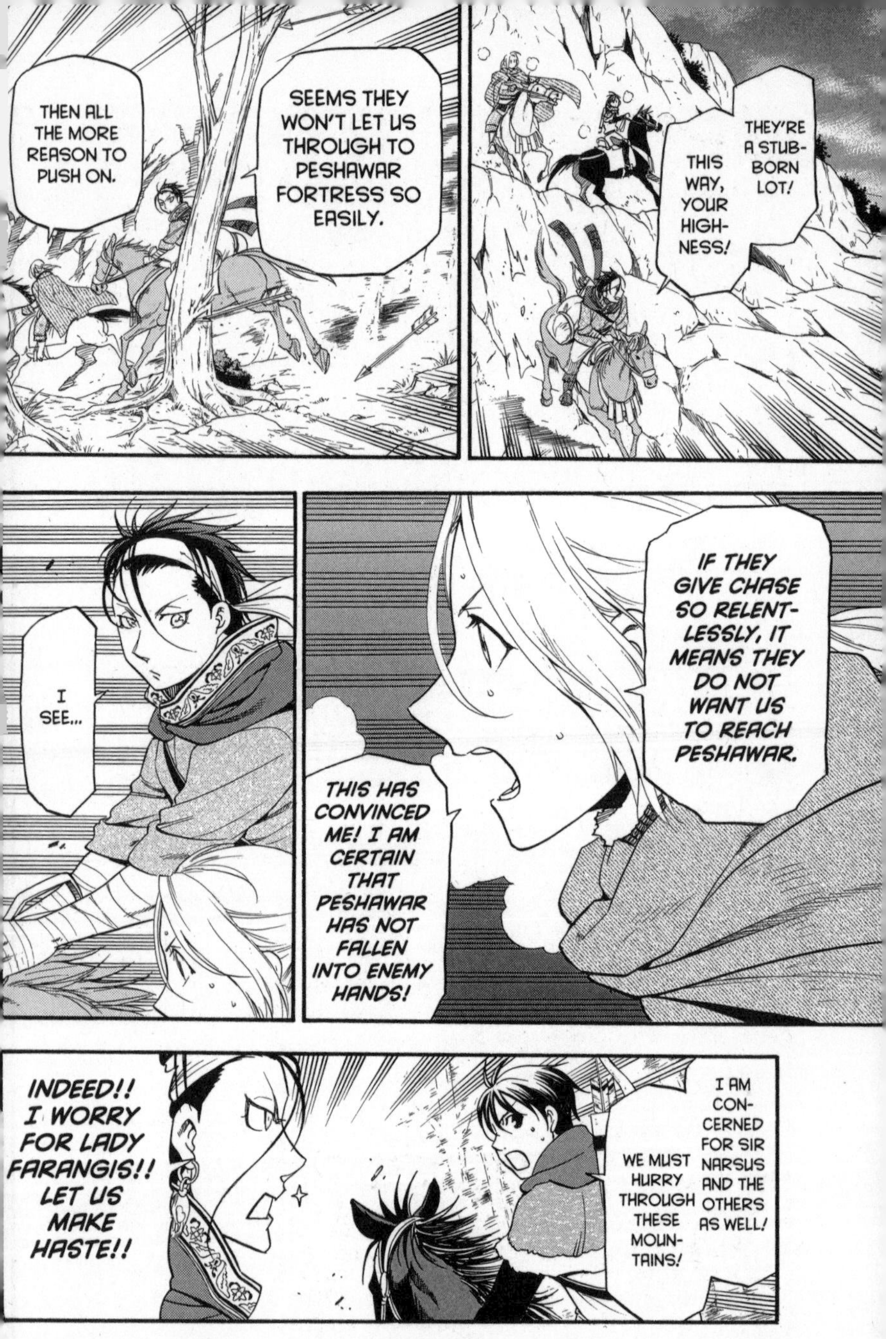
THEY'RE A STUBBORN LOT!
THIS WAY, YOUR HIGHNESS!
SEEMS THEY WON'T LET US THROUGH TO PESHAWAR FORTRESS SO EASILY.
THEN ALL THE MORE REASON TO PUSH ON.
IF THEY GIVE CHASE SO RELENTLESSLY, IT MEANS THEY DO NOT WANT US TO REACH PESHAWAR.
THIS HAS CONVINCED ME! I AM CERTAIN THAT PESHAWAR HAS NOT FALLEN INTO ENEMY HANDS!
I SEE...
I AM CONCERNED FOR SIR NARSUS AND THE OTHERS AS WELL!
WE MUST HURRY THROUGH THESE MOUNTAINS!
INDEED!! I WORRY FOR LADY FARANGIS!! LET US MAKE HASTE!!

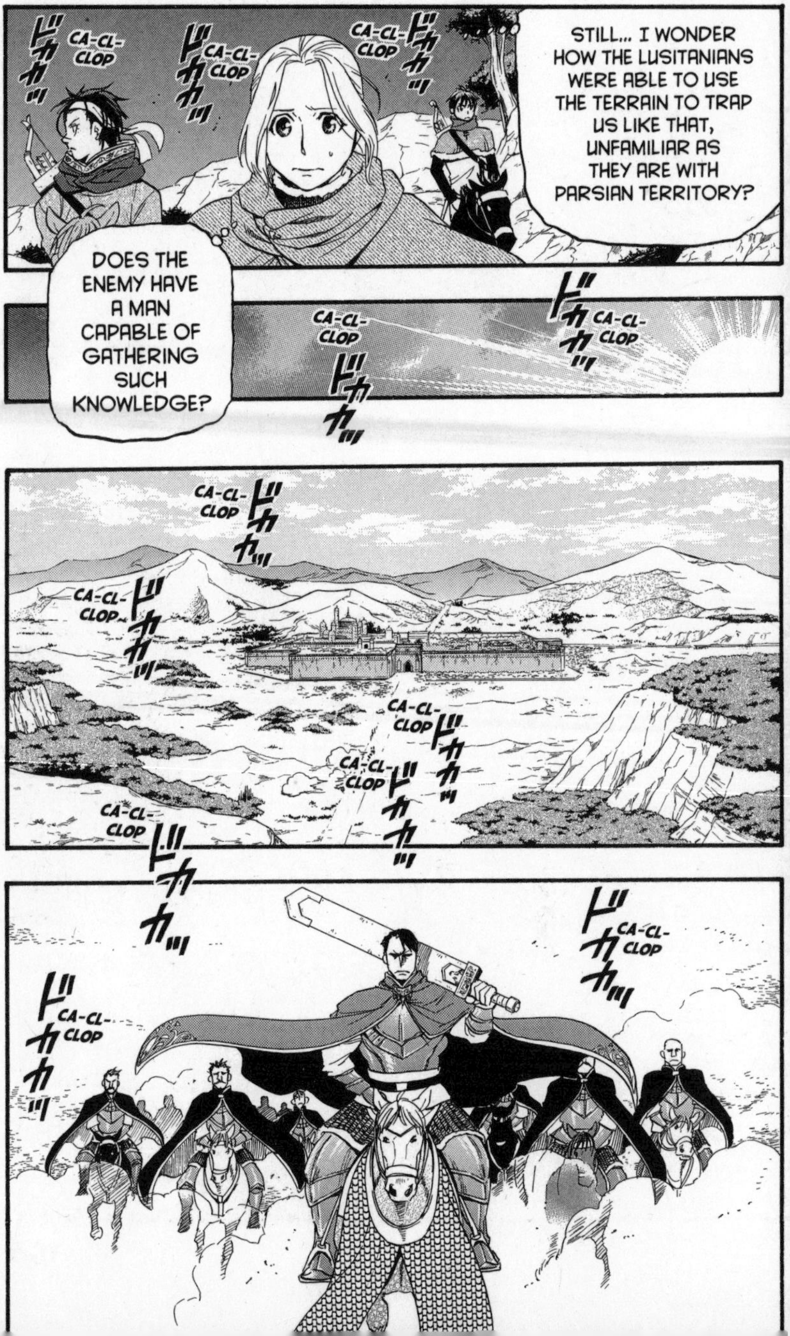
STILL... I WONDER HOW THE LUSITANIANS WERE ABLE TO USE THE TERRAIN TO TRAP US LIKE THAT, UNFAMILIAR AS THEY ARE WITH PARSIAN TERRITORY?
ドカカッ
CA-CL-CLOP
ドカカッ
CA-CL-CLOP
ドカカッ
CA-CL-CLOP
DOES THE ENEMY HAVE A MAN CAPABLE OF GATHERING SUCH KNOWLEDGE?
ドカカッ
CA-CL-CLOP
ドカカッ
CA-CL-CLOP
ドカカッ
CA-CL-CLOP
ドカカッ
CA-CL-CLOP...
ドカカッ
CA-CL-CLOP
ドカカッ
CA-CL-CLOP
ドカカッ
CA-CL-CLOP
ドカカッ
CA-CL-CLOP
ドカカッ
CA-CL-CLOP
ドカカッ
CA-CL-CLOP

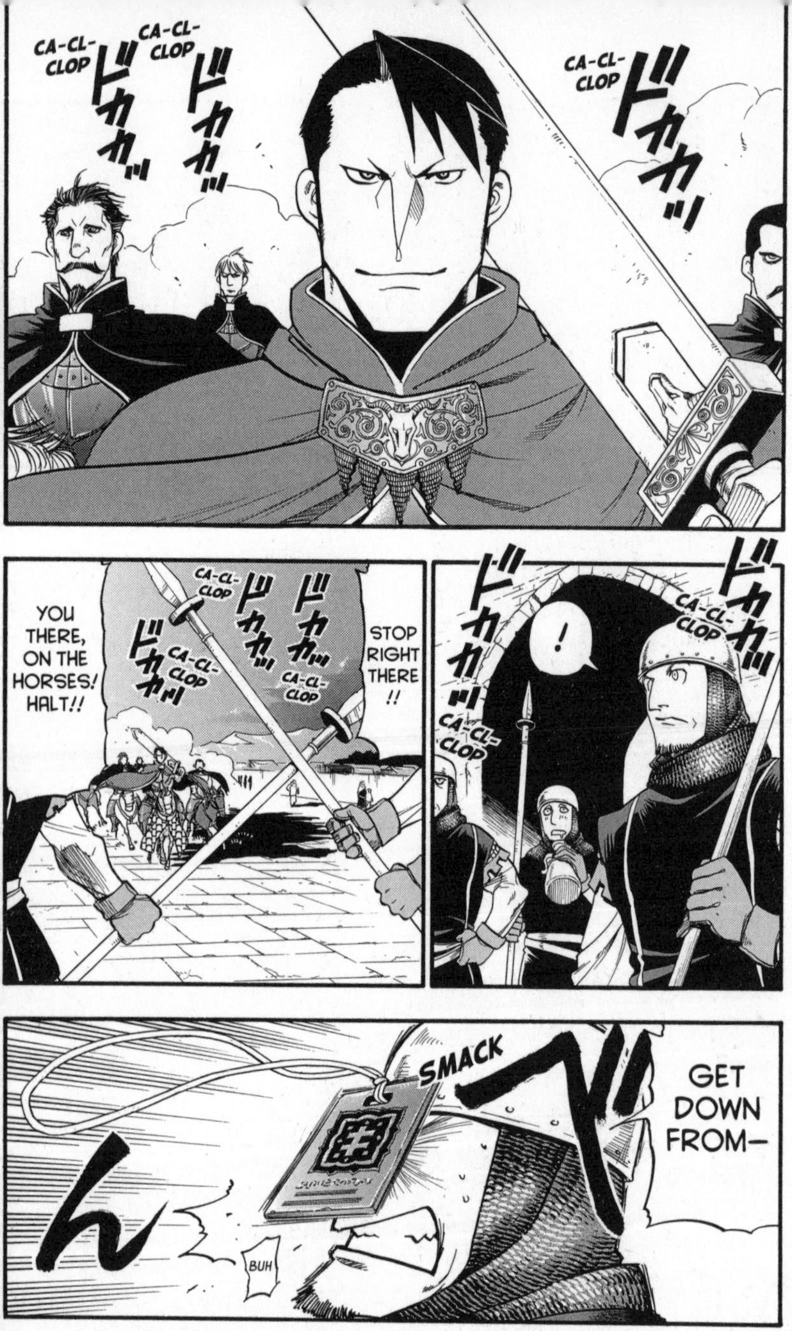
CA-CL-CLOP
CA-CL-CLOP
CA-CL-CLOP
CA-CL-CLOP
!
CA-CL-CLOP
STOP RIGHT THERE!!
CA-CL-CLOP
CA-CL-CLOP
CA-CL-CLOP
YOU THERE, ON THE HORSES! HALT!!
GET DOWN FROM—
SMACK
BUH

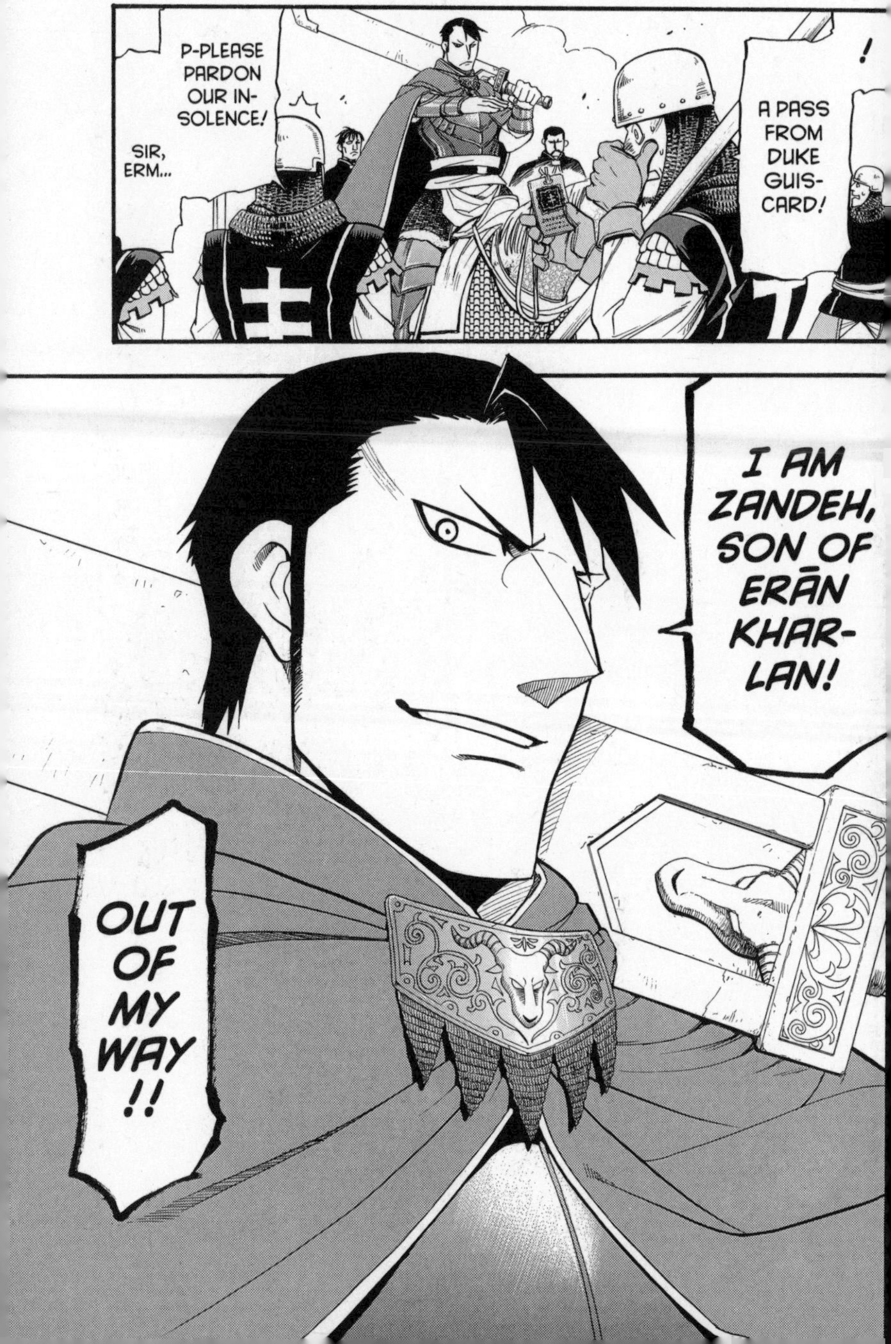
!
A PASS FROM DUKE GUISCARD!
P-PLEASE PARDON OUR INSOLENCE!
SIR, ERM...
I AM ZANDEH, SON OF ERĀN KHARLAN!
OUT OF MY WAY!!

THE HEROIC LEGEND OF
ARSLAN

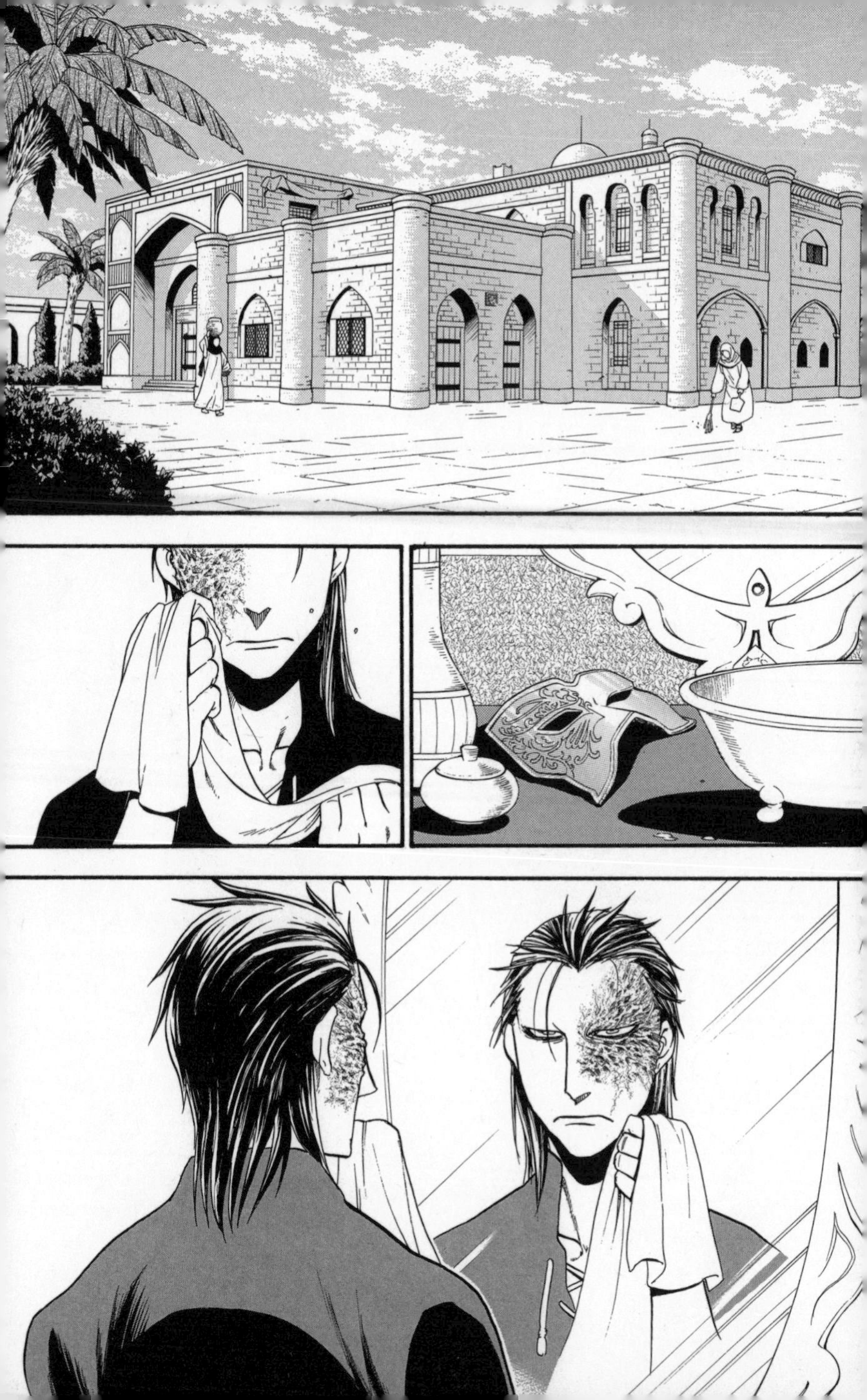

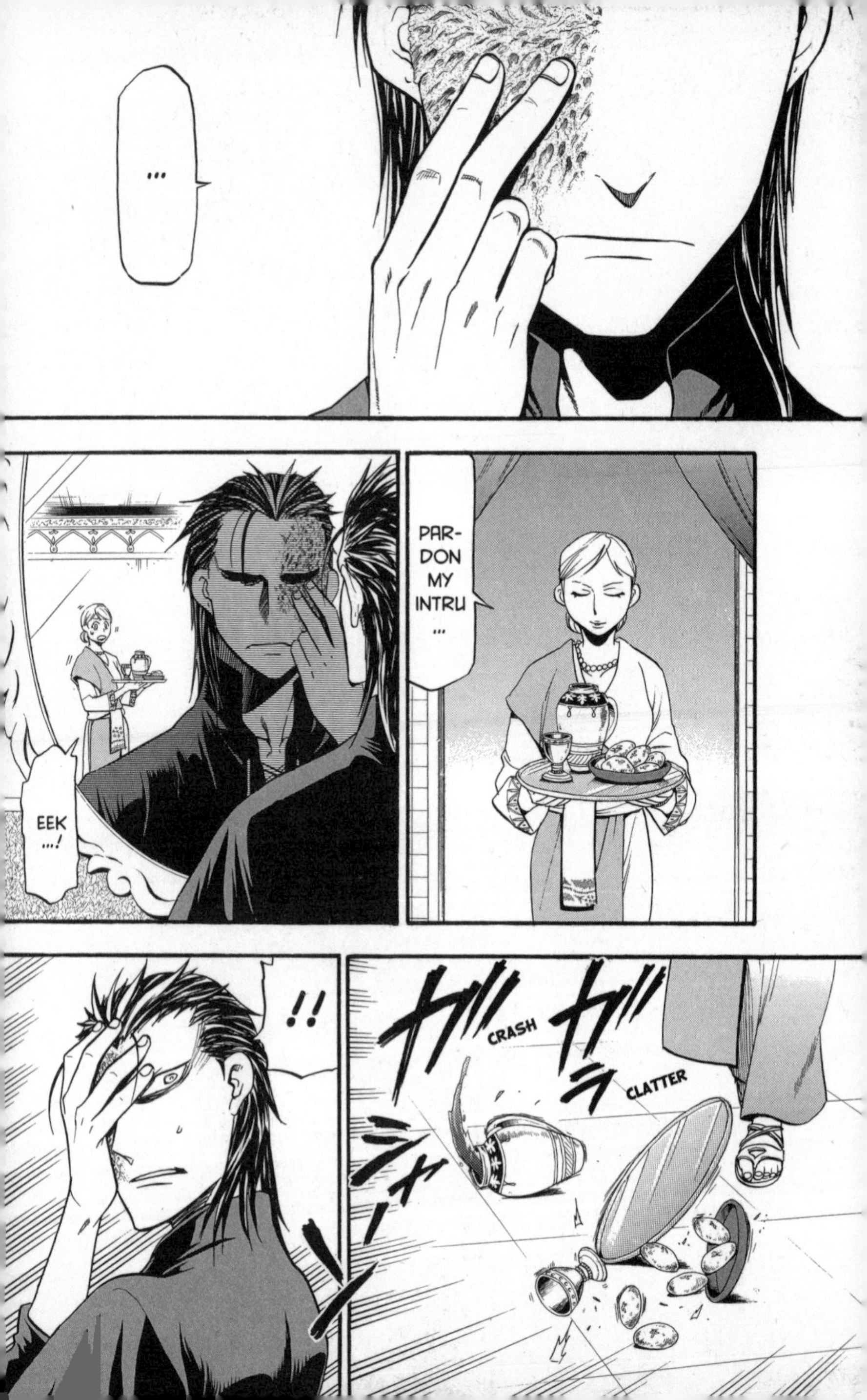
...
PAR-DON MY INTRU...
EEK ...!
CRASH
CLATTER
!!

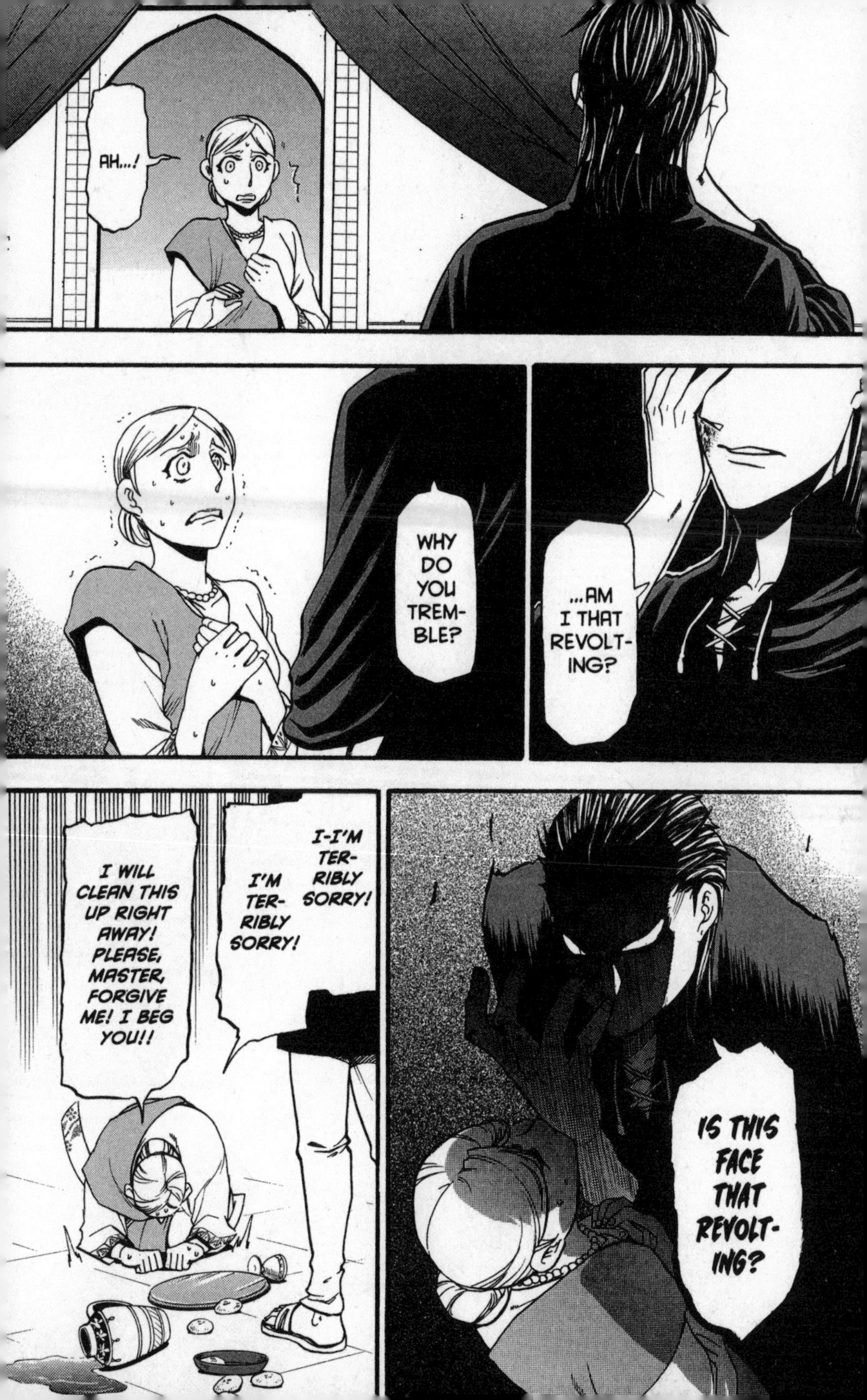
AH...!
...AM I THAT REVOLT-ING?
WHY DO YOU TREM-BLE?
IS THIS FACE THAT REVOLT-ING?
I-I'M TER-RIBLY SORRY!
I'M TER-RIBLY SORRY!
I WILL CLEAN THIS UP RIGHT AWAY! PLEASE, MASTER, FORGIVE ME! I BEG YOU!!

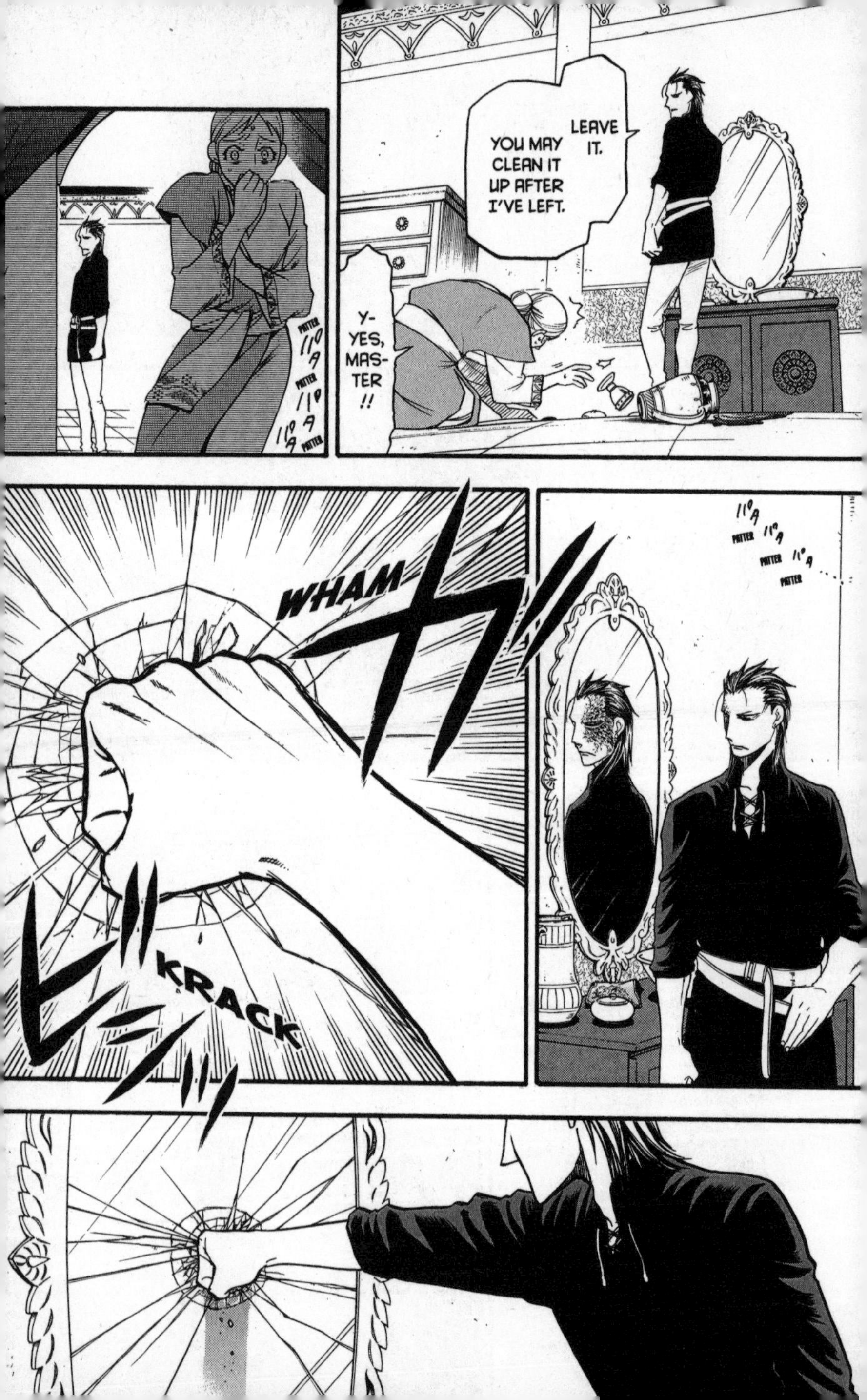
LEAVE IT.
YOU MAY CLEAN IT UP AFTER I'VE LEFT.
Y-YES, MASTER!!
PATTER
PATTER
PATTER
PATTER
PATTER
PATTER...
WHAM
KRACK

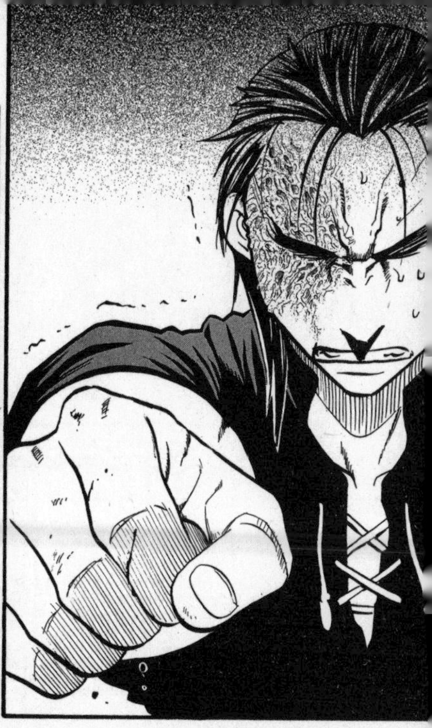

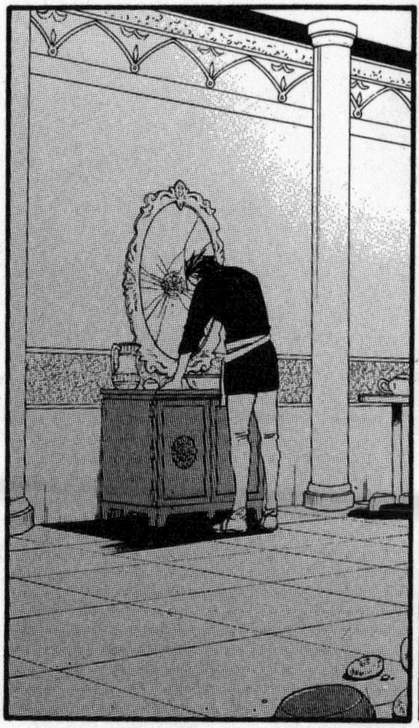

Chapter 27: Son of Kharlan

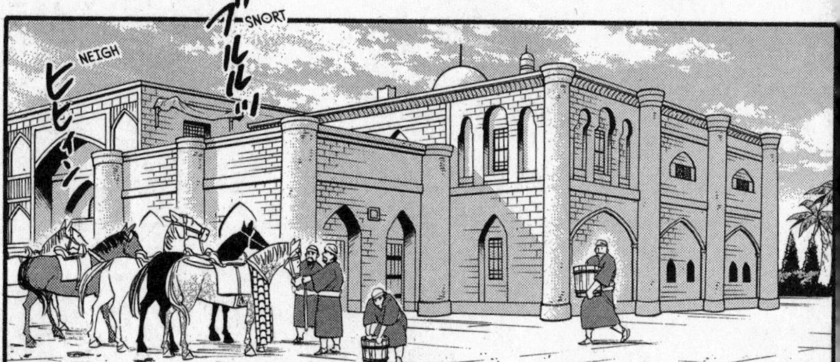
SNORT
NEIGH

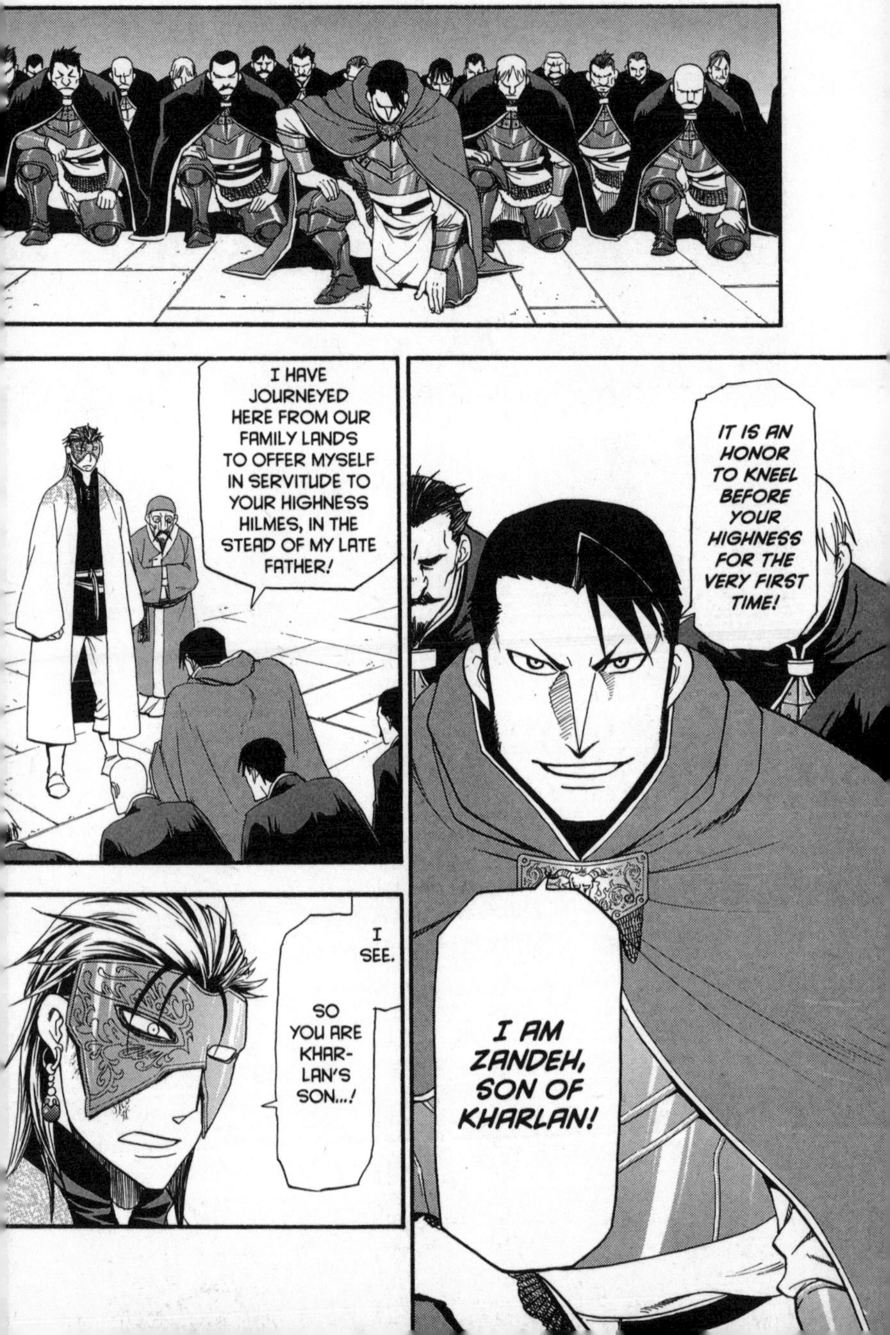
IT IS AN HONOR TO KNEEL BEFORE YOUR HIGHNESS FOR THE VERY FIRST TIME!
I AM ZANDEH, SON OF KHARLAN!
I HAVE JOURNEYED HERE FROM OUR FAMILY LANDS TO OFFER MYSELF IN SERVITUDE TO YOUR HIGHNESS HILMES, IN THE STEAD OF MY LATE FATHER!
I SEE.
SO YOU ARE KHAR-LAN'S SON...!

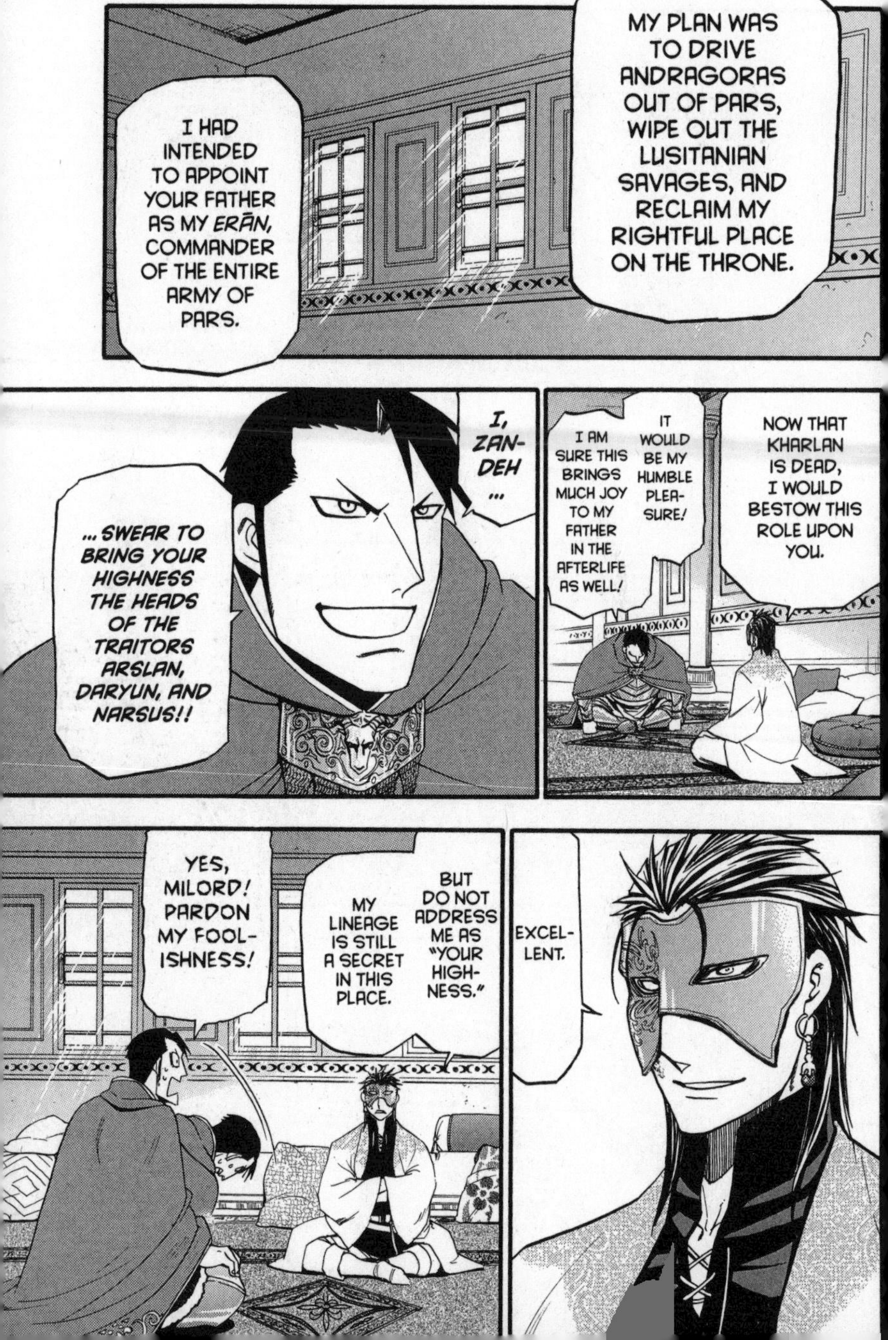
MY PLAN WAS TO DRIVE ANDRAGORAS OUT OF PARS, WIPE OUT THE LUSITANIAN SAVAGES, AND RECLAIM MY RIGHTFUL PLACE ON THE THRONE.
I HAD INTENDED TO APPOINT YOUR FATHER AS MY *ERĀN*, COMMANDER OF THE ENTIRE ARMY OF PARS.
NOW THAT KHARLAN IS DEAD, I WOULD BESTOW THIS ROLE UPON YOU.
IT WOULD BE MY HUMBLE PLEA-SURE!
I AM SURE THIS BRINGS MUCH JOY TO MY FATHER IN THE AFTERLIFE AS WELL!
I, ZAN-DEH...
...SWEAR TO BRING YOUR HIGHNESS THE HEADS OF THE TRAITORS ARSLAN, DARYUN, AND NARSUS!!
EXCEL-LENT.
BUT DO NOT ADDRESS ME AS "YOUR HIGH-NESS."
MY LINEAGE IS STILL A SECRET IN THIS PLACE.
YES, MILORD! PARDON MY FOOL-ISHNESS!

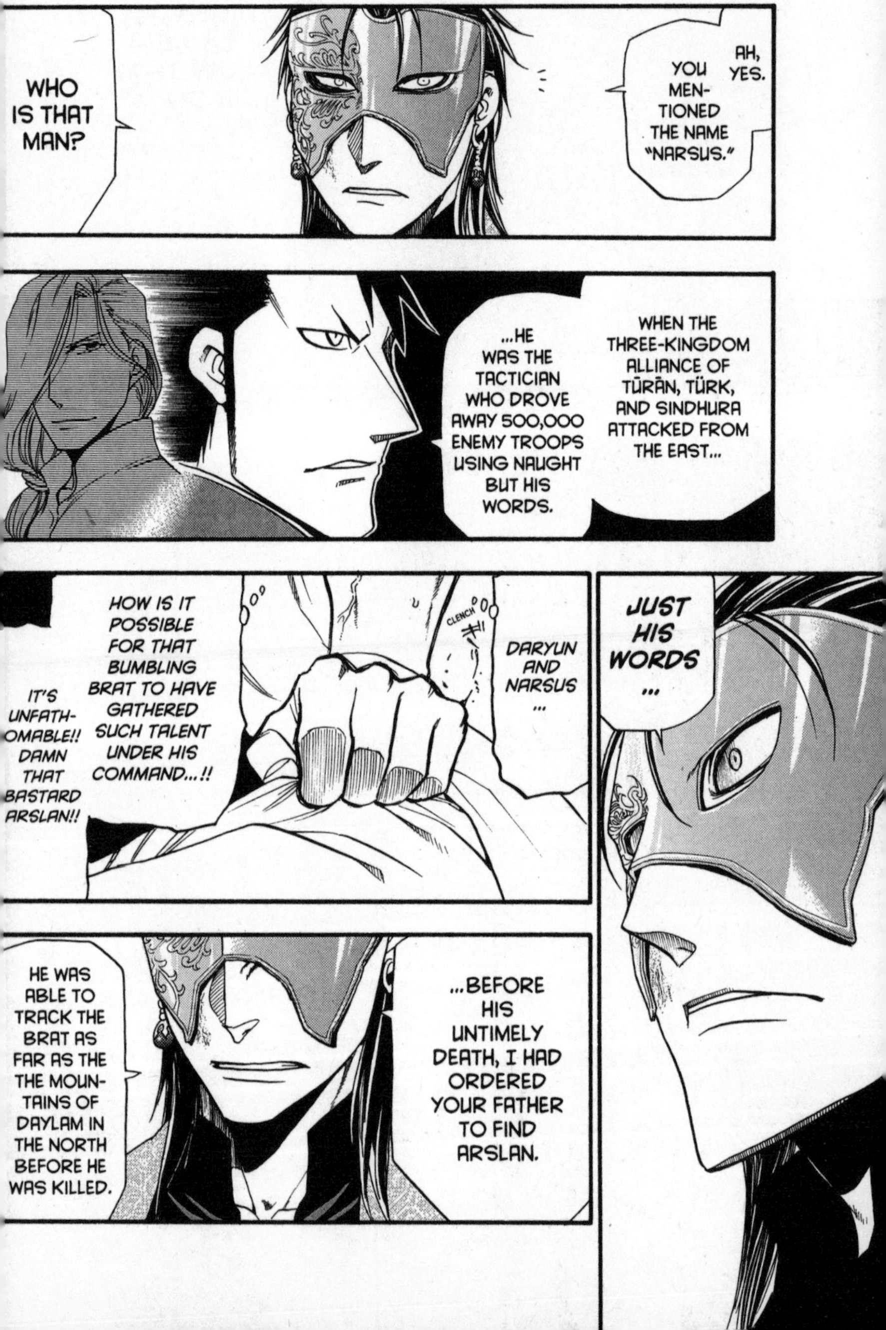
AH, YES. YOU MENTIONED THE NAME "NARSUS."
WHO IS THAT MAN?
WHEN THE THREE-KINGDOM ALLIANCE OF TŪRĀN, TÜRK, AND SINDHURA ATTACKED FROM THE EAST...
...HE WAS THE TACTICIAN WHO DROVE AWAY 500,000 ENEMY TROOPS USING NAUGHT BUT HIS WORDS.
JUST HIS WORDS ...
DARYUN AND NARSUS ...
CLENCH
HOW IS IT POSSIBLE FOR THAT BUMBLING BRAT TO HAVE GATHERED SUCH TALENT UNDER HIS COMMAND...!!
IT'S UNFATHOMABLE!! DAMN THAT BASTARD ARSLAN!!
...BEFORE HIS UNTIMELY DEATH, I HAD ORDERED YOUR FATHER TO FIND ARSLAN.
HE WAS ABLE TO TRACK THE BRAT AS FAR AS THE THE MOUNTAINS OF DAYLAM IN THE NORTH BEFORE HE WAS KILLED.

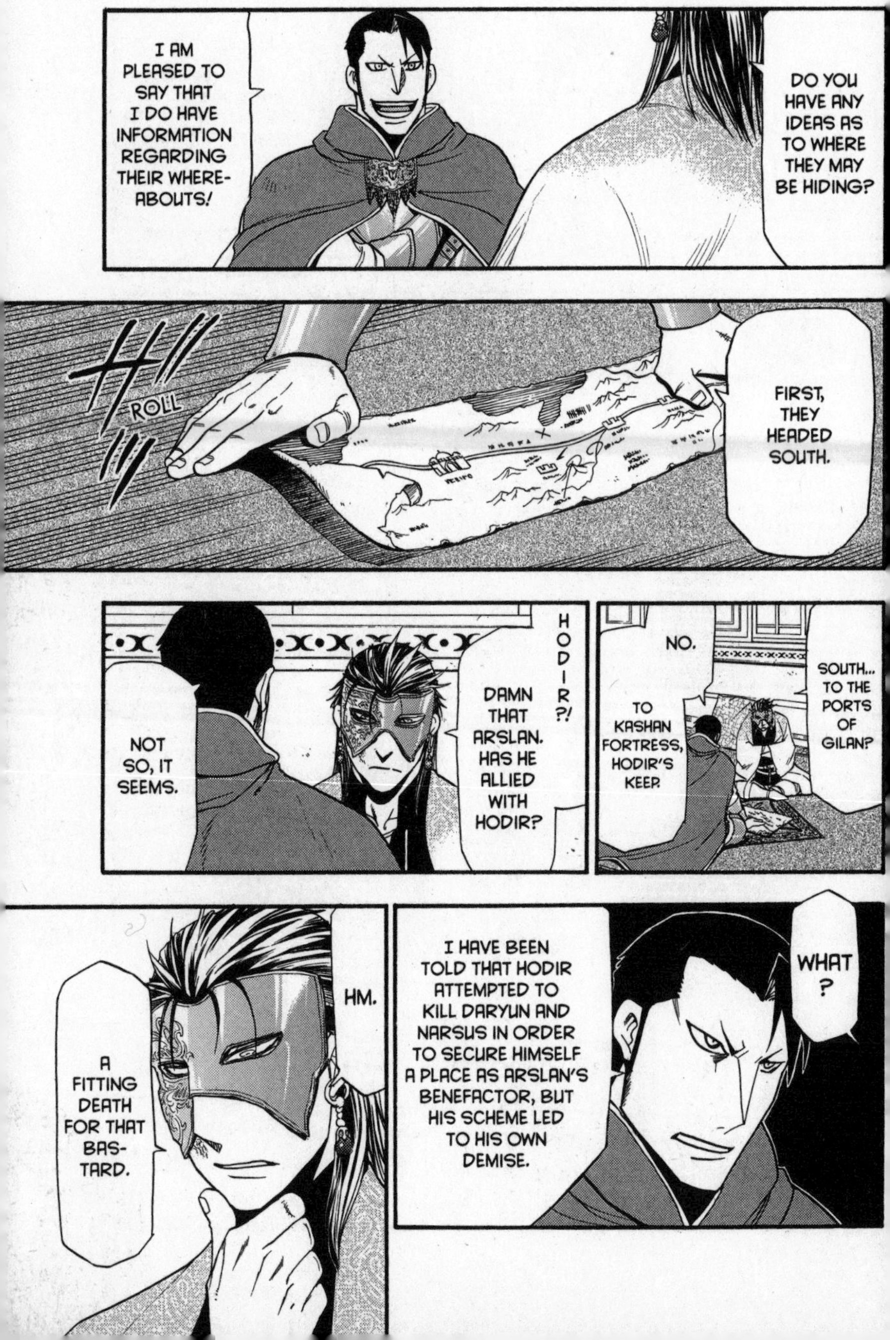
DO YOU HAVE ANY IDEAS AS TO WHERE THEY MAY BE HIDING?
I AM PLEASED TO SAY THAT I DO HAVE INFORMATION REGARDING THEIR WHERE-ABOUTS!
FIRST, THEY HEADED SOUTH.
ROLL
SOUTH... TO THE PORTS OF GILAN?
NO.
TO KASHAN FORTRESS, HODIR'S KEEP.
HODIR?!
DAMN THAT ARSLAN. HAS HE ALLIED WITH HODIR?
NOT SO, IT SEEMS.
WHAT?
I HAVE BEEN TOLD THAT HODIR ATTEMPTED TO KILL DARYUN AND NARSUS IN ORDER TO SECURE HIMSELF A PLACE AS ARSLAN'S BENEFACTOR, BUT HIS SCHEME LED TO HIS OWN DEMISE.
HM.
A FITTING DEATH FOR THAT BAS-TARD.

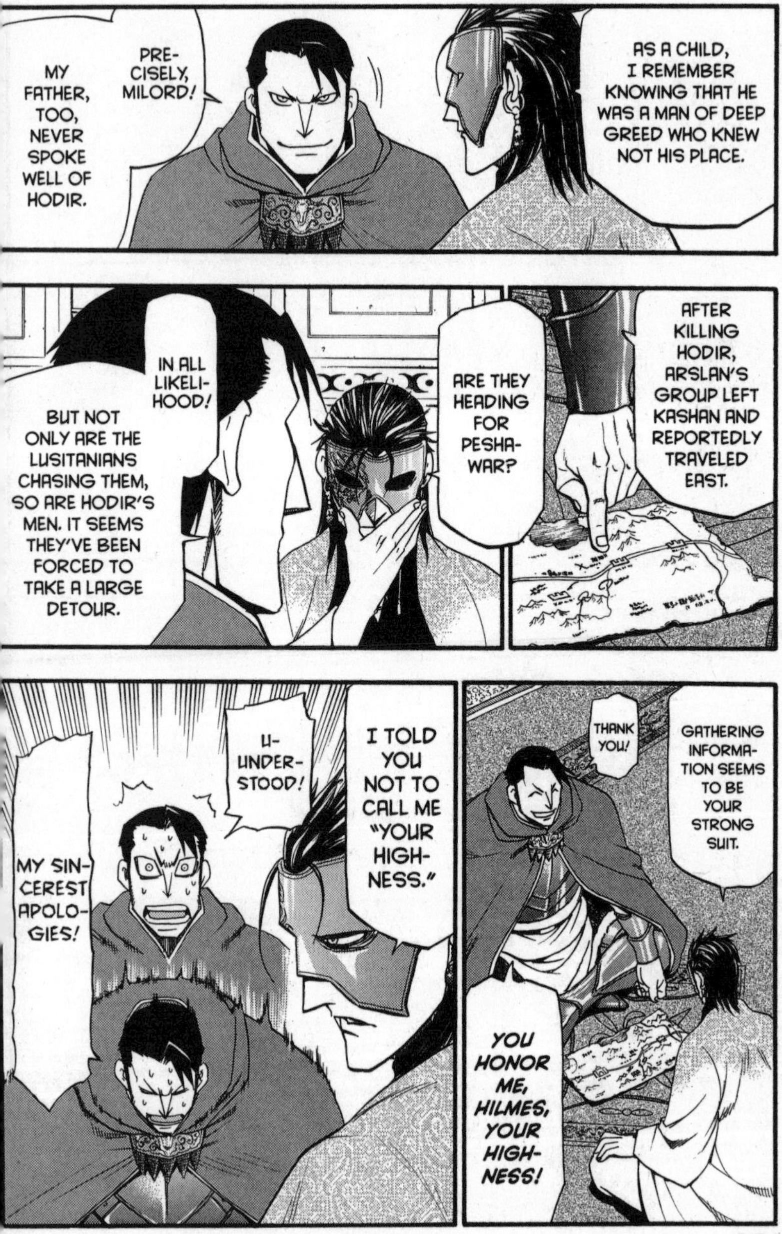
AS A CHILD, I REMEMBER KNOWING THAT HE WAS A MAN OF DEEP GREED WHO KNEW NOT HIS PLACE.
PRE-CISELY, MILORD!
MY FATHER, TOO, NEVER SPOKE WELL OF HODIR.
AFTER KILLING HODIR, ARSLAN'S GROUP LEFT KASHAN AND REPORTEDLY TRAVELED EAST.
ARE THEY HEADING FOR PESHA-WAR?
IN ALL LIKELI-HOOD!
BUT NOT ONLY ARE THE LUSITANIANS CHASING THEM, SO ARE HODIR'S MEN. IT SEEMS THEY'VE BEEN FORCED TO TAKE A LARGE DETOUR.
GATHERING INFORMA-TION SEEMS TO BE YOUR STRONG SUIT.
THANK YOU!
YOU HONOR ME, HILMES, YOUR HIGH-NESS!
I TOLD YOU NOT TO CALL ME "YOUR HIGH-NESS."
U-UNDER-STOOD!
MY SIN-CEREST APOLO-GIES!

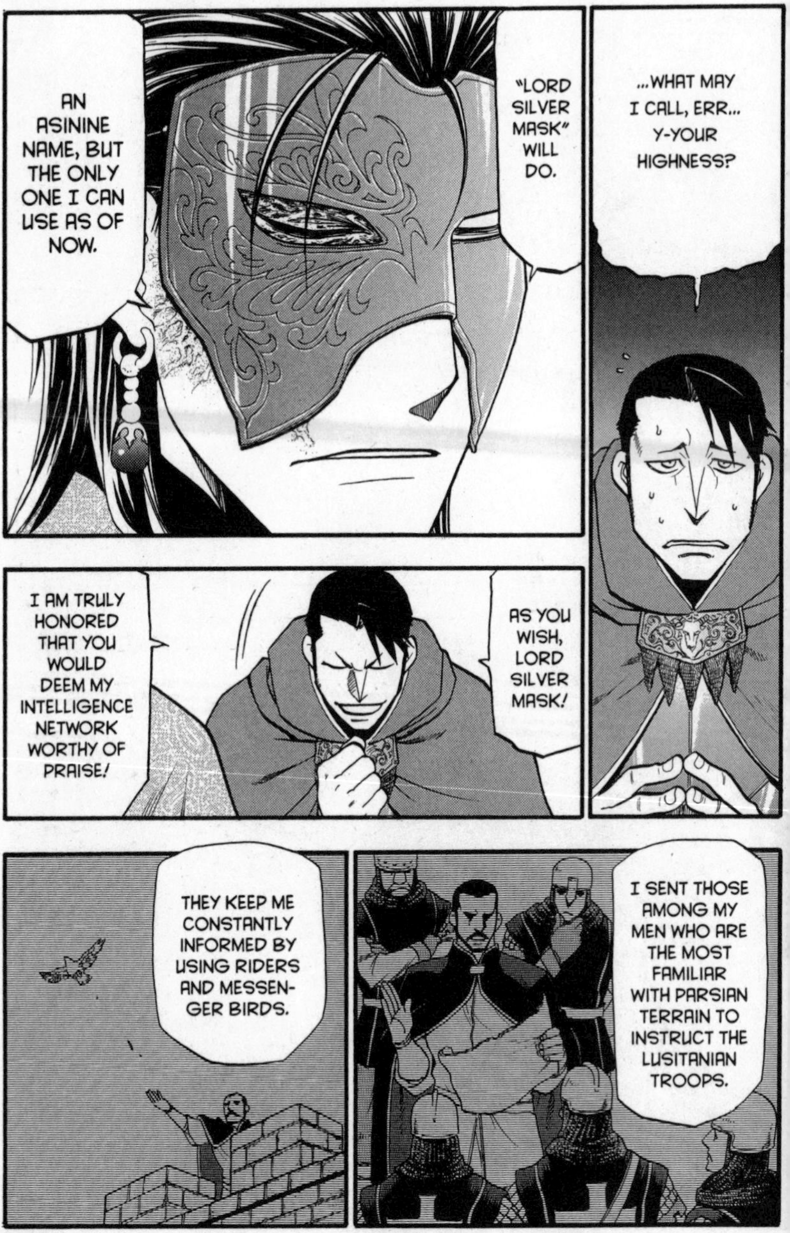
...WHAT MAY I CALL, ERR... Y-YOUR HIGHNESS?
"LORD SILVER MASK" WILL DO.
AN ASININE NAME, BUT THE ONLY ONE I CAN USE AS OF NOW.
AS YOU WISH, LORD SILVER MASK!
I AM TRULY HONORED THAT YOU WOULD DEEM MY INTELLIGENCE NETWORK WORTHY OF PRAISE!
I SENT THOSE AMONG MY MEN WHO ARE THE MOST FAMILIAR WITH PARSIAN TERRAIN TO INSTRUCT THE LUSITANIAN TROOPS.
THEY KEEP ME CONSTANTLY INFORMED BY USING RIDERS AND MESSEN-GER BIRDS.

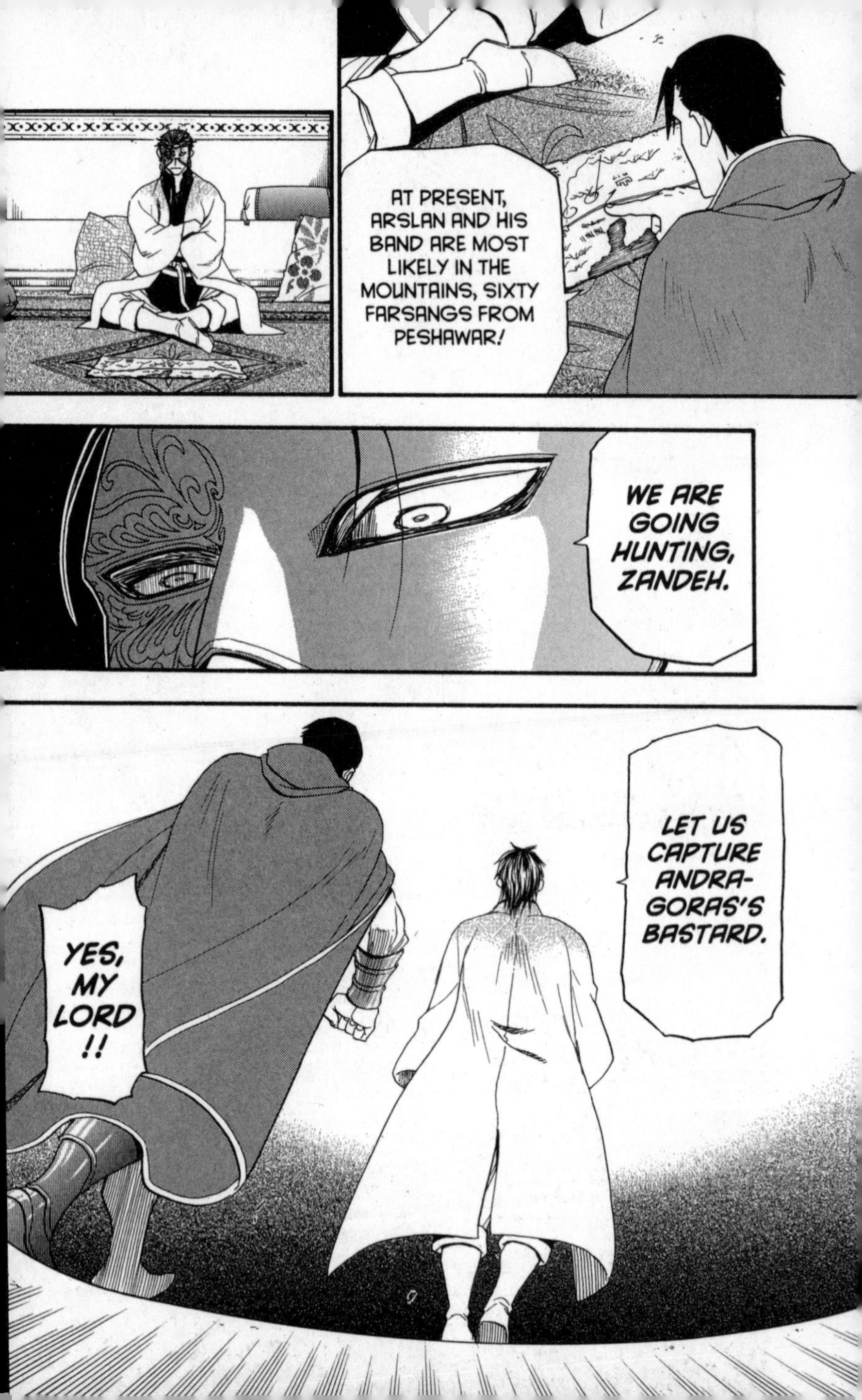
AT PRESENT, ARSLAN AND HIS BAND ARE MOST LIKELY IN THE MOUNTAINS, SIXTY FARSANGS FROM PESHAWAR!
WE ARE GOING HUNTING, ZANDEH.
LET US CAPTURE ANDRA-GORAS'S BASTARD.
YES, MY LORD !!

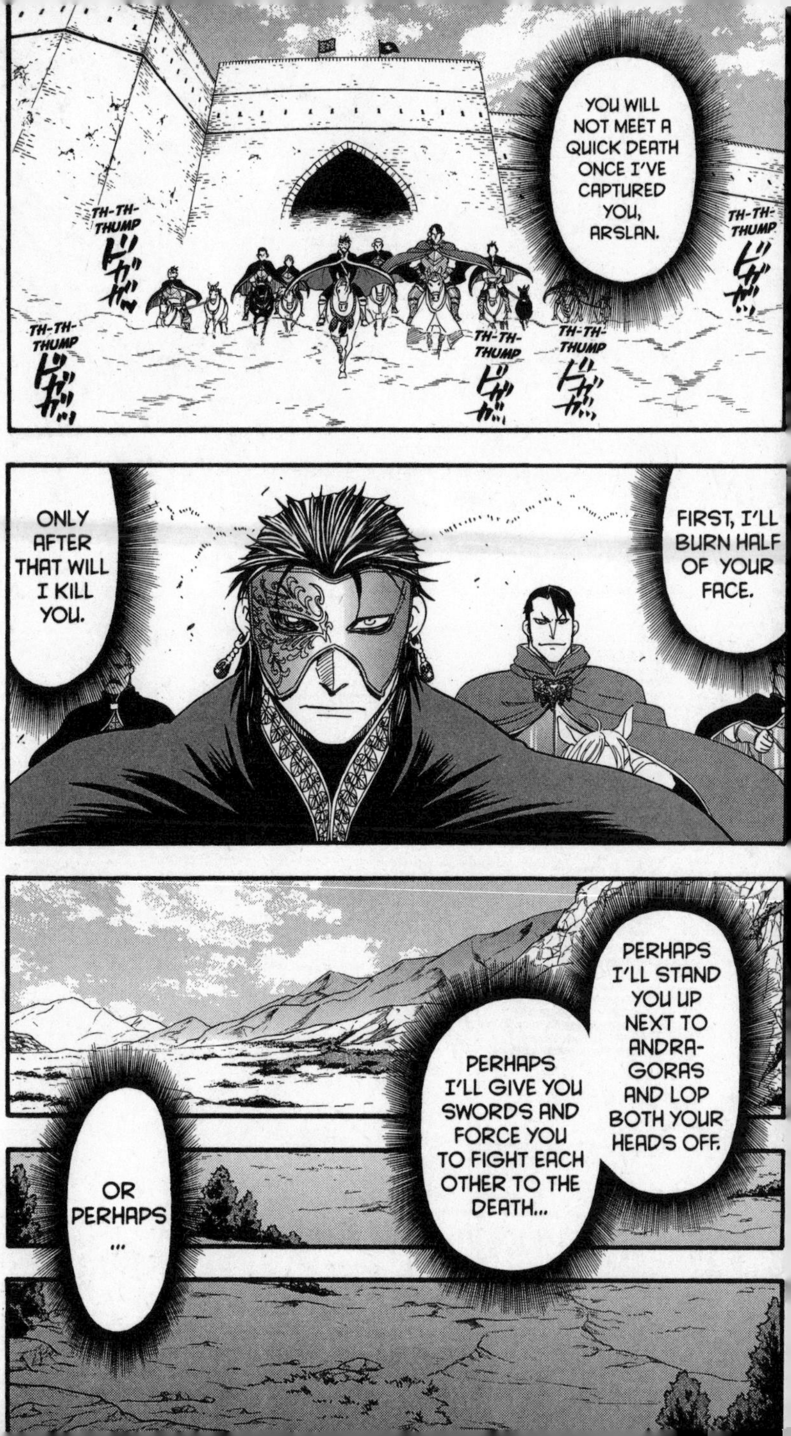
YOU WILL NOT MEET A QUICK DEATH ONCE I'VE CAPTURED YOU, ARSLAN.
TH-TH-THUMP
TH-TH-THUMP
TH-TH-THUMP
TH-TH-THUMP
TH-TH-THUMP
FIRST, I'LL BURN HALF OF YOUR FACE.
ONLY AFTER THAT WILL I KILL YOU.
PERHAPS I'LL STAND YOU UP NEXT TO ANDRA-GORAS AND LOP BOTH YOUR HEADS OFF.
PERHAPS I'LL GIVE YOU SWORDS AND FORCE YOU TO FIGHT EACH OTHER TO THE DEATH...
OR PERHAPS ...

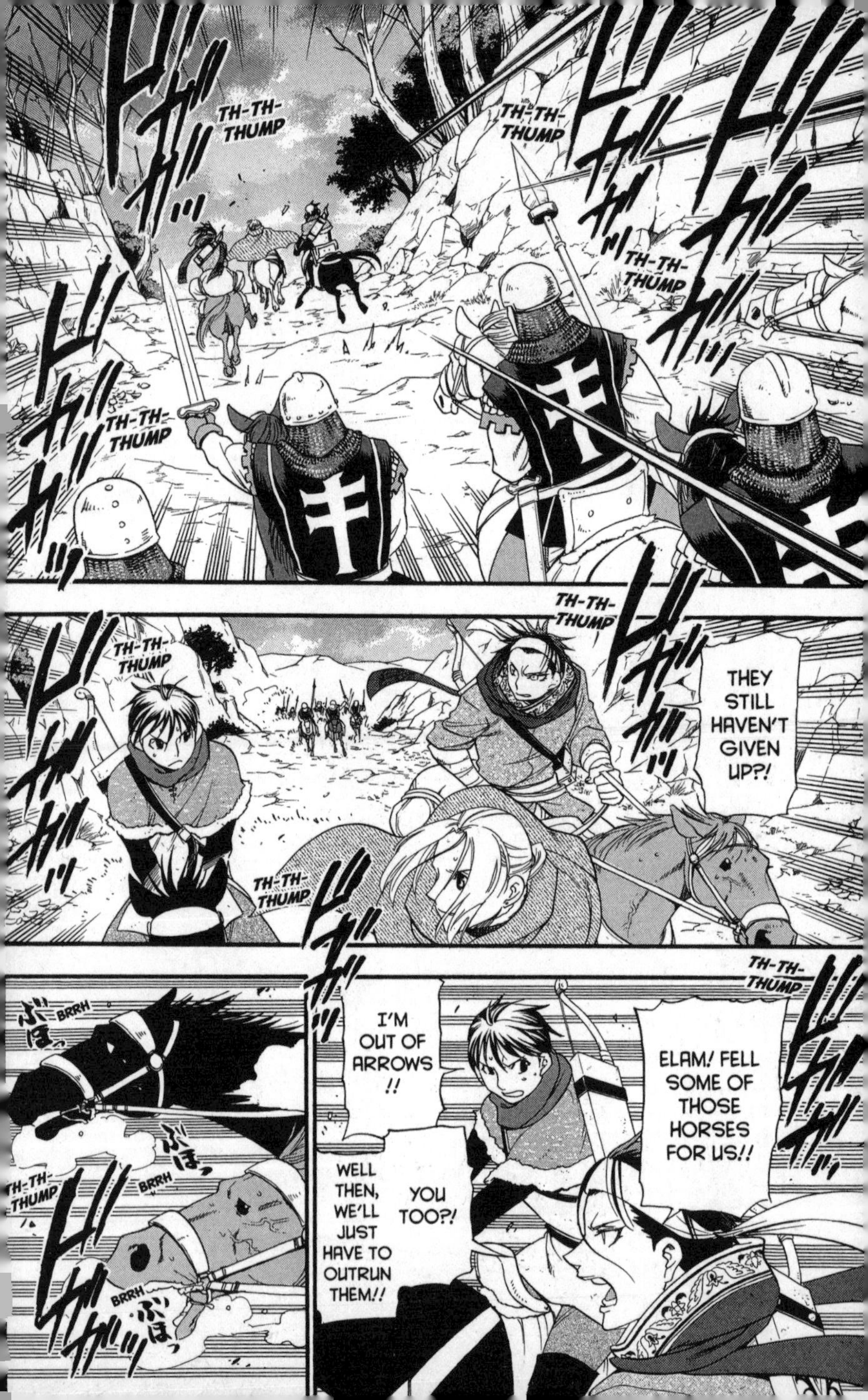
TH-TH-THUMP
TH-TH-THUMP
TH-TH-THUMP
TH-TH-THUMP
TH-TH-THUMP
THEY STILL HAVEN'T GIVEN UP?!
TH-TH-THUMP
TH-TH-THUMP
TH-TH-THUMP
ELAM! FELL SOME OF THOSE HORSES FOR US!!
I'M OUT OF ARROWS!!
YOU TOO?!
WELL THEN, WE'LL JUST HAVE TO OUTRUN THEM!!
ぶほっ BRRH
ぶほっ BRRH
TH-TH-THUMP
ぶほっ BRRH

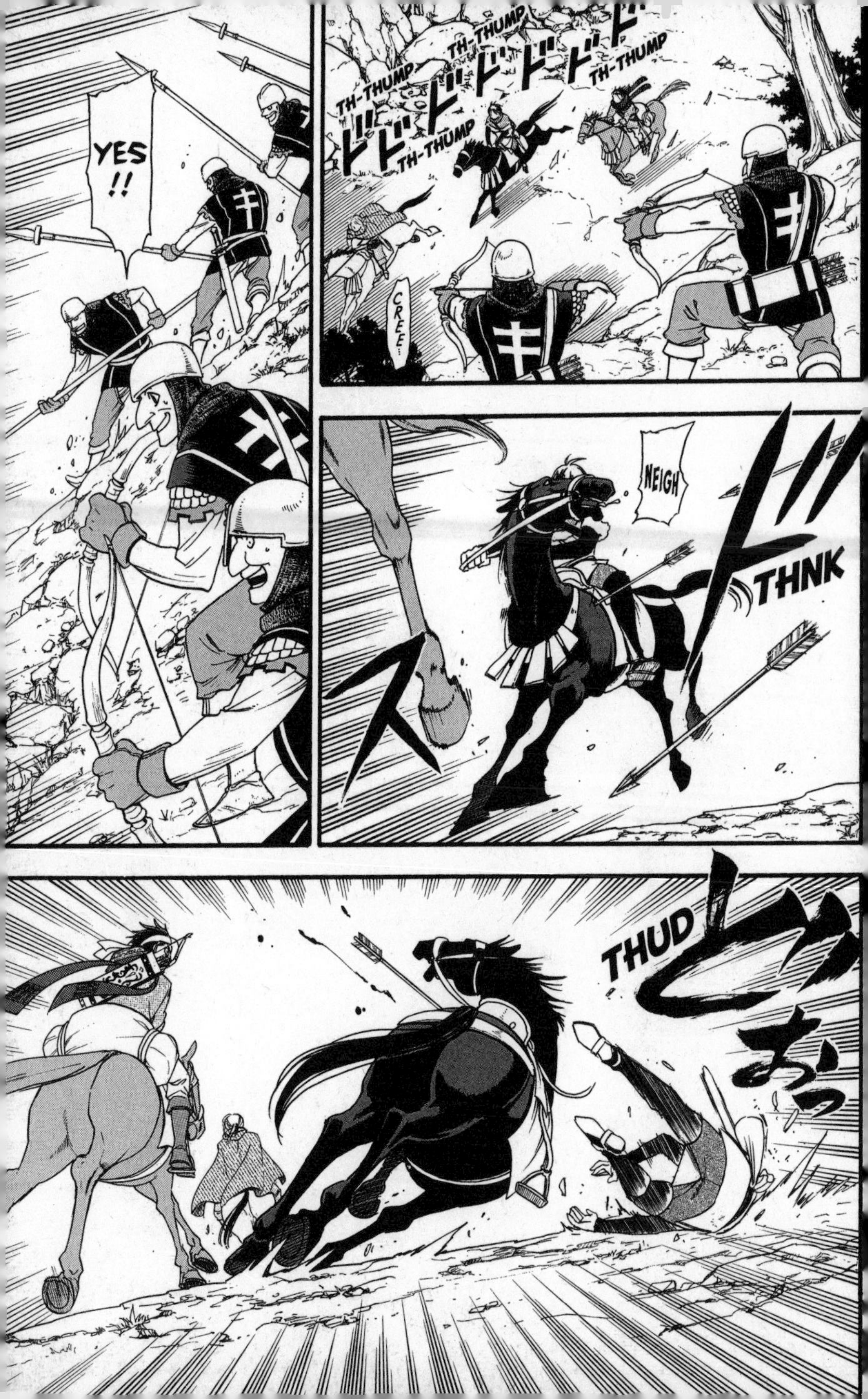

TH-THUMP
TH-THUMP
TH-THUMP
TH-THUMP
TH-THUMP
CREE...
NEIGH
THNK
YES!!
THUD

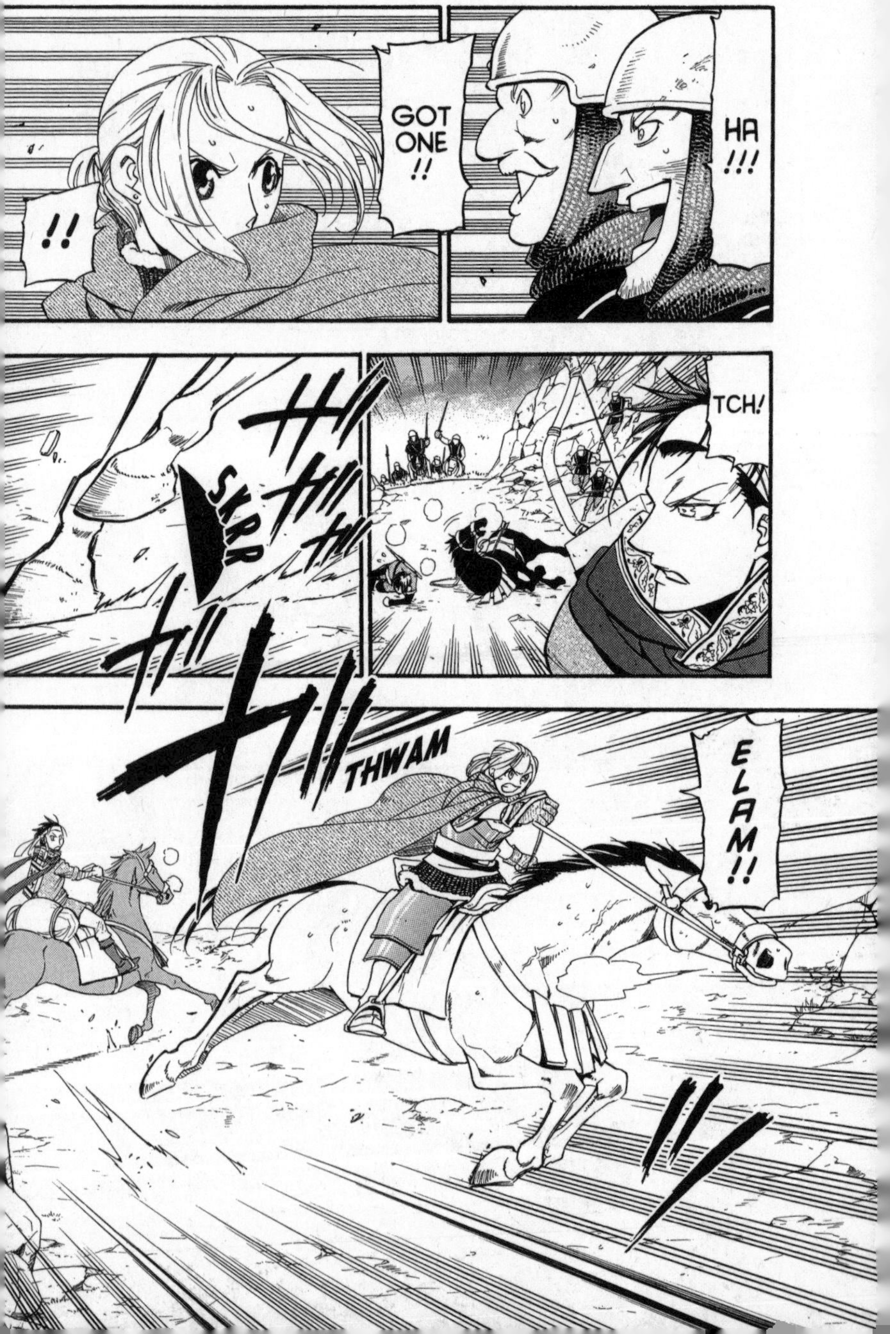
HA !!!
GOT ONE !!
!!
TCH!
SKRR
ELAM!!
THWAM

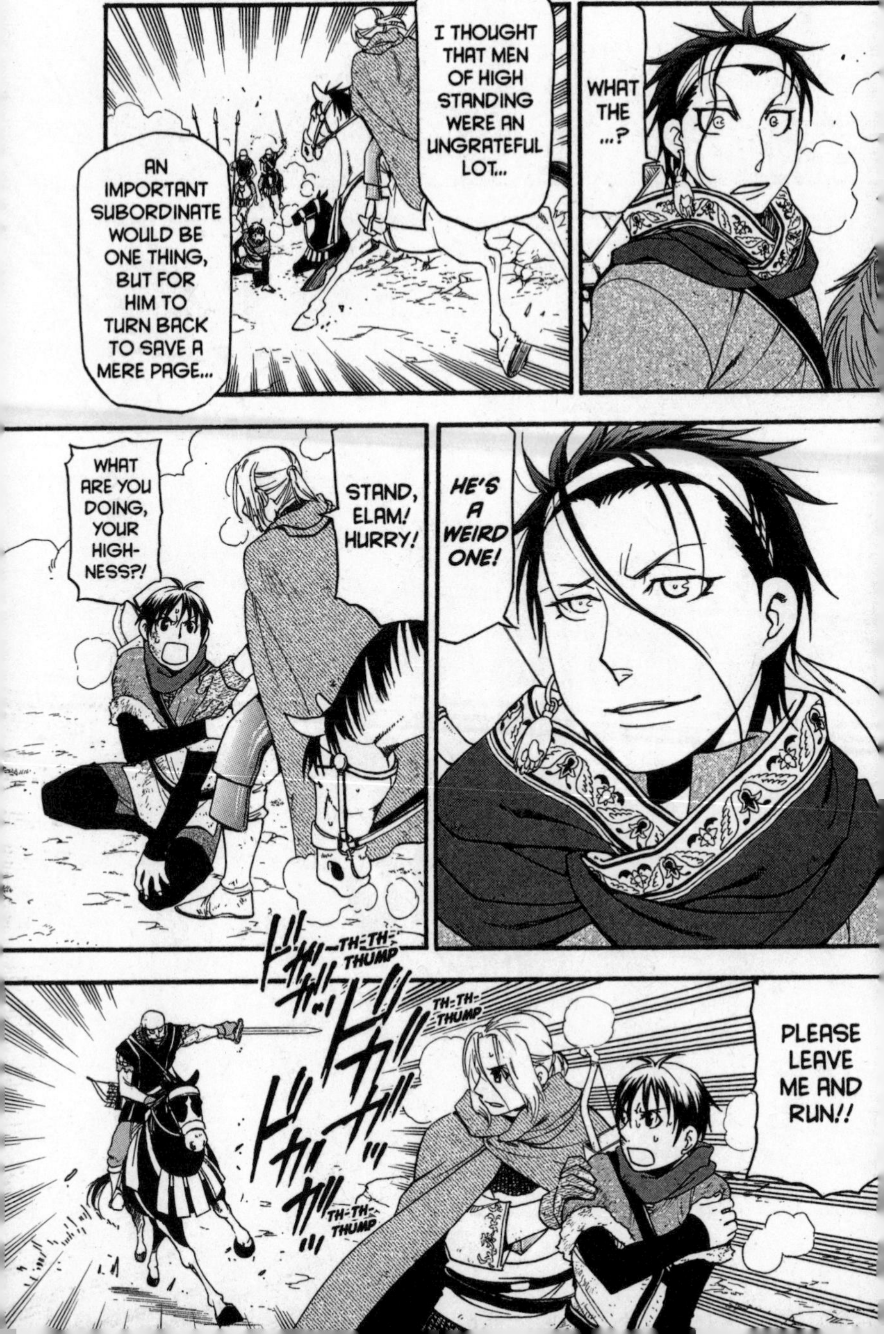
WHAT THE ...?
I THOUGHT THAT MEN OF HIGH STANDING WERE AN UNGRATEFUL LOT...
AN IMPORTANT SUBORDINATE WOULD BE ONE THING, BUT FOR HIM TO TURN BACK TO SAVE A MERE PAGE...
HE'S A WEIRD ONE!
STAND, ELAM! HURRY!
WHAT ARE YOU DOING, YOUR HIGHNESS?!
TH-TH-THUMP
TH-TH-THUMP
PLEASE LEAVE ME AND RUN!!
TH-TH-THUMP

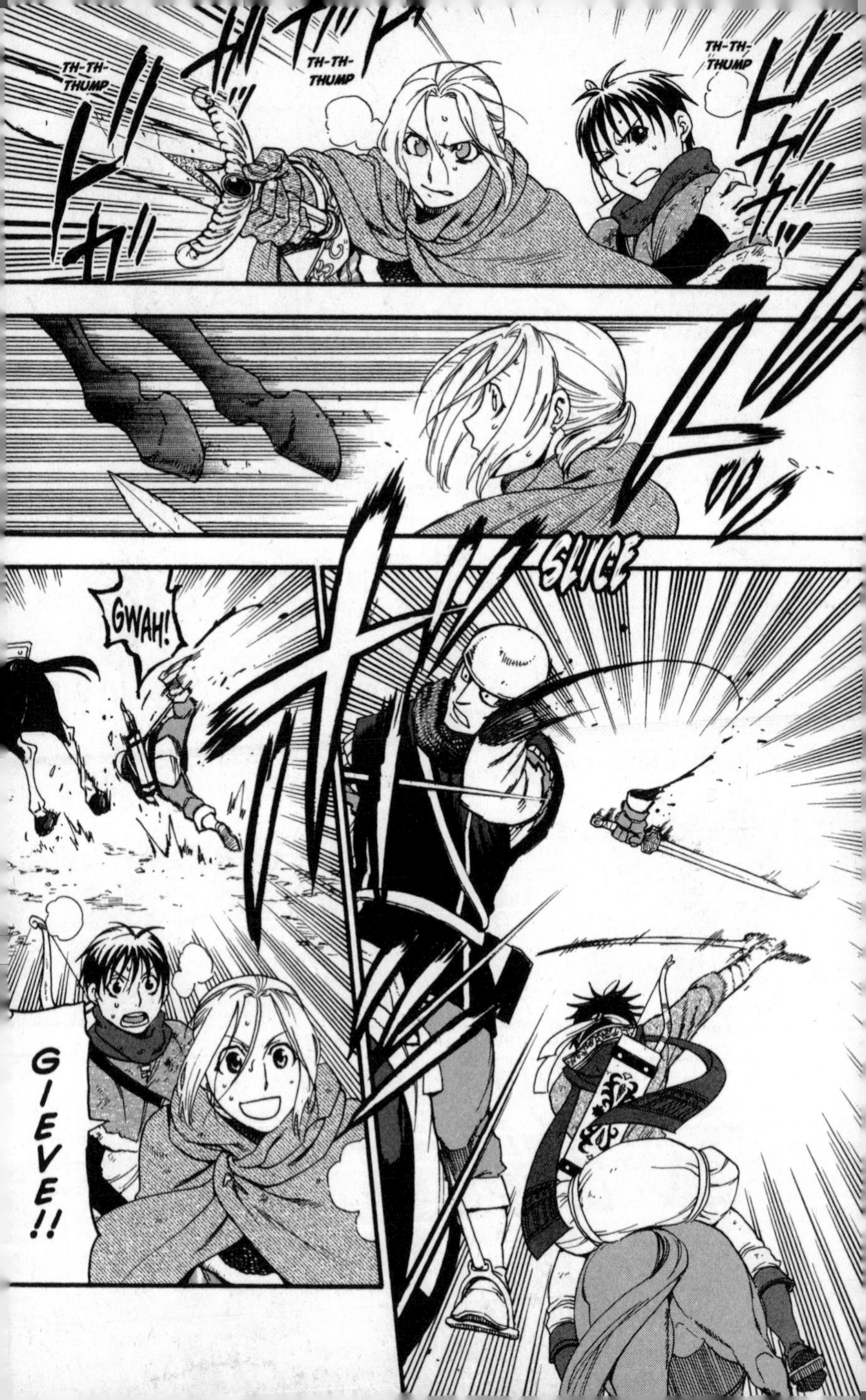
TH-TH-THUMP
TH-TH-THUMP
TH-TH-THUMP
SLICE
GWAH!
GIEVE!!

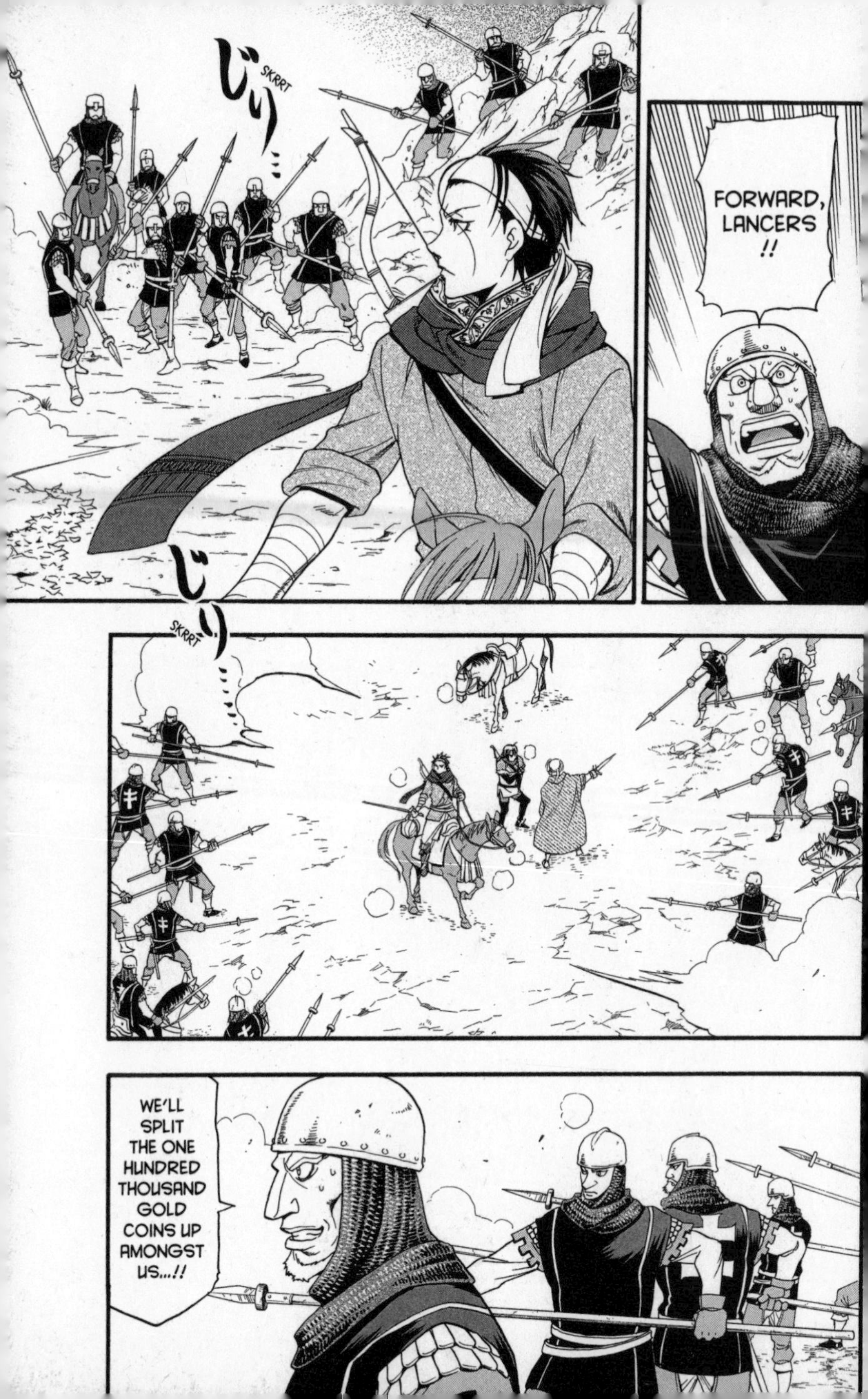
FORWARD, LANCERS!!
じり SKRRT
じり SKRRT
WE'LL SPLIT THE ONE HUNDRED THOUSAND GOLD COINS UP AMONGST US...!!

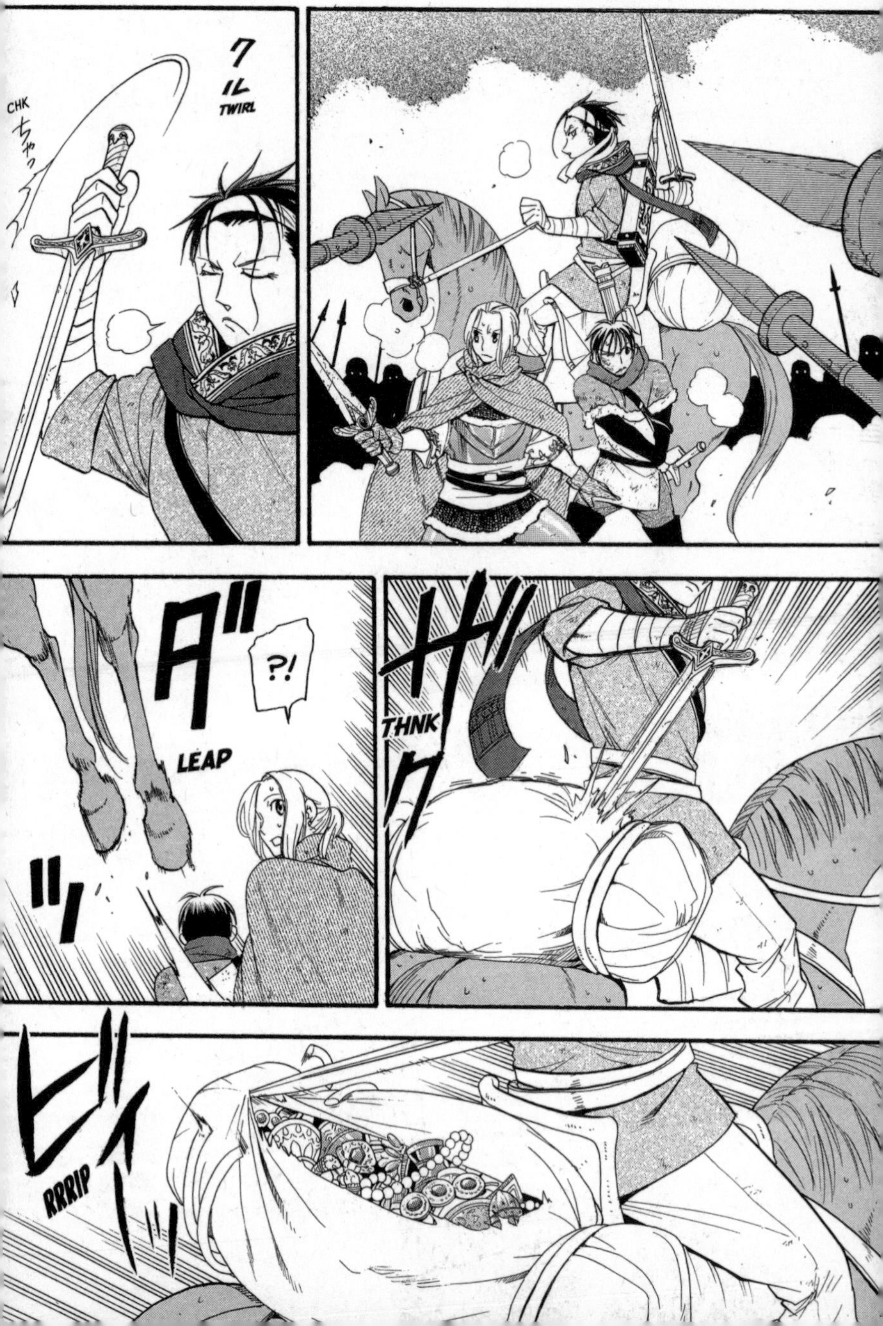
クル
TWIRL
CHK
ちゃっ
ザク
THNK
ダッ
LEAP
?!
ビイィ
RRRIP

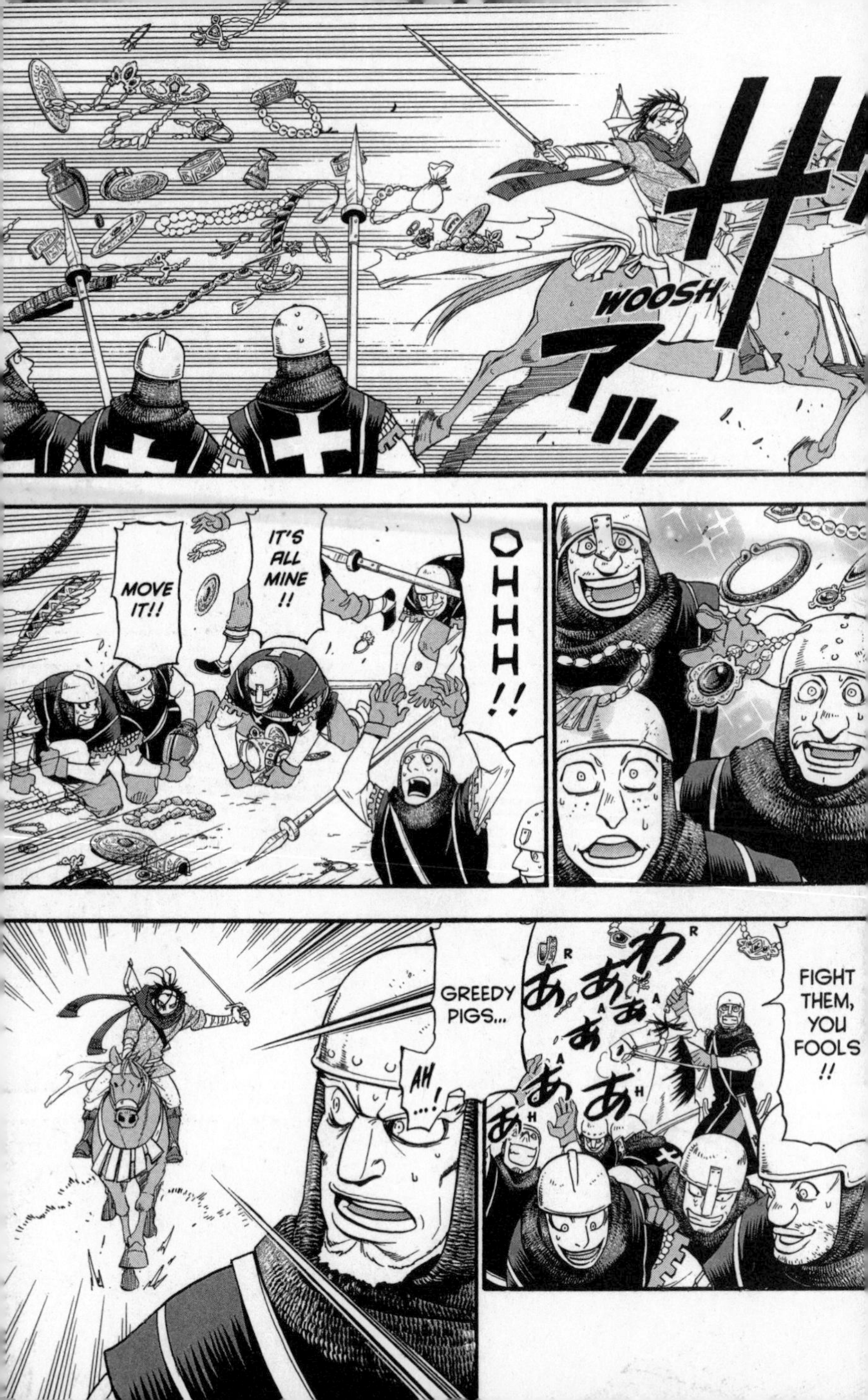
WOOSH
OHHHH!!
IT'S ALL MINE!!
MOVE IT!!
FIGHT THEM, YOU FOOLS!!
GREEDY PIGS...
AH ....!

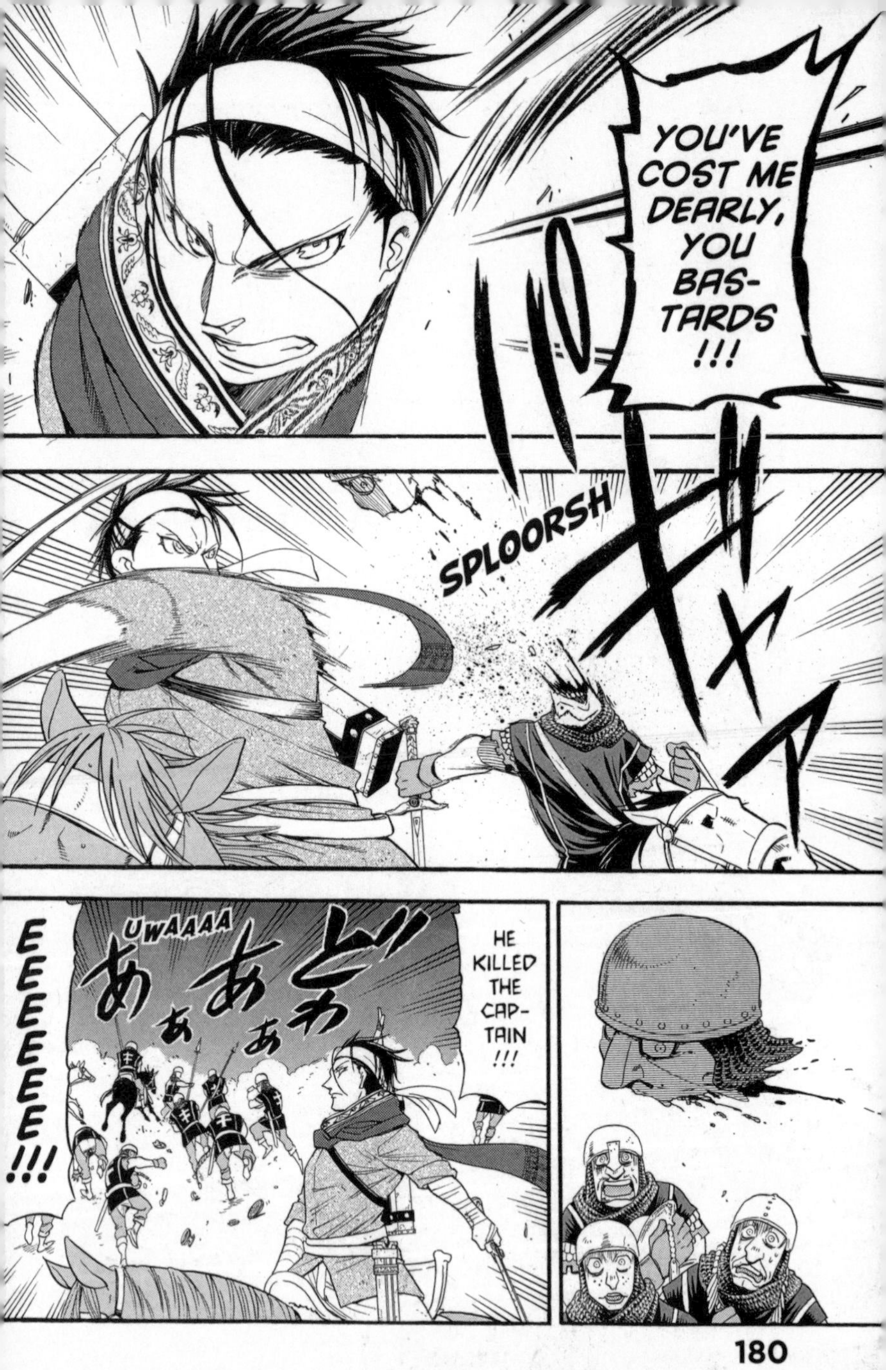
YOU'VE COST ME DEARLY, YOU BAS-TARDS!!!
SPLOORSH
HE KILLED THE CAP-TAIN!!!
UWAAAA
EEEEEEEE!!!

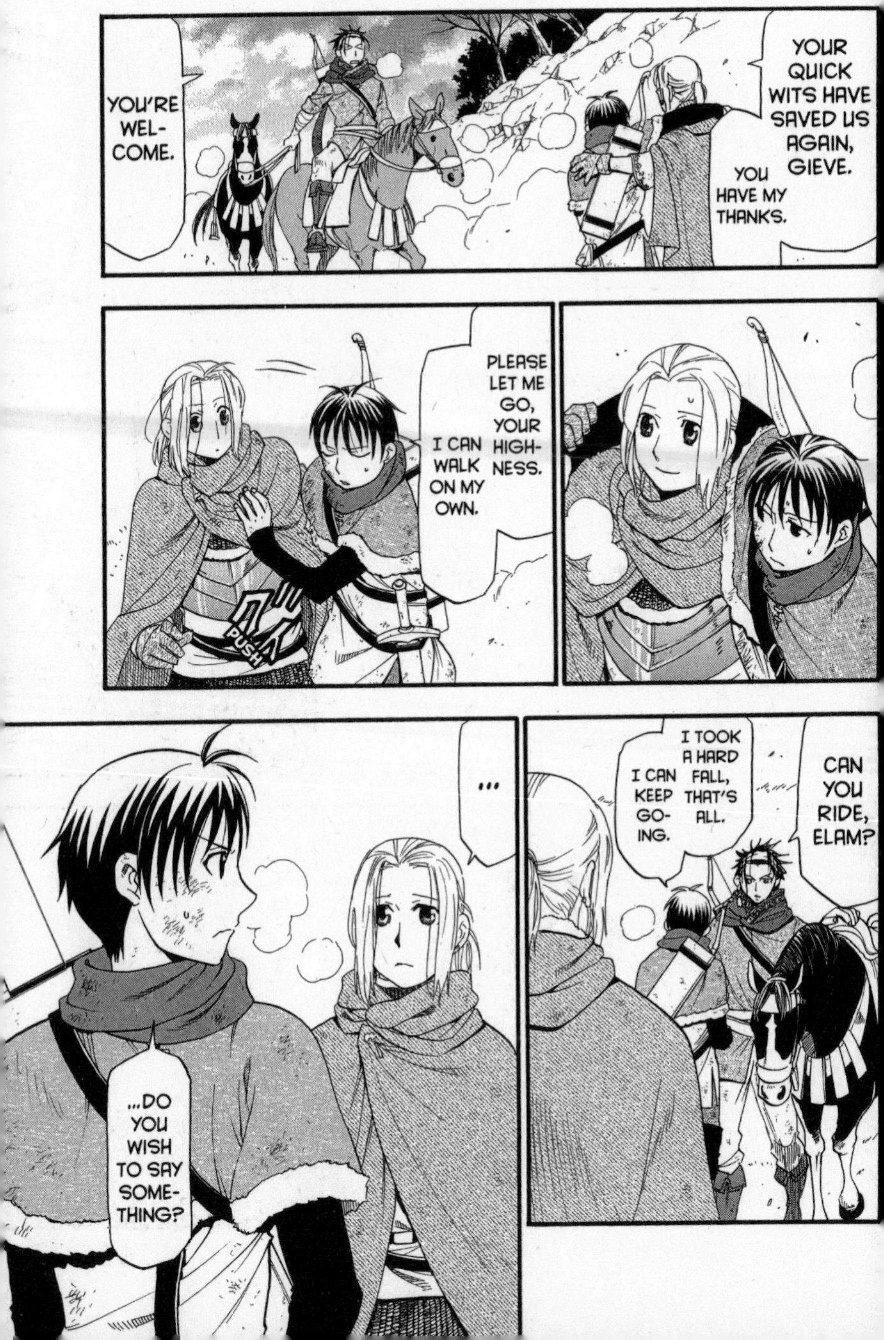
YOUR QUICK WITS HAVE SAVED US AGAIN, GIEVE.
YOU HAVE MY THANKS.
YOU'RE WEL-COME.
PLEASE LET ME GO, YOUR HIGH-NESS.
I CAN WALK ON MY OWN.
PUSH
CAN YOU RIDE, ELAM?
I TOOK A HARD FALL, THAT'S ALL.
I CAN KEEP GO-ING.
...
...DO YOU WISH TO SAY SOME-THING?

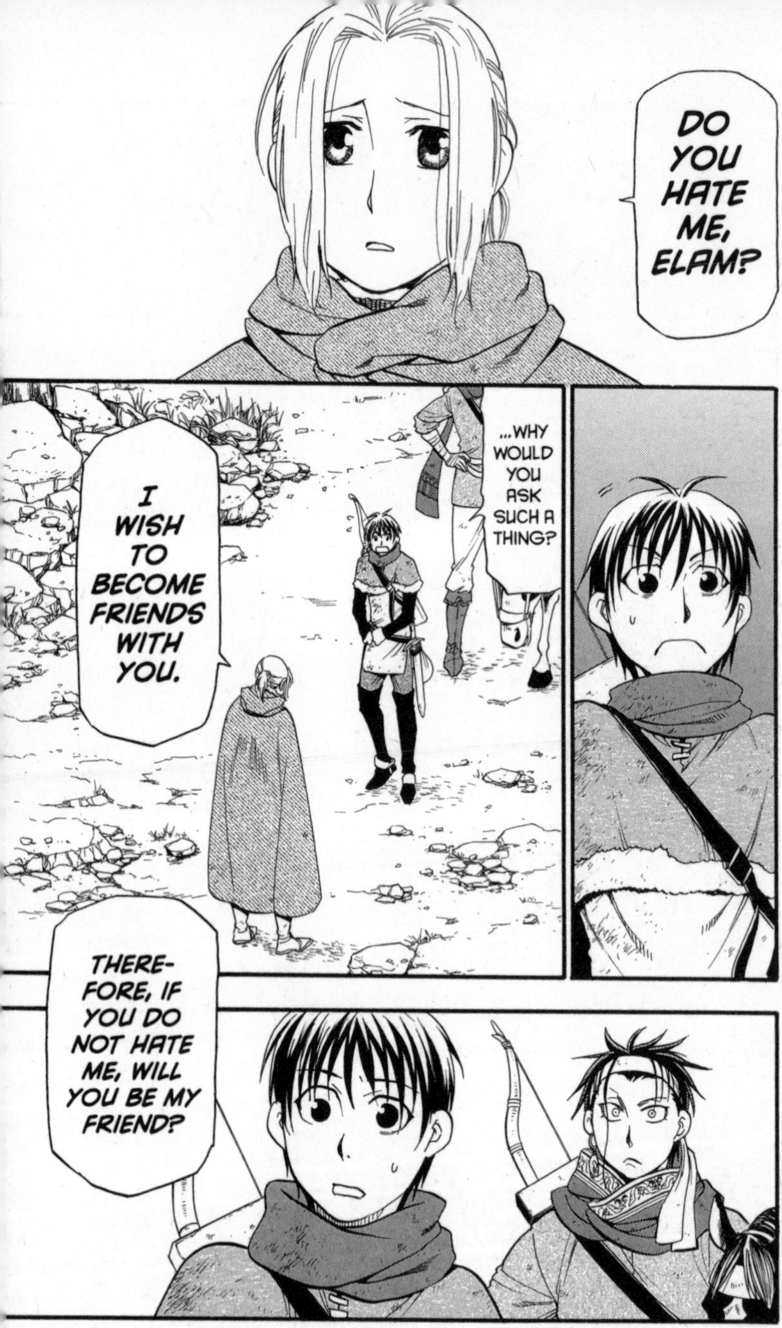
DO YOU HATE ME, ELAM?
...WHY WOULD YOU ASK SUCH A THING?
I WISH TO BECOME FRIENDS WITH YOU.
THEREFORE, IF YOU DO NOT HATE ME, WILL YOU BE MY FRIEND?

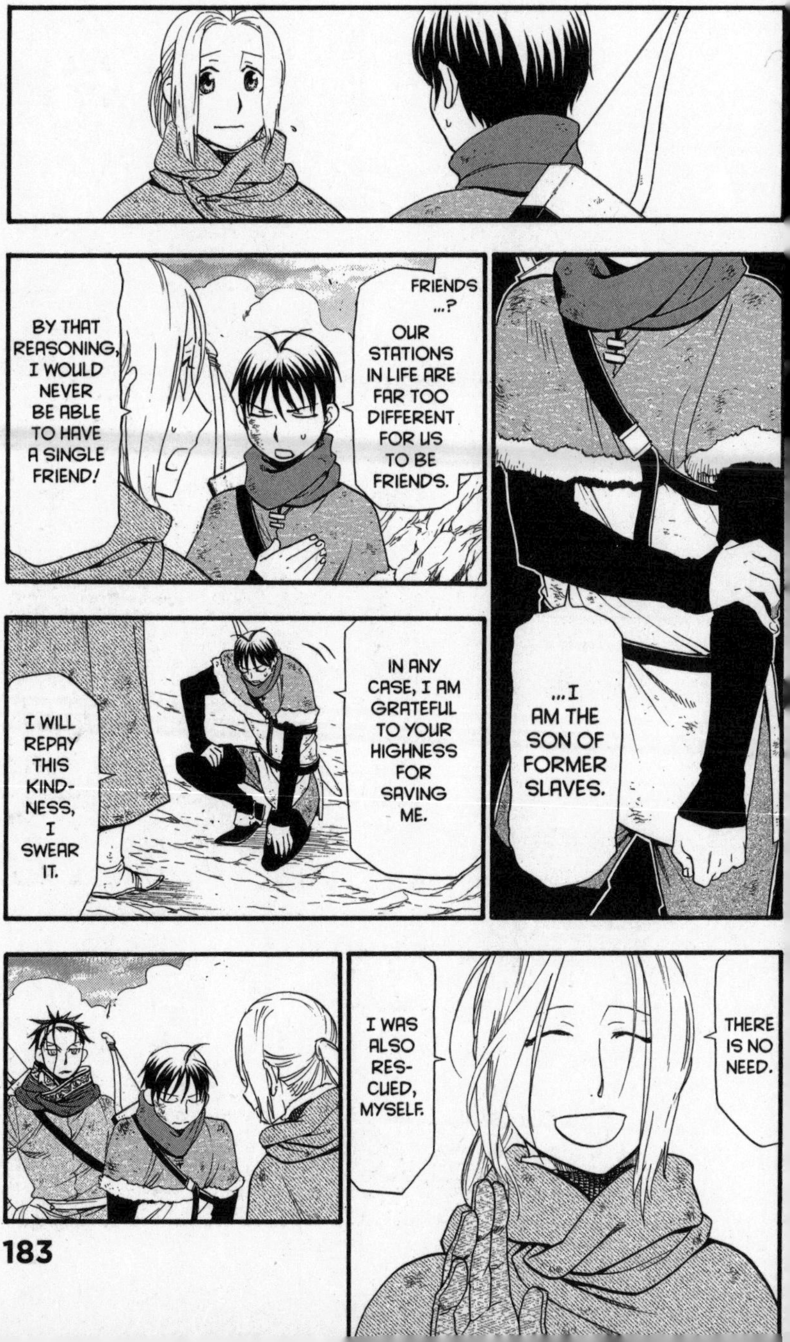
...I AM THE SON OF FORMER SLAVES.
FRIENDS ...?
OUR STATIONS IN LIFE ARE FAR TOO DIFFERENT FOR US TO BE FRIENDS.
BY THAT REASONING, I WOULD NEVER BE ABLE TO HAVE A SINGLE FRIEND!
IN ANY CASE, I AM GRATEFUL TO YOUR HIGHNESS FOR SAVING ME.
I WILL REPAY THIS KINDNESS, I SWEAR IT.
THERE IS NO NEED.
I WAS ALSO RESCUED, MYSELF.

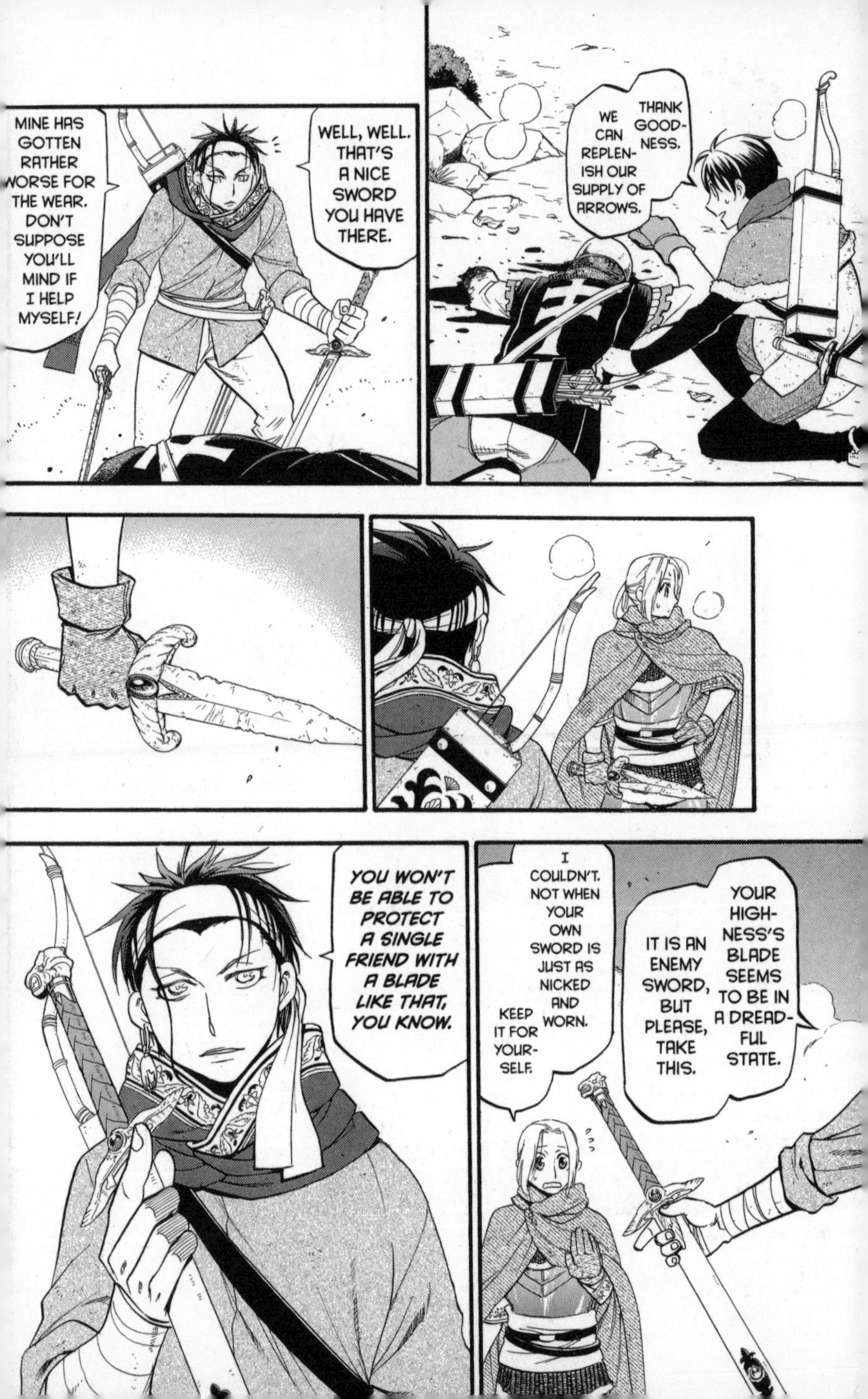
THANK GOODNESS. WE CAN REPLENISH OUR SUPPLY OF ARROWS.
WELL, WELL. THAT'S A NICE SWORD YOU HAVE THERE.
MINE HAS GOTTEN RATHER WORSE FOR THE WEAR. DON'T SUPPOSE YOU'LL MIND IF I HELP MYSELF!
YOUR HIGHNESS'S BLADE SEEMS TO BE IN A DREADFUL STATE.
IT IS AN ENEMY SWORD, BUT PLEASE, TAKE THIS.
I COULDN'T. NOT WHEN YOUR OWN SWORD IS JUST AS NICKED AND WORN.
KEEP IT FOR YOURSELF.
YOU WON'T BE ABLE TO PROTECT A SINGLE FRIEND WITH A BLADE LIKE THAT, YOU KNOW.

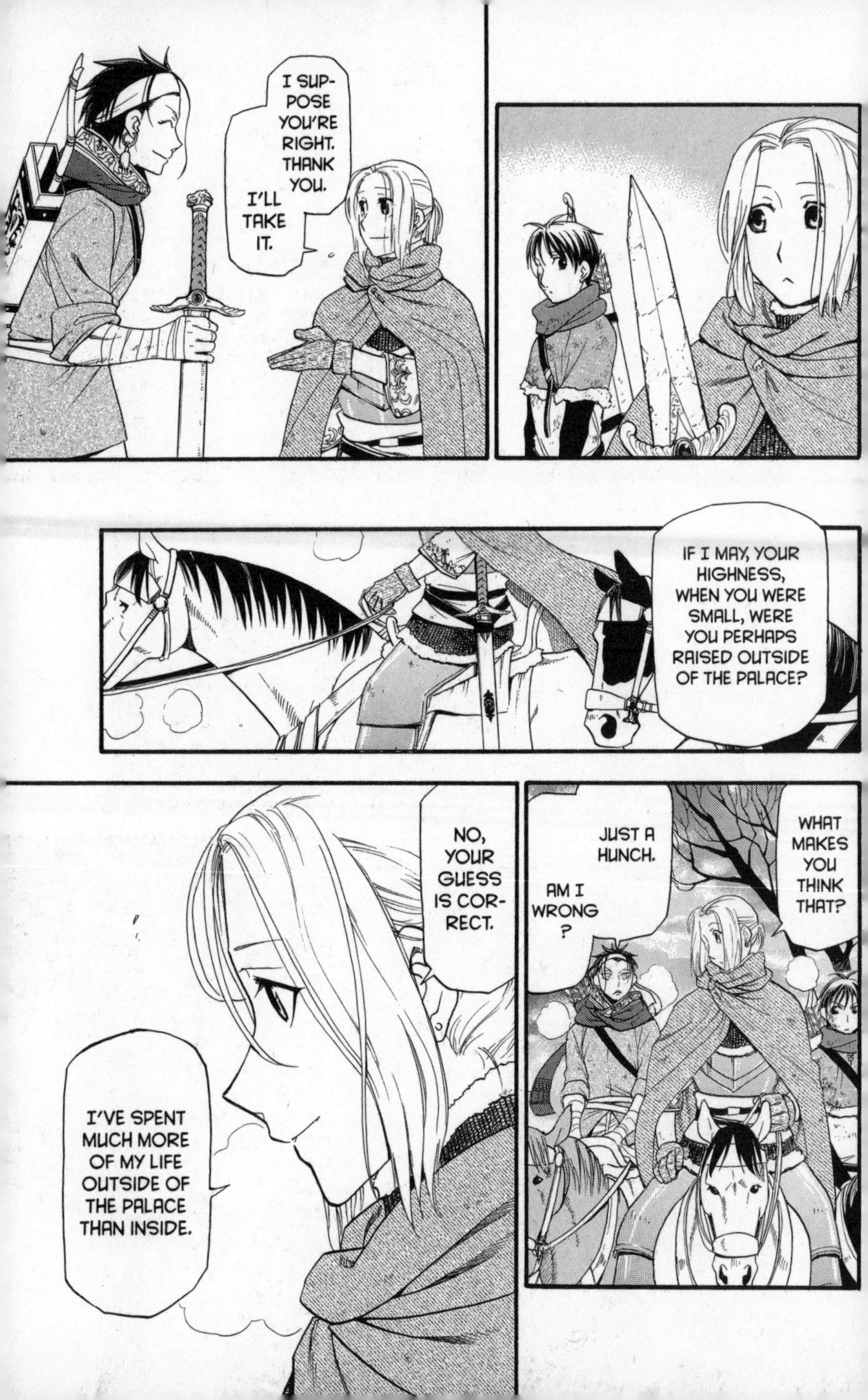
I SUPPOSE YOU'RE RIGHT. THANK YOU.
I'LL TAKE IT.
IF I MAY, YOUR HIGHNESS, WHEN YOU WERE SMALL, WERE YOU PERHAPS RAISED OUTSIDE OF THE PALACE?
WHAT MAKES YOU THINK THAT?
JUST A HUNCH.
AM I WRONG?
NO, YOUR GUESS IS CORRECT.
I'VE SPENT MUCH MORE OF MY LIFE OUTSIDE OF THE PALACE THAN INSIDE.

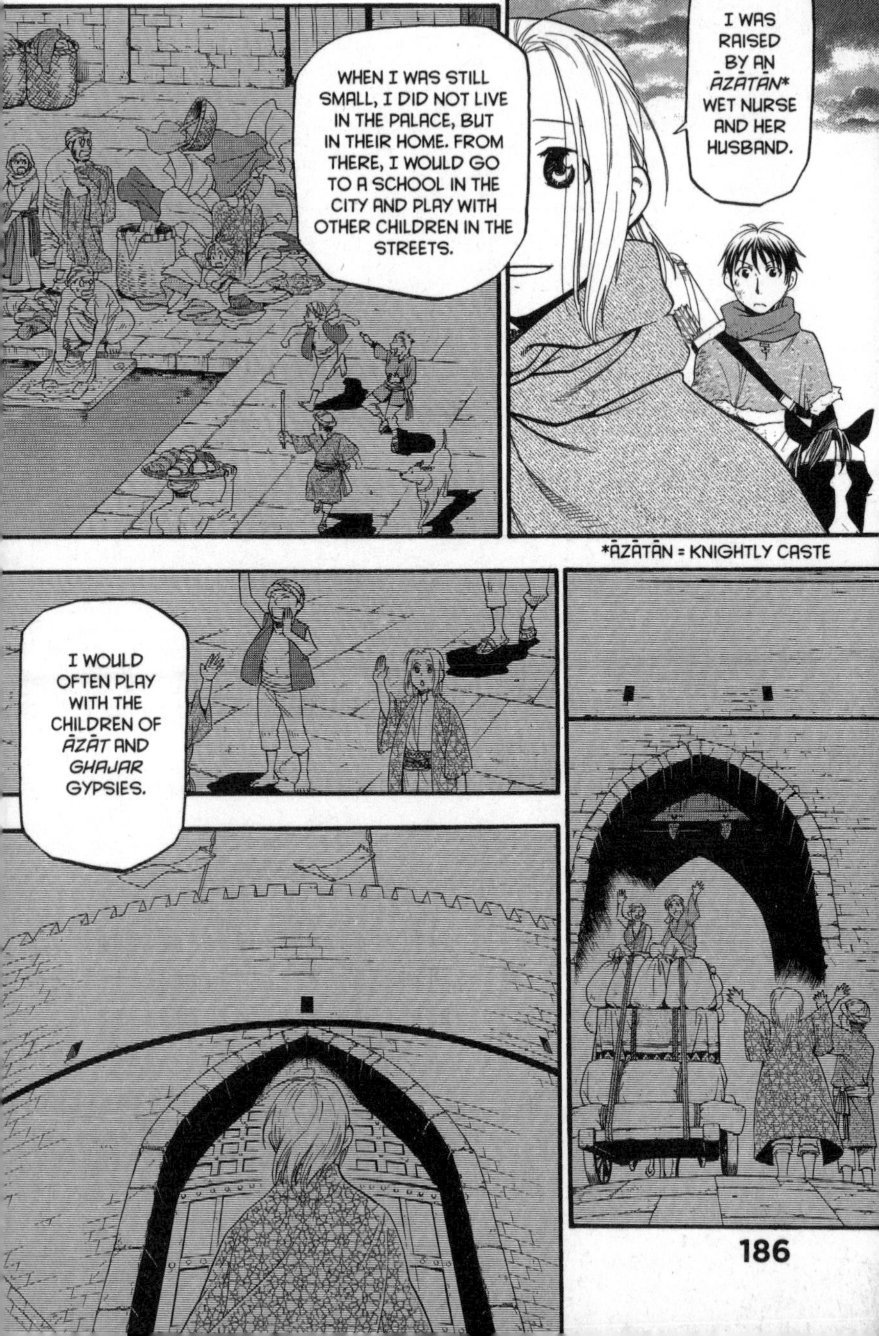
I WAS RAISED BY AN ĀZĀTĀN* WET NURSE AND HER HUSBAND.
WHEN I WAS STILL SMALL, I DID NOT LIVE IN THE PALACE, BUT IN THEIR HOME. FROM THERE, I WOULD GO TO A SCHOOL IN THE CITY AND PLAY WITH OTHER CHILDREN IN THE STREETS.
I WOULD OFTEN PLAY WITH THE CHILDREN OF *ĀZĀT* AND *GHAJAR* GYPSIES.

*ĀZĀTĀN = KNIGHTLY CASTE

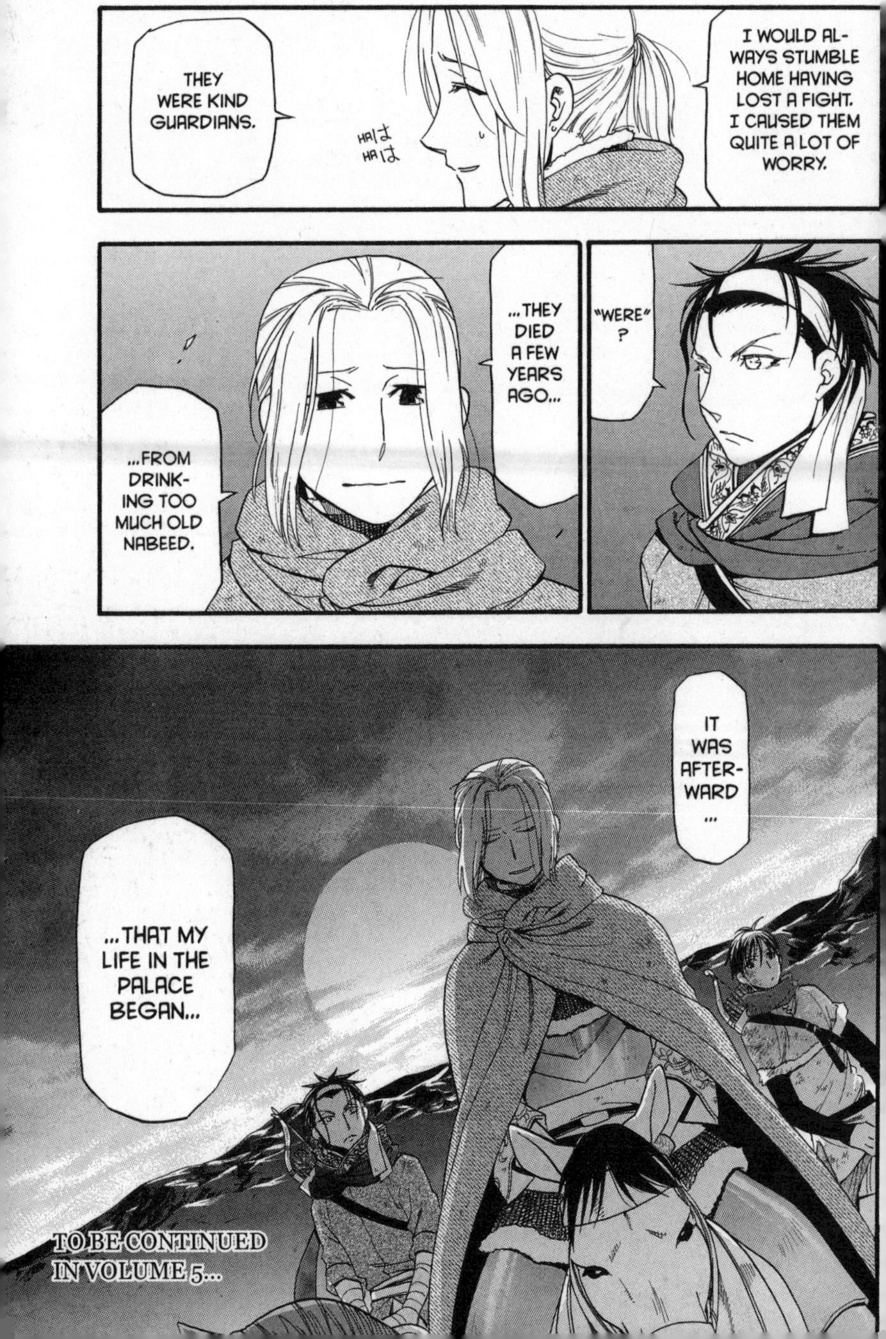
I WOULD AL-WAYS STUMBLE HOME HAVING LOST A FIGHT. I CAUSED THEM QUITE A LOT OF WORRY.
HA は HA は
THEY WERE KIND GUARDIANS.
"WERE"?
...THEY DIED A FEW YEARS AGO...
...FROM DRINK-ING TOO MUCH OLD NABEED.
IT WAS AFTER-WARD...
...THAT MY LIFE IN THE PALACE BEGAN...
TO BE CONTINUED IN VOLUME 5...

'SUNDAY 5 ᴾᴹ ANIME" BATON PASS INTERVIEW!!!

Hiromu Arakawa
My first series, *Fullmetal Alchemist (Monthly Shonen GanGan)*, started in 2001 and was a big hit. I'm currently drawing *The Heroic Legend of Arslan (Bessatsu Shonen Magazine)*, *Silver Spoon (Weekly Shonen Sunday)*, and *Hyakusho Kizoku (Monthly Wings)*. I love cows, and the inside of my house is filled with cow-themed items. The emoji I use in texts are mostly cows, too.

Hiromu Arakawa × Nakaba Suzuki

A COW AND A PIG! WHAT A DELICIOUS-LOOKING PAIR!!

Nakaba Suzuki
Debuted in 1998 with *Rising Impact* in *Weekly Shonen Jump*. My current series, *The Seven Deadly Sins*, is enjoying enormous success as my first series that has been turned into an anime. My other notable works include *Blizzard Axel*, *Kongo Bancho*, *(Weekly Shonen Sunday)* and others. My favorite beer is Belgian beer. I like to cut shochu (a type of Japanese liquor) with warm water.

As the super-popular *Seven Deadly Sins* TV anime reaches its final episode, *The Heroic Legend of Arslan* takes the baton and fills the 5pm Sunday time slot! We have arranged an interview with these two superstars and gotten them to open up about everything from their thoughts on each other's works and the joy of drawing manga to comments on their past careers!!

> **First impressions of each other?**

—The very popular anime *The Seven Deadly Sins* has reached its final episode, and the *Bessatsu Shonen Magazine* series *The Heroic Legend of Arslan* is getting ready to take over its 5pm Sunday time slot! As the baton is passed from Nakaba Suzuki-sensei to Hiromu Arakawa-sensei, we would love to hear how each of you feels about the other's work!

Hiromu Arakawa-sensei (hereafter, **Arakawa**): I read all of Nakaba-sensei's works! There was *Blizzard Axel* (*Weekly Shonen Sunday*), which was about figure skating. The way he drew the skaters' torsos while they were performing was so beautiful. I was all, "Wow!" and I started buying the graphic novels. I also like the character models in *Kongo Bancho* [*Indestructible Gang Leader*] (Ibid.). I loved the Hikyo Bancho [Underhanded Gang Leader]. Can I get your autograph later (ha ha)?

Nakaba Suzuki-sensei (hereafter, **Suzuki**): Of course! I actually brought a volume of Arslan for you to sign, too (ha ha)! When I first saw the armor for Al (Alphonse Elric, a boy who lost his body as the price for performing forbidden alchemy and had his soul fixed to a suit of armor) in *Fullmetal Alchemist (Monthly Shonen GanGan)*, I was really enchanted by your artistic sense. I knew you were a woman, so that surprised me. I tend to assume that when women draw armor, the design is more graceful and slender. But Al's armor was beautiful and practical, which was really cool. The story was so perfect, too, and I thought it was the work of an amazing new manga artist.

—Wow, torsos and armor, huh! I think it's interesting that both of you first noticed the art. Arakawa-sensei, how do you feel about *The Seven Deadly Sins*?

Arakawa: I went back and reread it, and I was shocked that it's only 13 volumes so far! There are so many characters doing their own things, and each has a past that is fully depicted in the series, but there's also so much story that keeps moving forward—each volume is packed with content. Of course, there are still a ton of unanswered questions, but it was really satisfying to read it all in one go.

As for the characters, I especially like the girls; they're all so cute. I like Jericho, too, and Guila is adorable. And Diane's feelings for the Captain and King really tug at my heartstrings!

Suzuki: Thank you very much! When I was writing *Rising Impact* (*Weekly Shonen Jump*), I would get letters saying, "You do not understand women!" (ha ha). So I got defiant, and now when I draw girls, my philosophy is that, instead of drawing realistic girls, I should draw girls that are so close to a guy's ideal that people would think there's no possible way they could really exist.

Arakawa: Women think they're cute, too!

Suzuki: *The Heroic Legend of Arslan* has peerless beauties alongside all those handsome warriors, too. The woman who was sent...or rather politely kicked out of her temple to protect Arslan...Kahina Farangis—she's the cutest of them all, and that includes how honest she is with herself! What's it like drawing her?

Arakawa: I'm not very good at drawing beautiful women (ha ha). But every character is so lovely and human on the inside that the more I draw them, the more it shows, and that's what gives them their charm.

—What do you like about *The Heroic Legend of Arslan*, Suzuki-sensei?

Suzuki: I'm a sucker for a story that starts out with a team of five against an army of thirty thousand, and of course the characters are all great. The hero, Arslan, is a little unusual. He's nothing! He doesn't have anything. But he's charismatic. He learns from Narsus (a genius-level strategist), grows stronger through experience in battle, and now he's in the process of getting everyone to accept him. I can't wait to see what happens! My favorite characters are Daryun (a Marzban of Pars, the kingdom where the series takes place, who swears his loyalty to Arslan) and Hilmes (a ruthless enemy who stands in Arslan's way as a general of the enemy army). I can't really draw men like them, who are firm in their convictions and purely awesome, so I really admire them.

Arakawa-sensei is stunned! The beautifully-torsoed jump! From the Nakaba Suzuki Short Stories Collection: The Seven Shortly Stories.

Arakawa: This series is based on someone else's story, so I'm not sure I could have created those characters from my own imagination. But I do have a habit, when I'm drawing enemy characters like Hilmes and the Lusitanians, of thinking really hard about their policies and what they consider to be justice.

Suzuki: I understand. I was the same way. Sometimes when I was drawing, I would be rooting for Hendrickson and company (ha ha). You said you're borrowing these characters, but I think you've made the characters of The Heroic Legend of Arslan all your own.

Arakawa: Maybe it's because I like *The Romance of the Three Kingdoms* [a Chinese legend that's famous in Japan]. I had a discussion with the creator, Yoshiki Tanaka-sensei, where I was like, "Daryun is all powerful and true to his convictions. So in *Romance of the Three Kingdoms*, would that make him Zhao Yun?"

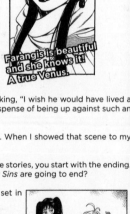
BECAUSE PRETTY LADIES, LET ALONE PEERLESS BEAUTIES ARE A RARE SIGHT.

Farangis is beautiful and she knows it! A true Venus.

Suzuki: So which character is the least likely to have been created by you?

Arakawa: I think Gieve, the wandering minstrel who joins Arslan. He's such a philanderer, and he says some pretty terrible things about women. So I thought he was a big jerk, but then I started drawing him, and it was super fun (ha ha).

—Incidentally, Suzuki-sensei, which scene in *The Heroic Legend of Arslan* shocked you the most?

Suzuki: This might be a spoiler, but the scene where Vahriz (Daryun's uncle and the old general who taught Arslan how to use a sword) met his gruesome death. I liked that character, so on the one hand, I was thinking, "I wish he would have lived a little longer," but on the other hand, it really made me feel the fear and suspense of being up against such an enemy, and I thought, "That's Arakawa-sensei."

Arakawa: He was one of those soothing characters; I really liked him, too. When I showed that scene to my assistants, they screamed, "Nooo! Not grandpa!" (ha ha).

—I've heard that one thing you two have in common is that when you create stories, you start with the ending. Do you already know how *The Heroic Legend of Arslan* and *Seven Deadly Sins* are going to end?

Suzuki: Yes. I already know exactly how it's going to end. The ending is set in stone, but how they get there depends on the characters.

Arakawa: Yes, that's right. If you already know how it's going to end, you can take out anything extraneous, and even if you do stray from the path a little, you can get right back to the main story. Even with Arslan, it's based on someone else's story, but I would imagine drawing the last chapter, and think about a destination point for the boy Arslan, and I had several meetings with my editor about the story.

Arakawa: Nakaba-sensei, this is your first fantasy series, isn't it? Did you always want to draw in this genre?

Suzuki: I grew up reading *Jump*, the golden standard of shonen manga, so when I started out, all I drew was fantasy. But it was terrible (ha ha). Then I did *Rising Impact*, and it was so much fun drawing a sports series that I left fantasy cold turkey. Now I have a better idea of how to develop characters, so I thought maybe I could try my hand at fantasy again.

Diane's love story pulls at Arakawa-sensei's heartstrings

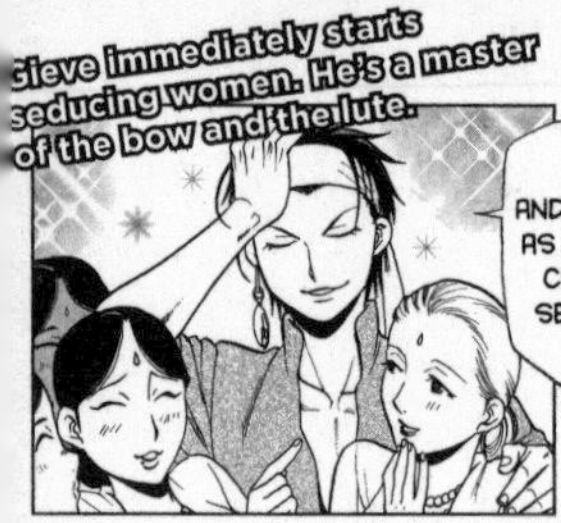
Gieve immediately starts seducing women. He's a master of the bow and the lute.
AND SO, AS YOU CAN SEE...

And Arakawa-sensei, in addition to this epic manga, your work covers a broad range, including the agricultural high school manga *Silver Spoon* (*Weekly Shonen Sunday*) and essay manga. And they're all fun to read. But did you start out wanting to draw a fantasy series like *Fullmetal Alchemist*?

Arakawa: No, I did that out of a vague idea to go with fantasy to match the taste of *GanGan*. I like reading it, and I had an idea already, then when I started doing it, I was surprised at how hooked I was. When I started *Silver Spoon*, people commented on how it's not fantasy, but that was another one that I drew because I was going to do it for *Sunday*, and when I asked myself what I wanted to draw for that magazine, that was the result.

Exposé?! The secrets of working for different publishers!

—You've both been published in a lot of magazines, haven't you?

Arakawa: People sometimes think, "Did you transfer over because you had trouble with your old publisher?" But it's more like it's just the natural flow of life. It's not because I ran into any problems (ha ha).

—Suzuki-sensei, you have experience with four different weekly shonen manga publishers: *Jump*, *Sunday*, *Champion*, and *Magazine*. Have you noticed any differences in working for different magazines?

Suzuki: First, it wasn't because I had any issues with any of them! (ha ha) This might be because of the individual editors, but when I wrote for *Jump*, they were fairly hands-off. My editor let me pretty much draw whatever I wanted. At *Sunday* they were a little more involved, and in *Blizzard Axel* I was dealing with a sport that's scored by judges, so I would stay up all night with my editor and a calculator and be very meticulous about how I drew that series. At *Champion*, it was a woman editor who asked me to draw for them. This was the first editor I'd had who couldn't drink, and I would get hammered all by myself! *Magazine* is more laid-back, too, but recently I've had so much work, I wonder if they couldn't just let me play my video games (ha ha).

Arakawa: Figure skating is pretty popular right now. I wish they'd do a reprint of *Blizzard Axel*.

Suzuki: No kidding. But the editor-in-chief at the great *Sunday*...uh! I mean, let's not talk about this right now (ha ha).

Expectations for The Heroic Legend of Arslan anime

—But you were playing games just yesterday, Nakaba-sensei! Let's get back to the subject. Is there anything you think our readers should watch for in the *Heroic Legend of Arslan* anime?

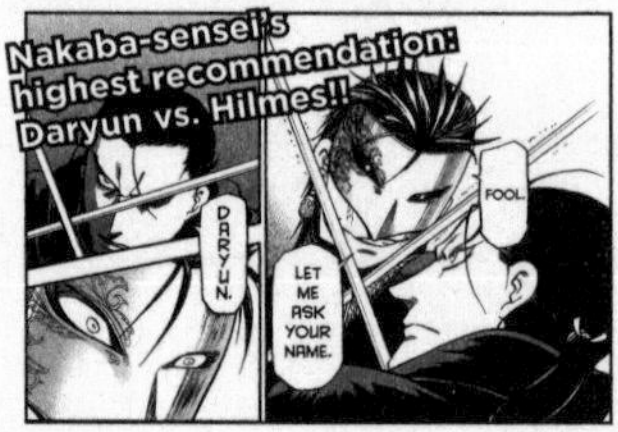
Nakaba-sensei's highest recommendation: Daryun vs. Hilmes!!
FOOL.
LET ME ASK YOUR NAME.
DARYUN.

Arakawa: The way the horses move! I think it's really hard to get horses to move right in animation. So I can't wait to see how they did these big cavalry battles. In anime, they have to draw the inbetweens—all the pictures between one manga panel and the next—to get characters to move, and they have to get to a good stopping point within a given amount of time. As a storyteller, I learn a lot from it. So I'm hoping to enjoy the series as another fan.

Suzuki: There really are a lot of things to look forward to, like the cavalry and the way they draw the fire attacks, but personally, I look forward to seeing how Yuki Kaji, who played the hero Meliodas, portrays my beloved villain Hilmes. He's using a deeper voice than he did for Meliodas, so you can really hear what a pro can do!

—Now, finally, we'd like a message from each of you to our readers.

Suzuki: Thank you to all of you who made the *Seven Deadly Sins* anime a hit!! In the manga, I'm going to take the story from where the anime left off and expand the world in a big way, so I hope you'll read the manga, too! But stay tuned to this channel (ha ha), and let's enjoy *The Heroic Legend of Arslan* together!

Arakawa: The original story has a lot of power, and there are a lot of fans in the anime staff, so they're really passionate. The anime is going to blend the novels and the manga together to make a new story, and I'm excited to see it, too! If you like the anime, I hope you'll pick up the novels and the manga, too!

This interview was first published in *Weekly Shonen Magazine* Issue 18, 2015.

- BONUS SKETCHES -

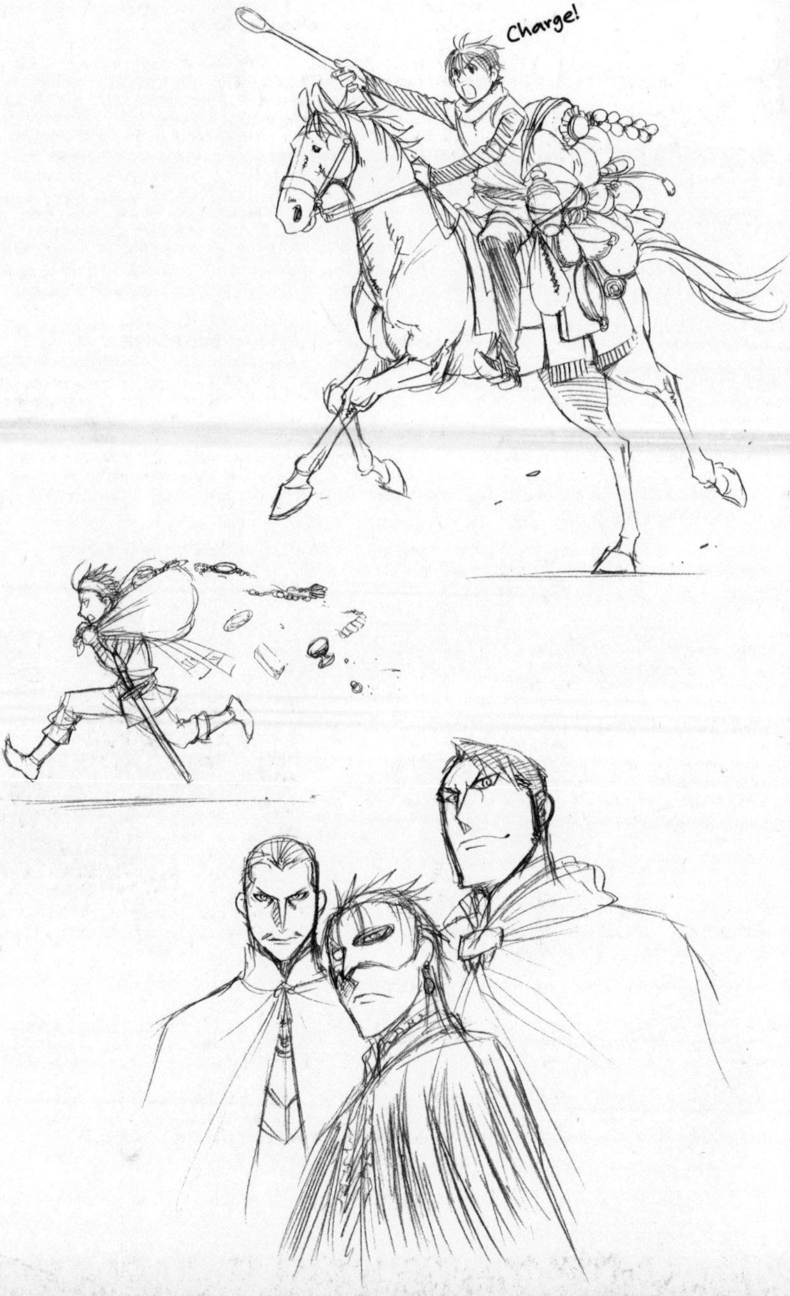
Charge!

The Heroic Legend of Arslan volume 4 is a work of fiction. Names, characters, places, and incidents are the products of the author's imagination or are used fictitiously. Any resemblance to actual events, locales, or persons, living or dead, is entirely coincidental.

A Kodansha Comics Trade Paperback Original.

The Heroic Legend of Arslan volume 4 copyright © 2015 Hiromu Arakawa & Yoshiki Tanaka
English translation copyright © 2015 Hiromu Arakawa & Yoshiki Tanaka

Published in the United States by Kodansha Comics,
an imprint of Kodansha USA Publishing, LLC, New York.

Publication rights for this English edition arranged through Kodansha Ltd., Tokyo.

First published in Japan in 2015 by Kodansha Ltd., Tokyo, as *Arslan Senki* volume 4.

ISBN 978-1-63236-111-0

Printed in the United States of America.

www.kodanshacomics.com

9 8 7 6 5 4 3 2 1

Translators: Lindsey Akashi, Alethea Nibley & Athena Nibley,
& Amanda Haley
Lettering: April Brown
Editing: Ajani Oloye